D1454426

Fishing and Foll_

Life and dialect on the North Sea Coast

compiled by Bill Griffiths

"Only those who have watched it at every season can tell the full beauty of the coast."
(Louise Creighton, 1904, 1/149)

This is the third book in Northumbria University Press "Wor Language" series, which includes the books *Pitmatic: The Talk of the North East Coalfield* and *Stotty 'n' Spice Cake* –
supported by the Heritage Lottery Fund.

Published by Northumbria University Press
Northumbria Graphics
Trinity Building
Newcastle upon Tyne NE1 8ST, UK
www.northumbriauniversitypress.co.uk

First Edition Published 2008

British Library Cataloguing in Publication Data. A Catalogue Record for this
book is available from the British Library.

ISBN-13: 978-1-904794-28-8

Designed and printed by Northumbria Graphics, Northumbria University.

Typeset in Original Garamond

Northumbria University is the trading name of the
University of Northumbria at Newcastle. 219787

Acknowledgements

As the dialect project 'Wor Language' proceeds, the harder it becomes to acknowledge everyone and every source involved, such has been the range of participation. The support of the Heritage Lottery Fund and the collaboration of the partners in the project has worked well – with particular thanks to Dr Bill Lancaster at Northumbria University, Jo Bath at Beamish North of England Open Air Museum and Andy Peden Smith at Northumbria University Press. The newsletters of the Durham & Tyneside Dialect Group have kept over 300 people regularly informed on the progress of the project, and brought in many extra stories and comments.

Additional thanks must go to the Coble and Keelboat Society, for their generous and friendly sharing of information, literature and contacts.

Among individuals, Katrina Porteous' (KP) permission to use her full list of dialect words from around Beadnell, Northumberland, is especially valued. This wordlist was compiled by her over the last 15 years plus and is a unique record of a local maritime vocabulary. I would also like to take this opportunity to thank very sincerely Dr Adrian Osler (AO) for his help in identifying and accessing a number of important texts, and many useful suggestions when the book was at draft stage; he is not of course responsible for the various opinions and conclusions with which I ornament the facts.

The many regional libraries, local history and community groups that invited me to talk to their members have been another major resource, and provided a valuable opportunity for group discussion.

Individuals who have sent in welcome information or who agreed to be interviewed for this book include: Ada Radford (AR) (Darlington), Alan Geggie (AG) (Ashington), Alan Illingworth (AI) (Hartlepool), Alan Myers (AM) (South Shields), Alf Sterling (AS) (Hartlepool), Mrs B.A. Allen (BA) (Seaton Sluice), Bart Taylor (BT) (Cullercoats), Bill Thomas (BT) (Whittingham), Carle and George Robinson (CGR) (Amble), Dave Davison (DD) (Ellington), Derek Rowell (DR) (Sunderland), Duncan Murdoch (DM) (Catchgate), Edgar Readman (ER) (Saltburn), Eric King (EK) (Seahouses), Florrie Merihein (FM) (Ashington), Frank Taylor (FT) (Cullercoats), Fred Short (FS) (Teesside), Fred Stainthorpe (FS) (Shotton), Gordon Dodds (GD) (Parkside), Gordon Patrickson (GP) (Seaham), Helen Hemingway (HH) (South Shields), Jack Ledger (JL) (Blackhall), Jim Cromarty (JC) (Spittal), Joe Henry (JH) (Seaham), Joan Philips (JP) John Foreman (JF) (Seaham), John Seed (JS) (Chester-le-Street), Margaret Reed (MR) (Seaham), Meg and Bill Stephenson (MBS), North Shields, Mel Deighton (MD), Mike Smyth (MS) (Cullercoats), Neil Johnson (NJ) (Hartlepool), Norman Conn (NC) (Seaham), Peter Adamson (PA) (Seaham), Tom Moreland (TM) (Parkside), Tony Sharkey (TS) (Co.Durham) … I am grateful to these and more, and hope they enjoyed the process of building the book as much as I did.

For help in assembling a rather striking set of illustrations, I depended heavily on Joan Taylor Phillips of Cullerocats and Bill Harris of Newbiggin. Adrian Osler contributed the excellent diagrams of named parts of a coble, and he in turn asks me to acknowledge the assistance of Hector Handyside, master coble-builder (retired) of Amble and Katrina Porteous.

Special sources include transcripts of oral material being currently developed by Jo Bath at the Beamish North of England Open Air Museum's Centre for Regional Resources; *BL MS Egerton 2868* (James Raine's dialect word list) and *BL MS Lansdowne 1033* (vol. 99 of Bishop Kennet's Collection, Bishop Kennet's 'Etymological Collections of English Words and Provincial Expressions'), with permission of the British Library; and *Bell-White MS 12* ('A Glossary for Newcastle, Durham and Northumberland') by permission of the Special Collections and Archives Librarian, Robinson Library Special Collections, University of Newcastle.

Websites are particularly difficult to list, as internet addresses change and websites appear and disappear. Special thanks are due to Tyne & Wear Museums Services for permission to quote their 'fishtales' website; and from Authorsden's Robert Harrison for his account of salmon tickling.

So many have participated, and yet I cannot pretend this is anything more than an initial treatment of a subject as challenging as the coast itself, with its scenery, wildlife, boats and fishing operations, communities and people. The combination of dialect vocabulary and literature as a way of explaining the coast and its social development is something of an experiment also – a history-by-vocabulary possibly unique to this project.

Bill Griffiths

Abbreviations

B'd Castle – Barnard Castle
B'p Auck – Bishop Auckland
C'd – Cumberland
Ch-le-St – Chester-le-Street
Cleve – Cleveland
D'm – Durham (county)
D'ton – Darlington
e – east
G'head – Gateshead
Hetton – Hetton-le-Hole
Ho'ton – Houghton-le-Spring
H'pool – Hartlepool
Ire – Ireland
Lx – Lancashire
n, N – north
N'd – Northumberland
Newc – Newcastle
N.I. – Northern Ireland
Nth – North of England
Sco – Scotland
s, S – south
S.Shields – South Shields
S'd – Sunderland
S'm – Seaham
Tyne – Tyneside
w – west

W'd – Westmorland
Yx – Yorkshire
Plus standard county name abbreviations

Note: in the context of distribution to 1900, reckoned via the *EDD* (English Dialect Dictionary), Nth imples counties of England from the Humber north; NE implies a combination of Northumberland, Co. Durham and Cleveland.

Abbreviations relating to language

Du – Dutch
Fr – French
OIce – Old Icelandic
MDu – Middle Dutch
ME – Middle English
Norw – Norwegian
OE – Old English (Anglo-Saxon)
ON – Old Norse (Viking)
Scand. – Scandinavian
Sw – Swedish

CONTENTS

The North Sea Coast

Coastal communities fascinate dialect and social historians, but they also pose many challenges. They are closely bound to their hinterland, exporting regional produce, distributing imports and, not least, feeding the wider population with the harvest of the sea. The coast since the eighteenth century has been a place of leisure, pleasure and rest. What began as an upper class pursuit was democratised by the coming of the railway. By nineteen hundred it was a rarity to meet someone who had never seen the sea. This book is largely concerned with lives of people who inhabit the North Sea Coast and its geography is by necessity broader than that of the other books on Northern dialect by Bill Griffiths. He was all too aware that the coast is a vital interface for the flow of language between the littoral and its region; between coastal communities that share the North Sea and between British maritime cities, towns and villages and those in other nations, particularly in Europe. Those familiar with the other books in this series will be all too aware, for example, of the Dutch contribution to North East dialect. We need to be aware of the mobile army of women fish workers who roamed the coast from Wick to Great Yarmouth, following the herring, well into the twentieth century. The Tyne and Wear colliers for more than a century regularly stopped at King's Lynn on their journey to London and much of the regions beer arrived from Edinburgh on a ship. Coastal crafts, centred on fishing and boat building, were practiced in communities along the North Sea often sharing techniques that were part of a wider European maritime tradition. Much of the research for this book took place in Northern England and this is reflected in its content. Readers are nevertheless urged to broaden their mental map of the region and embrace the richness and diversity of the North Sea Coast and its culture.

Bill Lancaster
Director of the Centre for Northern Studies, 1997–2008

Foreword

Bill Griffiths completed the preliminary draft of this book on the dialect of the North Sea Coast just days before his death in September 2007. It concluded a remarkable achievement, being the third book in Northumbria University Press' "Wor Language" series – supported by the Heritage Lottery Fund. The previous books *Stotty 'n' Spice Cake: The Story of North East Cooking* (2006), and *Pitmatic: The Talk of the North East Coalfield* (2007) received local and national acclaim and alongwith his *Dictionary of North East Dialect* (2004, 2005), established Bill's reputation as the region's foremost dialect scholar. He was a unique talent who possessed an unusual combination of skills. He came from an orchestra family, was trained as a classical pianist and had performed solo at the Barbican Centre. His musical education was followed by a degree in History at UCL and a Doctorate in Old English from Kings College, London. He also wrote poetry which was of the highest order; one of his many obituarists in the national press described his work as without equal in English since Ezra Pound. That he deliberately chose to publish with small presses, of which he was an ardent participant, partly explains why his work was not more widely known. In recent years, however, he had been appointed Visiting Professor in Poetry in many universities, particularly in the USA where his work is highly regarded. His role as a Fellow and a researcher at the Centre for Northern Studies at Northumbria University since 2000 provided a material security – unusual for Bill like many other poets – and it was during these years that he tirelessly researched regional dialect.

Bill moved from London to the North East, settling at Seaham in 1990. To many this seemed an odd choice as he had a growing reputation as a poet with a particular London focus. But, for Bill there was a strong logic to his northern journey. Since the 1960s he had frequently visited the region, drawn to the Morden Tower poetry scene and the poets who were emerging under the guiding influence of Basil Bunting. Bill was a strong admirer of Tom Pickard and their relationship of mutual respect produced the delightful collaborative work *Tyne Txts* in 2003. Above all it was the region's language that drew him here. Bill was a formidable student of Saxon literature who took great pleasure in living amongst the vestiges of Old English which forms the core of North East dialect. He quickly became part of the local cultural scene – in its widest sense. Professor Rosemary Cramp would visit his marvellously unkempt Tyneside flat at Seaham, surrounded by four pianos, including two grands! – to discuss aspects of Seaham's Saxon history. He wrote numerous books on Seaham from its Saxon origins to the Londonderry years. He was a champion of the local environment, drawing attention to the plight of the Durham Denes and attacking the local authority plans to develop the notorious *Get Carter* beach. These drew Bill into politics and he came within a few votes of winning a council seat as an Independent in this Labour stronghold. He became the leading figure and inspiration in the Seaham local history scene and helped to establish the Tyneside and Durham Dialect Society. He had a remarkable ability to blend in to local society; he could more than hold his own in academic circles, but it was his involvement with ordinary local people that gave him greatest pleasure. His half-time post at the Northumbria University allowed him to visit and talk to old people – Thursday afternoons were always reserved for making one elderly resident's lunch. He was well-known amongst teenagers, many who participated in his dialect projects. With his dishevelled appearance, tattoos that were a legacy of his involvement with the Hells Angels during the 1960s, and colourful American sportswear and shellsuits he developed an easy rapport with people who would normally be reluctant to participate in scholarly research. Indeed Bill always managed to invoke amongst those involved in his work a strong sense of shared ownership: he was there to help them preserve and defend 'their' language, a dimension all too apparent at his numerous dialect meetings when he was accompanied by an entourage of locals. To hear young men and women give demonstrations of contemporary dialect were memorable moments at these events.

Music, History, Poetry, as if this was not enough, stood alongside Bill's other great skill as an archivist. He was a member of the Society of Archivists; his membership was achieved in recognition of the important work he performed at the Kings College Poetry Archive during the 1990s. In recent years he catalogued the papers of the Northern Sinfonia and during the spring of 2007 he completed the task of listing over 100 hours of oral recordings of T. Dan Smith. Listening, studying and compiling were central to Bill's work. We can marvel at the thousand year plus etymologies to many local words; take surprise at his demonstration of the important Dutch contribution to the language of the region, and puzzle over the failure of Irish to have a linguistic impact upon the region despite the scale of nineteenth century immigration. Labour historians are indebted to his rescue and preservation of Pitmatic, the rapidly disappearing language of the Great Northern Coalfield – this alone is an achievement of historic significance. And in *Fishing and Folk* we witness Bill at the height of his powers. The community involvement is ever present – he visited and addressed the meetings of the Coble and Keelboat Society and he scoured the towns and villages of the region's coast in his quest. His research became more multi-dimensional and arguably this book is as important a work of the social history of the North Sea Coast as it is a record of the community's language.

At the time of his death we were planning a new project on the dialect of children's games and pastimes and it is the intention of all those involved with Bill that this work should be undertaken. Thanks to him the people of the North East have a wonderful cultural resource – a resource that Bill would insist was as much their making as his – and his greatest legacy is that he has created something that will be enduring. Bill died within a few weeks of Murray Martin – a founder and inspirational figure at Amber Films. They both shared a passion that working people of the region should be able to represent themselves whether in film or voice. The summer of 2007 so brilliantly explored in the Newcastle writer Gordon Burn's *Born Yesterday, The News as a Novel*, was miserable on many counts and there was much that we would rather forget. Bill's passing will not be forgotten and his life is a reminder that genius is often all around us.

Bill Lancaster
Director of the Centre for Northern Studies, 1997–2008.

Preface: Cuthbert on the Inner Farne

It is a good omen, surely, to start this vocal voyage around the North Sea coast and trawl for its maritime dialect, with Cuthbert, the saint who has symbolised the region since the beginning. His role in reconciling the Celtic and Roman traditions of Christianity firmly associated him with the unity of Northumbria to the extent that *Cuthberhteslond* (St Cuthbert's Land) and *Haligwerfolc* (holy-man's people) were often used where we would expect 'Northumbria' and 'Northumbrians'. To later Anglo-Saxons, he must have seemed an icon of the 'Golden Age' of Northumbria (essentially the eigth century AD), then as now honoured for its intellectual achievements, and through St Oswald for its military prowess.

After the disruption of the Viking incursions – for the large monastic estates were both specially attractive to and vulnerable to Viking ambitions – the uncorrupted body of the saint finally found rest with the construction of the new Durham Cathedral (998 AD), as a continuing symbol of reconciliation. There both the West Saxons and later the Normans found it expedient to honour the saint and promote through him a vision of the stability of the North East and its role in defending the borders of the Anglo-Norman state.

The rise of Scotland from the twelfth century on brought new centuries of disruption to the northern zone, and it is hard not to feel in the Border Ballads of the fifteenth and sixteenth centuries some sense of the misery of a land destabilised and in effect sacrificed to the defensive needs of the South.

This situation eased again with the Union of the Crowns in 1607; later on, many of its keelmen, miners and engineers on Tyneside would be Scots. The economic route to rebuilding the North East came through the demand for coal in the late sixteenth century and thereafter; it was coal that powered the world expansion of Great Britain – coal was the life-blood of its railways, ships and factories. New and improved ports along the North East coast took on the job of shipping it out, and in the early 1900s, the North East arguably enjoyed a higher standard of living than much of the South.

The wheel of fortune has since turned with a vengeance: pits and shipyards have literally vanished. The county system of local government, defined in 1888, has produced a Northumberland, a Durham, and ultimately a Tyne & Wear and Tees Valley, each with its claim to an honourable history, and each looking forward to a future with an improved environment. Which brings us back neatly to the early 'Green' credentials of St Cuthbert, preparing to lead the simple religious life on Inner Farne…

Then Cuthbert would live a hermit's life
entirely isolated.
He journeyed to Farne on the flowing tide,
an island all encompassed
by the salt wave in sea's midst.
The interior, though, at that time
was settled by swart spirits
so that nobody could bide there
for the danger of these dark demons.
Yet now they all fled away
and left that island quite empty
for the great saint. There solitary he lived
safe from their enmity by God's grace.
That island was altogether lacking
the benefit of fresh water so barren its rocks
but the holy man had them
dig in the hard ground
at the centre of the floor of his fair-built home
and suddenly a watersource sprang up
for his use and sweet to taste
just as once water to wine
he transformed by the favour of God.

The saint asked them then for seed:
he wished to grow a crop on the wasteland
if the Almighty God would allow him
to feed himself by his own effort.
He sowed wheat in well-worked soil
but it would not sprout and show,
not even grass managed to grow.
Then he had them bring him barley seed
and though out of season sowed it in the earth.
It grew readily and well ripened.

Then some ravens of his reward
would deprive him if they dared.
But the holy man said to the hard-bills
 "If the Almighty has allowed you to,
then you are welcome to take all you want;
but if the Lord has not given you liberty
get yourselves off, greedy birds
to your own home far from this island!"
Well then the ravens right away flew
off together over the salt wave
and left the saint the benefit of his labour.

Another time another two
black ravens arrived
and tore at his hut's thatch with their hard beaks
and carried it off to their nest to cosset their chicks.
These too the saint swiftly sent back
to their own land with one word of command.
But one of them after three days
came back, very contrite,
and flew to his feet seeking permission
to live in that land
if he made no mischief and his mate likewise.
Well then Cuthbert consented
and full of joy they flew back to Farne
and brought their protector a present
of pig fat to waterproof his boots;
and they lived there doing him no harm ever after.

(The passage above translates the free alliterative verse *Life of Cuthbert* by the West-Saxon monk, Aelfric, in the 990s.)

Part One: Coastal terminology

Eterne God, that thurgh thy <u>purveiaunce</u>   providence
Ledest the world by certein governaunce,
<u>In ydel</u>, as men seyn, ye no thing make,   without purpose
But, Lord, thise grisly <u>feendly</u> rokkes <u>blake</u>,   hostile…black
That <u>semen</u> rather a foul confusion   seem
Of werk than any fair creacion
Of swich a parfit wys God and a stable,
Why <u>han</u> ye wroght this werk unreasonable?   have

(Chaucer, *Franklin's Tale*)

Coastal feature-names may be a special case in place-name study: the features encountered – the cliffs, the rocky shelves, the isolated stacks, the areas of safe shelter – differ from those inland both in physical type and in how they relate to the needs of the map users. In the North East it is fishermen that have a claim on the naming process; but the number of charts appearing from the late seventeenth century onwards clearly respects the needs of the national coal trade. Standardisation toward 'Point' for headland and 'Rock' for an outcrop may reveal the influence of 'national' English and tidying up by Ordnance Survey rather than early-stage naming in Norman-French. (For example, Goldstone Rock (Holy Island) appears in 1540 as 'Golden Stonys'.) For us, the state of naming as printed authoritatively in the mid-nineteenth century has become a fixed standard that obscures pre-Ordnance Survey fluidity.

An older level of names subtends the whole, from the period of Anglian and Viking settlements. Anglians settled the North Sea coast from East Anglia to the Borders; the Vikings then made their claim along the Tees and in much of Yorkshire, etc. and a Viking Kingdom of York dominated the tenth century North. A factor relevant here, is that while Viking power inland declined after the Norman Conquest, Scandinavian influence continued to dominate the North Sea for many centuries afterwards, with a sustained opportunity of dominating the word pool.

Another puzzle forms when, amid the truly historic and the sensibly surveyed, we meet a level of what we might call 'opaque' place-names.* Little more than local mnemonics to help fishermen (and pilots, no doubt) remember points of risk or advantage, these jingles make little sense other than as local safety lore, and would probably have been transient in many cases if they had not been caught up and conserved by the map makers. In one case we catch a Sunderland keelman 'in the act':

> Upward of thirty years ago, I discovered a rock situate about a hundred yards without the bar, bearing from the Harbour South, about S.E. by E. I went… and found that it resembled, in figure, something like a soldier's centry box…but much larger…

> (Douglas, 1848, p.59, re 1810s)

Other examples abound: the 'Sow & Pigs' (detached rocks near Blyth), 'Spotty's Hole' (near Sunderland), 'Boardroom End' (near Boulmer), 'Priest's Fireside' (Lynemouth), etc. In a very few cases, it is possible to recover the reason for the name; more usually not.

And here it would be unwise to neglect the possible role of tourism. Walks were in place and the 'Romantic' beauties of Castle Eden Dene admired by the mid-eighteenth century; in the 1790s, inspired by the vaunted health benefit of sea air, the Milbanke family had Seaham Hall built overlooking dene and coast. A

---

*Some effort went into selecting the term 'opaque' (i.e. not understandable at a literal level); arguably they once exhibited a descriptive justification, rather as our many strange plant-names like 'foxglove' or 'toadstool' could be pre-literate guides to young trainees in herbs. But usually, the opaqueness has taken over.

century, later, the 'day by the seaside' was in full swing, and visitors would swim, take trips in boats, fish, photograph or paint seascapes, observe Nature on the foreshore, collect pebbles, fossils, moluscs or seaweeds at low tide, and much more... "Now yon crags there, we call them the Betty Muffet Rocks." "How interesting. Why is that?" and so on – the temptation to exploit a range of intriguing names can have been hard to resist. The Rev. T.W. Becan typically gilded the possible when seeking to explain 'Bessy's Hole' (Seaham seafront): Bessy, he wrote, "may have been the smugglers' galley [moll?], permanently or temporarily housed to receive the law-breaking, night-sailing, fortune-seeking men of the sea" (*Sunderland Echo*, 17 November, 1965).

To recover the etymology (origin) of a coastal place-name may not be a simple or logical process. Rather than treat each coastal feature-name individually, they are analysed below in terms of patterns within types of feature (the common names for headlands, for rocky shelves, etc.). This seems our best chance of understanding how and when the sea-forest of names came about. To unravel these layers may not be fully possible, but hopefully the process of attempt will provide some interesting evidence.

Chapter 1. Headland words

One of the most useful set of coastal place-names for analysis is the set of terms for 'headland', especially *snook, ness* and *nab*. To consider these in a fuller context, a full range of terms for the concept is explored here:

brigg – origin: < OE *brycg* ('bridge'); compare Old Norse bryggja 'landing-stage, gangway, movable pier'. 'Brij' is the southern pronunication, 'brig' the northern form, but exhibiting the southern not the ON meaning. early use: 1300+ *Cursor Mundi* "þai mad a brig/ouer a litel burn to lig" (bridge). c.1375 Barbour, *Bruce*, "A brig thai had, for till lat fall/Richt fra the bat [boat] apon the wall." (Gangplank.) In the broader sense of 'bridge' as a crossing place, the OE poem *Battle of Maldon* uses the word of a causeway, covered at high tide. Less clear is the case of Filey Brigg – just possibly there was once a landing facility, compatible with the Norse sense of the word 'brigg': "Filey Brigg is a most dramatic feature of the coast. A ridge of Lower Calcareous Grit stretches a mile out into the sea, like a great breakwater... There is said to be an artifical pier of stone running south from it, called by fishermen the Spittal, and built by the Romans, who made a harbour here" (Seymour, 1974, p.196). Local examples: Brig Head (detached rocks, Cresswell, N'd) OS 1899; Brig Head (path on sands, Lynemouth, N'd) OS 1899; Horsebridge Head (detached shingle, Newbiggin, N'd) OS 1899; Filey Bridge (MP, 1760s), Filey Bridge or Brig, LW 1794; Brigg End (Filey, Yx) modOS.

But do you know, sir, how the haddock came by these [black] marks? The legendary tale of Filey says, that the devil in one of his mischievous pranks determined to build Filey bridge for the destruction of ships and sailors, and the annoyance of fishermen, but that in the progress of his work he accidentally let fall his hammer into the sea, and being in haste to snatch it back caught a haddock, and thereby made the imprint, which the whole species retains to this day.

(William Hone, 1837, p.638)

cape – origin: from French < Latin *caput* 'head'. meaning: 'a piece of land jutting into the sea; a projecting headland or promontory' (*OED*). Early example: 1386, Chaucer, Prologue, "from Gootlond to the Cape of ffynystere".
(**note**: This later addition to the range of words is usually reserved to indicate promontaries abroad.)

end – origin: common Germanic. Meaning: termination of a feature. Local examples: Ness End (Holy Is.) WL 1819; Snookend (Holy Is.) WL 1819; Steel End (Holy Is.) OS 1899; Carr End (Nth Sunderland, N'd) OS 1899; Southrock End (Nth Sunderland, N'd) OS 1899; Boardroom End (Boulmer, N'd) OS 1899; Beacon End (Newbiggin, N'd) OS 1899; Hardend (south mouth of Tyne) MP 1760s; Sandsend (nYx) modOS.

(**note**: used to pinpoint part of a larger feature, often itself a promontory.)

gare – origin: possibly from French *gare*, in the sense of a 'basin' or 'jetty', i.e. mooring station; but likelier from OE *gar* 'spearhead', used of an angular point or promontory in the late ninth century. *EDD* – gore, EA, Sth; *gair* Sc, N'd, Yx, Linx. Early example: Alfredian, Orosius, "Ispania land is þry-scyte...an ðæra garena lið suðwest" (Spain is three-cornered...one of the points lies southwest). Local examples: Skeney Gar (south tip Farne Is.) OS 1899; North Gare Breakwater (Seaton Carew, D'm) OS 1899; North Gare Sands (Seaton Carew, D'm) OS 1899.

(**note**: with expected congruence between OE and N'd/D'm.)

head – origin: OE, *heafod*. Meaning: This seems to combine the sense of 'head' as 'the top, summit, upper end' (*OED*) with 'a projecting point of the coast, esp. when of considerable height' (*OED*). Early examples: c.1155 *Newminster Cartulary*, "Usque ad Gladenehefde". 1461 *Liber Pluscardensis*, "Apud locum qui Sanct Abbis Heid vocatur" (At the place which is called St Abb's Head). Local examples: Hud's Head (Tweedmouth, N'd) *LW*, 1794, OS 1899; Bear's Head (Spittal, N'd) OS 1899; Emmanuel Head (Holy Is.) *LW* 1794; Brig Head (detached rocks, Cresswell, N'd) OS 1899; Beacon Point and Element Head (Lynemouth, N'd) OS 1899; Broken Head (Seaham, D'm) LW 1794; West Carr Head (Teesmouth) modOS; Widdy Head (Whitby, nYx) modOS; Flamborough Head (eYx) *MP*, 1760s, *LW*, 1794.

(**note**: In some cases this may represent an abbreviation of 'headland'. Thus Flamborough Head appears in 1540 as 'Hedelonde'.)

headland – meaning: 'A point of land projecting into the sea or other expanse of water' (*OED*). Early examples: 1527 *Hakluyt Voyages*, "An head lond called Capo verde". 1769 *De Foe's Tour of Great Britain*, "The Cape or Head-land of St. Bees... still preserves its Name".

(**note**: Equivalent to 'cape' and perhaps originating as a translation of that word – but rarely used in placenames, where the shorter alternative 'head' is preferred.)

nab – origin: < ON. *nabbr / nabbi* 'a projecting peak or knoll', compare Sw. nabb (dial. *nabbe*) 'nab, promontory, prominence'; ?plus OE *cnæp*. *EDD* as *knab* Sc, Nth, Mids, Sx, Hants. Meaning: 'A projecting or jutting out part of a hill or rock; a peak or promontory; a rocky or outstanding hill, a summit, etc.' (*OED*). 1787 Grose: nab – 'the summit of a rock or mountain'. 1827 Brockett: nab, nabb – 'a protuberance, an elevated point, the rocky summit and outermost verge of a hill'. 1849 Dinsdale, Tees: nab – 'abrupt termination of a hilly ridge'. 1855 Robinson *Whitby Gloss.* 'Nab, a rocky projection from the land into the sea'. 1868 Atkinson (Cleveland): nab – 'a rocky headland'. 2006 'sharp fall at a hill range edge' (Vic Wood, nYx). Early examples: 1360s "le nabb de Bles clif"? near Bilton, Yx. (*BL MS Egerton 2868*). 1400–50 *Alexander*, "And...in þe nabb speris" (and on the rock climbs). Local examples: Nab Nab (Redcar, NYx) OS Online Gazetteer; Eston Nab. "It slopes gently up from the southern Guisborough side but then there is a sharp drop down to Teesside on its north side" (Vic Wood, nYx); Highcliffe Nab above Guisborough (nYx) (Vic Wood); Hod Nab – "Point on cliff near Staithes used as landmark" (nYx) (Umpleby); Redhouse Nab (Staithes, nYx) modOS; Cowbar Nab (Staithes, nYx) modOS; Old Nab (Staithes, nYx) modOS; Scab Nab (Kettleness, nYx) modOS; The Nab (Robin Hood's Bay, nYx) modOS; Miller's Nab (Robin Hood's Bay, nYx) modOS; Saltwick Nab (Yx) Robinson *Whitby Gloss*, 1855; Birk Nab (nYx) OS Online GazeteerBirkby Nab (nYx) OS Online Gazeteer; Black Nab (nYx) OS Online Gazeteer; Nab End x2 (nYx) OS Online Gazeteer; Nab Ridge (nYx) OS Online Gazeteer; Nabs (nYx) OS Online Gazeteer; White Nab (Scarborough) Admiralty Survey to 1951; Yons Nab (Scarborough) Admiralty Survey to 1951; Long Nab (Scarborough) Admiralty Survey to 1951; Cunstone Nab (Filey) modOS.

(**note**: This is a useful marker of Viking influence. The OS Online Gazeteer gives over fifty place-names including 'nab', all in the Viking-settled North. These include (not listed above) Nab Farm x2 (nYx) and Nabb Farm (D'm). It is applied to both coastal and inland features.)

Naze – origin: < local version of Fr *nez*? Compare also OE *nasu* 'nose', ON *nasar* 'nostrils'. Meaning: 'A promontory or headland, a ness' (*OED*). Local example: Carr Nase (Filey Brigg, Yx) Admiralty Survey to 1951.

(**note**: a rare example, the word is only recorded from the eighteenth century. Compare Walton-on-the-Naze (Essex).)

neb – origin: OE *nebb* 'bill, beak, nose'. (*EDD*) in general use. Meaning: 'a point, a beak, also the nose, the mouth' (Brockett, 1829). Example: lacking – only the ON cognate *nab* is used in this sense, but note southern 'Portland Bill'.

nese – origin: a further variant of 'nose' or 'naze', esp. Scottish, distinguished by the long /e/ vowel. meaning: 'A ness or headland' (*OED*). Early example: 1497 via *Aberdeen Reg.*: "It was… ordanit that ij kelis… be brocht to the neyss" (it was ordained that 2 keelboats be brought to the nese).

ness – origin: OE *næs* 'headland' (cf. OE *nasu*, *nosu* 'nose'); ON nes. *EDD* – Sc, Yx, Lx, Man, Lincs, Shrop, Kt. Meaning: 'a promontory, headland, or cape' (*OED*). Early examples: 778 Kemble charters III, 382, 28: Tucingnaes. 801 Kemble charters I, 216, 25: "on Taemise fluvio ubi dicitur Fiscnaes" (on the River Thames at a place called Fishness). 1049 *OE Chronicle* (MS. C): "þa oðre foron on East Seaxon to Eadolfes næsse" (then others travelled into Essex to Eadolf's Ness). Local examples: Ness End (Holy Is.) WL 1819; Sharpness Point (N'd). Heslop 1880s: "[ness] appears only once in Northumberland (Sharpness Point)" – or does Harkess Rocks (Bamburgh, N'd) represent a second?; Sandsend Ness (nYx) modOS; Kettle Ness (Whitby, nYx) LW, 1794; Ness Point or North Cheek (Robin Hood's Bay, nYx) modOS; Ness Rock (Robin Hood's Bay, nYx) modOS; Crook Ness (Hundale, nYx) modOS; Scalby Ness (Scarborough) Admiralty Survey to 1951.

(**note**: Bosworth and Toller observe "the word ness, found in English local names, is mostly of Scandinavian origin." Certainly the main concentration of –ness place-names is in the Orkneys and Shetland; the OS Online Gazeteer also gives a few examples in the south, e.g. Sheerness, Dungeness, Kent). The word is used in Anglian poetry (e.g. *Beowulf*) and occasionally in Anglo-Saxon charters as noted above, and cannot be considered purely a footprint of Viking presence. In North Yorkshire, it is typical of the stretch Whitby to Scarborough, while nab is used rather more widely on the Viking coast. Nonetheless, the existence of the two similar terms is thoughtworthy. Most famous of the Anglo-Saxon occurrences of 'ness' is the siting of Beowulf's burial mound on 'Hronesnæs' (Whale's Ness), not alas, to be sought on the North East coast of England, but conveying the respect felt to headlands where, in current English terms, a ruined abbey or castle might be expected.)

Then the Geats constructed
a mound on the headland; it was high and wide
to be visible to seafarers from afar;
and over ten days built
the hero's memorial, surrounded
the ashes of the pyre with a wall, as most properly
wise elders could devise.
They placed in the mound rings and jewels,
along with such treasures as were found in the
[dragon's] hoard
that graceless men had formerly hidden,
riches left for the earth to keep,
gold in the ground, where it still remains
as useless to men as it ever was.
Then round the mound rode warriors,
sons of the leaders, twelve in number;
they wished to speak their grief and mourn the
king,
make their word-chant and commemorate the
man,
express his courage and brave acts,
praise his goodness, as it is fitting
any man praise his amicable lord,
think well of him, when the soul onward
from the body is conducted.
So the Geatish people mourned
the fall of their lord; his hearthmen
professed that of world-kings
he was the mildest of men and most merciful,
most caring of his people and keenest for glory.
                                    (*Beowulf*, 3156–3182)

nose – origin: OE *nosu*. Local example: Noses Point (Dawdon, D'm) OS, 1899.

(**note**: the idea behind several of the words for 'headland', but rarely found itself.)

nook – origin: *OED* says "a Scandinavian origin seems probable" – cf. Norw. dialect nok 'hook'. Not recorded in common English before 1300.

EDD re exterior angle – Sc, Nth. Meaning: 'a point of land running into the sea; a headland or promontory' (*OED*). 'neuk, nyuk, nuick, nuik – a nook, a corner' [either recessed or projecting] Heslop, 1880s. Early examples. 1487 Barbour's *Bruce*: "On Turnberyis nwk [variant: snuke] he may mak a fyre". 1577 Harrison via Holinshed, "As for Galloway it selfe, it yeeldeth out a great point, promontory or cape (which the Scots call a Mule or Nuke) into the Irish Sea". Local examples. Blyth Nook (headland north of Blyth river mouth) *LW* 1794; Ryhope Nook (D'm) OS 1899; Blue Nook (end of rocks, Saltburn, nYx) modOS; Low Nook (end of extended rocks, Robin Hood's Bay, nYx) modOS.

(**note**: used here of an obtruding corner, the temptation is to think of an Old Norse word permeating Anglian areas; but the few examples do not permit a clear conclusion.)

point – origin: from French < Latin *punctum*. Meaning: 'The tapering extremity of any promontory or piece of land running into the sea' (*OED*). Early example: 1553 "He discovered a corner or poynt of the sayd mayne land" (1st example). Local examples: There are at least fifty-eight examples, between Berwick and Filey Head and little to be gained from a full listing. Many simply reflect the neighbouring settlement name, e.g. Beadnell Point (N'd), Horden Point (D'm); some are less specific, e.g. Castle Point (Dunstanburgh, N'd), Crag Point (Whitley, N'd); with relatively few 'opaque' names. In a few cases, 'Point' qualifies an earlier promontory name, as in Snook Point (Beadnell, N'd), Noses Point (Dawdon, D'm)…

(**note**: The relatively late date of 'Point' coming into use suggests it is not a direct effect of Norman-French rule, but the application of a time when it has become the standard English word, and (perhaps) the preference of cartographers.)

snab – origin: /s/ + nab? but compare Flemish *snabbe* 'point of land' 1460. *EDD* – Sc. Meaning: 'the projecting part of a hill' (Heslop, 1880s), 'a rugged rise or point' (OED). Local examples: Black Snabb (point and rocks, Howick, N'd) LW 1794; Snab Rocks and Snab Point (Cresswell, N'd) OS 1899.

(**note**: it is hard to determine whether this is an original Old Northumbrian term or a later adaptation of *nab*. The three examples given by the OED come from Scotland.)

snook – origin: Old Northumbrian? Either an independent form or /s/ + *nook* (see *nook* and *snab* above, and cf. Norw. dial. *snoðka* 'to snuff, smell'). To 'cock a snook' is to extend the hand in front of the nose, to deride someone. *EDD* – N'd and Som, 1891. Meaning: 'A projecting point or piece of land; a promontory' (*OED*); 'a beak-like, projecting headland' (Heslop, 1880s). Early examples: 956 Sawyer charter 606 (Kemble V, 344, 33) of King Eadwig re Bleadon, Somerset: "…of þære dic on færsc mærus west sn can, of þam sn can on fulan mære east weardne…" (from that ditch into the fresh ?marsh west of the snook; from the snook into the foul ?marsh eastward…). c.1236 *Newminster Cartulary*: "In illa parte agri quæ vocatur le Snoc" (In that part of the field which is called The Snook). c.1297 *Documents Illustr. Hist. Scotl.* (1870): "In factura pontis castri Berwyci, muri lapidei juxta mare subtus le Snoke" (In making the bridge of the castle of Berwick, walls of stone near the sea below The Snook). 1648 Blaeu Atlas Engl.: "The Snewke or Conny warren" (Holy Island). Local examples: Snookend (Holy Is.) (*WL*, 1819) ("a long sandy point, with small hillocks" (Baharie, 1849, p.19); Snook or Sunderland Point (N'd) (WL, 1819); Snook or North Sunderland Point OS 1899; Ebbe's Snook or Beadnell Point (N'd) OS 1899; Snook and Snook Point (headland with rocks running forth, Beadnell) OS 1899; Dawden Snook (D'm) OS, 1850s; Seaton Snook (clifftop than headland?, Seaton Carew, D'm) OS, 1899, ?LW, 1794; Snook Banks (Easington, D'm) OS, 1899.

(**note**: The concentration in N'd/D'm is striking. While the possibility remains that its root is /s/+nook and therefore shows ON influence, it is notable that 'snook' is not typical of Viking-settled North Yorkshire. Rather, a small number of early examples from the south suggest this was a valid OE word, while the cluster of occurrences in the North-East suggest it may have once been specifically Old Northumbrian. Other examples include Snook Bank, a farm near Glantlees, Swarland, N'd (inland) and Snooks Farm inland near Walhampton, Hants (from OS Online Gazeteer), The Snook "which was a quiet spot on the River Allen. A tributary of the Derwent, it could be described as 'headlandish'", Jack Gair; Snook Hill near Winlaton (Tyne), Snook Acres Farm (Witton Gilbert, D'm – ?re bend in R.Browney) and one Seaton Snook on Shetland (these via Google online search to term 1300).)

Some headland anomalies

Ebbs Hook (point and rocks) N'd, (*LW*, 1794). A sharp bend or angle, e.g. a bend in a river. Perhaps in some cases influenced by Du. *hoek* 'corner, nook' (*OED*) though Northern 'nook' would be expected.

Loom (headland, Easington, D'm) (OS, 1899). Possibly from dialect *loomy* 'misty'; the *OED* gives 'loom', as a noun, of something looming, as especially maritime. "'Loom': at sea at night is the 'loom of a light[house]', the over-the-horizon illumination seen before you can discern the actual flashes; a useful early warning" (Adrian Osler); *EDD* – 'the hazy appearance of land towards the horizon', Sc, nYx.

The Snood (Holy Is.) (OS, 1899). Presumably after *snood* 'a piece of fishing line' – see Part Three: Fishing.

Conclusion

Although a variety of usage is found on the North Sea coast, the gradation from 'snook' (Old Northumbrian?) in Northumberland to 'nab' (Old Norse) in Yorkshire is surely significant of the identity of the dominant name-givers in these areas who are also the last dominant settlers.

A number of uncertainties revolve around the question of forms with initial /s/. North East dialect has a number of examples where initial /s/ was added to a word (*spiles* for *piles*, *skwits* for *quits*, and (nationally) the link of *sneeze* to *nose*). If *snook* and *snab* (and less probably *scar*) fit this process, then it attests to Old Norse influence throughout the North Sea coast, subject to local modifiation. However, forms with initial /s/ are more likely valid and perhaps distinct Old Northumbrian terms.

One other line worth exploring might be the geology of the rocks involved: in North Yorkshire this is the Jurassic Lias series; in Co.Durham the Permian (Magnesian) Limestone; north of the Tyne, the Coal Measures, and further north in Northumberland, a Mountain Limestone from the Carboniferous Age, with some whinstone and basalt intrusions. However, while the geological formation of a headland might intrigue modern man, initial naming was surely more practical – and related to usefulness as seamark or as danger to shipping, no doubt taking account of height, shape, colour...

Chapter 2. Rock shelves and isolated rocks

The standard term for an isolated rock is, understandably, rock, plural rocks (from French). Somewhat less common are forms in –stone (from Old English). The dominant form may not come from French influence as such, but via the common use of rock in Standard English. To save undue repetition, the comparison below concentrates on the less usual terms.

bus – origin: perhaps from Northern and Scots form of 'bush'. Meaning and local examples: bus – 'seaweed-covered rock; also, **ware buses**; e.g. The Bus a the Born, Skyenney's Bus, Falloden Bus, Gapsey Bus. Andrew Rutter suggests also *bush*' Katrina Porteus (KP, Beadnell). "The best Northumbrian example surely is Pan Bush, the dangerous breaking shoal just east of Amble entrance; meaning the Bush within sight of (salt) Pan point" Adrian Osler (AO).

carr – origin: *OED* as Old Northumbrian, but compare Welsh *caer* 'a rock', etc. *EDD* – Sc, N'd, e.g. Bondi Carr, Pan Carr, Togston Carr. Meaning: carr – 'rock or reef' (KP, Beadnell). The word seems to cover a single rock or an area of rocks. Early example: mid-tenth century *Lindisarne Gospels Gloss*. "Se ðe getimbres hus his ofer carr" (he that builds his house on a rock) (*Matt.* 7:24). Local examples: Big Harcar (Farne Is.); Scarcar (Inner Farnes) OS 1899; Shorestone Outcarrs (Bamburgh, N'd) OS 1899; Carr End (North Sunderland, N'd) OS 1899; Burn Carrs (Beadnell) OS 1899; Comely; Carr (Beadnell) OS 1899; The Hurkars (variously spelt). A striking feature in Eyemouth entrance, per AO; Little Carr (Beadnell, N'd) OS 1899; Muckle Carr (Beadnell, N'd) OS 1899; Ice Carr (Newton, N'd) OS 1899; Pern Carr (Newton, N'd) OS 1899; Fish Carr (Embleton, N'd) OS 1899; Lobster Carr (Embleton, N'd) OS 1899; Bally Carrs (Boulmer, N'd) OS 1899; Brady Carrs (Boulmer, N'd) OS 1899; Birling Carrs (Alnmouth, N'd) OS 1899; Silver Carrs (Hauxley, N'd) OS 1899; Bondy Cars (Druridge Bay, N'd) LW 1794, Bondi Carrs OS 1899; Broad Car (Druridge Bay, N'd) *LW* 1794; Delis Carrs (Newbiggin, N'd) OS 1899; Spital Carrs (Newbiggin, N'd) OS 1899. (Named after an old hospital inland); Outer Carrs (detached rocks, Newbiggin, N'd) OS 1899; Out Carr (Embleton, N'd) OS 1899; Thorns Carr (Dunstanburgh, N'd) OS 1899; West Carr (detached rocks, Teesmouth) modOS; Redcar (nYx) modOS; Ravenscar (nYx) modOS.

(**note**: car is rarely used in North Yorkshire, confirming its Northumbrian status. If 'carr' and 'scar' have unrelated origins, so may also snook/nook, snab/nab...)

crag – origin: a Celtic word (cf. Gaelic creag). Meaning: 'A steep or precipitous rugged rock' (*OED*). Early examples: c.1300 Cursor M.: "þis castel..es hei sett a-pon þe crag" (this castle is high set upon the crag). c.1350 Will. Palerne: "þat witty werwolf...kouchid him vnder a kragge" (the clever werewolf hid himself under a rock). 1375 Barbour, Bruce: "Betuixe ane hye crag and the se" (between a high crag and the sea). Local example: The Crags (Hendon) OS 1899.

(**note**: Although the word has long been in use in the North, and in 'standard' English, the Hendon example seems to be the only one in this region.)

Scar – Several etymologies and pronunciations seem to contribute to the generous use of this word:

1. **scar** – 'the face of a precipitous rock' (Atkinson, 1868, Cleveland). Origin: scar 'a break or broken piece' < ON *skarð*. According to Atkinson (Cleveland), ON, *skarð* 'is a cliff, an abrupt rock'. *EDD* – Sc: *scaur*, NE: scaar. Compare also the ON adjective skaer 'sheer' – Durham Account Rolls c.1340 mention "ij skers" (two plough-shares or sickles).

2. **scar/sker** 'a rocky surface at the foot of the sea-cliffs, or below the narrow beach, and lying, as regards the water-level, nearly awash', Atkinson; 'skeea(r) – seaweedy rocks', Bart Taylor (BT), Cullercoats. *EDD* – Sc: *skeer*, NE,Lx: *skaar*. Origin: <ON *sker* 'reef', cf. Norw. *skjær*. But Gael. sgeir 'a rock in the sea' is believed to come from the ON (thus *OED*). However, as these sources have long become confused and are often used as near-equivalents, it will be easier to treat them together: Meaning: Scar – 'rock, crag, cliff, sunken or low rock cf. skerry' (*OED*). scarre – 'a cliff or lone rock on the dry land' (Grose, 1787). Scarr – 'a rock' (*Bell-White MS 12, 1815*). Scar, skar – 'a bare and broken rock on the side of a mountain or in the high bank of a river' (Brockett, 1829). skear/skeer/skerr – 'applied to some coast rocks, as in Hadstone Skeers, etc.' (Heslop, 1880s). Scar – 'sometimes pronounced *scaur* – the face of a precipitous rock, or stony bank; a rocky surface, at the foot of the sea-cliffs, or below the narrow beach, nearly awash' (Atkinson, 1868, Cleveland). Scar, scarth – 'a line of rock bare of vegetation' (*Lonsdale Gloss*, 1869). Skeer – 'rock,

exposed reef, e.g. Iron Skeers (Howick). Andrew Rutter suggests a shore-based reef' (KP, Beadnell). Scar – 'rocky wave-cut platform' (http://geology.about.com/). Early example: Salt Skare / Salt Skars, Long-Skares – rocks off the Tees per John Seller, *The English Pilot* (London, 1671, vol.1 p.11). Local examples: Red Skirs (Tweedmouth, N'd) OS 1899; Far Skerr (Goswick, N'd) OS 1899; New Skerr (Goswick, N'd) OS 1899; Scarcar (Inner Farnes) OS 1899; Iron Scars (Howick, N'd) OS 1899; Marmouth Scars (Boulmer, N'd) OS 1899; Broad Skear (Cresswell, N'd) OS 1899; Seal Skears (detached rocks) OS 1899 (Cresswell, N'd) OS 1899; The Scarrs (Cresswell, N'd) OS 1899; Black Score (Newbiggin, N'd) OS 1899; Whitehouse Scears (Newbiggin, N'd) OS 1899; Seaton Scars (Cullercoats, N'd) *LW* 1760s; Inscar Point (Hartlepool) OS 1899; Throston Scar (Hartlepool) OS 1899; Salt Scar (detached rock, Teesmouth) modOS; Saltburn Scar (nYx) modOS; Hummersea Scar (nYx) modOS; Bias Scar (Boulby, nYx) modOS; The Scar (Whitby, nYx) modOS; High Scar (south of Whitby, nYx) modOS; West Scar (Robin Hood's Bay, nYx) modOS; Landing Scar (Robin Hood's Bay, nYx) modOS; East Scar (Robin Hood's Bay, nYx) modOS; Cowling Scar (Robin Hood's Bay, nYx) modOS; Low Scar (Robin Hood's Bay, nYx) modOS; Flat Scars (Robin Hood's Bay, nYx) modOS; High Scar (Robin Hood's Bay, nYx) modOS; Billet Scar (Robin Hood's Bay, nYx) modOS; Iron Scar (Cloughton, nYx) modOS; Hundale Scar (nYx) modOS; Flat Scar (Hundale, nYx) modOS; High Scar (Scarborough) modOS; Scarborough (nYx).

(**note**: only Northumberland examples hint at the original /e/ vowel. Examples in the south of the region seem normalised on 'scar'. The use of a long or short vowel appears arbitrary. That both scar and car occur in N'd confirms these are two separate words, and that *scar* in N'd is not just /s/ + carr – the compound use in 'Scarcar' further confirms this. Awkwardly, the two meanings of scar – as a tide-covered platform of rock and the vertical feature of a cliff fall or precipitous rock – have become inextricably confused. Nonetheless, *scar* seems to be one important example of an ON word significantly penetrating N'd.)

scarp – origin: from French *escarpe* 'steep bank'. Early example: in form 'scarp', 1589, 'escarpe', 1688 (*OED*). Local examples: Law Scap (Budle, N'd) OS 1899; Oyster Scap (Budle, N'd) OS 1899; Mussel Scarp (Coquet Is., N'd) OS 1899; Whitby Scarf (nYx) LW 1794.

(**note**: the integrity of the above group is doubtful. Its application would seem to be relatively modern, with the core meaning 'a sloping feature'?)

skerry – origin: ON, *sker* via Orkney dialect (*OED*). Meaning: 'a rugged insulated sea-rock or stretch of rocks, covered by the sea at high water or in stormy weather; a reef' (*OED*). 'A skerry is a small rocky island, usually defined to be too small for habitation. It may simply be a rocky reef', Neil Johnson (NJ). Skerry – 'a level rock outcrop lying just above low tide' (http://geology.about.com/)

(**note**: no local examples – suggestive of lack of influence from second-wave Norwegian (Viking) settlers.)

stack – origin: ON, *stakk-r* 'haystack', but more immediately from Faeroese *stakkur* 'high solitary rock in the sea'. Meaning: a detached section of cliff, standing like a tall solitary rock. 'A columnar mass of rock, detached by the agency of water and weather from the main part of a cliff, and rising precipitously out of the sea' (*OED*). Early examples: 1769 Pennant, *Tour Scot.*: Great insulated columns, called here Stacks. So also in Shetland and Orkney Islands. 1878 Huxley, *Physiogr.*: "[Rocks] completely isolated in the form of 'needles', 'stacks', and 'skerries'". 1944 A. Holmes, *Princ. Physical Geol.* xiv. 287, "Later the arch falls in, and the seaward portion of the headland then remains as an isolated stack". Local examples: Maw Stack (Seaham, D'm) OS 1899; Marstack or Dogger Rock (Horden, D'm) OS 1850s; Limekiln Stack (Whitby, nYx) modOS.

(**note**: it is likely, given the few examples, and the lack of general early usage, that this term was introduced in the NE as a common geological term in the nineteenth century.)

steel – origin: there is no detectible entry for this word in the *OED*, for it is surely a different word from metallic steel. A source is likely in OE *stægel* 'steep, abrupt' (Bosworth-Toller), a rare word in OE, but with cognates in Danish: *stejl* 'steep, precipitous' and Norw.: *steil* 'steep, abrupt'. Its limited distribution suggests a valid Old Northumbrian word, even allowing for Scandinavian cognates. Meaning: steel – 'ridge, point of tongue or land, a precipice, a rock'. *EDD* – example. N'd, Roxb); Steel – 'a rocky prominence, e.g. Boulmer Steel, Cusha Steel' (KP, Beadnell). Local examples: Parton Stiel (Budle, N'd) OS 1899; Stiel (one of the Farne Islands) WL 1819; Longhoughton Steel (Howick, N'd) OS 1899; Cushat Stiel (Dunstanburgh, N'd) OS 1899; North Steel (Coquet Is., N'd) OS 1899; South Steel (Coquet Is., N'd) OS 1899; Steel Rock (Whitburn, D'm) LW 1794; White Steel (Whitburn, D'm) OS 1899; Penny Steel (rocks from shore out, Staithes, nYx) modOS; Keldhowe Steel (rocks, Goldsborough, nYx) modOS; Bulmer Steel (south of Whitby, nYx) modOS; Peak Steel (Robin Hood's Bay, nYx) modOS; Blea Wyke Steel (Ravenscar, nYx) modOS.

(**note**: the OE online Gazeteer confirms the above limited use of 'steel' – the only other possibilities being Steel Bank (wYx) and Steelend (Fife). The term is surely useful in view of slack use of 'scar'. Regarding use of 'Steel' in nYx, an Old Northumbrian (OE) word penetrating the Viking zone is entirely possible.)

Some other forms

hoolibaloos – 'blowers' (Umpleby, Staithes, 1930s).

knaps – 'a local name for a part of the rocks' (Umpleby, Staithes, 1930s); but Brockett (1829): 'knap – the brow or projection of a hill' – *EDD* 'small hill', esp. Sth [OE cnæp].

nogglets – 'local name for part of the rocks' (Umpleby, Staithes, 1930s).

The **Torrs** (Boulmer, N'd) (OS, 1899). This may reflect the Celtic word tor 'a rock' (*EDD* – esp. SW).

South **Cheek** and North **Cheek** (Robin Hoods Bay, Yx) *LW* 1794. This describes features each side of the bay, thus 'cheeks'. *EDD* – esp. Sc. Rumble Churn (Dunstanburgh, N'd) (OS, 1899), Rumbling Kern (Howick, N'd) (OS, 1899). The Churn (Farne Is.) (*WL*, 1819). These are explained in the following note: "The Churn is a cavity in the rock near the northwest point of Farn Island, that has a hole at top through which the water is forced by the sea, and produces a beautiful *jet d'eau*, particularly when the wind is from the North-East with a heavy swell" (*WL*, 1819). Presumably the noise was felt to resemble the rumbling sound of a churn.

The Northern form *kern* either reflects ON *kirna*, or may come via Common Northern English /k/ for /ch/.

Other names for rocks may be more descriptive/opaque, e.g.: King and Queen Rocks (Filey Brigg), Admiralty Survey to 1951. Darning Needle (detached rock), (Ryhope, D'm) (OS, 1899), Needle's Eye (Newbiggin, N'd) (OS, 1899).

Black Middens (Tynemouth) (OS, 1899) – a 'midden' being a refuse heap.

Lintycock Stone (Hummersea, nYx) (modOS) (*linty* for *linnet*).

Lingrow Knock (detached rock, Runswick, nYx) modOS.

Fillet Tail (Kettleness, nYx) modOS

Clock Case (south of Whitby, nYx) modOS

Cow and Calf (south of Whitby, nYx) modOS

Sailors' Grave (rocks, Scarborough) modOS

Betty Muffet Rocks (Scarborough) modOS

Coffee Pot (?) modOS (Scarborough) modOS

Perilous Rocks (Scarborough) modOS.

Conclusion

The problem in this group comes about when words have possible origins in either OE or ON. Further study 'in the field' may provide some clarification, but in the interim it is equally valid to assert that a useful word could be borrowed from ON into Northumbrian, and vice versa. As these are often specialist terms, we can suspect direct borrowing and therefore the emergence of intercultural borrowing along the coast.

A View of the Farnes

Opposite to Bambrough lie the Farn Islands, which form two groups of little isles and rocks, to the number of 17, but at low water the points of others appear above the surface; they all are distinguished by particular names. The nearest isle to the shore, is that called the House Island, which lies exactly one mile 68 chains from the coast: the most distant is about seven or eight miles. They are rented for 16£ per annum: their produce is kelp, some few feathers, and a few seals, which the tenant watches and shoots, for the sake of the oil and skins. Some of them yield a little grass, and serve to feed a cow or two, which the people are desperate enough to transport over in their little boats.

Visited these islands in a coble, a safe but seemingly hazardous species of boat, long. narrow, and flat-bottomed, which is capable of going through a high sea, dancing like a cork on the summits of the waves.

Touched at the rock called 'Meg', whitened with the dung of cormorants, which almost covered it; their nests were large, made of tang [seaweed], and excessively foetid.

Rowed next to the Pinnacles, an island in the farthest group; so called from the vast columnar rocks at the south end, even at their sides, and flat at their tops, and entirely covered with guillemots and shags: the fowlers pass from one to the other of columns by means of a narrow board, which they place from top to top, forming a narrow bridge, over such a horrid gap, that the very sight of it strikes one with terror.

Landed at a small island, where we found the female Eider ducks, at that time sitting: the lower part of their nests was made of sea plants; the upper part was formed of the down which they pull off their own breasts, in which the eggs were surrounded and warmly bedded... The nests are built over the beach, among the loose pebbles, not far from the water... The people of this country call these St. Cuthbert's ducks, from the Saint of the islands.

(Mr Pennant, qu. W. Hutchinson, 1778, vol.2, pp.180–81)

Marsden Rock

Sensational Rock,
swimming in light.
Bird-cries clinging to ancient ledges,
Kittiwakes smashing against time.
What tales you could tell.

Your face is so moody,
flickers with breezes,
crumbles in a hot afternoon.

Climbing your powdery steps,
we look down on the sea
thrashing at you.

We join a choir of birds at your peak,
cry out to the sky
in good spirits.

Nesting for the sake of it,
our lyrics are remnants on the shore.

We keep chipping away,
do we not?

We slip
through the pebbles,
splashing
with babies.

We leave our mark,
a grain
on the ancient landscape.

We go.

We dance like the sunlight
on your scarred body:

tripping,
falling,
singing

away.

(Keith Armstrong)

Chapter 3. Hills and dales

These are worth including as they sometimes also feature as coastal names, or in the case of the Durham denes, connect directly with the coast.

bank – origin: probably ON, cf. Old Icelandic bakki, 'ridge'. Meaning: hill, slope on road. Bank, bank-top – 'edge of land, small cliff or sand-dune above sea' (KP, Beadnell). Local example: Hummersea Bank (nYx) modOS. Brae – 'a bank' (KP, Beadnell). [ON *bra* and thence to Common Northern English]. Cop – the top of anything – Yx; 'in N'd it means a high hill' (Brockett, 1829). Only used inland? [OE (Old Northumbrian?), *copp*; ON *koppr*].

dale – origin: OE dæl, pl. dalu, ON dalr. Meaning: A valley; "In the northern counties, the usual name of a river-valley between its enclosing ranges of hills or high land" (*OED*). Local examples: principally used of the main river valleys in the west of the region, e.g. Teesdale, Weardale, Tynedale, plus: Dunsley Dale (Runswick, nYx) modOS; Hun Dale (nYx) modOS.

(**note**: as a regular part of place-names in Yorkshire, surely a Viking feature.)

dene – origin: OE *denu* 'valley'. Meaning: 'the picturesque wooded hollows, each traversed by a stream, which line the sea-coast of Durham, are called denes' (Palgrave, 1896, Hetton). Dene, dene, den – 'a valley through which a burn flows' (Heslop, 1880s). Local examples: Roker Dene (Sunderland) OS 1850s; Ryhope Dene, also Cherry Knowle Dene higher up (D'm) OS 1850s; Seaham Dene (D'm) OS 1850s; Dawdon Dene (D'm) OS 1850s; Dalton Field House Dene (Dawdon, D'm) OS 1850s; Hawthorn Dene (Hawthorn, D'm) OS 1850s; Foxholes Dean OS 1850s, Horden Burn Dene OS, c.1919 (Horden, D'm); Castle Eden Dene (D'm) OS 1850s; Crimdon Dene, OS 1850s, or Thorpe Bulmer Dene, OS c.1919 (D'm).

(**note**: the dene is in effect a function of the East Durham plateau, through which the watercourses (and perhaps ice before them) cut a route downward. Though an authentic OE term is used for most of these, a few smaller examples, debouching on the coast, are listed under 'gill' – the ON equivalent. It seems two equivalent terms have been given differentiated meanings in D'm: 'large valley' and 'small valley'.)

dodd – origin: uncertain; first noted in Middle English. Meaning: 'a rounded summit or eminence, either as a separate hill, or more frequently a lower summit or distinct shoulder or boss of a hill' (*OED*); 'bare hill'. *EDD* – Sc, N'd, Cum. Dodd – 'a blunt hill or butt end of a hill. Its occurrence is noted thirteen times in place-names in N'd' (Heslop, 1880s). Local example: inland than a coastal feature.

Gill, Ghyll (/g/ pronounced hard) – origin: ON gil 'a dep glen'. Meaning: 'A deep rocky cleft or ravine, usually wooded and forming the course of a stream' (*OED*). Gill – 'a small glen or dell, properly a narrow valley with steep and rocky banks on each side, and with a stream of water running through it' (Brockett, 1829). A gill runnel – 'a rivulet or thread of water coursing along a deep dell' (Robinson, *Whitby Gloss.*, 1855). Ghyll – 'a bit of wild ground hollowed out by nature; a ravine. A common place-name in the Lake country' (Palgrave, 1896, Hetton). Local examples: Warren House Gill (Horden, D'm); Ash Gill (Easington, D'm) OS 1850s; Whitesides Gill (Easington, D'm) OS 1850s; Blackhills Gill (Easington, D'm) OS 1850s; Limekiln Gill (Easington, D'm) OS 1850s; Cross Gill (Crimdon, D'm) OS 1850s.

(**note**: this is pre-eminently the ON term for a water-cut valley, used widely in Northern counties, e.g. Cumbria. In the NE, like *beck*, it is only found in D'm outside of original Viking-settled areas.)

heugh – origin: < OE h h 'a heel, an obtruding piece of land', but also note early link with elevation: "ða hean hos" (the high heughs). Meaning: 'a precipitous or hanging descent; a craggy or rugged steep; a precipice, cliff, or scaur; most commonly, one overhanging a river or the sea' (*OED*); *EDD* 'crag, cliff' – Sc, Ire, Nth. Early examples: c.1300 Cursor Mundi, "bath ouer hil and hogh" (both over hill and heugh). c.1450 St Cuthbert, "Him thoght þat abouen þat hough he and his men lay sure ynogh". Local examples: Heugh Hill (Holy Is.) OS 1899; The Heughs (Dunstanburh, N'd) OS 1899; Craster Heugh (N'd) OS 1899: "strange [basalt] cliffs, called 'heughs'" (Creighton, 1904, 1/149); Long Heugh (Craster, N'd) OS 1899; Red Heugh (North Seaton, N'd) OS 1899; The Heugh (headland at Hartlepool).

(**note**: There are no examples on the nYx coast – though ON *haugr* ('hill, mound') develops into how as in Stanghow; *haugh/haw* 'low lying land beside a river', from OE *healh* is recorded by the *EDD* in Scotland and the North.)

hope – (i) OE *hop*. Meaning: 'land enclosed by marsh'. Early examples: 1323–24 Merton Coll. Rec. (Essex): "Unam hopam marisci continentem duas acras" (a marshy hope comprising 2 acres). 1500 Will of N. Brown: "Crofts, lands, marshes, hopes & walles". Local examples: – believed lacking. (ii) ON. h p 'a small land-locked bay or inlet, salt at flood tide and fresh at ebb' (*OED*) Given as the source for hope meaning 'valley' by the *OED*, with distribution in Scotland and the NE. Meaning: 'A small enclosed valley, esp. a smaller opening branching out from the main dale, and running up to the mountain ranges; the upland part of a mountain valley; a blind valley' (*OED*); 'a small upland valley or hollow enclosed at the upper end...' *Scots Nat. Dictionary*; Howp – 'of land, a prominence, or the cut defined by it?' (KP, Beadnell). Early examples: c.1400–50 *Alexander*: "So þai come till a caue...Betwene twa hillis in a hope". 1542 Newminster Cartul. "Such as inhabyte in one of those hoopes, valyes, or graynes" (grayne = branch or side-valley). 1596 Dalrymple tr. *Leslie's Hist. Scot.* "Ouer hil and hoip, bank and bra". Local examples: Hecla Howp, Seahouses (KP, Beadnell); and in the phrase 'skeers an' howps' (hills and hollows?). Ryhope (D'm).

how – origin: ON. *haug-r* 'mound, cairn'; 'small detached hill or mound'; *EDD* – Sc, Nth esp. Yx. Meaning: 'a hill, hillock' (*OED*). Local examples: Saltpan How (Spittal, N'd); Gallihowe (Hummersea, nYx) modOS; Lingrow Howe (Port Mulgrave, nYx) modOS; Gnipe Howe (Whitby, nYx) modOS.

(**note**: the one ex. in N'd need not negate an ON origin.)

knob – origin: probably Germanic but first appearing in Middle English. Meaning: 'A prominent isolated rounded mound or hill; a knoll; a hill in general' (*OED*); 'low roundish hill';

EDD – esp. Lx. Local example: Huntley Foot or Old Knob (Whitby) LW 1794.

(**note**: *OED* record higher use in United States place-names, perhaps reflecting its vase in Lancashire (and so possibly from Norwegian Vikings?).)

knowe – origin: OE *cnoll*. Meaning: 'knoll, hillock, rising ground' (*OED*); 'small hill'; *EDD* – Sc, Ire, Nth. Local example: Toppy Knowe (Spittal, N'd) OS 1899.

(**note**: *OED* record as limited to Scots and North dialect.)

law – origin: OE *hlāw* 'hill, mound'; *EDD* – Sc, Nth, wMids. Meaning: 'A hill, esp. one more or less round or conical' (*OED*).

North Berwick Law (N'd) *OED*
Cushat Law (Cheviots, N'd) *OED*
Bible Law (Holy Is.) OS 1899
Black Law (Bamburgh, N'd) OS 1899
Law Scap (Bamburgh, N'd) OS 1899
Old Law (Bamburgh, N'd) OS 1899

Hare Law (Bamburgh, N'd) OS 1899
Oxberry Law (Craster, N'd) OS 1899
The Lawe, South Shields 'the hilltop overlooking the Tyne entrance, where pilots had their residences' (AO).

(**note**: the cluster of 'laws' around Holy Island may alert us to the subsidiary use of the word in OE for a burial mound. Law is also used inland in Co.D'm, e.g. Maiden Law, Tow Law, but not clearly in nYx or elsewhere in the UK. Another Old Northumbrian word?)

pike – origin: likely from ON, compare West Norw. dial. *pik* 'a pointed mountain'. Meaning: a conical hill, a cairn. Pike – 'a pointed hill [esp. N'd] – dodd, in contrast, is a truncated hill; pike – a temporary haystack' (Heslop, 1880s) – but I can find no coastal examples. *OED* records as typical of Cumbria.

warsit – meaning: 'hill: Humersty Warsit, Huntcliffe Warsit, etc.' (Umpleby, Staithes, 1930s).

A little more on the denes…

It would be remiss to talk of the coast without more on the series of great denes that make the coastal zone so remarkable and 'picturesque' between Sunderland and Hartlepool. The claims of Castle Eden Dene were early recognised, and paths and a spectacular bridge in place in the eighteenth century to give access to its awesome chasms with romantic feature-names like 'Gunnar's Leap'. Here is an account of a visit to the dene by the ailing lyricist, Joseph Blackett, in a letter of 23 October 1809:

> Naturally curious, and an impassioned lover of romantic scenery, I have explored the celebrated Dean or Glen of Castle Eden. The morning seemed to promise fair, the western sky was burnished; and at nine o'clock, I left Seaham, for a sight of that rural, yet magnificent prospect. In an hour and half's riding, I reached Castle Eden, put up my horse, (the Baronet's, and who seems now perfectly acquainted with me,) at an inn; and by half past eleven, found myself in the centre of one of the wildest glens mine eyes ever beheld: Judge of my rapture, and share the transport which I then experienced.
>
> From the shelving sides of regularly sloping rocks, hung trees 'of all hues'; the light green youthful ash, the sombre yew, the sun-burnt beech, and dark shaded holly, formed to the eye the finest contrast of colours

imaginable. Mine eyes dwelt on this scene with delight; and shortly after, witnessed another with astonishment and awe – for piercing through the bosom of the Dean in a western direction, and clambering over some precipices, I came to a horrid chasm, through which the waters rushed with a force that made the adjacent perforated rocks, 're-bellow to the roar.' This is the true sublime of scenery, said I, here may the eye revel, here may the eye contemplate, on daring pinions soar beyond the little scenes of art, and glean the ears [i.e.wheat-ears] of wisdom from inspiring nature...

(The Remains of Joseph Blackett, 1811, vol.1, pp.66–67)

The great brick viaducts of the Sunderland-Miidlesbrough Railway (1900s) that span the dene mouths accenutate rather than mar the scale and solemnity of the occasion (and do not interrupt the free passage of wildlife the way filling in a dene to carry a road over it does). Despite the attempts to liberate this stretch of coast from the clutches of a now-ghostly coal trade, a new trend of industrial expansion along the coast south from Seaham is underway and should set the warning bells ringing and the watch-beacons flaring. To conserve rare examples of the natural environment is not a matter of selfishness – a pandering to our sense of Romantic Nature – but a simple act of respect to the non-human world, and an appreciation of the claim of all life-forms.

Much could (and should) be written about the risks of loss, but we'll make do with one short anecdote:

A lady from a university once came to visit the largest of the denes in search of a rare orchid believed only to grow only there, if not already entirely extinct. The local policeman fell in love with her at first sight and devoted his spare hours to working out ways to impress her. Now then, one morning, he set out to pick her a special bunch of flowers from the dene, for he knew every nook and corner of it. Imagine her surprise on being presented with a bouquet containing a few examples – possibly the very last – of the very orchid she had set out to rescue.

(Gordon Patrickson, Dawdon)

Chapter 4. Rivurine and water features

batts – 'islands in rivers or flat ground adjoining them' (Bailey, D'm, 1810), sim. (Brockett, 1829). *EDD* give as limited to N'd, nYx, but there is Low Batts (OS, 1850s) in Castle Eden Dene (D'm). Examples in nYx could sometimes refer to areas of rock: South Batts (Whitby), Pursglove Stye Batts, Normanby Stye Batts (south of Whitby).

beck – 'a mountain stream or small rivulet, a brook' (Brockett, 1829); 'a small stream... occurs about sixty-three times in the county of Durham. Thirty-eight of these are within the Tees district' (Heslop, 1880s); 'beck. Used indifferently with burn. A stream' (Palgrave, 1896, Hetton)[ON].

burn – 'a brook, or rivulet... any runner of water that is less than a river' (Brockett, 1829); 'a burn, the name in N'd for a considerable stream' (Heslop, 1880s); 'born – burn, a stream' (KP, Beadnell) [OE].

canch – 'a ledge of rock' AR, Seahouses; kansh – 'ridge of rock, sand or other obstacle in a **waterway**: "Sha's gitten ov a kansh", i.e. coble had run ashore on a ridge in the harbour' (Umpleby, Staithes, 1930s); *EDD* gives ex., N'd, of canches or steps in a river bed giving rise to mill-race like turbulence [source unknown; compare Mids. cank-stone]; *EDD* – Nth, Mids, EA.

carr – 'a marsh' [only x1 in N'd: Prestwick Carr] – 'a rocky place' [x20 in N'd] (Heslop, 1880s) [the roots are: carr = rock, ONorthumbrian/Celtic – see above; carr = marsh, ON].

cleugh – 'a rocky valley' (*Bell-White MS 12*). [OE *cloh*]; *EDD* – Sc, Nth, Mids.

drumley – 'muddy or thick water' (Grose, 1787); drumly, drummely – 'muddy, thick; as applied to the mind, confused' (Brockett, 1829); drumly – 'muddy, thick cf. jumly' (Heslop, 1880s).

dub – 'a pool of water' (Grose, 1787).

forse – 'a cascade' (Bailey, 1810, D'm). [ON *fors*]; *EDD* – Nth only.

goit – 'a watercourse; any channel for water; a stream' (*OED*). Bird Flight Goit (Saltburn, nYx), Seal Goit (Saltburn, nYx) modOS. [*OED* as variant of *gote* < OE *geotan* 'to pour' or MDu. *gote*]; *EDD* – Yx, Lx.

gut – narrow passage, waterway: Fish Quay Gut (North Shields), Fittin Oot Gut (Readheads Shipyard, South Shields) MBS; Piper Gut (Farne Islands), The Benty Gut (KP, Beadnell); Willington Gut, Nth of Tyne; "canny Teamgut" – mouth of R. Team. C19/1 (Harker, 1985, p.94); New Gut (passage through rocks, Hummersea, nYx) modOS; Old Gut (Hummersea, nYx) modOS; *EDD* – general

hole, hyel – 'an inlet. The Benty Hyel' (KP, Beadnell) [cf. *howle*] *EDD* – esp. nYx.

holm – 'low flat land caused by alluvion – a small island' (Brockett, 1829). [ON *holmr* 'creek' or 'shore meadow'].

howle – an access or inlet. Examples. in modOS come from Marske (nYx): Mill Howle, Millclose Howle, Red Howle, Bydale Howle, Church

Howle, Hurries Howle. [*OED* gives as variant of *holl* < OE *hol* 'a hollow place; a cave, den; a hole'].

kaims – 'gravel ridges or banks' (AR, Seahouses). [geologically, 'elongated mounds of post-glacial gravel' (*OED*); in the sense of 'crest', *OED* relates this to *comb*, but compare also dialect *cams* 'hills'].

linn – 'a cascade' (Bailey, 1810, D'm); lin, linn – 'a cascade' (D'm and N'd) (Brockett, 1829) [OE *hlynn*, Gaelic *linn*].

a mizzy – 'a quagmire' (*Kennet BL MS Lansdowne* 1033), as Northern [?from *moss*]; *EDD* – Lx, NE.

moss – 'bog' (KP, Beadnell). [OE *meos* 'moss, bog']; *EDD* – all Nth.

ratch – 'the straight course of a navigable river. The word is used on the Tyne in the same sense as Reach on the Thames. The Newcastle keelmen generally call it Rack' Brockett 1829; rack / ratch – 'reach of navigable river: Hebburn Rack' (Heslop 1880s) [N and S forms of 'reach'].

sike – small watercourse: "to Wallington by the seevy sike" (Harker, 1985, p.173). ?C18/2 [OE *sic*, ON *sik*]; *EDD* – Sc, Nth, Mids.

slack (noun) – 'an inlet' (KP, Beadnell); 'Jarra Slaks' MBS [same as next word]; *EDD* – esp. Nth

slakes – 'mud-flats, e.g. Waren Slakes' (KP, Beadnell). [*OED* 'mud, slime']; *EDD* – Sc, Nth, Mids.

sleck – 'mud at a river where the tide comes in and out' (AG, Ashington); 'slimy mud, sludge' (BA, Seaton Sluice) [source unknown, compare 'slakes'].

stank – 'an embankment for damning back water' (Heslop, 1880s) [properly 'a pool', OF *estanc*].

stell – 'tidal drainage channel' M'bro per BG ['an open ditch or brook' *OED* but compare *stell*, in fishing section]; *EDD* – N'd, D'm, Yx.

This word group is not essentially coastal, but contains some interesting evidence. Thus, ON-based *ghyll* and *beck* parallel the OE-based *dene* and *burn*, and are typical of, repectively, Teesside and Northumberland. However, all four terms are used side by side in East Durham, which suggests an early affinity, as the words are not widely available through Common Northern English.

Erosion is a practical problem with settlements like Robin Hood's Bay and Runswick especially vulnerable. It is worth remembering that cliff erosion can come equally from surface water at the top as from sea action at the base. Flooding inland from sea water is not expected in our region, given the cliffs along much of the coast, but a river in spate can cause considerable damage...

The Sheel Raw Flud

'S lang as aw live awl nivor forget
One Setorday wen it was se wet,
Ivory body wis nearly <u>bet</u>   overwhelmed
  Fra th' Setorday till th' Sunda', O!
The ducks did quack an' the cocks did craw,
For wat wis up thae diddent naw,
It neerly droon[d]ed awl Sheel Raw,
  That nasty Sunda' mornin', O!

Mall Jonson tiv hor husbind sais:
"Reech me ma stockens en ma stais,
For God' suaik let me heh ma stais,
  Or else aw will be droonded, O!"
"Tha clais," said he, "thor <u>guain we</u> mine,   gone with
Like <u>Boyd</u> an' <u>Elliott</u>, up the Tyne;   (professional rowers)
Aw've leukt fra five, an' noo its nine,
  This nasty Sunda' mornin', O!"

On the bed she began to rowl,
An' flung hor airms aroond th' powl,
Sa'en, "Lord heh marcy on maw sowl
  This nasty Sunda' mornin', O!"
Th' vary cats thae ran up staires,
Got on thor nees ta sae thor prairs,
Thinkin' thae wor gon <u>for fairs</u>   for real
  That nasty Sunda' morning', O!

Aw wis sorry for Sally Clark,
Th' fire wis oot, an' awl wis dark,
She gat oot i' bed wi nowt but hor <u>sark</u>,   shift
  That nasty Sunda' mornin', O!
She muaid a splash we sic a <u>clattor</u>,   row, noise
Thit Bob cried oot, "Sal, wat's th' mattor?"
She sais, "Aw's up to me eyes i' wattor,
  It must be a nasty mornin', O!"

Bob jump'd oot of he's bed an' awl,
He went where ivor he heerd hor squal,
But th' wattor wis alwis shiften Sal,
  That nasty Sunda' mornin', O!
At last th' wattor brust opin th' dor,
An' weshed away buaith Bob an' hor,
At <u>Tinmith</u> they wer wesh't ashore,   Tynemouth
  That nasty Sunda' mornin', O!

(Tommy Armstrong)

Chapter 5. Bay and harbour words

bay – origin: *Fr baie*. Meaning: 'an indentation of the sea into the land with a wide opening' (*OED*); in general usage, 'a sheltered, recessive stretch of coast between two headlands'. Early examples: 1385 Trevisa Higden: "In that grete mouthe and baye, beth ilondes Calchos, Patmos, and others". 1596 Shakespeare, *Merch.*: "The skarfed barke puts from her native bay". Local examples: there are twenty-one examples, by my count, from Berwick to Filey, making this the standard word here as on the rest of the coast.

haven – origin: OE hæfen. Meaning: 'A recess or inlet of the sea, or the mouth of a river, affording good anchorage and a safe station for ships' (*OED*) – thus a natural harbour. Early examples: 1031 OE Chron., "þa hæfenan on Sandwic" (the havens at Sandwich). c.1205 Layamon, "þat hauen of Douere he hauede inumen" (that haven of Dover he had captured). Local examples: Meadow Haven (Berwick); Brownsman Haven, Pinnacles Haven, (Farne Is.); Stamford Haven (Inner Farnes); Beadnell Haven (N'd; St Mary's or Newton Haven (N'd); Craster Haven (N'd); Howick Haven (N'd); Boulmer Haven (N'd); Hauxley Haven (N'd); Prior's Haven (Tynemouth); Man Haven (north of Marsden, D'm); Soft Leas Haven (Hartlepool); Wine Haven (south of Robin Hood's Bay, nYx).

(**note**: the vast majority n Northumberland, in accordance with its Anglo-Saxon origin.)

pool – origin: OE p l 'a pool' cf. ON *pollr*, but also Welsh *pwll*. Meaning: large area of calm water, from 'a deep and still place in a river or stream' (*OED*). Early examples: 1000+ Birch, Cart. Sax., I. 57: "endlonge burne in þane pol buue Crocford" (along the stream to the pool above Crockford). 1632 Massinger, *City Madam*, "The ship is safe in the Pool, then?" Local example: Hartlepool, only. Hartlepool possesses a considerable natural harbour, prominent in the Middle Ages; compare Liverpool, Poole in Dorset, etc.

wyke – origin: from ON *vik* – used of the inlets on the Scandinavian coast from which the Vikings received their name. Meaning: 'a creek, inlet, or small bay' (*OED*); *wik, wyck, or wyke* – 'a crook or corner, as in a river or the sea shore' (Brockett, 1829); *EDD* gives wick/wyke 'corner, hollow' – Sc, Ire, Nth, eMids. Local examples: Hole Wyke (Boulby, nYx) modOS; Rosedale Wyke (Port Mulgrave, nYx) modOS; Overdale Wyke (Sandsend, nYx) modOS; Deepgrove Wyke (Sandsend, nYx) modOS; Maw Wyke Hole (Whitby, nYx) modOS; Ground Wyke (Robin Hood's Bay, nYx) modOS; Blea Wyke (area of water, Hayburn, nYx) modOS; Blea Wyke Steel (Hayburn, nYx) modOS; Hayburn Wyke (nYx) modOS; Cloughton Wyke (bay, nYx) modOS; Longhorn Wyke (Scarborough) modOS; The Wyke (Filey) modOS.

(**note**: a feasible ON alternative to the 'havens' of N'd?)

Working in Harbour

The North Dock was not a pleasant place then. The discarded guts from the butchers and the muck from all the drains emptied into the North Dock direct. My Dad used to smoke cigarettes in harbour to avoid the smell. And of course it was ideal for rats. They lived in holes in the cliff all round the dock. I remember once we were putting nets over the side and there was a rat caught up in it; we just hoyed it overboard with the net.

To work on the boat, we would strand it on the slope outside the North Dock. The bottom would be covered with tar you could purchase from the Gas Works. The upperwork was painted – with whatever was at hand – ours was painted green and white, but blue was a favourite colour. Cobles and mules were open boats in those days – no canvas covers (we call them 'dodgers') in the bow – that would have interfered with stepping the mast. You would wear whatever you could to keep warm – but not gloves. You needed to be able to use your hands: the very work seemed to keep them agile in the cold weather. Once I had to take my oilskins off and lay them over the engine, I recall – for fear the magneto and leads would get wet in the rain. It was more important to protect the engine than me.

Many fishing boats would work like this on a daily basis. The fish caught would be eaten locally, though if the wind were seriously strong, a sailing vessel might have to make for Sunderland or Hartlepool and sell the catch there. Today, still, there are traditional cobles in Seaham Harbour, but tending to rely on motors rather than sails, and with a canvas-covered shelter at the very bow.

(Joe Henry, Seaham)

Chapter 6. Shore and beach terms

The seashore

bent – 'a long coarse kind of grass, which grows in the counties of Northumberland and Durham, near the sea, and is sometimes used for thatch' (Brockett, 1829); 'a coarse kind of grass, usually growing on wet land, or on sand hills upon the sea shore; hence *the Bents*, a name for grassy sand dunes' (Heslop, 1880s) [bents – 'grassy field or surface' (*OED*), esp. North] *EDD* – general.

braid – 'a solid and secure place for a boat to be parked' (Joan Philips re Cullercoats, Amble).

dabba – 'a stick with point on end for catching flat fish on sand (children)' (KP, Beadnell).

a hard, noun – 'a piece of hard ground, e.g. Boulmer Sooth Hard, Byre-End Hard' (KP, Beadnell).

hole, hyel – 'rockpool' (KP, Beadnell).

kythin – 'worm casts on the beach sand' (AR, Seahouses) [OE *cyððan* 'to make know', here in the sense of evidence?]; *EDD* – N'd only.

links – dunes. 'Alang the links' (KP, Beadnell); 'undulating sandy ground near the sea-shore' (*OED*). In N'd, sometimes equivalent to 'golf course' [OE *hlinc*].

pee-wit-land – 'cold, wet, bad land which the pee-wit generally haunts' (Brockett, 1829).

sand-cowpees – 'people who took sand for sale' (BA, Seaton Sluice); [cowp 'to swap, sell'].

sands – the beach: "Aa yes gannin doon the sands – are you going to the beach?" (Helen Hemingway (HH), S/Shields). Principal name in NE for a beach. [The origin of 'beach' is unknown, though typical of the south coast usage; could it be a southernisation of ON *bakki* 'bank'?].

sandy-lowpers – 'sand-hoppers, small flea-like creatures which live in seaweed on the beach' (KP, Beadnell) [lowp – to leap, from ON].

seaves – rushes. Seaveybog Hill (Goldsborough, nYx) modOS. [ON *sef*].

spart / spret – the rush: "the grun's varry sparty here aboot" (Heslop, 1880s) [earlier forms: *sprat, sprot* – *OED* as Scots]; *EDD* – Sc, Nth, D'm.

swath – 'a small piece of land among rock on the shore' (Amble / Newbiggin only) (KP,Beadnell) [?swarth].

tath (noun), **tathy** (adjective) – 'rough grass. "Tathy grass"' (KP, Beadnell) [ON *tað* 'dung', i.e. manured land].

trink – 'dip in sand holding deeper water' (KP, Beadnell). [AN *trenque* 'trench'].

wetter-hyels – 'rockpools' (KP, Beadnell).

willik – 'winkle shell on beach' (AG, Ashington).

plus

hole – cave, fissure [< OE *hol*]. Main examples (unchecked as yet for variant meanings): Braidstone Hole (North Sunderland, N'd), Collith Hole (Beadnell, N'd), Nacker Hole (Beadnell, N'd), Liverpool Hole (Newton, N'd), Lady's Hole (Benthall, N'd), Football Hole (Newton, N'd), Oxberry Law Holes (Craster, N'd), Black Hole (Craster), Fluke Hole (Alnmouth, N'd), Coquet Hole (Coquet Is.,

N'd), Quay Hole (Coquet Is.), Headagee Hole (Lynemouth, N'd), Lishey Hole (Lynemouth), Sandle Holes (Lynemouth), Byers Hole (Whitburn, D'm), Potter's Hole (Whitburn), Spotty's Hole (Roker, D'm), Maud's Hole (Hendon, D'm), Bessy's Hole (Seaham., D'm), Busiers Holes (Hawthorn, D'm), Fox Holes (Easington, D'm), Goat Holes (Teesmouth), Hob Holes (Runswick, nYx), Saltwick Hole (Whitby, nYx), Maw Wyke Hole (Whitby, nYx), Dungeon Hole (Robin Hood's Bay, nYx), Boggle Hole (Robin Hood's Bay, nYx).

Beach Life – 'Spottie'

"Come all ye good people and listen to me
And a comical tale I will tell unto ye,
Belanging' yen Spottie – leev'd on the <u>law quay</u>,   i.e. Tyneside
That had nowther hoose or harbour he.

The poor auld wives o' the North side dissn't knaw what for to dee,
For they daurna' come to see their husbands when they come to the quay:
They're feared for their sels, an' their infants tee,
For this roguish fellow they ca' Spottie.

But noo he's gyen away unto the <u>seaside</u>,   i.e. Whitburn
Where mony a yen wishes he may be weshed away wi' the tide,
For if Floutter's flood com' as it used for to dee,
It'll drive his heart oot – then where'll his midred be?

The poor auld wives of Whitburn disnn't knaw what for to <u>dee</u>,   do
For they daur na come alang the sands wi' their lang-tail <u>skyets</u> i' their hands,   skates
to Jacob Spence's landin' as they used for to dee,
They daurna come alang the sands wi' their <u>swills</u> i' their hands,   baskets
But they're forced to tyek a coble an' come in by the sea.

As Laird Forster was riding alang the sands,
As he, or ony other gentleman might chance for to <u>dee</u>,   do
Spottie cam' oot – his <u>tanter-wallups</u> did flee –   tattered clothes
His horse <u>teuk the boggle</u>, an' off flew he.   shied, reared

He gethers coals i' the day-time, as he's well knawn for to dee,
An' myeks a fire on at neet, which <u>kests</u> a leet into the sea,   casts
Which <u>gar'd</u> a poor <u>sloopy</u> cry, "hellem a lee!"   made / sloop crewman?

An' aback o' the <u>Carcasses</u> cam' poor she.

remains of wooden
north pier, Sunderland

Alack! an' well-a-day, said the Maister – "What mun we dee?"
"Trust to Providence" said the Mate, "An' we're sure to get free."
There was a poor little lad 'at had come a trial viage to sea,
His heart went like a pair fo bellowses, an' he didn't knaw what for to dee.

Johnny Usher, the Maister, wad ha'e carried <u>him</u> away,

i.e. Spottie

But the ship's company swore, de'il be their fate it they wad wi' him stay;
We'll first forfeit oor wages for not gannin' to sea
Afore we'll gan wi' that roguish fellow they ca' Spottie."

Possibly from the 1820s, this woeful song represents a deep distrust of outcasts – Spottie is portrayed as little better than a wrecker. But people living in beach caves was not such a rare or dangerous phenomenon:

On the Blast Beach, Dawdon, between the Wars, there were at least three people lived in caves: the brothers Kenneth and George, and a third, who occupied a solitary cave, and was nicknamed 'Loppy Dick'. All quite harmless, it seems.

Kenneth and George boarded the front of their cave with planks thrown up by the sea, and made beach fires of driftwood to cook on. Rabbits (and it is rumoured, rats) were their staple fare, cooked into a stew in a large pot. They would be seen up at Struthers' shop buying a ha'pnyworth of herbs to flavour the soup. Also they would pick up any cigarette ends that looked viable. Rabbit skins, it is said, would be used to repair their boots. Come World War 2, the Army arrived to blow up the Nanny Goat's Path, the main access to the Blast Beach and to the cave-homes. The brothers were picked up, with their bedding of blankets or sacks, and moved to some empty brick-kilns Sherburn way. Although occasional beach parties have been noted since, and the odd night fisherman lighting a fire to signal hopefully to the fish, no one has been reported living on the Blast recently. For a start, the slurry and spoil tipping has filled the caves up to nearly the roof...

(Gordon Patrickson)

Seaweeds

may tops – 'brown seaweed that washes ashore when the may is on the trees' (KP, Beadnell).

old maids' laces – 'long thin strands of sea-weed' (KP, Beadnell).

peysey-ware – 'bladderwrack' (KP, re Seahouses).

sea-tang – 'sea-wrack (seaweed)' (Atkinson, 1868, Cleveland). [ON tange 'point', here a reference to the fingered form of seaweed?].

swad – 'fine green weed which grows on ropes, etc. On Holy Island, the term is used for zostra' (KP, Beadnell) [source unknown].

tang'el – 'long seaweed' (KP, Beadnell); **tangle** – 'seaweed' (FK, Berwick).

ware(s), **weir**(s) – seaweed; 'ware-cow: long, thick-shanked seaweed – 'cow' meaning clump as in heather-cows? Ware-bangs – 'bangs' meaning fringe as in American usage? Pillar-wares (pillow?)(Boulmer). Peysey-ware – bladderwrack (Seahouses)' (KP, Beadnell); 'sea-ware – sea-weed', Nth N'd (Heslop, 1880s) [OE *war*]; *EDD* – sporadic.

wrack – 'seaweed thrown on the shore by a storm' (Luckley/Alnwick, 1870s); 'rack, rach or wrack – sea-weed, field weeds' (Heslop, 1880s). Wrack Hills (Runswick, nYx); wreck, wrack – 'seaweed' (Umpleby, Staithes, 1930s) [AF/ON]; *EDD* – Sc, Nth.

(**note:** the local distribution of ware/wrack is typical of OE/ON contrasts.)

Swimming

dook (noun) – 'a bathe' (KP, Beadnell).

drook, drouk – 'to drench with water: "Drooked ti the skin"' (Heslop, 1880s); *draak'd*, ED'm.

druned – 'drowned' (Heslop, 1880s); **droonded** (S'd, Newc).

labbering – 'floundering, struggling, or labouring in water' (Brockett, 1829).

plodge – 'paddle, wade. Also: **plode** (Seahouses)' (KP, Beadnell) [imitative].

soom – 'to swim' (Luckley/Alnwick, 1870s); 'suum – swam' (KP, Beadnell).

soomer – 'a swimmer: "a top soomer"' (Brockett, 1829).

Chapter 7. The sea

Tides

away – 'turned, of tide. "Tide's away" – tide has turned' (KP, Beadnell).

bend (noun) – 'full flow of tide: "The bend a the tide"' (KP, Beadnell).

big tide – 'spring tide' (KP, Beadnell).

coonter-tide – 'tide which runs opposite to the normal direction, found around rocks and islands' (KP, Beadnell).

deed tide – 'dead, small or neap tide' (KP, Beadnell).

flow (verb) – 'to reach high tide: "Tide flows at haa'f six"' (KP, Beadnell).

mek – 'to make or grow, as in: "Tide's mekkin' – tide is coming in"' (KP, Beadnell).

ootrogue – 'undercurrent from shore, taking sand out with it' (KP, re Amble).

put up (of tide) – 'to increase, grow towards spring tide: "Tides is puttin' up"' (Opposite of 'tyek off') (KP, Beadnell).

running (tide) – 'incoming tide' (FK, Berwick).

slack (adj) – 'time at high and low water when tide is not moving, e.g. slack tide; high-wetter slack' (KP, Beadnell).

split, splet – '(of tide) turn? "i' the split a the tide"' (KP, Beadnell).

true tide – 'north and south flowing tide-flow, unaffected by islands, rocks or land' (KP, Beadnell).

tyek off – 'to diminish (of tides, after spring tides)' Opposite of 'put up' (KP, Beadnell).

watter – tide: "when the watter leaves ye" (John Green, S'd, 1879, p.36).

(note: mostly common words than specialised vocabulary?)

Surface

acker – 'to curl, as the curl of water from the wind; noun, a ripple on the surface of the water' (Brockett, 1829). [*OED* links to *eagre* 'tidal bore' but compare *ackersprit* 'curling shoot of potato']; *EDD* – Sc, N'd, Yx, EA.

berrel – 'a whirlpool' (KP, Beadnell) [?pril/birl 'to spin'].

the brik – 'where the sea breaks' (KP, Beadnell).

caal of the sea – 'movement of water driven by the wind on its surface (the opposite is **keld**, smoothe, re the Tyne)' (Heslop, 1880s).

clock calm – 'very calm; windless day; smooth sea' (KP, Beadnell).

coulpress – 'continued breaking of sea: "it's breeakin' coulpress ower t'arbour mooth"' (Umpleby, Staithes, 1930s); *EDD* has only coulpress 'a crowbar'.

a dog before its master – 'sea starting to change though no evident wind to account for it yet' Eric King (EK), Seahouses; 'the growing swell, unaccompanied by any significant amount of wind, which is generated by a far off but approaching storm' (AO re W. Runciman, 1924, p.208); 'dog afore its maister – sea which reaches land [before] wind which caused it' (KP re Seahouses).

droomly – 'cloudy, of liquid: "Droomly wetter" – muddy water' (KP, *WW*, Beadnell). [drubly < OE *droflic*' disturbed']; *EDD* – Sc, N'd.

grund – 'a swell on the sea' (EK, Seahouses).

gurrelly – 'rough, gloomy (of sea or hard wind on gloomy day)' (KP, Beadnell).

hike – 'to swing... the hiking of a boat' (Brockett, 1829) [source unknown].

hobble – 'short seas, surface ridges on sea caused by wind. "A bit hobble on." Also adj, 'hobbly': "Hobbly the day." On Holy Island this is 'wabble', 'wabbly', in Seahouses 'rabble'. "A top-rabble."' (KP, Beadnell) [Du hobbelen 'to toss or rock'].

jumping sea – presumed to be a breaking and toppling wave crest of the kind that occurs in the 'surf zone'; velocities in the tips of these crests can reach 100 mph: "... and we were hit by a jumping sea..." (inquest witness, *Sunderland Daily Echo*, 27 March 1911).

keld – 'the smooth part of a stretch of water' (Heslop, 1880s). [ON kelda, 'spring', also deep, smooth water]; *EDD* – N'd, C'd.

knot (a watter) – 'a sea' (Holy Island, Craster) KP; knott – 'a bad sea: "sha teak a nasty knott there"' (Umpleby, Staithes, 1930s).

lift (noun) – swell: "there's a nasty bit ov a lift on [the sea]" (John,1879, S'd, p.64); 'a rolling sea' (KP, Beadnell).

lipper – 'white caps on sea, breaking, choppy, often accompanying southerly wind, etc. A confused sea: "There's a bit lipper on"' (KP, Beadnell); "against a lipper she bumped upon the tops of the waves" (Salmon, 1885, p.16); lipper, stiff lipper – 'wind-driven waves, rather than swell, of sufficient height to merit care and attention in a sailing coble' (AO). [ON *hleypa* 'to make leap']; *EDD* – Sc, N'd, Yx.

lownd – 'smooth of sea, calm of weather: "this lownd day"' (*Yorkshire Dialogue*, 1673); "to seik

some lowner harbore thayre" (*Legend of St Andrew*, 1583) [ON *lugn, compare Ice. lygn; *OED* exx. mostly Scottish]; *EDD* – Sc, Nth.

mek – 'to make or grow, as in: "Sea's mekkin" – sea is getting rougher' (KP, Beadnell).

rabble – see hobble.

range – 'long seas, rollers: "A bit range on"' (KP, Beadnell).

rowelly – 'rough, rolling (of sea): "A right rowelly day"' (Beadnell). Also: **roolly** (Seahouses) KP [roll].

run – 'swell; the distance seas travel up beach, into harbour, etc. "Theer's a hell of a run on!" Also verb: "Sea's runnin'" – i.e. big swell' (KP, Beadnell).

saliers – wake of ship: "lads swimming in the Fish Quay Gut would wait for the wake of passing boat and dive into the saliers" (MBS). *EDD* as standing feet wide in a boat and rocking it.

sea – 'a wave: "A sea hit him." Also used to describe condition of sea when rough, especially in expression 'sea on': "Plenty sea on the day"; "a canny bit sea on"' (KP, Beadnell).

sugar loaves – 'presumed to mean a squall of such strength that it tears the wave crests into white fragments (i.e. far more severe than common 'white horses')' (AO); "he saw a huge wave coming behind them which lifted the sea into sugar loaves." (inquest witness, *Sunderland Daily Echo*, 27 March 1911); Sugar Loaf Sea – 'high turbulent waves with little wind' (Smyth, 1867).

sweel – 'swell' (KP, Beadnell).

toppy – choppy sea (Hutton Henry).

tummelly – 'rough (at sea)' (KP, Beadnell) [tumble].

wabbly – see hobble.

(**note**: this group contains a fair proportion of ON-based words, even in N'd. The cause would seem to be Viking influence along the coast, especially in the art of sea-faring.)

The sea floor

douffie – 'soft, useless ground' (KP, Beadnell). [?Du *doof* 'benumbed. spiritless']; *EDD* – *duffie* 'blunt, stupid'.

easy – 'soft (of ground)' (KP, Beadnell).

grund – 'ground, sea-bed that is good for catching' (KP, Beadnell). [OE *sæ-grund*].

shad – 'shoal, shoal water, shallow place or sand-bank, e.g. Islestone Shad, Glororum Shad (Farne Islands), Tughall Hall Shad' (KP). [?OE *sceadu* 'shade'] EDD – Sc: *shade*, N'd *shad* 'open piece of ground'; shad (adj.) – shallow: "where it's a bit shad at the back o' Coquet…" (AO, noted Amble, 2007).

shite an' sugar – 'useless, muddy ground (at sea)' (KP, Beadnell).

smooth (a/the) – 'sandy ground, e.g. Craister Smooth (Craster), the Benty Smooth' (KP, Beadnell).

soft – 'general term for fishing grounds with sandy bottom (Hummersty Soft, Bullfit Soft, etc.)' (Umpleby, Staithes, 1930s).

Chapter 8. Weather

Astronomical and electric phenomena

brattle – 'any great noise, as a brattle or clap of thunder' (*Bell-White MS 12*); 'the noise of a peal of thunder: "what a brattle o' thunner that was!"' (Luckley/Alnwick, 1870s); 'a peal, as "a brattle of thunder"' (Robson, Birtley); brattle – 'a loud noise, a peal of thunder' (Heslop, 1880s), Tyne; 'the noise thunder makes: "A brattle a thunn'er"' (KP, Beadnell). [*OED*: imitative; exx. esp. Scots].

bruff – 'a halo round the moon' (Robson, Birtley); bruff – 'a ring around the moon. Also, "a bruff moon"' (KP, Beadnell). [ON *brog* 'enclosure']; *EDD* – Sc, Ire, Nth, Linx.

cock's comb – 'a ring around the moon' (KP, Beadnell).

haggering – 'distortion of objects by atmospheric refraction' (AR, Seahouses).

leetnin – 'lightning; dawn' (Dinsdale,1849, Tees).

merry-dancers – see **streamers**.

rowly rattle bags – 'thunder clouds' (*Bell-White MS 12*).

streamers – 'the Northern Lights' (*Borderers' Table Book*, vol.7, 1846, p.164); **merry-dancers** – 'the glancings of the *Aurora borealis*' [OED as Scots]...[also] **pyrrhy-dancers**. (Brockett, 1829) [pyrrhic – warlike?].

sun-dog – 'an isolated spot of prismatic colours, usually seen well up in the northern parts of the sky' (Heslop, 1880s); *EDD*: general. **weathergaa'** – 'a sundog or small patch of rainbow in fine sky, usually presaging weather change or wind from its direction' (KP, Beadnell) [see *OED* wind-gall]; *EDD* – Sc, Nth.

thunnor – 'thunder' (Brockett, 1829); **thunder-pash** – 'thunder-storm' Dinsdale; **thunner-splet** – 'a thunder storm' (KP, Beadnell); "God whaling the tatties" (sorting and grading potatoes) – thunder re Newham (Crocker, 1990, p.31).

weathergaa' – see **sun-dog**.

The Northern Lights

Perhaps the most impressive of these phenomena (with no disrespect to Thor) is the Northern Lights. They are surely implied (as dire indications of disaster) in the Anglo-Saxon Chronicle for 793 AD:

Her wæron reðe forebecna cumene ofer Norðanhymbra land, 7 þæt folc earmlice bregdon; þæt wæron ormete ligræsas, 7 wæron geseowene fyrene dracan on þam lyfte fleogende; þam tacnum sona fyligde mycel hunger, 7 litel æfter þam þæs ilcan geares on vi. idus Ian'r earmlice heðenra manna hergung adiligode Godes cyrican, in Lindsifarena ee, þurh reaflac, 7 mansleht...
[ð and þ = th]

(In this year were terrible portents observed throughout Northumbria, that seriously alarmed the people; these were exaggerated flashes of lightning, and fiery dragons were seen flying in the sky. Straight after these tokens a great famine occurred, and slightly later still in the same year, on the 6th day before the Ides of January an army of heathen folk miserably afflicted God's church, on the Island of Lindisfarne, looting and slaying...)

Another, more lyrical account comes from Elgey's *Star and Weather Gossip* in the 1910s:

Warm and placid was the last night but one of that September. Away from the city lights, where Nature brooded solemnly silent, a mystical glow suffused the northern horizon long after the sun had departed. Towards eight o'clock a clearly defined luminous arch could be seen stretching from N.E. to N.W., with its crown some fifteen degrees above the sky-line. It was like a star-surmounted silver portal that led to the region of eternal ice and snow.

Barely had I time to remark upon the beauty of the scene, when an auroral ray shot up over Arcturus in the north-west to level with Corona Borealis. It had no tint: merely duskily luminous against the greater luminosity on which it was projected. Then other rays darted upward under the Great Bear, whoe gigantic figure was feet down toward the horizon.

From due north the rays worked round to the nor'-nor'-east. One glowing, quivering shaft, indeed, sprang up almost as far round eastward as Capella, which at the moment was blazing with great splendour...

Shortly before nine o'clock a fan-shaped series of sreamers appeared under the western side of Boötes and the tail of the Bear. One inexpressiblybeautiful beam immersed Cor Caroli, which almost had its light extinguished.

For nearly an hour aferward the northern sky remained quiescent. Yet there was still that fascinating, mystical glow. The display ended at five minutes past ten with a superb streamer which pierced Corona Borealis. It was but a momentary apparition, and ehen it faded from view the glow departed with it...

More recently:

It was a New Year's Eve way back during WW2, I can't remember which year it was. My father was away at sea, and there being generally a shortage of men around, I was sent out with the usual piece of coal and a silver coin to be the 'first-foot'. Although just a lad and neither tall, dark or handsome, as the only male on hand at the time I was happy to do the honours.

This turned out to be a memorable experience; one I shall never forget! There was a perfectly clear sky which appeared a brilliant and luminous pale green. With no light pollution, the 'black-out' being in force ay the time, a myriad of stars and the planets shone brightly, in addition the Northern Lights swept across the whole sky like curtains constantly moving. The marvellous silence which pervaded the scene added to the dramatic effect. It was most spectacular and beautiful and had a dream-like quality as I recall. All this made me reluctant to go back into the house after the hour of midnight had struck and the ships in the river sounded their welcome to the New Year.

I have not seen a display of the Northern Lights since to equal the above. Perhaps we shall not experience such a wonderful show again, with all the background luminescence in today's world...

(Edgar Readman, Redcar)

Precipitation

bleachin' – 'lashing (of rain or snow)' (KP, *WW*, re Beadnell); *EDD* – Sc, N'd, Ches.

bleezin' – "in South East Northumberland I've heard this used as a weather description as in 'It's bleezin down a snaa/rain' to mean it is raining or snowing heavily" (*Cate Dobson*).

brash – 'melted snow: "snow brash", "brashy weather", "brashy wettor"' (Heslop, 1880s); 'snaa-brash (Nth N'd) – melted snow: "the snaa-brash had ruined me shoes"' (Heslop, 1880s). [*OED* only as *brash* 'shower']; *EDD* – Sc,N'd.

clashy – 'wet e.g. weather, road' (Dinsdale, 1849) Tees.

coarse – 'poor, rough, of weather; denotes wind and rain: "A coarse day"' (KP, Beadnell).

dag – 'to drizzle; dag - a drizzling rain' (Brockett, 1829); to rain, 'to drizzle: "it's daggin on", "it's daggin weather"' (Heslop, 1880s); 'dag (to dag on) – to spit with rain' (KP, Beadnell). [ON döggva]; *EDD* – general.

dagling – "15 Apr [1672] mizling, drizling, dagling, small rain", Diary of John Swale of Askham, nr York/Raine from *BL MS Egerton 2868.*

daggy – 'damp, wet: "A daggy day"' (Brockett, 1829); 'daggy – drizzly' (Dinsdale, 1849, Tees); 'daggy, daggly – wet, drizzly: "It's varry daggy thi' day"' (Heslop, 1880s).

fewles o' muck – 'bad weather' (Umpleby, Staithes, 1930s).

flite (of rain, snow, etc.) – 'to fall lightly, to fall in showers. "It's flitin' on"– it's showery. Also noun: "Flites a rain" – streaks of rain on sky in distance' (KP, Beadnell) [?flight].

fleead – 'flood' (Umpleby, Staithes, 1930s).

freshes – 'floods: in the great freshes we have had of late' (Berwick-on-Tweed, 1647). Raine from *BL MS Egerton 2868*; fresh – 'a flood; mild weather in winter' (Luckley/Alnwick, 1870s); 'fresh. – a thaw. "There's a heavy (or, thick) fresh on." Common word among countrymen' (Palgrave, 1896, Hetton); 'fresh (noun) – a spate' (KP, re Amble).

haggles – 'it hails' (John Ray, 1674), *Kennet BL MS Lansdowne 1033* as Northern [OE hagalian, ON *hagla*].

har – see Lights, clouds and visibility.

hashy (nth N'd) – 'wet, sleety: "Eh! what a hashy day"' (Heslop, 1880s) [cf section (d)] [form of *harsh?*].

h'yel-water – whole water; said of a heavy fall of rain (Brockett, 1829; Seaham; 1992 per BG).

missling – drizzly: 'If ye morning bee wette and misling, ye best way will bee to stay att hoame' (Best's Farming Book, 1641, p.49); 'March...misling oft' (Askham, 1667/68 per Raine from *BL MS Egerton 2868*; mizzle – 'slight rain' (Dinsdale, 1849, Tees); mizzle – 'drizzle' (Dobson 1973). [Du *miezelen*].

pash – 'a heavy fall of snow or rain' (Heslop, 1880s). [*OED* as imitative]; *EDD* – Nth.

plash – 'a downpour of rain' (Heslop, 1880s); plash – 'to splash or spatter: "plashin wet" soaked with wet' (Heslop, 1880s); 'a plash of rain' (Luckley/Alnwick, 1870s). [?splash]; *EDD* – general.

plennet – 'rain falls in plennets' (partially) (Dinsdale, 1849) Tees/ [<planet. *EDD*: Nth].

pule – 'to sleet, or to fall as a mixture of snow and sleet: "pules an' snaws sae"' (Atkinson, 1868, Cleveland); *EDD* – Sc, N'd, Yx.

scud – 'a heavy shower' (KP, Beadnell) [*OED* as C16th].

slattery – 'wet, rainy: a slattery day' (Heslop, 1880s).

snaa-brash – see **brash**.

snew – snowed; "it snew all day" (Brockett, 1829); snew – 'did snow' (Dinsdale, 1849, Tees). [OE *sniwan*, ON *snjóva*].

soft – 'wet (of the weather). The common salutation on a rainy day is, "Soft!"' (Palgrave, 1896, Hetton).

tanking – "It's tanking down" of rain (H'pool via BG, 2005).

wankle weather – weather which is unsettled and dry (*Bell-White MS 12*). [OE *wancol*, shaky].

weet – 'to rain, to wet; [noun] slight rain, wet weather' (Brockett, 1829).

whitening – "Looks like it's whitening outside." Meaning of course that it looked like it would snow later' (DM, Catchgate).

Wind

air – 'a breeze. "A fine air a wund"' (KP, Beadnell).

airt – 'the point from which the wind blows: "The wund's the wrang airt"' (Luckley/Alnwick, 1870s); airt or art – corner: "the wind is in a cold airt" (*Kennet BL MS Lansdowne 1033* re Yorks); 'airt, art – a point or part of the horizon or compass; a district or portion of the country' (Brockett, 1829); airts – [directions]: "fra a' airts 'n' pairts" (Egglestone, Weardale); airt (pronounced -art) 'part of the compass, direction: "what airt's the wind in thi day?"' (Heslop, 1880s). [Gaelic/Scots].

arsle – '(of wind) to back. "Wund's arsellin" '(KP, WW, re Boulmer).

breead winnd – 'N.N.-W.' (Umpleby, Staithes, 1930s) [?broad].

bruckle – 'like to break': "t' weather was bruckle like"' (Egglestone, Weadale); *EDD* – vb 'to dirty', N'd.

It [i.e. the wind] came away… rose markedly, and maybe unexpectedly, in strength: "The wind came away from the north-east as we were making for the harbour" (*Sunderland Daily Echo*, 27 March 1911); (AO from S. Shields) foyboatmen c.1980; still in common usage amongst local coastal sailors.

coarse – see Precipitation.

chop – 'sudden retrograde movement: "the wind chopped round to the nor'rard"' (Heslop, 1880s); custard-winds – 'the cold easterly winds prevalent on the N.E. coast in spring' (Atkinson, Cleveland, 1868) [<coastward].

dacker – 'uncertain, unsettled, as applied to the weather' (Brockett, 1829). [MDu?]; *EDD* – Sc, Lx, N'd.

daflin – 'a light breeze blowing from no definite direction – "divven nar which ole te blar frae"' (AI, Hartlepool). [?ON *dauf*].

easter – 'to come round to the east: "Wund's eastered"' (KP, Beadnell).

flam – 'a sudden, light breeze. Cf 'flan', Shetland. Verb: Flammin' aboot – of wind, variable. "Wund's flammin' aboot"' (KP, Beadnell).

hashy – 'rough, windy: "She's hashy at the cutter" – it's a gusty day' (KP, Beadnell) [cf. Precipitation].

hask – 'roughened, dried-up [drying, harsh]: "a hask wind", "hask lips"' (Heslop, 1880s). [harsh].

hooley – 'very windy: "It's blowin a hooley out there"' (NC, Seaham).

lazy wund – 'a cutting wind, one that 'gans straight through ye' (KP, Beadnell).

lound – 'quiet, calm: "it's varra lound ti-neet"' (Umpleby, Staithes, 1930s) [ON *lugn*].

nantlin' – 'wandering: "t'au'd wind's nantlin' aboot finndin' a 'ooal ti blaw in"' (Umpleby, Staithes, 1930s).

piner – 'a penetrating, cold south-easterly wind. "By, yon's a sooth-east piner, aa'reet!"' (KP, Beadnell). [OE p n 'torment'; in this usage possibly an Old Northumbrian term]; *EDD* – pine 'to blow strongly', Sc, N'd, Yx.

smolt – calm (of weather) (*Lindisf. Gosp.* Matt. xvi). Term survived in Scots till sixteenth century. [OE smolt]; *EDD* – Ex, EA, Sx, Hants.

a snithe wind – 'cutting or piercing' (Grose, 1787). *EDD*: Yx. [ON *sniða*, OE *sniðan* 'to cut'].

tatty – 'blustery, of wind or weather (KP, Beadnell): "A tatty day". In Seahouses, tattery' (KP)

waff – 'a slight motion of the hand; a slight puff of wind' (Brockett, 1829); [compare Norw *veift* 'puff of wind'].

From earliest times up till the mid-nineteenth century (and later), wind was the key to navigation – there was no other effective source of power for a voyage of any length, yet none so undependable – it could fail, it could change, it could blow directly contrary to the desired direction; if strong enough it could risk a ship being driven ashore ('on a lee shore'). The wind direction was crucial to the colliers on their way to London:

Fleets of loaded vessel leaving the coal ports bound south, get up [i.e. south] as far as Flamborough Head, where, becoming baffled by the wind, they are unable to 'weather' the Head, and consequently congregate there in large numbers, often to the exent of many hundreds – not unfrequently of a thousand sail. In this position they are caught by a S.E. gale, and there being no port capable of entry during a storm, they are scattered along the coast as far as the Firth of Forth, strewing the shores with wreck or foundering by the way, and in the latter case usually carrying all hands to the bottom. Those ships who have succeeded in reaching the shelter of the Forth – battered, damaged, and leaky, from their struggle with the storm, often with spars carried away and scarcely a rag of canvas left – still have their whole voyage before them, and after refitting, start again…

(Cortis 1871, p.4)

A Storm at Sea (Hartlepool)
As the night advanced the wind heightened. When dawn glimmered, unearthly-like, through the wilderness of murk, the hurricane hailed it with the shriek of ten thousand furies. The great salt wind blew dead inshore. It did not come gustily, but with a steady, mighty, roaring pour.

When a glimpse of the water was caught through the obscurity one looked, as it were, on a snow-covered moor lashed into white chaos by a blizzard. The waves had no regularity, no rhythmic succession. Ere they could assume definite shape and sequence they were shipped into the air, torn into spray, blown ashore in perfectly horizontal lines, hurled against the face of the cliff and sent pouring over its edge like steam. The grim North Sea is terrible in its rage.

At the margin of the tide the foam lay knee-deep. With every run of the sea it floated, an undulating snow-field. Then while it was still buoyant the hurricane shipped it into a rapid vortex, drew it high upwards, and drove it over the town. By it the Moor had its carpet of green changed to quivering white. It was a lonely Moor that day.

Noon saw the storm at its height. To be then at the sea-front was utterly bewildering. The senses were stunned by the terrible turmoil. The merciless might of the ocean beat down all feelings save that of an overpowering oppression. The heavens themselves seemed to have fallen on sea and land. The sun's light was lost. An awful shadow eclipsed the face of nature.

A few pilots and fishermen stood braving the storm at the heugh. Oilskinned and sou'westered, they huddled behind the lighthouse-yard wall, on the New Pier side. They made an interesting group. While the lowering scud flew over their heads, and the sea-spray stung their faces and rattled on their oilskins, they tried to talk to one another. but shouting their loudest they made themselves heard with difficulty, and when the wind suddenly swept round the seaward end of their sheltering wall it clopped off their words with vicious abruptness.

Of course, their disjointed conversation was of wrecks and rescues. 'Tis ever so with these hardy fellows when tempest falls on the North-East coast. What more appropriate surroundings, indeed, could be conceived for recalling such stirring sea-tragedies as the loss of the French barque Français on Middleton beach, a mile away; or the heartrending wreck, almost at their feet, of the Rising Sun, of Sunderland; or the heroic attempts to rescue the crew of the Granite, over the hurricane-swept bay yonder!

Starting from the northern side of the lighthouse was the great Headland Protection Wall, built to preserve the crumbling cave-eaten cliffs from the onslaught of the sea. The storm played fearful havoc upon it. While the wind wrenched off the heads of the tall, substantial lamp-standards and shivered them to fragments, the waves snapped the thick, heavy iron stanchions on the edge of the wall, and even tore some of them from their bed of solid masonry.

At the New Pier – its construction is one of the memories of my boyhood – the mountainous masses of water made sport with the loose giant blocks of concrete. The North Sea storm-waves toy with mere tons. Through the spray-mist I had wonderful glimpses of the raging sea attacking this long, massive breakwater. As I stood in the wind, fascinated, the ground beneath my feet quaked with the perpetual impact between the forces of nature and the works of man. The great creamy breakers rushed out of the haze with a speed that would seem incredible to an inlander. Straight for the pier they went, and struck the high, smooth, curved wall with a noise that resembled the explosion of a huge shell. Then up, up they would shoot, eighty or a hundred feet into the air with the swiftness of a cannon-shot, and before they could descend again the wind would blow them into fine spray and sweep the mist with a seething hiss into the calm water beyond.

Those waves – all chaotic – which were not thus dissipated, or which did not make a clean sweep of the pier, would rebound from the glistening wall and would meet another oncoming wave (perhaps a confusion of two or three of them) with a crash like violent overhead thunder. Such collisions invariably resulted in a tremendous upheaval of water. As may be imagined, these contending seas, while adding to the general clamour, churned the water into foam, which above the tide at this part of the shore lay quite four feet deep.

Away from the sea, down in the ancient town, desolation reigned. No vehicles were astir; the shops were closed and shuttered, to save the windows. The storm was in absolute and undisputed possession; its tumult penetrated every corner of the homes of the inhabitants, who for the most part did not venture out to run the risk of being blown off their feet or injured by falling masonry.

It was exceedingly dangerous being out in the streets at all that day. Slates were ripped from roofs and carried away on the wind like so many pieces of paste-board, as I myself witnessed in various quarters of the town. The crash of a falling chimney-stack continually broke on the thunder of the gale. The shivering of glass was one of the common sounds of the day.

The main approach to the docks was deep in débris torn from the house-tops. Passing that way was a most hazardous proceeding. It was necessary to hug the doorway, taking breath and a glance aloft from every place of refuge. I saw several slates blown across the street to an opposite roof, and on one occasion a chimney-stack fell with an ear-splitting crash a few yards from where I was sheltering.

This thoroughfare led to the ferries, which for so many years have plied across to Middleton, but the row-boats were suspended that day. It is only in the severest weather that they cease running. Even could they have been kept going there would have been no passengers to ferry over.

On the Town Wall, which skirts the narrow channel leading from the bay to the harbour, a small group of men stood leaning against the wind and gazing fixedly in the direction of West Hartlepool sands. What they say through such a smother of spindrift I was at a loss to imagine. Suddenly, however, there was a slight clearance that

way. The dim outline of a ship on the beach slowly revealed itself; then the spray-mist closed in again...
A tug heaved slowly into the little harbour at day-break on the following morning.

The skipper told me that for twenty-six hours he had fought with the hurricane in the bay, almost within hailing distance of land. During the whole of that anxious time he was unable to see more than a few yards away, and could only keep steaming in the teeth of the wind and sea.

His vessel moved in a circle, he believed. All around was the white, ghostly spindrift, and so precarious was their situation that not a single man of them expected to set foot on shore again. He described the waves as the queerest he had ever experienced; they spurted into the air twice the height of the funnel.

How the men kept the fires going no one seemed to know clearly; once they were quenched nothing could have saved the tug and her crew. Sea after sea flooded the stokehold, and all hands worked unceasingly to get the water passed up in buckets. When I went down into it the cinders were knee-deep.

One golden afternoon, when the bay had fallen as quiet as a lake, I saw a waterlogged Norwegian barque towed into port. Her main and mizzen masts had gone; so, too, had her foretopmast. The jagged stumps of the missing masts protruded gauntly a few feet above the deck.

A trawler had the vessel in tow, and as she passed through the lock I scrambled aboard of her. Her deck felt like pulp to the tread. Little of her bulwarks remained; they had been carried away by the great seas, and also, no doubt, by the falling spars. How she had kept afloat with her decks almost awash was a mystery until it transpired that she was timber-laden.

The deck-house, always so conspicuous a feature of Scandinavian timber-ships, was left standing, but the doors had disappeared, and the interior was stripped bare. A prison cell could not have been more uninviting than that skeleton of a deck-house. It was clear that the seas had played hide-and-seek in and out of it at will; and while bursting continually over the crippled vessel, as over a log, they had made a clean sweep of the deck cargo, not a stick of which remained.

Those who were left of the crew were visibly affected. Cowed by their terrible experience aboard this battered barque, they shuffled along the soddened decks wearily and with vacant stare, indifferent alike to kindly enquiries and to the fact that they had at last reached a haven of refuge. When the seas were running at their highest two of the sailors were swept overboard like a flash, and their dying shrieks were smothered by the louder shrieks of the hurricane. Another of the men had his leg broken. He lay helpless in the captain's cabin.

On the board the trawler that brought her in a begrimed member of the crew told of how the barque, before they picked her up, had been in tow of another trawler, and how that one of the men of this later vessel got fast in the bight of the warp and was cut in two, whereupon the barque was cast off to the mercy of the gale again.

But such harrowing incidents as these were many during that memorable storm. Yet how gently, and how insinuatingly, did it not come from over the ocean to the little promontory! A discoloured dwell under a blue sky in the daytime; a nightfall troubled with hollow draughts of air and sighing sounds that mingled weirdly with the dull rumour of the sea.
That was all.

(Joseph H. Elgie, c.1915, pp.70–76)

Light, clouds and visibility

black-men's heeds – 'small, black clouds' (KP, re Craster).

climpers – 'cumulous cloud' (AR, Seahouses) [?clump].

clinkers – 'clouds rising up from the east, out of the sea' (KP, Beadnell). Cf. Andrew Rutter, 'climpers'.

darkening – 'twilight' (Dinsdale, 1849, Tees).

dole – 'gloomy (Amble/Newbiggin)' (KP, Beadnell) [dowly?].

dowfy – 'dull, damp, mild weather' (AR, Seahouses) [cf. douffie in Wind].

dowlee – 'dark or dismal' (MD); *EDD* – SC, Nth. [ON *daufligr*].

fining – 'improving: "it's fining away to a poor day" – weather improving from awful to just poor' (EK, Seahouses); **fine** (verb) – 'to brighten (of weather)' (KP, Beadnell).

fret – 'a mist, or sea-fog' (Palgrave, 1896, Hetton); 'summer sea mist' (KP, Beadnell); *EDD* – N'd, D'm, nYX.

grey – 'twilight' (EK, Seahouses).

hag – 'a white fog or mist' (Atkinson, 1868, Cleveland).

har – 'small rain [D'm]; it harrs – it rains in small drops' (*Kennet BL MS Lansdowne 1033*); 'har or harr – a mist of thick fog' (Brockett, 1829); harr – 'a strong fog or wet mist, almost verging on a drizzle' (Atkinson, Cleveland); 'har – a sea fret, a drizzling rain or fog; [adv] moist, damp' (Heslop, 1880s); 'haar – winter mist with frost' (KP, Beadnell) [from Dutch; cf **Precipitation**].

harl – 'a mist' (John Ray, 1674), (*Kennet BL MS Lansdowne 1033*) as Northern [not *EDD*].

lax – 'cloud: "sha's (t'sun) gannin' doon intiv a lax"' (Umpleby, Staithes, 1930s) [for racks?] [not *EDD*].

owergaffen – 'heavy, overcast sky' (AR, Seahouses).

rook – 'mist, rooky – misty – the mist or sea fret' (*Bell-White MS 12*); rook, rouk – 'a mist or fog' (Brockett 1829); 'roke – a thick fog' (Atkinson, Cleveland); rook – 'fog, mist' (Nth N'd) (Heslop, 1880s); 'rook (roo:k). thick fog, damp: "It's a thick rook the neet" (to-night)' (Palgrave, 1896, Hetton) [ON].

rouky – 'misty, damp, foggy' (Brockett, 1829); 'roky – foggy (Atkinson, 1868, Cleveland)'; 'rooky' (Palgrave, 1896, Hetton); 'roopy' (Brockett, 1829) [cf. reek 'smoke'].

scud – 'common meteorological term for wispy fragments of wind-driven low level cloud (*stratus fractus*)' (AO; cf. Salmon, 1885, p.55).

sea-fret / (Nth N'd) 'a damp fog from the sea' (Heslop, 1880s); 'sea-fret' (Oxnard/Hetton, 1990s); *EDD* – N'd, W'd, nYx, eYx.

shy (adj) – poor weather. "A shy day" – a poor day' (KP, Beadnell).

snell – see **Temperature**.

soft – 'damp, drizzly: "it's a very soft day"' (Luckley/Alnwick, 1870s).

thick (noun) – 'fog ("a thick come on")' (KP, Beadnell).

upcasting – 'a rising of clouds above the horizon, especially as threatening rain' (Brockett, 1829)

weather – 'good weather: "wa'll gan if it's weather"' (Umpleby, Staithes, 1930s).

windsuckers – 'rapidly developing cumulus (cumulus castellanus), foretelling increased wind?' (AO): "see! there's a number of wind suckers arising in the west. These latter are small clouds like the wisps or puffs of vapour which are caused by the explosion of shells in the air." (Salmon, 1885, p.55).

Fog was a particular risk for a sailing ship near the shore. The following dark story relates to Toney Joblin, pilot, of Sunderland, and is titled:

A New Way into Sunderland Harbour
As the vessel drew near the port, the shades of evening began to fall, the coming darkness being considerably increased by the aid of a dense fog, so thick that poor Toney, in attempting to grapple his way into the harbour, put the schooner ashore behind the north pier. The sea was fortunately as smooth as a mill pond, and there being but little wind the vessel came gently to the beach – as Toney afterwards observed, 'she wadn't ha' brocken a hegg-shell.'

It being ebb-tide, she soon fastened herself, and Toney was for a moment or two in a frightful state of agitation.

'Hiven bliss us all!' he piously ejaculated under his breath, 'the ship's ashore; an' eff aw cannot get out o' this mess, aw'll loss mee brench [licence] altigither.'

Toney, however, proved himself quite equal to the occasion, for after a brief inward converse he went boldly up to the captain and said, with all the sincerity that pure inborn innocence might be supposed to command – 'Now, sir, ye're all reet; the tide's ebbin' an' ye'll seun be fast agrund. When the watter leaves ye, just run out a line frev the starbut bow an' another frev the pote quarter, an' ye'll lie as snug as a bug in a rug, an' fust thing iv the moanin' Sir Hedwith's cairts 'll be down for yer ballas'. And now, sir,' continued Toney, 'as aw hev a little Scotchman for ti tak ti sea this tide yet, an' as ye nee doubt knaw yersel, neebody can afford for ti let nowt gan past them these times, aa wad thank ye for the pilotage an' a put ashore; siven fut an' a half at fifteen pence.'

Toney was paid his pilotage, landed by the ship's boat on the beach, and speedily vanished in the darkness.

Early next morning a large number of people covered the sands to the northward of the harbour, drawn thither by the at all time startling report of 'a ship ashore'; and the poor captain found, to his horror and astonishment, that instead of his vessel being, as he expected, safe in a harbour, she was lying on a main beach, and that a stiff breeze from eastward for six hours would knock her into more pieces than Toney's pilotage would represent when changed into half-farthings. Neither the captain nor any of his crew were able to speak positively as to the pilot, and it was not until some years after that Toney consented to take credit for this famous exploit."

(Green, 1879, pp.36–37)

Temperature
   bleary – 'damp, cold' (KP, Beadnell).
   callar – 'fresh, cool: "callar air" (Grose, 1787); 'caller – cold, icy, frosty' (elsewhere, fresh). (AR, Seahouses); *EDD* – Sc, N'd, D'm, Yx.
   daized – 'numb from cold' (Dinsdale, 1849, Tees).
   nether'd – 'starved with cold' (Grose, 1787); 'netherin – biting, blasting, shrivelling: "a netherin wund"' (wind) (Heslop, 1880s).
   rozzla – 'very hot day' (MD).
   skinner – 'a cold day' (KP, Beadnell).
   smoothy (the th sounded as in thin) – 'dank, damp and warm [humid]: "it's a smoothy day"' (Heslop, 1880s) [? > muthy].
   snell – 'sharp, cold, as a "snell wind", a sharp piercing wind, "a snell morning", a bitter cold morning [D'm]' (*Kennet BL MS Lansdowne 1033*); snell – 'sharp, keen, applied to the weather: "it's gey snell thi' day"' (Heslop, 1880s) [ON]; *EDD* – Sc, Ire, Nth.

urled – 'pinched with cold' (Dinsdale, 1849, Tees); *EDD* – Nth.

Conclusion

Given the importance of weather, and notably the wind, to sea-faring, it is not surprising to find a number of Old Norse terms here, and some Dutch, beside some survivors from Old English – piner, smolt.

Chapter 9. Names for fish

Aelfic's 'Colloquy' – The Fisherman

Aelfric was a monk and teacher at Cerne Abbas in the 980s when he composed a Latin grammar and reader for the use of his young pupils in the monastery. This reader takes the form of an interviewer talking to various different craftsmen about their work, hence the usual title of 'Colloquy' (conversation). Perhaps a generation later, an Old English version or crib was added, as names of fishes, animals and the like, as everyday items were of special use to monks who, like members of any institution, had to keep records of goods received from their estates, or as tithes. Of particular interest to us is the passage in which Aelfric's questioner addresses a fisherman:

Q. Qualem artem scis tu?
Hwylcne cræft canst þu?
What skill know you?

A. Ego sum piscator.
Ic eom fiscere.
I am (a) fisherman.

Q. Quid adquiris de tua arte?
Hwæt begyst þu of þinum cræfte?
What gain you by your craft?

A. Uictum et uestitum et pecuniam
Bigleofan ond scrud ond feoh.
Food and clothing and cash.

Q. Quomodo capis pisces?
Hu gefehst þu fixas?
How catch you fish?

A. Ascendo nauem et pono retia mea in amne, et hamum proicio et sportas, et quicquid ceperint sumo.
Ic astigie min scyp ond wyrpe max mine on ea, ond, ancgil ic wyrpe ond spyrtan, ond, swa hwæt swa hig gehæftað ic genime.
I board my ship and cast net mine in (the) river; also, (a) hook I cast and baskets; and whatever they entrap I take.

Q. Quid si inmundi fuerint pisces?
Hwæt gif hit unclæne beoþ fixas?
What if it (turns out that) unclean are (the) fish?

A. Ego proiciam inmundos foras, et sumo mihi mundos in escam.
Ic utwyrpe þa unclænan ut, ond genime me clæne to mete

I throw the unclean away, and take to-me (the) clean for food

Q. Ubi uendis pisces tuos?
Hwær cypst þu fixas þine?
Where sell you fish yours?

A. In ciuitate.
On ceastre
In town.

Q. Quis emit illos?
Hwa bigþ hi?
Who buys them?

A. Ciues; non possum tot capere quot possum uendere.
Ceasterwara. Ic ne mæg swa fela gefon swa ic mæg gesyllan
The townsfolk. I not can as many get as I can sell.

Q. Quales pisces capis?
Hwilce fixas gefehst þu?
What fish catch you?

A. Anguillas et lucios, menas [small fish] et capitones [?chub], tructas et murenas, et qualescumque in amne natant.
Ælas ond hacodas, mynas ond æleputan, sceotan ond lampredan, ond swa hwylce swa on wætere swymmaþ
Eels and pike, minnows and blenny/burbot, trout and lampreys, and whatever in the water swims.

Q. Cur non piscaris in mari?
Forhwi ne fixast þu on sæ?
Why not fish you at sea?

A. Aliquando facio, sed raro, quia magnum nauigium mihi est ad mare.
Hwilum ic do, ac seldon, forþam micel rewyt me ys to sæ
Sometimes I do, but seldom, because much rowing for-me it-is at sea.

Q. Quid capis in mare?
Hwæt fehst þu on sæ?
What take you at sea?

A. Alleces et isicios, delfinos et sturias, ostreas et cancros, musculas, torniculi, neptigalli, platesia et platissa [plaice] et polipodes [octopus] et similia.
Hæringas ond leaxas, mereswyn ond stirian, ostran ond crabban, muslan, winewinclan, sæcoccas, fagc ond floc ond lopystran ond fela swylces.
Herrings and salmon, dolphin/porpoise and sturgeon, oysters and crabs, mussels, winkles, cockles, plaice and flounder and lobsters and many such.

Q. Uis capere aliquem cetum?
Wilt þu fon sumne hwæl?
Wish you to-take a whale?

A. Nolo.

Nic

Not-I.

Q. Quare?

Forhwi?

Why (not)?

A. Quia periculosa res est capere cetum. Tutius est mihi ire ad amnem cum hamo meo, quam ire cum multis nauibus in uenationem ballene.

Forþam plyhtlic þingc hit ys gefon hwæl. Gebeorhlicre ys me faran to ea mid scype mynum, þænne faran mid manegum scypum on huntunge hranes.

Because (a) perilous thing it is to-take (a) whale. More-agreeable it-is to-me to-go to (the) river with boat mine than to-go with many ships a'hunting (the) whale.

Q. Cur sic?

Forhwi swa?

How so?

A. Quia carius est mihi capere piscem quem possum occidere, quam illum, qui non solum me sed etiam meos socios uno ictu potest mergere aut mortificare.

Forþam leofre ys me gefon fisc þæne ic mæg ofslean, þonne fisc, þe na þæt an me ac eac swylce mine geferan mid anum slege he mæg besencean oþþe gecwylman

Because preferable it-is to-me to-take fish that I can kill, than a fish which not only me but also my companions with one blow can sink or slaughter.

Q. Et tamen multi capiunt cetos, et euadunt pericula, et magnum pretium inde adquirunt.

Ond þeah mænige gefoþ hwælas, ond ætberstaþ frecnysse, ond micelne sceat þanon begytaþ…

And yet many do-capture whales, and escape harm, and much money thence obtain…

A. Uerum dicis, sed ego non audeo propter mentis meae ignauiam.

Soþ þu segst, ac ic ne geþristge for modes mines nytenyssæ.

Truth you speak, but I not dare (to go after whales) for mind's mine timidity.

Though co-operative (with a little prompting), the fisherman does not emerge as a particularly admirable figure. It was, after all, in Aelfric's interest to stress the dangers faced by and the short-comings of his characters, thus reaffirming the comparatively safe life of the novice monk. Allowing for a certain monastic bias, the following useful points still emerge:

1. The fisherman already had at his disposal a variety of fishing techniques: the net, the hook and line, and a 'basket' – perhaps a sort of eel pot.
2. The fisherman does not rule out working at sea, but his boat is clearly more suited for river or estuary work; it has oars but not a sail. We are not told if it is made of hide or wood, but one suspects the former.
3. A distinction was made between fish useful for

food and 'unclean' or less edible species. The latter are not named, nor is the criterion for rejection made clear – though there is a hint at Matthew 13:47–48. (It would be topical, but incorrect, here, to substitute 'undersize' for 'unclean'.)

4. A ready market for fish was available in any town, we are telled. An added boost would be the Church's insistence on no eating of meat on Fridays – though fish was allowed.

5. Note that deep sea fish like the cod, turbot and haddock are not mentioned; and were presumably beyond this fisherman's resources. Herrings and salmon head the list.

6. Whaling, it is noted, required not only a stouter sort of boat than the fisherman possessed, but co-operation of a number of such vessels (the embryo whaling fleet?) – and a good measure of courage! This was particularly so in Medieval times, when the whale mouth was a symbol for the entrance to Hell, and the story of Jonah and the Whale would be part of everyday folklore. Nonetheless, Aelfric makes it clear that whaling did take place in the tenth century, a point not often given due weight.

General

alevin – 'recently hatched salmon' (FK, Berwick).

baggie – 'the stickleback' (Heslop, 1880s); baggies – 'immature coal fish' (KP, Beadnell); *EDD* – Sc, N'd.

baggit-fish – 'a salmon on the eve of depositing its ova' (Heslop, 1880s); baggit 'unspawned female salmon in spring', Scots. [Scots form of 'bagged', first noted 1848].

bastard sole – 'the lemon sole or lemon dab' (Heslop, 1880s).

bedroom fish – 'the skate' (KP, re Craster).

black-back – 'flat fish found among seaweed' (KP, Beadnell).

black-jack – 'the colesay, often called rock salmon by fishermen' (Heslop, 1880s); **blackjack** – 'fully grown coal-fish' (KP, Beadnell).

blast, gurnet blast – 'gurnet's bladder' (Umpleby, Staithes).

brandling – 'a name given to a species of trout caught in the rivers of Northumberland' (Brockett, 1829); brandling 'a river trout caught in the Tyne' (cf brandlings – multi-coloured peas) (Heslop, 1880s).

brat – 'name for a turbot on the Northumberland coast' (Heslop 1880s; brat – 'turbot' Umpleby, Staithes [bret, first noted c.1460]; *EDD* – N'd, Yx.

bully beshers – 'a kind of fish in the local streams' (Harry Peart, South Gosforth).

but – 'an abbreviation of holibut' [sic] (Heslop/Tyne, 1880s); butt – 'flounder' (KP, Beadnell) [implying flatness].

byennie – 'blenny' (KP, Beadnell).

chips – a fish 'chips' when it cuts the surface of the water without leaping [re a salmon] (Heslop, 1880s).

coal-say, the coal-fish – 'a species of cod' (Brockett, 1829); coalsay, colesay – 'the coal-fish' [black jack, rock salmon – when young: podlie] (Heslop, 1880s).

codlin' – 'codling: **Robbie codlin'** (Amble) – small codling; **Tommy coddlin'** (Amble) – larger codling' (KP, Beadnell).

cuddy's legs – 'herrings' (Heslop, 1880s).

dab – 'the sole' (KP, Beadnell); *EDD* – Ire, Yx, London.

eliator – 'a very small eal' (*Bell-White MS 12*).

fetther-lasher – 'sea-scorpion, gurnard' (KP, Beadnell).

flatty – 'a flat fish' (Heslop, N'd, 1880s).

fluck – 'a flat fish' (Grose, 1787); 'a flounder, a small fish' (*Bell-White MS 12*); **fluke** – a flounder. The Fluke-Hyel, Seahouses (KP, Beadnell); fluck, **flucker**, or **jenny-flucker** – 'a flounder' (Brockett, 1829); 'lady fluke', Scots [OE flóc, ON flóke]; *EDD* – general.

gibby – 'salmon with 'gib' or barb on its lip' (KP, Beadnell).

ginny – 'a skate' (KP, re Amble).

go'nets – 'gurnets' (Umpleby, Staithes) (Fr).

green-bone – 'the gar-fish, or needle-fish; taken on the coast of N'd' (Brockett, 1920); greenbyens, **greenhorn** – 'the garfish' (KP, Beadnell).

gurnet blast – see **blast**.

grilser – 'young salmon returning to the spawning grounds for the first time after a year or so at sea' (FK, Berwick).

haa'f-fish – 'a young cod about 9 to 12 pounds' (AR, Seahouses).

haa'f waxties – 'half-grown coal fish' (KP, Beadnell) [to wax – to grow].

haddock: tid haddocks (Amble) – 'small haddocks'; **danny haddocks** (Craster, Amble) – 'middle sized haddocks' (KP) [origin unknown].

halibut – 'holy + butt (flat) - so called from being so commonly eaten on holy-days'; *OED* – see turbot.

hallan – 'the fry of the coal fish' (Brockett, 1829).

harrin – 'herring' Dodd; harrin' (KP, Beadnell); heerin, harrin – "four twopence caller harrin"; (Brockett, 1829); "man with horse and cart shouted 'caller harrin'" (BA, re Blyth) [OE *haering*, Du haring].

jackie doory – 'the John Dory' (KP, Beadnell).

jenny flucker – 'a smal fluck or flounder' (*Bell-White MS 12*); jenny-flucker – 'a flounder' (Heslop, 1880s).

keek (noun) – 'pout whiting' (KP, re Craster).

keekies – 'Scotch haddocks' (KP, re Seahouses).

kelks – 'the salmon in the river Tyne after it has spawned' (*Bell-White MS 12*); kelk – 'codfish spawn' (Umpleby, Staithes); 'kelt – a female salmon or trout which has spawned and is on her way back to the sea. Local saying 'as seek [sick] as a kelt' (Jim Cromarty, Spittal/Berwick); also **kelt** or **keltie** (spent fish) Scots; kelks 'the salmon in the river Tyne after it has spawned' (*Bell-White MS 12*). ["Kelt is the normal 'scientific' name for a spawned salmon – whether male or female. Mortality among spawning males is high, and at this stage both male and female fish are emaciated and quite inedible, even if it was legal to catch them. Surviving fish rapidly regain condition down river, and some spawn for several years" (AO).]

kipper – smoked herring. Also 'male salmon at spawning time', Scots [?copper-coloured].

kilks – 'haddock rows (eaten as a delicacy)' (KP, Beadnell).

leeat – 'small coal-fish' Umpleby, Staithes; *EDD* – *lait* 'pollack' Sc, Ire, Yx; 'coalfish' Sc.

mattie – 'a fat young herring before roe or milt has developed (this term was used beyond Northumberland)' (KP, Beadnell); mattie – 'herring' Scots. [from Du *maatjes* 'female herring', first noted in English in 1858]; *EDD* – Shetland, Sc, EA.

maze – 'herring eggs' (KP, Beadnell).

meddoms – 'minnows' (KP, re Craster).

minnims – 'minnows' (KP, Beadnell).

mops – 'small codlings' (Umpleby, Staithes).

orgin – 'young codling' (Umpleby, Staithes).

paddle-hoosh – 'lump-sucker' (Beadnell, in Craster, **paddle**) (KP).

parr – 'young salmon about a year old' FK, Berwick; *EDD* – Sc, Yx.

podler (Beadnell), **podlie** (Seahouses), **puddler**

(Holy Island) – 'small coal-fish' (KP); podler – "children caught these in the harbour" (BA, Seaton Sluice); **poadla** – 'fish, probably immature coalfish' (FK, Berwick); *EDD* – *podley*, Sc, *poodler*, N'd.

podlie – see **coalsay**.

rede fyshe – ?salmon Cuth.Fair C16; red fish – salmon (Eric King, Seahouses); red fish (male salmon at spawning time) Scots – see also **kipper**.

roondy – (adj and noun) 'round, as of ungutted fish: roondies' (KP, Beadnell).

rown (ruuwn) 'roe of a fish. The milt is called melt' (Palgrave, 1896, Hetton); rowen – 'row, eggs' (KP, Beadnell).

run (of herring) – 'to spawn' (KP, Beadnell).

sailor's purse – 'skate's egg-case' (KP, Beadnell).

sea-cat – 'cat-fish, rock turbot' (KP, Beadnell); *EDD* – Sc, N'd.

sea-divvil – 'the monkfish' (KP, Beadnell); *EDD* – N'd.

sea-sow – 'the rock goby' (KP, Beadnell); *EDD* – N'd.

skeeat – 'skate' (Umpleby, Staithes) [ON skata].

skelly – 'the dace and the roach' (Brockett, 1829) [?scaley].

skidder – 'the common skate' (Heslop, 1880s).

skurff – 'grey trout (not red)…principally on the Tees' (Herrtage, 1881, p.326, p.xx).

skyell – 'a scale, e.g. salmon skyells' (KP, Beadnell).

slunk – 'thin, as of spent fish' (KP, Beadnell).

smeears – 'fish spawn' (Umpleby, Staithes).

smolt – 'an 18 month old salmon that has yet to go to sea for the first time' (FK, Berwick) {smolt as 'shiny'?]

soocker – 'the lamprey' (KP, Beadnell); *EDD* – 'young cod and other fish' Sc.

spaa'n – 'spawn'; **spaa'ny** – 'spawny' (KP, Beadnell).

spent (noun and adj) – 'herring which has spawned' (KP, Beadnell).

sprag – 'codlings' Umpleby, Staithes; sprag – 'large codling' (KP, re Craster) [first noted 1787, Grose]; *EDD* – N'd, Yx.

spur-dog – 'dogfish' (KP, re Craster).

squids – 'small herrings' (Umpleby, Staithes).

stang – 'a weever fish (sting on the back of his fin)' (KP, re Amble/Newbiggin).

sweet wulliam – 'male dogfish' (KP, re Craster).

thorn ears – 'large dog fish' (Umpleby, Staithes).

turbot – 'In the Newcastle fish market, the hallibut is called a turbot' (Brockett, 1829); turbot – 'the common name for halibut on the N'd coast' (Heslop, 1880s) [OFr *tourbout* a turbot]. See also **brat**.

tuck – 'the miller's thumb (fish)' (KP, Beadnell); **tuft** – 'the miller's thumb' (KP, re Craster); *EDD* – N'd.

watther bo'n – 'phosphorescence of herrings: "T'watther bo'ns on"' (Umpleby, Staithes, 1930s).

whick – quick, alive – 'used in the cry of fresh fish at Newcastle: "whick-an-alive"' (*Bell-White MS 12*).

willietuck – 'fish caught at the mouth of the Tweed' (FK, Berwick).

witch – 'a sole' (KP, Beadnell); EDD – Gromsby, Sx.

wrangham – 'odd lots of miscellaneous under-sized fish' (Umpleby, Staithes) [wrong'un].

It is notable in the above, that apart from a very few common names, going back to ON or OE, the terms for fish are invented and/or local, arguably reflecting the individual initiatives of separate fishing communities and relatively modern skills of deep-sea fishing.

Crustaceans

baccy boxes – '?spawning crabs' (KP, Beadnell).

barr'l – 'the barrel or main body of a lobster, which is measured for size' (KP, Beadnell).

beetle – 'a small prawn' (Blyth area, not used in north Northumberland) (KP).

berries – 'eggs on lobster. Berried hen – female lobster carrying eggs' (KP, Beadnell).

boast – 'breast (of crab)' (Newbiggin/Amble). Cf. **brisket**. (KP).

brisket – 'the main body of a crab' (cf. 'boast) (KP, Beadnell).

clonker – 'a large prawn' (Blyth only) (KP).

craaler, craalin' boockie – 'hermit crab' (KP, Beadnell).

crab cart – 'empty shell of crab' (Umpleby, Staithes).

deedmen's fingers – 'the inedible grey lungs inside a crab' (KP, Beadnell).

doggers – see **Fishing…bait**.

gowdie (Holy Island only) – 'squat lobster' (KP, Beadnell); *EDD* – 'goldy' Holy Island.

limmitter – 'a lobster with one claw missing' (Elsewhere, a disabled person) (KP, Beadnell).

miffy – 'lobster without large claws' (Umpleby, Staithes).

nancy – 'squat lobster' (KP, Beadnell); *EDD* – 'a small lobster' (EA).

nannycocks – 'undersized lobsters' ('**Pawks**' and '**linties**' at Whitby) (Umpleby, Staithes).

paddy (Eyemouth and Holy Island) – 'smooth spider crab' (KP, Beadnell).

peelers – see **Fishing…bait**.

piper – 'spider crab' ('tyed' [toad] in Seahouses) (KP).

pistil – 'a lobster with no claws' (KP, Beadnell).

poos – 'crabs' (Holy Island, also used on Scottish East Coast) (KP, Beadnell).

runch (Holy Island only) – 'small smooth spider crab' (KP, Beadnell). [*OED* only has 'runchie' as a Scots word for seaweed].

shear claa' – 'sharp claw of lobster (as opposed to numb claa', blunt claw)' (KP, Beadnell).

sheiler – 'a soft crab' (KP, re Holy Island).

shelpy -'soft (of crabs)' (KP, re Seahouses).

sixpenny man – 'squat lobster' (KP, re Seahouses).

softies – 'tiny crabs before shell appears' (Umpleby, Staithes).

squat lobster – 'muddy brown kind of lobster – very short – different species; (FT,Cullercoats);

swap lobster –'a small orange lobster, you eat them, you can only eat the tail' (CR, Amble).

toes – 'claws (of crab)' (KP, Beadnell).

tommy – 'small crab, thrown back' (KP, re Holy Island).

tyellier (Holy Island only) – 'smooth spider crab (also '**paddy**')' (KP, Beadnell).

tyed – 'spider crab' (Seahouses) (KP) [toad]; *EDD* – *tod* 'a small species of crab', Sc.

tyed-legs – brittle star (KP, Beadnell/Craster).

velvet swimmers – 'other sort of crabs found in pool' (Eric King, Seahouses).

wasp – 'a small prawn further south' (Blyth?) (KP).

white crab – 'soft crab, one that has shed its shell' (KP, Beadnell).

wiggy – 'name used for squat lobster farther south, Blyth area' (KP).

Whereas 'crab' (OE crabba, ON krabbi) and 'lobster' (OE loppestere) are well established terms, the detailed words for types or parts are inventive and local, e.g. variety of terms for a squat lobster: nancy, sixpenny man, wiggy. Like the opaque terms for coastal features, there is a kind of logical humour behind many of the by-names, but they comprise a level of everyday detail that evades regional or historical unity.

From the Sea-floor
Dicker hoyed his line oot ower far
To wheer the crabs 'n' lopsters are.
They thranged aroon' it one an' aa'
An' nicked the bait wi' crafty claa'
Then tugg'd three times to let him knaa'
They'd luv sum mair — it woz five-star!

("Not e'en a thankyou note," said Dicker, "Na,
"Aa'll save ma raggies, man, let's hev a jar.")

Deep unnerneeth the ocean's lip
The crafty lopster keeks wor ship
That stopped an' garr'd a hook ti dip;
Sez he, 'Young crabs for a sov'rein tip
Aa'll gie yi a clinkin' roon'-world trip,
Jus' queue up here, an' gerra grip!'

(The babby crabs went up an' doon,
An' 'greed it woz a rare bit fun.)

Shellfish

barnitickle – 'barnacle' (KP, Beadnell).

boockie – 'whelk. Slavvery boockie – whelk shell with snail inside. **Craa'lin' boockie** – whelk shell with hermit crab inside' (KP, Beadnell); EDD – buckie 'any spiral shell' esp. Sc.

checkers – 'periwinkles ("Thoo's browt checkers like mice een")' (Umpleby, Staithes).

chuck – 'a sea shell'; chucks – 'a game among girls; played with five of these shells, and sometimes with pebbles, called chuckie-stanes' (Brockett, 1829); chuck – 'a shell, usually of snail or winkle' *Hull MS* wNewc 1880s; *EDD* – Sc, N'd, Yx, Lx.

Easter-shells – 'the pinpatch or periwinkle' (Atkinson, 1868, Cleveland).

flithers – 'limpets' (Umpleby, Staithes) [not in OED]; *EDD* – nYx only.

jenny groats, john o' groats – 'cowrie shells' (KP, Beadnell).

mushel – 'mussel' (KP, Beadnell) [OE *muscle* from Latin].

oyster-scaup, -scappy – 'oyster-bed – cf. mussel-scaup' (Heslop, 1880s) [from Latin *ostrea*].

pennywilk – 'the winkle' (Heslop/Tyne, 1880s) [OE *pervinca*, from Latin].

shells – 'specifically, clams' (KP, Beadnell).

slavvery boockie – 'the whelk, as opposed to 'craa'lin' boockie – whelk shell containing hermit crab' (KP, Beadnell).

willicks – 'the shell fish periwinkle' (Bell-White MS 12); **wilk/willok/wullok/wulk** (Nth N'd), **penny-wilk** – 'a periwinkle, the edible sea-shell fish *Turbo littoreus*, L.' (Heslop, 1880s); 'willock – standard black whelk on rocks below high tide' (JH, S'm) C20/mid; willick – whelk: 'the willick or periwinkle is a small univalve mollusc found on the rocks of the Geordieland coast' (Dobson, 1972); whullick, whulk – 'a winkle' (KP, Beadnell); willoughs, (BA, Seaton Sluice) [OE *weoloc*]; *EDD* – Sc, East and South coasts.

The number of Latin-based standard terms perhaps reflect the known Roman fondness for shellfish, possibly loaned direct to Anglo-Saxon.

Other sea creatures

badger – 'starfish' (Umpleby, Staithes).

barr'l-arse – 'squid. Baa'ld-arse at Seahouses' (Also – **inkfish**) (KP, Beadnell).

cat o' nine tails – 'squid or octopus spawn' (Craster) (KP, Beadnell).

cock's comb – 'a red jelly-like creature found on the sea-bed 5 or 6 miles off Dunstanburgh Castle' (KP, Beadnell).

frone – 'starfish. Kyel-frone – sun starfish' (KP, Beadnell) [cf. thoorns].

haddock bags – 'sea squirts (haddocks eat them)' (KP, Beadnell).

ink-fish – 'squid' (Holy Island) (KP, Beadnell).

jilly – 'jelly, jellyfish; also used for a sea-anemone' (KP, Beadnell).

kyel-frone – see **frone**.

miller's thumb – 'properly a kind of fish, but used in Craster for big red starfish' (KP, Beadnell).

musk-shell, musk – 'cuttlefish' (KP, Beadnell).

paps (Holy Island) – 'sea-anemones' (KP, Beadnell); 'paup – a green anemone which sticks to rocks in the intertidal zone' NC, Seaham [?pap = teat]

pap-styens – 'soft coral, dead men's fingers' (KP, Beadnell).

sale – sandeels (KP, Beadnell).

sandels – 'sandeels' (Amble / Newbiggin) (KP, Beadnell).

sand-hopper – 'large, woodlouse-like creature which lives on the sea bed (?)' (KP, Beadnell).

skate's egg – 'the sea-potato, a small white sea-urchin' (KP, Beadnell).

slater – 'woodlouse; sea-slater – large, woodlouse-like creature found at sea' (KP, Beadnell); *EDD* – 'woodlouse' Sc, Ire, N'd, C'd.

snig – 'an eel; hence, to **sniggle**, to fish for eels' (Brockett, 1829); *EDD* – general [?Mdu *snigge* 'a snail'].

sookers – 'sea anemones' (Umpleby, Staithes) [contrast 'sookers' under **General Fish**].

swatter – 'jelly-fish' (KP, Beadnell): **swither** – Scots (Eyemouth & St. Monans).

thoorns – 'thorns' (starfish) (Umpleby, Staithes).

Few if any of these curiosities of the sea have names of any detectable antiquity, suggesting their low status in the fishing hierarchy.

Sea mammals

finner – 'killer, pilot or minke whale in Beadnell area. Elsewhere used for dolphin' (KP, Beadnell); *EDD* – Shet, Ork.

harrin' whale – 'whale commonly seen around shoals of herring (probably Pilot and Minke whales)' (KP, Beadnell).

piker – 'killer whale' (KP, re Newbiggin).

plasher – 'a porpoise or dolphin' (plash = splash) (KP, Beadnell).

puffy – 'porpoise' (KP, re Seahouses); *EDD* – puffy-dunter, N'd.

skeldie – 'porpoise' (KP, Beadnell).

wallerin' – 'waddling, moving as a seal on land' (KP, WW, Beadnell).

Conclusion

Besides certain well-established terms, there is a curious lack of consistency, even for the all-important commercial fish. The Fishery Board for Scotland in the 1920s compiled a list of names (now online); thus for cod, north of the border, we have:

Blawn cod (split and half dried), Block Codling (medium-sized, hardly adult), Blockie (half-sized fish), Coddie (small cod), Codling (small- and medium-sized in Banffshire), Droud, Dunean (half grown fish), Keelin' (large adult fish), Killine, Kleg, Kylling, Poor John (cod in poor condition), Poullach, Purr (small fish), Redware Cod (cod of a red colour), Ruggie (an old cod), Ruggie (small fish), Scots-Willie (small codling), Shingler (cod with large head and thin body), Slinger, Slink, Sousler Cod (badly fed fish with big head), Sprag, Stock Fish (medium- sized cod between codlin' and keelin'), Stuckie (a 'thick' codling), Warey Codlin' or Keelin' (from the rocks), and Wind Fish (dried in air) – none of which, except 'codling', are reflected (as far as I can detect) in our North-East region.

If we look at the ever popular Salmon, the Scots offer:

Baggit (Unspawned female in spring), Beastie, Beikat (male fish), Ben (small spring salmon), Black fish (female at spawning time), Braddan or Bradhan, Branlie (parr), Brannock (parr), Bull (Trout salmon on second return from sea), Bykat (male fish), Candavaig (foul salmon),

Caul Iron, Dropper (fish returning down river before spawning), Duke's fish, Finnie (salmon not a year old), Gerrat or Gerrit (parr), Graulse or Graul, Grey Salmon (autumn salmon), Grey schule, Grilse, Gilse, Girlss, Girsill, or Glysort (adolescent stage), Ieskdruimin, Kelt or Keltie (spent fish), Kipper (male at spawning time), Lax fish or Lax salmon (salmon on second return from sea), Liggar (foul salmon), Marled salmon, Orange fin (smolt), Parr (young in river on way to sea), Pyrre (parr), Rawner (unspawned female in Spring), Red fish (male at spawning time), Reister (salted and dried salmon), Ronnal (female fish), Samlet (parr), Sheddar Salmon (female), Slinger (spent fish), Soldier (male at spawning time), Spring fish, Wair-ben (spring salmon)...

Whereas the modern word *salmon* derives from French (and ultimately Latin), the OE for a salmon was leax. The Old English *Boethius* (Metre 19) refers to 'leax [or] cyperan' – the first term here is a salmon, thus 'Lax fish or Lax salmon – salmon on second return from sea' (Spey district and Aberdeen); the second OE term implies 'copper-coloured' and may well refer to the male salmon at spawning time, thus a Scots law 1597 talks of 'redde fish or kipper' as equivalents, and see 'red fish' in Scots list (above).

The first recorded application of *kipper* to preserved fish (in fact salmon) is from Defoe's *Tour* 3, 336 ca. 1700 and it may be from preserved salmon the word transfers to preserved herring.

However, a reference from 1614 mentions North-East fishermen catching herring off Yarmouth: "and all the herrings that they take, they sell fresh unto the Yarmouth men to make red herrings" (*Journal of the Coble & Keelboat Society,* 27, 2006) – which suggests that smoking herring was already common, though under another name.

The overall lack of unity – especially when it comes to detailed terms – runs contrary to the unity suggested by the common use of the coble-type of fishing craft; the general cultural tie of a Northern dialect from East Anglia to Scotland; and the mobility and contact inherent in the herring fishing industry. It may simply be that details of fishing are everyday (commonplace) matters for which local words are inevitable and that it would be wrong to place too much emphasis on diversity at this level.

A celebration of the role of fish in the nineteenth century diet is the song William Watson composed in 1842, a lullaby filled with secrets:

When the Boat Comes In
Come here me little Jacky,
Now ah've smoked me baccy,
Let's hev a bit of <u>cracky</u>,   talk, chat
Till the boat comes in.

Dance to thee Daddy, sing to thee Mammy,
Dance to thee Daddy, to thee Mammy sing;
Thou shalt hev a fishy on a little dishy,
Thou shalt hev a fishy when the boat comes in.

Here's thy mother humming,
Like a canny woman;
Yonder comes thy fatha,
Drunk - he cannat stand.

Dance to thee Daddy, sing to thee Mammy,
Dance to thee Daddy, to thee Mammy sing;
Thou shalt hev a fishy on a little dishy,
Thou shalt hev a haddock when the boat comes in

Our Tommy's always fuddling,
He's so fond of ale,
But he's kind to me,
I hope he'll never fail.

Dance to thee Daddy, sing to thee Mammy,
Dance to thee Daddy, to thee Mammy sing;
Thou shalt hev a fishy on a little dishy,
Thou shalt hev a bloater when the boat comes in

I like a drop mesel',
When I can get it sly,
And thou, my bonny bairn,
Will like't as well as I.

Dance to thee Daddy, sing to thee Mammy,
Dance to thee Daddy, to thee Mammy sing;
Thou shalt hev a fishy on a little dishy,
Thou shalt hev a mackerel when the boat comes in.

May we get a drop,
Oft as we stand in need;
And weel may the keel row
That brings the bairns tha breed.

Dance to thee Daddy, sing to thee Mammy,
Dance to thee Daddy, to thee Mammy sing;
Thou shalt hev a fishy on a little dishy,
Thou shalt hev a salmon when the boat comes in.

Denounced by Terry (1931, p.ix) as "all very silly and foolish, and a libel on the Northumbrian fisher folk," I cannot help wondering if he has missed something.

Chapter 10. Sea birds

In Anglo-Saxon poetry, birds command a special respect, either as the fierce 'birds of battle' that haunt the battlefield in anticipation of feeding, or as sea-birds that represent the flight of the soul over the ocean, in the loosening of sleep or vision of death. In the Old English poem Seafarer they reinforce the sense of isolation of the hermit-outcast, in a passage many reckon to have been written with reference to the coast of Northumbria:

> þær ic ne gehyrde butan hlimman sæ
> iscaldne wæg hwilum ylfete song
> dyde ic me to gomene ganetes hleoþor
> ond huilpan sweg fore hleahtor wera
> mæw singende fore medodrince
> stormas þær stanclifu beotan þær him stearn oncwæð
> isigfeþera ful oft þæt earn bigeal...

> ...there I nothing heard but the murmuring of the sea,
> the ice-cold wave; sometimes the swan's song
> made I my entertainment, ganet's outcry
> and curlew's call in place of the laughter of men,
> the sea-mew singing as my mead-drink;
> storms there on rocky-cliffs beat where the tern responds
> and icy-winged full often the eagle calls out...

Stearn as 'tern', *ganet* as 'gannet' survive in Modern English; 'whaup' (<*huilp* 'curlew') and 'mew' (<*maew* 'gull') have limited modern (dialect) use. Our all-purpose 'gull' is seemingly derived from Celtic sources. There is now a pretty complete set of names for the various different seabirds, but to the fisherman they are not so much admirable as awkward; relatively few have valid traditional identities; more usually nick-names or local names.

alluns – 'The little auk (*alle alle*) "The'r leyke alluns efther't"' (Umpleby, Staithes).

annets – "common gulls – here annets" (Hutchinson, re Farnes, 1778, p.181).

au'd wife – see bleg.

bleg – 'seahen ('au'd wife' at Whitby)' (Umpleby, Staithes).

brocket – "sea larks – here brockets" (Hutchinson, re Farnes, 1778, p.181).

cuddy duck – 'eider duck, St Cuthbert's duck. Also, **culbert duck**' (KP, WW, Beadnell).

cuddy – 'eider' (WS, Seahouses) via Ada Radford.

dokie – 'auk, such as guillemot or puffin' (Newton) (KP, WW, Beadnell) [from Northern form of 'duck'].

dot bo'ds – 'dotteril' (Umpleby, Staithes, 1930s) [related to dote, dotard].

go west – 'pintail duck' (WS, Seahouses) via Ada Radford; **gau-west, lang-tailed gau-west** – 'the blue-neb or long-tailed duck' (KP, WW, Beadnell).

gormer – 'cormorant' (WS, Seahouses) via Ada Radford [OE gor (dirty) + maw]; *EDD* – Sc, N'd, C'd, Yx.

kep-shite – 'skua, so called because it chases other birds until they drop their food, thought by fishermen to be droppings' (KP, Beadnell) [kep 'catch' ?i.e. the dropped food].

mullymac – 'fulmar. Also **mully**, very similar to Shetland name, maly' (KP, Beadnell); mully mac – 'fulmer' (WS, Seahouses) via Ada Radford; **mallimawks** – 'guillemots' (Umpleby, Staithes) [?from Gaelic mull 'headland'?]

(**note**: "The fulmar is such a recent 'entrant' (post-war) to the area that it seems to have received no dialect name other than 'mollymawk' which, in various forms, was applied rather indiscriminantly by seamen to seagull-like birds, including the cape albatross!" (AO).)

pee-wit, peez-weep – 'the lapwing' (Brockett, 1829); **peas weep** – 'a plover so called from its crie' (*Bell-White MS 12*); peesweep (paez:waep) 'lapwing, or peewit' (Palgrave, 1896, Hetton); **pee'sit, pee'sweep** – 'lapwing or peewit' (KP, Beadnell) [imitative of call]; *EDD* – Sc, Ire, Nth, eMids, EA.

pets – 'seagulls' (Umpleby, Staithes).

pickie – 'a tern' (KP, Beadnell); **pickle peck head** – 'arctic tern' (WS, Seahouses) via Ada Radford [< *picky* 'small' (Sc) or *picky* – 'pitch-like'?].

pilot, sea-pilot – 'oyster-catcher' (KP, Beadnell) [see sea pie].

roach – 'little awk' (WS, Seahouses) via Ada Radford, (KP, Beadnell) [*OED* s.v. *rotche*, from Du *rotge* (?*rotgoes*) – brent goose)].

scoot – 'the guillemot, so-called near Spittal' (Heslop, 1880s); scoot – 'guillemot' (KP, Beadnell); **skout** – 'the auk' (N'd 1790) (Heslop, 1880s); "a[u]ks – here skouts" (Hutchinson, re Farnes, 1778, p.181) [*OED* s.v. *scout*, source unknown].

seagulls – "I remember the kids I taught in Hull in the 70s divided birds into two kinds – spuggies and seagulls; i.e. land birds and sea birds" (JS).

sea-mice – 'small wading birds such as knots or sanderling (usually plural). Also used at Newbiggin for sea-slater' (KP, Beadnell).

sea pheasant – 'long-tailed duck' (WS, Seahouses) via Ada Radford.

sea pie – 'oyster catcher' (WS, Seahouses) via Ada Radford [pie(d) 'particoloured']; *EDD* – Shet, Ork, Sc, N'd, Lx, EA.

sea pigeon – 'black guillemot' (WS, Seahouses) via Ada Radford.

sea-pilot – see **pilot**.

sollan – 'gannet or solan goose' (KP, Beadnell) [ON súla 'gannet'].

tarrock – "kittiwakes or tarrocks" (Hutchinson, re Farnes, 1778, p.181).

tearn – 'sandwich tern' (WS, Seahouses) via Ada Radford; **teerum** – 'tern' (KP, re Seahouses); tarree – 'arctic tern' (KP, re Craster), WW [ON *þerna*, OE *stearn*].

teddelum – 'wader' (WS, Seahouses) via Ada Radford; **tudelems** – 'small sea birds, such as knots, dunlin' (KP, re Seahouses, Beadnell); tudelems – 'small birds with long red legs' Seaton Sluice; **ch'dlums** – 'of any number or kind of shore birds' (Eric King, Seahouses) [?tootle sound].

teufit / tuifit – 'the peewit' (Heslop, 1880s) [cf. Du tivit].

tommy-noddy – 'the coulter-neb or puffin' Brockett 1829; tommy noddy – 'puffin' (WS, Seahouses) via Ada Radford; tommy noddy, **tommy** – 'puffin cf. Shetland, Tammy Norrie' (KP, Beadnell); *EDD* – *tommy-noddy* 'dwarf or misshapen person', N'd, 'puffin' Ork, N'd.

waffler – 'the green sand-piper' (Brockett, 1829); *EDD* – N'd – 'so called from its undulating odd flight'.

waregoose – 'barnacle goose' (KP, Beadnell); **wore goose** – 'brent goose' (WS, Seahouses) via Ada Radford [ware – seaweed].

whaup – 'curlew' (FK, Berwick) [OE *huilp* – cf. Du *whulp*]; *EDD* – Sc, Ire, C'd, Linx.

witter-hen – 'moorhen or coot' (KP, Beadnell).

wullemot – 'guillemot' (Heslop, 1880s);

wulliemot – 'guillemot' (WS, Seahouses) via Ada Radford; **wullymint** – 'guillemot' (KP, Beadnell) [Anglo-Norman, ultimately from *William/Guillaume*].

plus:

hard-shells – 'guillemots' eggs' (KP, Beadnell).

Wild fowl – especially around Holy Island and the Farnes, as Adrian Osler points out to me – were an important food source, witness records of Abbey of Whitby in 1394 that detail 2,000 oysters, salmon, 2 swans, 12 teals, 12 lapwings, 12 partridges, 12 plovers, 24 fieldfares, 12 small birds, 50 roasting eels, 3 barrels white herrings, 3 pike, etc. Later, not eating but shooting of any gull was a practical recreation in the nineteenth century: "From some years after I came to Seaham Harbour I used to be frequently on the sea shore within these manors, shooting sea birds which at that time were numerous on the coast…" (George Howey, re 1830s). The eggs of virtually any bird were also valued food. See note on Farne Islands, above; here, more fully, about re Flamborough Head:

The climmers [sic] operated thus. A team of three men would set forth to the cliff top, secure a safe anchor a few feet back from the clifftop, and from this secure the main rope. Two men would remain up above, to haul the climmer up or lower him down according to his signals. The climmer himself…would lower himself over the cliff edge, with a second lighter rope in his hand for signalling. Down he would go, down the vertical cliff face, and with great skill he would swing himself to and fro, often for amazing distances, to pluck the eggs off isolated ledges. ..

Into his satchel he would put the eggs. If he wanted up or down he would send up signals of so many tugs on his signal rope. These cliffs are four hundred feet high in places, and quite vertical, so climming was not a job for the faint-hearted. When his bag was full he would come up.. In a good day he could take two to three hundred eggs." p.215. Continued to 1954 when Law passed. cliffs worked every year starting mid-May, but also sometimes left fallow a for a year. "The eggs they sold, and they were very good to eat (thye sold in London hotels for enormous prices – as 'plover eggs').

(Seymour, 1974, p.215)

Generally, the dialect terms collected here are seldom as specific as the Latin species names – an anticipated gap between popular and scientific usage. Correctly identified or not, for the modern observer, the mass of gulls landing to nest and raise chicks, might be reckoned today one of the glories of the North East coast.

Conclusion

In dealing with 'culture' of the coast, from Anglian settlement to the present, we are faced with a number of historical strata, each overlaying the other, and evidenced in the changes of vocabulary. Proceeding (archaeologically) from the surface down:

On top we can recognise a long tradition of giving 'pet' names to rocks, fish and weather that affect everyday life – these are necessarily local and show little consistency, other than in a tendency to use graphic, easily remembered images (though often 'opaque' to modern understanding). This diversity implies a society of separate and settled (not necessarily 'isolated') fishing villages. A degree of Dutch influence is also evident in words like *hook, goit, hobble, douffie, mizzling, dacker* – a reminder that contacts can as easily be cross-sea as along coast.

Of similar age is the official terminology for coastal feature and coastal proceedure, encouraged by map-makers, legislation on safety and like official usage, tending to obscure local variety and historic divergence.

Behind these lies yet another more unified layer, when vocabulary and technology was shared along the coast, and there is interchange of Old Norse and Old English terms. While it is possible this was encouraged by super-local communications like the overall presence of the pre-Reformation monasteries (all the North-East coast lay within the Archbishopric of York), it seems likelier that it was a specific phenomenon of the coastal zone. As Scandinavian influence over the North Sea persists throughout the Middle Ages, we need not date this interchange of words to any particular century. This is a process similar to the growth of a Common Northern English, in which Old Norse-based words appear in non-Norse settled areas, but has special application to the coast. It is also the time when the practice of the coble (itself a fusion of British and Anglian/Norse skills) is distributed along the coast. It seems fair to dub it an Anglo-Viking culture.

Ultimately, behind all these is the layer that distinguishes Anglian from Viking, clearest in coastal feature name and settlement place-names, which show division along the lines of first settlement of each group, clealy fossilised. This enables us to add to and confirm the list of specifically Northumbrian words in Old English: *shield, snab, snook, steel, carr, dodd, piner, law (hill), staello (stell)* …

This model or framework is necessarily conjectural, but allows for periods of cultural fluxion and cultural individuation during the history of the coast, which has left unique traces in its vocabulary and technology.

Part Two: The boats

Now is this ship well made
Within and without, thinks me.
Now home then will I wend
To fetch in my <u>meney</u>.   household
Have good day both old and young,
My blessing with you be.

(Newcastle Noah Play)

Clinker shipbuilding was a genuine craft, in which the shipwright remained close to his materials. The size of the ship depended on the timber he could find in the nearby woodland. The width of the planks depended on the girth of the tree; the curvature of the ribs depended on the natural curvature of branches in the wood. Long clinker-built ships required the existence of tall, slow-grown, knot-free trees typical of 'wildwood' environments which became increasingly rare in England by the 14th century.

(www.britarch.ac.uk)

Chapter 1. General terms

Structural systems

clinker (or **clench**) built – with overlapping planks (strakes); strakes define the shape; a strong construction; less planing of wood, therefore quicker, less technologically demanding. Strength depends on hull rather than frame. Cobles are an example of the clinker-built style where the hull is constructed first, then the ribs fitted in [probably from Dutch *klinken*].

carvel – "A 'frame first' method in which the pre-formed frames (ribs) are put in place first and the hull planks are then fitted flush, edge to edge, around them. Popularised first in the Mediterranean, carvel construction had spread to most of Atlantic Europe (including Britain) by the late 1500s" (AO) [OFr *carvel*, a type of small ship].

variant: **scarbel-built** – 'carvel-built, built with smooth planks' (KP, Beadnell).

> With the old method, clinker-building, northern carpenters built the hull first overlapping the planks to give strenth and watertightness. With the new method the frames were set up first and then the hull planking was added on, pinned to the internal timbers. The hull planks with skeleton construction were thus fitted edge-to-edge rather than overlapping as before.
>
> (Ungar 1985 p.155)

Tools

(with help from Nigel Gray, Coble & Keelboat Society)

adze – does main shaping. "Although adzes are quite out of fashion today, because the steel saw has taken their place, it is safe to say that without the invention of the adze boat-building could never have advanced from the dug-out stage" (Lethbridge, 1952, p.15).

auger – to drill holes for bolts and rivets.

draa'-knife – 'tool used to shape planks when building coble' (KP, Beadnell).

draw plane – secondary shaping, e.g. rounding masts, spars.

backing-out plane – to hollow inside of planks for carvel.

prodder – 'small hand drill' (KP, Beadnell).

rebate chisel and plane – for sockets for planks at stem and stern posts.

spokeshave – similar to draw-knife, on smaller scale.

The Tweed coble-builder's tools are essentially those of the small boat-builder anywhere in Britain – an adze for shaping the stem and timbers...and a draw-knife for shaping the planking; screw and shell augers...hammer and copper rooves and nails for clinching; a jumper for removing **rooves** or bent nails where a claw-hammer is ineffectve; and boat-builder's tongs [used for a vice].

(Sanderson, 1969, p.276)

To the modern boat-builder, electric tools like the sander, grinder, chainsaw are a great asset – as illustrated in the film *The Last Galway Hooker* (John Helion, *Classic Boat*, 1995), which nonetheless provides a vivid and sympathetic account of the hand-building tradition.

For the rest of us, a hint: "You know when you put a screw in, you give it an extra turn, you've hardened it up. The younger generation stop when it's flush…" (Ernie Keedy, Beamish, 2005/84).

Wood words

   fay or **fey** – 'a word used by ship carpenters before a piece of timber is placed: "It fays fair" (it is likely to fit)' (Brockett, 1829) [OE *fegan*]; *EDD* – N'd, Lx, esp. Sth.

   frass – 'sawdust made by woodworm' (KP, Beadnell); [< Gm *Frasz*, adopted in C19th].

   haze – "the stempost is shaped from an oak 'haze' cut from a part of the tree grown with a natural bend" (Sanderson, 1969, p.277) [plus fn.6, p.280: "O.Norse hals = neck; halsar = the curved planks abutting on stem or stern-post"; cf. OE *heals*].

   hog piece – "When a boat is first started, a non-coble will be laid and built on a hog piece which gives support to the keel" (DR, S'd).

   lofting – providing with planks; *EDD* – Sc, N'd, D'm.

   rabbet – 'a deep groove or channel, cut in a piece of timber longitudinally, to receive the edge of a plank' (Falconer, 1780) [OFr *rabat*].

   ruff – "neither ryff nor ruff" (*Newc. Noah Play*); *ryff* is probably 'sail'/'reef'; in which case *ruff* will be 'roughtree' (mast), rather than *rugh* (a rove).

   scarf joint – "a joint in which the two parts are tapered away and overlapped, thus not increasing the thickness of the whole" (AO) [root uncertain,

possibly ON; *EDD* records *scarf* as Shetland, *scare* as the expected form in Sc, N'd, Yx < ON *skera* 'to shear, cut'].

   spelk – pliable lath of wood: "four spelkes athwart, and one top spelk are sufficient" (in constructing a hive) 1648 via Raine (*BL MS Egerton 2868*); any small piece of wood [OE spelc]; *EDD* – Sc, N'd, Linx.

   spell, **speal** – a splinter, thin piece of wood: "spelles" 1641 via Raine (*BL MS Egerton 2868*) [ON *spela*]; *EDD* – Sc, Ire, Nth, Mids. Equivalent to previous entry.

   spront – *Newc. Noah Play* – possibly a misreading for 'sprout' in the sense of new wood, brushwood, withies.

   sprot – *Newc. Noah Play* – ?sprote 'a small piece of wood', which is supported by the rhyme (boat); or perhaps 'pole' – compare: 'a sprete – a pole, a long staff [D'm]' (*Kennet, 1695, BL MS Lansdowne 1033*), and modern 'bowsprit'; but also 'sprat, sprot – the rush' – (Heslop, 1880s).

   sprund – *Newc. Noah Play* – ?for *sprunt* 'a short, stiff piece of wood' – a peg?

   spyer – *Newc. Noah Play* – beam for ship; compare: "essh spyres et ellyrspyres" (of ash and alder) 1361/62 via Raine (*BL MS Egerton 2868*); spear – 'a spar, a wooden bar e.g. a pump rod' – (Heslop, 1880s); "spares 4 inches deep and 3 inches in thickness" as rooftrees – late seventeenth century via Raistrick (*Yorkshire Dales*, ch.4); *EDD* – Sc, Yx, Lx [ON sperra].

   stang – wooden bar or long pole: "The people...bett them with great stanges", (N'd, 1630) via Raine. [ON/OE]; *EDD* – Shet, Ork, Sc, Nth, Mids, so likely of ON origin.

   steaming – "planks are bent by direct exposure to steam, e.g. in an enclosed pipe" – (Derek Rowell, S'd); "risky as knocks nature out of it (the wood)" (Bart Taylor, Cullercoats); "ribs are made from one straight piece of timber, which is put in the steambox – that long, coffin-like thing there – and cramped to shape in a mould" (Hargrave, Hopwood, qu. March 1970, I, pp.113–14).

stobb – a post or stump: "hankt [tied?] him to a stobb", 1673, Raine (*BL MS Egerton 2868*) [OE/ON]; *EDD* – Sc, Ire, Nth.

stower – 'a stake or long pole', Raine (*BL MS Egerton 2868*) [ON staurr 'stake'].

trinnels – 'trenails or trunnels, used in common shipwright practice to fasten planking and other elements to a ship's (or large boat's) frames, usually used in combination with metal fastenings' (AO).

A group of these words occur in the fifteenth century Newcastle Noah Play, where Noah declares his lack of skills and supplies to build the Ark, but accuracy may have been subordinated to amassing sound effects:

For I was never since I was born,	
Of kind of <u>craft</u> to <u>burthen</u> a boat;	skill...create
For I have neither <u>ryff</u> nor <u>ruff</u>,	sail...mast
<u>Spyer</u>, <u>sprund</u>, <u>spront</u>, no <u>sprot</u>."	spar...?
	peg...?
	withies... ?
	small wood

Rivets

clench – 'to knock over nails when building coble' (KP, Beadnell); 'copper nails...clenched up with burrs' (Wood, 1937, p.45) [OE form of *clink*].

suein' nail – 'sewing nail, copper nail or rivet used to make coble' (KP, Beadnell).

rowe – blank for rivet *Newc. Noah Play*; 'The rove is that little iron plate into which the clinch nails are clinched' (*The Seaman's Dictionary* [1620s]);

rugh – (DR, Sunderland); **reeve** (KP, Beadnell) [ON. ró – with /v/ as later 'excrescence' (OED); however *rugh*/*ruff* could be a valid later Viking form, e.g. Færoes rógv; (Durham Account Rolls, *1406*) [*rufe* – which could give rove or rugh]; *EDD* – *rove* Shet, Sc, N'd.

For a rivet: hole drilled first; the rivet or nail inserted from outby, and kept tight to wood by a hodder [holder up]; then rugh driven over rivet using hollow punch to get it tight to wood; nail is clipped to rugh level; nail is flattened over rugh; last is 'hoddin' off' – the rivet head is recessed into wood.

(Derek Rowell, Sunderland Maritime Heritage)

The planks were copper fastened, with square nails, and roves. The shipwright would drill a hole, smaller than the nail sizes, square nails. Then he'd hammer, tap it in. A smaller drill hole, you didn't want a big hole for the nail to wobble about. Then on the inside, you could buy a copper washer with a square hole, you'd fit these over, your copper nails would protrude through the timber, and you'd stick about that much on the inside, you put a copper rove on with a square hole, cut it off and rivet it over.

(Ernie Keedy, Beamish, 2005/84)

Planks fixed with copper nails every 2½ " – in pattern 3 nails, rib, 3 nails etc. First drill hole, drill bit equals width of side of square nail so nail grips, and put on rove; cut away extra length of nail to surplus that equals width of the rove, then offset it with a small hammer – first spread nail end with round of hammer, then shape it with flat head of hammer. Hold nail in place flush against side with a heavy dolly – any lump of timber with an indent, or metal – can also be used to tap nail through. Can be done single-handed but ribs need two to rivet.

(Bart Taylor, Cullercoats)

Two shipwrights worked for us, we had a floating dock. You put a patch on, and in those days there was no power tools, it was an auger with a wooden handle, was the only way you could put a hole in, there was no power. The planks were copper fastened, with square nails, and roves…

(Ernie Keedy, Beamish, 2005/84)

Shipyard rivetting
In the days of hand rivetting in shipyards it actually took about 5 men to put in a single rivet:
A Heater – he heated the rivet on his bellows fire. When the rivets were red hot he picked them out with his tongs and threw them to…
A Catcher – he picked them up with his tongs and placed the rivet in the rivet hole…
A Hadda-on – then held the rivet in place at the back; then
Two Hand Rivetters – hammered and clenched the rivet over. They took alternate strikes, one right-handed and one left-handed.

(Bill Stephenson, N.Shields)

Caulking

blare (noun) – 'a strong caulking material composed primarily of dried animal, usually horse, dung' (AO); 'mixture of cow-dung and tar used for caulking' (KP, Beadnell); *EDD* – N'd, EA.

caulking iron – 'scraper like, to drive tow into gaps between planks' (Nigel Gray).

caulking mallet – 'used in combination with caulking iron' (Nigel Gray).

hobby – 'caulker's or riveter's tool' (Newc. via BG); *EDD* – 'block that holds nail in place for rivetting' – N'd only.

theet – 'watertight: "Them beeats [boots] is as theet as a bottle" (used also at Flamborough) (Umpleby, Staithes, 1930s).

yetlin – 'three-legged iron pot, used for cooking and also for boiling tar' (KP, Beadnell).

The wherries used to sink, and I used to make this oakum and blare – that was an old shipwrights' name for it, like a pudding, mixed up with sticks and put onto the wood before you harden it up…

(Ernie Keedy, Beamish, 2005/84)

The Gokstad ship of ca.900 AD was rivetted, and has a caulking of tarred rope (Kemp, 1978, p.48).

Samples of hair caulking from medieval boat timbers excavated in London showed, on analysis, a mix of cattle hair (48%), goat hair (38%) and sheep's wool (18%) (Ryder, 1998). In general, though, caulking would not be applicable to a clinker-built boat, where the strakes would swell and lock together in water.

Painting
The colourful appearance of many a present-day coble ensures its visibility at sea, and is part of tradition of simple colour-coding, by which, for example, a foyboat would be usually black with a white topstrake, or certain colours be preferred at a particular harbour. But effective industrial paint is a relatively modern product, especially in a range of colours and Edgar March surely trips when he asserts "the brightly coloured planks may go back to the days of King Harold" (March, 1970, I, p.93) citing as evidence the boats on the Bayeux Tapestry. The tapestry has wonderful horses, too, in blue, red and mustard – but none such would be found in William's army!

For the 1930s boat, sober green or blue were said to be preferred externally, light blue inside; colour was indeed available up to a century earlier (see Osler & Barrow, 1993, 2, pp.264–45), but plain patterns obtained in the eighteenth century:

> …black-strakes – a range of planks immediately above the wales in a ship's side: they are always covered in a mixture of tar and lamp-black, forming an agreeable variety with … the scraped planks of the side, covered with melted turpentine or varnish of pine, above.
>
> (Falconer, 1780)

Bitumen was one source of tar; a similar preservative could be distilled from conifers ('Stockhom Tar'); coal-tar was a useful by-product of the processing of coal to coke. At one point on his voyages (1777) the resourceful Captain Cook noted: "As we had neither pitch, tar, nor rosin, left to pay [smear] the seams, this was done with varnish of pine."

Locally:

> I went to mind the pitch pots, etc. for Thomas Harbottle, a shipwright, who had a keel hove up by means of a crab [windlass] and slide balks, upon the Gill Quay [Wearside]… [later] I went to Ayre's Quay, as a shipwright, to Richard Metcalf. There I stayed until we launched the Auspicious, during which time I had to mind the boilers for steaming the planks, this requiring my presence in the yard at 2 or 3 in the morning.
>
> (Sanderson 1873, pp.14–15)

Problems

bowelt – 'graithing bolt, grappling iron used to drag for lost gear' (KP, Beadnell).

grades – 'grappling gear for recovering lost lines. (Y'u ma' graade all t'daay an' nut tak' 'o'd.)' (Umpleby, Staithes, 1930s).

graith (verb) – 'to drag for lost gear; grapple: Graithin' bowlt. Graithin' irons. Graither – a grapnel' (KP, Beadnell) [ON *greiðe* 'equipment'].

howsing – 'bailing' (Yx) (Bradley, 2, p.31)

jogged – pumped: "when we jogged her [the ship] out this moanin' we didn't get two buckets out on her" (John Green, S'd, 1879, p.48).

leks – 'leaks: "sha leks leyke a baskit"' (Umpleby, Staithes, 1930s).

rent – (noun) 'split which opens up between planks of a wooden boat when left to dry out' (KP, Beadnell).

rove – torn, split: "we heard she'd rove a plank through and sank" (Amble per BG) [ON *rífa*]; *EDD* – rive: Sc, Ire, Nth, Mids, EA.

spring (verb) – 'to open out (of planks of a boat)' (KP, Beadnell).

tingal – 'a patch of wood over a rent in a coble to prevent it leaking' (Heslop, 1880s); **tinggel** – 'wooden patch nailed onto boat, doubling planking' (KP, Beadnell); 'a sheet of metal, usually copper, used for making temporary repairs on a small wooden boat when it has been holed' (*OED*) [?Du].

tyek up – '[to] close up, of rents in a wooden boat' (KP, Beadnell).

Eventually these craft became so expensive, the damage, you used to get windshakes…

Getting rid of wherries – we towed them out to sea, you were supposed to go three mile out, used to take the plugs out in the harbour, because it took too long to sink, so I used to smash the planking at the fore-end so the water would come rushing in. As long as we cannot see them – you can see them underwater, but they weren't visible from the shore, you knew they were going down. I think, when I read they've found a Spanish galleon, it could have been our wherry! There's quite a few…

Plug holes – in those days, how they got a three inch hole, they had the old-fashioned augurs, probably had to chisel it to get a hole – most of these wooden boats took water in. So whenever you were somewhere where you were going to go on the ground, you would take your plug out to let the water out. The plug was there all the time. It wasn't a big pit prop, you cut a chunk out. And when the tide started coming in, you put your plug back in.

(Ernie Keedy, Beamish, 2005/127)

The Weary Coble o' Cargill

This local ballad, which commemorates some real event, is given from the recitation of an old woman, residing in the neighbourhood of Cambus Michael, Perthshire. It possesses the elements of good poetry, and, had it fallen into the hands of those who make no scruple of interpolating and corrupting the text of Oral Song, it might have been made, with little trouble, a very interesting and pathetic composition.

Kercock and Balathy are two small villages on the banks of the Tay; the latter is nearly opposite Stobhall. According to tradition, the ill-fated hero of the ballad had a leman [lover] in each of these places; and it was on the occasion of his paying a visit to his Kercock love, that the jealous dame in Balathy Toon, from a revengeful feeling, scuttled the boat in which he was to cross the Tay to Stobhall.

David Drummond's destinie,	
Gude man o' appearance o' Cargill;	
I <u>wat</u> his blude rins in the flude,	reckon
Sae <u>sair</u> against his parents' will.	sorely, tragically
She was the lass o' Balathy toun,	
And he the butler o' Stobhall;	
And many a time she <u>wauked</u> irate,	waked, or possibly walked
To <u>here</u> the coble o' Cargill.	hear
His bed was made in Kercock <u>ha'</u>,	hall
Of gude clean sheets and of the hay;	
He wudna rest <u>ae</u> <u>nicht</u> therein,	one night
But on the prude waters he wud <u>gae</u>.	go

His bed wes made in Balathy toun,
Of the clean sheets and of the <u>strae</u>;　　　　　straw
But I wat it was far <u>better</u> made,　　　　　?more effectively
Into the bottom o' bonnie Tay.

She bored the coble in seven pairts,*
I wat her heart might hae been sae sair ;
For there she got the bonnie lad lost,
Wi' the curly locks and the yellow hair.

He put his feet into the boat,
He little thocht o' any ill
But before that he was mid waters,
The <u>weary</u> coble began to fill.　　　　　cursed

"Woe be to the lass o' Balathy toun,
I wat an ill death may she die;
For she bored the coble in seven pairts,
And let the waters perish me!

"O help! O help! I can get none,
Nae help o' man can to me come!"
This was about his dying words,
When he was choked up to the chin.

"Goe tell my father and my mother,
It was naebody did me this ill;
I was a-going my <u>ain</u> errands,　　　　　own
Lost at the coble o' bonnie Cargill."

She bored the boat in seven pairts,
I wat she bored it wi' gude will;
And there they got the bonnie lad's corpse,
In the <u>kirk-shot</u> o' bonnie Cargill.　　　　　literally church-fee, here churchyard
O <u>a'</u> the keys o' bonnie Stobha',　　　　　all
I wat they at his belt did <u>hing</u>;　　　　　hand
But a' the keys of bonnie Stobha',
They now ly low into the stream.

A braver page into his age
Ne'er set a foot upon the plain;
His father to his mother said,
"O sae sune as we've <u>wanted</u> him!"   ?missed

"I wat they had mair love than this,**
When they were young and at the scule;
But for his sake she wauked late,
And bored the coble o' bonnie Cargill.

"There's ne'er a clean <u>sark</u> gae on my back,   dress or shirt
Nor yet a <u>kame</u> gae in my hair;   comb
There's neither coal nor candle <u>licht</u>   light
Shall shine in my bower for ever mair.

"At kirk nor market I'se ne'er be at,
Nor yet a blythe blink in my <u>ee</u>;   eye
There's ne'er a <u>ane</u> shall say to anither,   one
That's the lassie gar'd the young man die.   made

Between the <u>yetts</u> o' bonnie Stobha'   gates
And the kirk-style o' bonnie Cargill,
There is many a man and mother's son
That was at my love's burial."

                                    (Motherwell, 1846, pp.104–107)

* That the holes were 'bored' and the time taken for the boat to fill indicates this was a wooden coble.

** I take the speech from here on to be that of the lass of Kercock, i.e. the one not guilty of his death.

Decommissioning

Decommissioning, that is, a payment for putting a commercial fishing boat out of action, is a recent system, designed, like limiting the number of days fishing a week a boat can work, to help moderate the amount of fish caught. Introduced in the European Union in 1983, payment was dependent on the boat being scrapped, transferred out of the EEC, or used 'for purpose other than fishing for profit'. In UK terms, this has come to mean consigning the boat to a scrapyard for breaking: "Decommissioning always leads to breaking and in some cases burning of boats (the wooden ones)" (NC). This irreversible process bodes ill for conservation in general since it sets a notional barrier between the options of working boat or no boat.

The establishment of an Advisory Committee on National Historic Ships in 2006 may promote better public awareness of what is at risk for exceptional ships, but the outlook for many fine vessels, large and small, remains bleak. An example is the *City of Adelaide*, one of three surviving 'composite' ships of its kind with wooden planking over a metal frame – another being the famous *Cutty Sark* of Dumbarton. Built on Wearside in 1864 and with an overall length of 244 feet, the City of Adelaide is now berthed in Scotland, and despite well-intentioned attempts to conserve her is deteriorating to the point where she is likely to be 'deconstructed'. The listed status of the vessel is reported to have been provisionally revoked (early 2007) to permit her breaking – a sad comment on the lack of funds and poor level of expectation when it comes to our maritime heritage.

At a more modest level, the paddle tugboat *Reliant* from Seaham Harbour was claimed by the National Maritime Museum in Greenwich. There it featured for a while on display before 'disappearing' – i.e. being dismantled and offered to other museums as spare parts. Contrast this with her sister tug, *Eppleton Hall*, on honoured display in San Francisco, and you get some idea of the effort needed to change attitudes in this country. The local communities that built the ships or commissioned them are too often left without a trace of their own past endeavours.

Chapter 2. The coble

The traditional coble, with its flat bottom, 'horseshoe' stern and gracefully flaring hull, is properly regarded as native to the North-East coast, and found from Spurn Head in the South to the Tweed in the North – along some 160 miles of coast. It is ideal for hauling up onto and launching from moderately sloping beaches, as at Redcar to the south, and Newbiggin in Northumberland; the custom continues though concrete ramps may now be in place (grooved ramps were earlier known as **coble-sleds** (nYx). In some measure the angle of slope of the foreshore predicts the design:

> At Filey, Holy Island or Cullercoats... where the incline of the landing is gentler, a deeper, prouder forefoot was possible, producing the ability to sail closer to the wind and make less leeway.
>
> (Bradley, I, p.28)

As a type of boat, the coble's closest visual parallel is the Irish *curragh*, with similar sharp prow and square stern. The curragh, however, was built of hide over a grid frame of thin branches or 'withies', whereas the coble as we know it is built of overlapping planks with a frame fitted inside the hull. Could the coble be a curragh type of boat, translated into wood? T.C. Lethbridge (1952, p.187) asserts: "[the] coble...is nothing more or less than a clinker built version of a skin boat." The relationship between curragh and coble remains obscure; there is little evidence, archaeological or documentary, to help. As Kemp notes of the Anglo-Saxon period: "the old records of the time are strangely silent: all through these years fishing was a considerable industry, but there is no description of the craft which fished the North Sea or more distant waters" (1978, p.51).

In terms of skill and time in construction, and the avoidance of use of metal, a hide boat would be more economical than one of wood and nails. Though the Anglo-Saxons and Vikings were skilled woodworkers, the everyday boat of British fishing, both before and after the Angles arrived, is assumed to have been a hide boat, and one argument for 'coble' being originally applied to such a boat lies in it not being a Germanic word, but a Celtic or Celtic-Latin one.

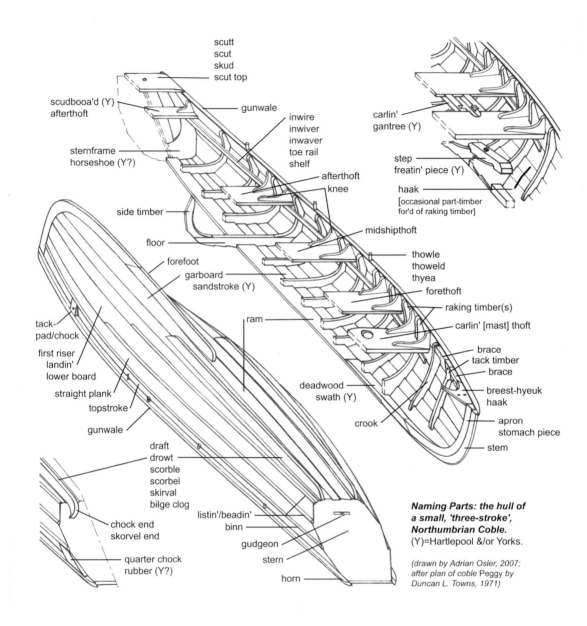

scutt
scut
skud
scut top

gunwale

scudbooa'd (Y)
afterthoft

inwire
inwiver
inwaver
toe rail
shelf

carlin'
gantree (Y)

sternframe
horseshoe (Y?)

afterthoft
knee

step
freatin' piece (Y)

haak
[occasional part-timber
for'd of raking timber]

side timber

midshiptoft

floor

thowle
thoweld
thyea

forefoot

garboard
sandstroke (Y)

forethoft

raking timber(s)

ram

carlin' [mast] thoft

tack-
pad/chock

brace
tack timber
brace

first riser
landin'
lower board

breest-hyeuk
haak

deadwood
swath (Y)

straight plank

topstroke

apron
stomach piece

gunwale

crook

stem

draft
drowt
scorble
scorbel
skirval
bilge clog

**Naming Parts: the hull of
a small, 'three-stroke',
Northumbrian Coble.**
(Y)=Hartlepool &/or Yorks.

listin'/beadin'
binn

chock end
skorvel end

gudgeon

*(drawn by Adrian Osler, 2007;
after plan of coble Peggy by
Duncan L. Towns, 1971)*

stern

quarter chock
rubber (Y?)

horn

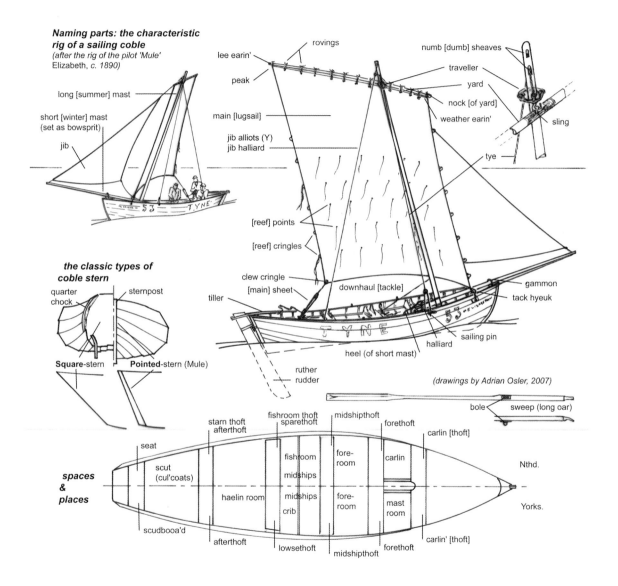

Naming parts: the characteristic rig of a sailing coble
(after the rig of the pilot 'Mule' Elizabeth, c. 1890)

long [summer] mast

short [winter] mast (set as bowsprit)

jib

rovings

lee earin'

peak

main [lugsail]

jib alliots (Y)
jib halliard

[reef] points

[reef] cringles

clew cringle

[main] sheet

tiller

numb [dumb] sheaves

traveller

yard

nock [of yard]

weather earin'

sling

tye

downhaul [tackle]

gammon

tack hyeuk

sailing pin

halliard

heel (of short mast)

ruther
rudder

the classic types of coble stern

quarter chock

sternpost

Square-stern

Pointed-stern (Mule)

(drawings by Adrian Osler, 2007)

bole

sweep (long oar)

spaces & places

seat

scut (cul'coats)

scudbooa'd

starn thoft
afterthoft

haelin room

afterthoft

fishroom thoft
sparethoft

fishroom

midships

midships
crib

lowsethoft

midshipthoft

forethoft

fore-room

fore-room

midshipthoft

carlin [thoft]

carlin

mast room

forethoft

carlin' [thoft]

Nthd.

Yorks.

71

The history of the word 'coble'

Early forms of the word cable are attested in Latin and Celtic sources, but do not occur widely in the Germanic languages. Its origin as a word is therefore reasonably to be sought in the Latin or Celtic tongues. The Latin *caupulus* has the air of a diminutive suffix (compare bibulus 'inclined to drink' from the verb *bib-ere* 'to drink', or *dracula* from *drac-o* 'dragon')* – there is, however, no obvious word in Latin of which caupulus serves as a diminutive form. All Latin references date from the time after the Celts made contact with the Roman world; forby, the coble (whether skin boat or clinker-built) does not conform to mainstream Roman boat-building practice.

A range of Celtic forms of the name exist, suggesting the word could well be native to the Celtic language. Curiously, there is no equivalent in Irish or Scottish branches of Celtic ('Gaelic') – Thier (2002) discounts a connection with the Irish *coblach* 'fleet'. If the word is current in Celtic only in those areas dominated by Rome, then we may be best advised to talk of 'coble' as a Celtic-Latin word, that is, one Celtic in origin but reinforced, disseminated and ultimately sustained by the authority of Latin (and Roman rule). (The *OED* ventures an ultimate root in cau- 'hollow', but the Celtic and Latin forms seem too close to be independent derivations from such a root.)

Beside Latin *caupulus* we have:

Welsh *ceubal*, *ceubol* 'ferry-boat, skiff, lighter' from assumed Old Welsh **caupol* – with lenition of /p/ to /b/ medially; on /eu/ from /ou/ and /au/ (see Jackson, 1953, p.373).

Breton *caubal* – with similar change of /p/ to /b/ – as gloss to Latin lembus (a short boat).

Lenition is a process Jackson dated conjecturally to the fifth century AD (1953, p.695) – however, "its existence is rarely betrayed in the written sources of the time" and the new forms are not found regularly in writing until the post-Conquest period (p.552). Thus the *cuopl* of the *Lindisfarne Gospel Gloss.* could be written with /p/ even if pronunciation had shifted to /b/, and need not be derived from Irish (where the /p/ was retained in spelling and pronunciation).

Forms in the Germanic languages are rarer, being limited to:

OE *cuopl* – a light boat (one single occurrence only, in the *Lindisfarne Gospel Gloss.*).

ON *keipull* – coble (OIce) – while *keip(r)*, according to Zoega's online dictionary of Old Icelandic, means 'rowlock'. Thier (2000, p.131) cites ON keipla-brot 'fragment of a boat', and *húðkeipr* 'skin-boat'; re *keipl* she notes "it appears to have been borrowed from the British in the eighth century at the earliest" (*ibid*., p.133).

---

*Manuscript variants in Aulus Gellius' text (caupolus/caupilus) show uncertainty in the spelling of the medial vowel, which points to an unaccented syllable and short vowel, compatible with a diminutive suffix; the Leipzig Thesaurus by contrast gives forms cauplus and caupillus, implying a long second syllable, incompatible with the short vowel of the Latin suffix.

Foerster (1941, pp.188–190, fn.4) takes 'coble' as ultimately a loanword from Latin, but then somewhat undermines his position by assuming the Lindisfarne cuople comes from an Irish origin – yet the fact that a 'coble' word is not found in Irish Celtic is the strongest argument for a Latin origin for the word.* His argument for an Irish source for *cuople* is based on the medial /p/ (since lenition would not occur in Irish Gaelic), and the possibility that the /cuo-/ spelling reflects an earlier (second–fourth century) change from Latin /quo/ to Old Irish /ko/ – if so, misapplied in the case of cuople where the initial /c(u)/ has no relationship to an earlier Latin /q(u)/. Foerster's theory assumes Irish influence in the *Lindisfarne Gospel Gloss.*, not impossible if the gloss was contemporary with the manuscript and its context of the early link (sixth–seventh centuries) between Irish Christianity and Northumbria. However, the gloss was added in the mid-tenth century, and contains words that could not be derived from Irish Gaelic, e.g. by in the phrase "hus vel lytelo by" (a house or small farmhouse, probably Old Norse) at *Mark* 5:3.

In the context of the *Lindisfarne Gospel Gloss.* it is one of a number of /cuo/ spellings (e.g. *cuom, cuoeð*) equivalent to /cw/ elsewhere in the text and general OE usage. Admittedly, the initial /cu/ in cuople is difficult to account for in Old English: I can only suggest that the *Lindisfarne Gloss.* scribe considered /cuo/ a reasonable spelling for /c/ plus long /o/, on analogy with the long /o/ in OE *cw'm, cw'mon*. (Though not directly comparable, the form cuoeð occurs three times in the lines immediately above *cuopl*.)

In British Medieval Latin, Latham (1965) notes: *caupullus*, 690 AD, *cobella, cobellum* (1228,1319), gobellum (thirteenth century). It seems that insular Latin was changing in line with British pronunciation, giving medial /b/. Vernacular English followed suit, hence the modern word coble. Whether the /o/ of coble should be a long vowel (as north of the Tyne) or short (as south of the Tyne) is a delicate point; the *Michigan Middle English Dictionary* gives *c'bel* with a long /o/, as one might expect if derived from a diphthong (double vowel). However, changes in vowel length do occur, and the shorter-voweled Durham coble is likely to have the validity of several centuries' use: the *Scottish National Dictionary* records a short vowel in Scotland vying with a long vowel in south Scotland, supporting Foerster's contention (1941, pp.189–190) that Scots has a tendency to shorten long /o/.

The history of the concept 'coble' as boat

Research on this point is complex and far from conclusive; the name and design of a boat may alter independently, yet (paradoxically) remain linked.

Typically unhelpful is the occurrence in Aulus Gellius – a mid-second century Latin author, associated with Rome and Athens. His sequence 'Attic Nights' mentions the coble at X, 25,5 as part of a long list of boats, none of which, however, is further defined or described:

---

*Foerster's proposed Old Irish *cópal* has no existence in the Irish record; indeed it would be odd for the Irish to apply the word *curragh* to a structure comparable to a coble, if they already possessed the word *cópal*. Conversely, if the Anglo-Saxons had in turn borrowed the concept from Irish rather than British Celts, they would surely have called it *curragh* not *cuopl*.

The *Leipzig Thesaurus of Latin*, under the heading *caup'lus*, *caupillus* gives a fourth century reference:

> "iam non caupulis Germanorum repletur, sed Romanorum liburnis" (Hegesippus De Bello Iudaico, 2,9)
> (For now it is not supplied with the cobles of the Germans, but the liburnae of the Romans).

(**Note:** *liburna* – 'a light, fast sailing vessel' – probably *liburna* and *caupulus* are to be contrasted here, as are 'German' and 'Roman', and the usage in both regards may be rhetorical rather than literal. The contrast could be between a sailing and a rowed type of vessel.)

From the *Laws of the Burgundians* (fifth–sixth centuries):

> quicumque navem aut caupulum involare praesumpserit, inferat ei cuius est navis, solidos XVII (Leges Burgundium)
> (whoever will dare to steal a ship or coble shall pay to him that owns the ship 17 solidi)

Here the standard word navis ('ship') is contrasted with caupulus, and our assumption is that the coble would be the lighter of the two types; yet equal in value (as generating income), the one perhaps as a trading the other as a fishing vessel?

Isidore (a Spanish bishop, 560–636 AD), in his extensive catalogue of Latin terms (*Etymologiae or Origines*) gives slightly different information:

> Lembus, navicula brevis, quæ alia appellatione dicitur et cymba et caupolus, sicut et lintris, id est carabus, quem in Pado paludibusque utuntur.' (Etymologiae XIX, 1, 25)
> (Lembus: a short boat, which by another name is called cymba and coble, and also lintris, that is a carabus, such as are used on the River Po and in shallow swamps.)

(**Note:** *lembus* 'a small fast-sailing vessel with a sharp prow' but *carabus* – "parva scapha ex vimine facta, quae contecta crudo corio genus navigii praestat" (Isidore, *Origines*, 19, 1, 26) – 'a small boat made of withies, which type of vessel, covered with raw hide, predominates' (*vimen* ' a pliant twig, a switch, withy, osier'); while *scapha* is 'anything scooped out, a light boat, a skiff'.)

Glosses to Placidus' Sermons are apparently not earlier than the eigth–ninth centuries, although Placidus was a companion of St Benedict in sixth century Italy; the glosses to his sermons were available to Abbo (of France and England) in the late tenth century:

> Caupilus lignum cavatum [quasi] cumba, id est velut cavabum valde brevissimum.
> (Glossae Placidi)
> (a coble [is made of] hollowed wood, like a cymba, that is like a very short cavabum)

(**Note:** *cymba* – 'boat, skiff'; *cavabum* ?unknown. The phrase 'hollowed wood' could imply a primitive dug-out, or simply 'boat-like'. This is however the first reference to a coble as being made of wood.)

Definitions above vary widely, but there is a sense of lightness, shortness and shallow draught, which may cover dug-outs*, hide boats and planked ones alike. Perhaps *caupulus* was applied to a class of short, light boats, irrespective of construction.

Turning to the British evidence, we have uniquely the *Lindisfarne Gospel Gloss*. The text of this beautiful North-Eastern manuscript was in Latin; but written in between the lines is a later (mid-tenth century) gloss, that is, a literal translation or 'crib', in Old English. Here is the relevant verse (Mark, 8:23) in Latin and Old English:

> …Et ascendente eo in navicula secuti sunt eum discipuli eius.
> and ofstigende hine vel ða he ofstag in lytlum scipe vel in cuople gefylgdon hine vel him ðegnas his.
> (and ascending he, or when he ascended, on a little ship or on a coble, followed him or to-him disciples his.)

In subsequent verses, a great storm arises and threatens to swamp the little boat (*navicula*) while Jesus sleeps. The terrified disciples wake Jesus up, begging him to save their lives.

Elsewhere in the same gospel, at Mark 1:29 the vessel from which James and John are fishing is called *navis* in the Latin, and scip ('ship') in the OE. The implication there is surely of a sturdier work vessel. At Matthew 13:2 *navicula* is translated as *scipp*, without invoking the alternative of a coble. The conclusion seems to be that *lytlum scipe* and *cuopl* are used at Mark 8:23 to emphasise the frailty of the vessel, as one quite unsuited to weathering a storm in the open sea. It may not be a particularly small vessel, if it is capable of holding twelve disciples, plus room for Jesus to lie down and sleep (did the glossator take this into account?); and clearly lacked in stability, despite the 'ballast'.

Again, if the glossator had intended to refer only to a smaller type of boat, then *lytlum scipe* would have sufficed. That he introduced an extra and special word, 'coble' – this is the only instance of its use in the whole Old English record – suggests he had in mind something different from what the wider world understood by 'ship', and that something different could well have been a hide boat after the Celtic/British fashion.

Old English did not adopt or use the word *coracle* – indeed in the Anglo-Saxon Chronicle (891 AD) the word *bat* (boat) is used for what is in reality a coracle. And this leads us to the possibility that coracle and coble were originally applied to the same type of light rivurine vessel: *cwrwc* would be the earlier Celtic term, still current in Wales, in Ireland as *curragh*, in Scotland as *currach*. The more Romanised Britons of the east coast favoured the term cuopl, as did the Anglo-Saxons after them; only the Welsh, half way between Rome and Ireland (as it were) used both terms. (The demarcation is almost, but not quite the same as that between P-Celtic ('British') and Q-Celtic ('Gaelic').)

Irish *curragh*, Scottish *currach*, Welsh *cwrwc* and later English *coracle* are all from the same root; but whereas the Irish curragh defined (developed into?) a special built form, the Scottish currach was more basic.

---

*Though we regard dug-out boats as primitive, "Thousands of dug-outs have been found in marshes and lakes all over Scandinavia, the oldest from the Stone Age and the most recent from our own times" (Landstrom, 1961 p.130).

The *Scottish National Dictionary* describes it as 'a small wickerwork boat covered in hides', 'in shape oval, near three feet broad and four feet long' and as 'the shape and about the size of a small brewing-kettle, broader above than below, with ribs or hoops of wood in the inside, and a cross-stick for the man to sit on' – that is, equivalent to the hide-built Welsh coracle.

Thier (2000, fn.55) and Hill and McKee (1978, p.4) both give quotations that equate 'coble' with a hide-built boat; e.g. "a salmon coble or currach..." 1822 re Ayrshire (qu. Their, 2000, fn 55); St Ninian's boat is explained in 1895 as "cobbe – coble, a small boat then consisting of a wooden frame over which an ox-hide was streched" (*ibid*.) A fuller example comes from an addition to Walton's *Compleat Angler*:

> They [a type of trout] are not easily to be got at without a boat, or wading, for which reason those of that country use a thing they call a thorocle, or truckle; in some places it is called a coble, from the Latin corbula, a little basket: it is a basket shaped like the half of a walnut-shell, but shallower in proportion, and covered on the outside with a horse's hide: it has a bench in the middle, and will just hold one person, and is so light that the countrymen will hang it on their heads like a hood, and so travel with a small paddle, which serves for a stick till they come to a river; and then they launch it, and step in; there is great difficulty in getting into one of those truckles for the instant you touch it with your foot it flies from you: and when you are in, the least inclination of the body oversets it.
> (Isaac Walton, *The Complete Angler*, 6th edition with notes by Sir John Hawkins, 1797, p.124, fn.)

One or two references to a Scottish coble as built of planks (see 'Tow a Cow', p.???, and 'The Weary Coble', p.???), and the Irish 'hooker' and smaller 'puchan' which are wooden, with the sloping transom of a coble, but built on a keel and frame base – are to be regarded as more recent developments.

The situation is: the British cuopl or coble and the British cwrwc or coracle may in fact have been synonyms, from different Celtic language traditions, both referring to a light hide-covered vessel. In Ireland this developed into a more advanced hide structure but retained the dominant name 'curragh'. On the North-East coast of England a separate development in wood occurred, and kept the traditional local term for a small boat, viz. *coble*.

Structural factors

Its unique form makes the coble difficult to fit into the known development of historic boats. It has the clinker planking and tall, sharp prow of a Germanic vessel, but shares its shallow draught, square sloping stern and lack of keel with the Irish curragh. This is quite possibly a case of parallel, independent development*, arising from the practicalities of day fishing from a beach. The apparent Celtic-Germanic collusion over the name 'coble' may not extend to structural matters, and who can say whether the Irish curragh is a forerunner of or a copy of the

---

*Various other types of square stern are reported: the Portuguese *muleta*, the Swiss *weidling*, the Breton *bisque* – without any obvious connection to the coble. Other theories of origin, such as the need to remake a damaged double-ended boat, or cutting one in two, are uncomfortable, as they attribute the careful design of the coble to the accidental.

North East coble. It is by no means impossible that the Irish curragh was a retro adaptation of a wooden Anglo-Viking design to a more basic technology. After all, the Vikings could as easily have exported design to Ireland as the Irish to Northumbria, with examples enduring on the conservative west coast: not the source, but an echo. That Anglo-Vikings called a 'new' type of vessel after the native cople/coble need not deter us if both fulfilled the same function viz. a beach-based inshore fishing vessel.

In favour of a Germanic genesis, we may note that most of the features of the wooden coble are in some way foreshadowed in earlier North Sea boat design.

Most early Viking boats probably did not have keels. Rock carvings of the later Bronze Age seem to show a sort of keel which projects visually beyond bow and stern, curved upwards at the forward end, but the general opinion is that what at first looks to be a form of keel was, in fact, a runner, to keep the hull clear of the ground when it was hauled across land (Kemp, 1978, 39–40). An excavated example of such a boat, in wood, is dated to AD 200–300, Jutland. (This is some evidence that the Vikings were familiar with the principle of 'scorbles' or 'drafts' from an early time.) As late as c.630 AD the Nydam Boat from Schleswig "was not intended for sailing, was double-ended and clinker built, but had no keel" (Sandahl, 1951, p.17).

A square stern was experimented with, oddly enough, in dug-out boats. Thus a log-boat excavated on the Tyne at Derwenthaugh "appeared to have a fitted transom" (*The Mariner's Mirror*, 71, 1985, p.337) and Lethbridge notes re dug-outs – "one early form, with a transom board let into grooves in an open stern, is often found in Britain in peat bogs or old river courses" (1952, p.104). The point was perhaps that removing one end of the tree-trunk first gave better access for hollowing out the whole, to the extent that it worth refitting the missing end afterwards as a transom.

Generally speaking, the coble as we know it fits more into the line of development of wooden boats than into withy-and-hide techniques. For example, in the fourth century, thwarts for rowers and oars pivoted on the gunwhale are believed to have been introduced. About the same time, a more formal structural division of bow, keel and stern blocks emerged that parallels the ram-and-forefoot structure in the coble. These important developments would have been in time, and indeed may have been essential, for the Saxons to have raided the British coast in the fourth century, leading the Romans to counter with the imposing forts of the 'Saxon shore' and the signal towers on the coast between Filey and Saltburn. The same type of boat was presumably the vehicle that brought the Anglo-Saxons to settle here in the fifth and sixth centuries. However, whether these were rowed or sailed is less clear. According to Sandahl (1951, p.17) sail was adopted 300–500 AD, and, according to Kemp (1978) only in the seventh–eigth centuries. Friel (2003, p.24) comments: "Sails were known in northern Europe before the Romans came, and it seems unlikely that the Saxons would have been much of a seaborne menace to the late Roman Empire if they had only possessed oar-driven boats." Of course, we need to bear in mind the likely different grades of ship available at any time – from the high-tech warship commissioned by a tribal leader, to the simpler vessel of a local fisherman. The Oseberg ship of c.800 AD and the Gokstad ship of c.900 AD are both classed as long ships: "Equally adapted to rowing and sailing and chiefly used for fighting purposes" (Sandahl, 1951, p.18). In both cases, the beam was sufficiently broad to lead to a high prow and stern as the strakes were gathered together. All these boats were double-ended.

Anglians and Vikings

Whether the modern coble borrowed design features or only the name from British Celts, it is reasonable to assert that the wooden coble was developed in the Anglo-Viking age on the North East coast. We can also suggest that the reason it is found here and not obviously widely in the British Isles is that the common Celtic 'cople/coble' was a hide boat not a fully wooden one, while the wooden coble was an innovation specific to the North East coast.

Its design can be accounted for by the need to evolve a boat suited to day fishing in particular conditions on the coast, but more seaworthy than existing types. Considering that a daily fishing expedition would involve a great deal of launching and recovery over time, it is not unlikely that boat-builders would have experimented with a sloping square stern to make beaching easier. (Admittedly not all the North East coast has suitable beaches, but fishing villages would inevitably develop where good access to a beach was available, so that the relationship of boat to beach remained to the fore.)

The coble is launched and recovered stern-to-beach (the rudder being unshipped), so that an oblique transom permits better access at the stern from outside and less opposition to sand or shingle on beaching. An upright stern would be more likely to dig into the sand or shingle and obstruct recovery – likewise if one tried to beach bow-first. (The stern rudder is not thought to have introduced until about 1200, and is not itself the reason for the shape of the coble transom.) Again, a square and vertical stern would not be a viable sailing feature, as waves in a following sea would soon break over it. With a sloping stern, the wave energy tends to lift the boat not swamp it. In work terms, also, a square stern afforded extra access for lifting and lowering equipment.

Regarding the lack of keel in a coble, only the forefoot is both structurally basic and obtrudes below the hull; the two drafts or scorbles are external additions, helping to spread the weight of the coble on land and aid beaching. A full keel would disadvantage handling onshore by concentrating resistance onto one focus, and risk overbalancing on land.

The search for the initiators of the 'modern' coble reasonably focuses on the Anglians (from the sixth century on) or the Vikings (from the ninth century on) – though it may be unwise to make too great a distinction between the two. Adrian Osler in *The Mariners' Mirror* (2000) suggests the 'proto-coble' fits early Northumbria and an Anglian context: "Does not the seagoing coble's geographic concentration mirror that of the early religious establishments, and the run of their river-going salmon?" The point here seems to be that the monasteries of seventh–eigth century Northumbria would need a boat specific to salmon fishing, and that the later distribution of the coble fits well enough the scope of influence of Anglian Northumbria. Support for the Anglian role in shaping the coble comes from Katrin Thier, who points out "…Irish type curraghs could have been introduced into Northumbria by the foundation of Lindisfarne. This would explain the lack of survival of the type anywhere else in Britain" (Their, 2000, p.136). This is part of her contention that the word and the boat alike came from Ireland to Northumbria, probably before 700 AD (*ibid.*).

For salmon fishing in a river or even an estuary a hide boat would surely suffice – remember that Aelfric's 'typical' Anglo-Saxon fisherman only casts his net in the river, and does not fish at sea. It was the Vikings who were the great sea-travellers of the age. If developed in early Northumbria, the design of the coble might be expected to extend further than the North-East coast – for Northumbrian influence extended at a maximum to Cumbria on the west coast and up the east coast to Edinburgh. Viking influence was strongest in Yorkshire and East Anglia. Neither profile coincides precisely with the current distribution of the coble from Northumberland to Yorkshire, and it is risky to assert what its original historic distribution might have been. It would be useful here to know more of examples of cobles in Yarmouth and Kings' Lynn (Norfolk) and whether they represent an authentic local tradition of use. In 1844, for example, we learn, "It is called very often a Yarmouth coble, from the frequency of these boats on the coast of Norfolk, as in-shore fishing vessels" (*Dictionary of Trade, Commerce and Navigation*).

Of the Walthamstow Boat (now dated to the mid-eigth century) Lethbridge reports: "There was no keel in the true sense, but instead there was a plank 14" wide. All strakes were fastened together with clinch-nails...the whole skin was pegged with tree-nails to the timbers, which were of oak" (1962, p.129). The information is confirmed in Marsden (1964): there was apparently an outer and an inner skin of planks, with ribs between. The boat was found in 1900, supposedly upturned over a skeleton and sword: if so, then no self-respecting Anglo-Saxon would be buried in this fashion in the eigth century – though a Viking very likely would. Again, from Lethbridge:

> It is a remarkable thing that, whereas all the Viking age and earlier Danish boats on the Continent are double-ended, two out of three Anglo-Saxon [sic] boats found in East Anglia have had square sterns. As far as one can judge, they were both boats of the coble type.
>
> (1952, p.156)

It hardly needs saying that East Anglia was part of the Viking Danelaw, though not historic Northumbria.

The Anglo-Saxons were no match for the Vikings at sea, but this tells us little about their ability at smaller boat building. Given equal skills, it still seems significant that the wooden coble does not develop overall on Anglo-Saxon or Celtic coasts, but predominantly on that sector where Viking and Anglian came together, with Vikings dominating.

Medieval evidence

A number of medieval deeds give us further evidence of the status of the coble. An *Inquisition Post Mortem* of 1248–49 (33, Hen, III), relating to Warkworth in Northumberland, describes (in translation): "Werkewrth manor including...the borough and new town...a mill...and a fishery with a small ship called 'cobel'" (*Calendar of Inquisitions Post Mortem*, vol.1 (PRO: 1904) item 164, p.41).

This underlines the likelihood that many medieval fishing vessels would not have been in individual ownership, or at least not owned by the fishermen as such, but part of a larger estate. A role in promoting the coble by monasteries, boroughs or feudal estate owners would have given a degree of authority and consistency to the design, and facilitated its adoption along the North East coast. (On the monastic role, see further Friel,

1995, p.28.) Excavations at London, Nottingham, Lincoln and York have revealed plentiful fishbone evidence and suggest the eleventh century saw "a move toward eating more marine species of fish such as cod, herring and mackerel. This, in turn, implies an increase in sea fishing activity" (Friel, 2003, p.44). (Gillian Hutchinson, 1994, p.129) considers that before 1200, fishing was a simple subsistence industry.) Friel's evidence supplies a good context for the development of a reliable inshore fishing craft.

Specific to the monastic world, the documents of Coldingham Priory include an inventory of 1374, with some detail on the boats under the priory's control:

Item cordae pro piscaria apud Haytmouth, i magnus limbus cum omnibus pertinentiis.
(Item: cords [?lines, nets] for fishing at ?Eyemouth [and] one large boat with all its tackle)

Item alius magnus limbus cum mastis et saylyerd cum antiquo velo tantum.
(Item:another large boat with masts and sailyard with an old sail also)

Item i smalynbat cum omnibus pertinentiis, I scheffe cum iiii remis, I cobil cum iiii remis.
(Item: one ?salmon-boat with all its tackle, I skiff with four oars, one coble with four oars)

Item ad portum de Coldyngham i smalynbat cum mastis et velu cum vi remis, i scaffe, i cobil ad Louyffh cum ii remis."
(Item: at the harbour of Coldingham, one ?salmon-boat with masts and sail, with six oars, one skiff, one coble at the ?lough [inlet] with two oars.)

(Raine, *Coldingham*, 1841, p.lxxvii)

This is our clearest indication of the state of the coble in the Middle Ages: it could take two or four oars, implying cobles of different lengths were used; and four oars implies that the basic means of propulsion was rowing – surely only one set of oars would be needed, if they only supplemented a sail. Significantly, in the case of the coble here, there is no mention of a mast or a sail – valuable items in their own right, even when 'antique', and clearly worth mentioning in the case of other larger boats in this document. A relatively late addition of a sail to the coble design is quite possible: "It is curious too, to observe that no small boat of the Anglo-Saxon or Viking age is known to have carried a mast or sail" (Lethbridge, 1952, p.156).

From 1420 AD, the will of Matilda, wife of William de Bowes, survives, relating to Dalton-le-Dale and Seaham area.

I tem do et lego Galfrido Mawer meliorem cobyll; item lego uxori Johanis Yole alium cobyll.
(I give and bequeath to Geoffrey Mawer my better coble; item, I bequeath to the wife of John Yole my other coble.)

(Raine, *Wills*, 1835, p.64)

Here the coble is seen in the context of the secular world, and from hereon it will be individuals rather than institutions that are reckoned as owners. However, these references do not tell us anything about the form or material of the coble, other than it existed in various grades (lengths?).

The first fuller reference comes from an Elizabethan description, which it is worth quoting more fully....

> Truly it may be sayd of these poor men, that they are lavish [unstinting] of their lives who will hazard twenty of forty myles into the seas in a small troughe so thinne that a glimpse of the sunne may bee seene through yt*, yet at eleven or twelve of the clocke in the mornynge, when they come from the sea, they sell their whole boatys lading for 4s [shillings], or if they doe get a crown [5 shillings] they suppose to have chaffered [bargained] fayre. Three commonly come in one boate, each of them having twoe oares, which they governe by drawynge one hande over the other. The boate ytself is built of wainscotte; for shape excels all modeles for shippinge: two men will easily carrye yt on lande betweene them, yet are so secure in them at sea that some in a storme have lyved aboarde three dayes. Their greatest danger is nearest home, when the waves break dangerouslye...
>
> (qu. March, 1970, I, p.94)

Another Elizabethan reference in a will of 1565, confirms our expectations that we are dealing by now with a sea-going vessel, not some hide-covered rivurine boat: "I will that my wyffe shall haive the best sea coble in hir custodye" (qu. Their, 2000, p.134, fn 45).

The earliest extant reference to a coble as possibly made of wood comes from the Placidus Glosses of the tenth century. *The Lindisfarne Gospel Glosses* of the mid-tenth century emphasise frailty, and could well refer to a hide-built 'cople'. The development of the modern 'coble' can feasibly be placed in the centuries either side of 1000 AD: earlier than late, for the simple arrangement for oars, the non-evolution (if this is the case) of a proper keel, the absence of references to sails and the retention of the sharp rising Viking prow (abandoned in later medieval boat design, e.g. *cnear* or *cob*) – all point to early development of the coble design. The first use of the Latin term cobellum in 1228 could well be significant, and my best suggestion is that the coble design was well established by 1200.

Whether it changed much after that is problematic. Hill and McKee's contention (1973, p.3) that the tumble-home on the upper strake of a coble may derive from Dutch fishing vessel design suggests the modern coble may not have been finalised until the seventeenth century,** though this accords ill with Heslop's contention that 'cat-built' meant an "old style of shipbuilding" with much tumble-home, "on the Norwegian model." However, it may well have been the Dutch initiative in exploiting the herring fishery in the

---

* – presumably of cobles stored on land and left to dry out somewhat.

**Of this period, we are told "northern European ships were transformed [as] builders gradually came to appreciate the advantages of constructing vessels to do one job or set of jobs. Specialised design made the vessel more durable, more efficient and more practical" (Ungar, 1985, p.154). However, the coble is essentially a medieval design and unlikely to have participated in this era of (largely) carvel-built progress.

sixteenth–seventeenth centuries that encouraged the building of more fishing boats with sails* on our coast, to claim a share of the harvest. An expansion of all forms of fishing is indicated at this time, if only to feed the rapidly increasing population.

The coble in the Twentieth Century

The design of the coble, however and whenever developed, was aimed to suit local fishing conditions.

The lack of keel meant a flatter base with less resistance, suitable for drawing up on a beach after a daily fishing stint; the square stern gave working access and a profile suitable to a following sea, the sharp prow gave efficiency when rowing and sailing. With the development of harbours during the nineteenth century, the need for beaching was reduced, yet the design continued to prove valuable.

It was modified, as regards scorbles and hull, with the fitting of an engine, from the 1930s on. Often the propeller and shaft would be built into a 'tunnel' inset in the hull that modified the build. Reduced space inside the boat and the balance of the weight of the engine had also to be taken into account. Nonetheless the advantages of an engine overrode more traditional considerations, bringing greater speed and reliability at sea.

As a final note, we need to record that at the time of writing no wooden coble is under construction on the North East coast, though some energy goes into renovating older cobles. The skills of coble building, which are both traditional and individualistic, seem set to be lost. Controversially, the coble hull is duplicated in resin, and examples for recreational use will be found in most marinas. Is this a denial of the coble's identity ("tupperware" Bart Taylor calls them) or another technological adaptation to be accepted with grace? Few boats need nowadays to be drawn up daily onto a beach, or to work unassisted by engine power, so the special design of the coble has become a traditional or aesthetic consideration; it can no longer – to the regret of many – claim to be the indispensable small fishing boat of the east coast.

---

* The parallel development of windmills is worth noting here: first introduced to England about 1200, there was an apparent burst of windmill building in the seventeenth century, in reaction to demand for flour from an increasing population.

"The boat was called the Betsy Hughes. It was a Keel Boat and belonged to Robert Dawson and family. Keel boats were popular in Newbiggin at the beginning of the [20th] century" (Mary Dickman).

Photo courtesy of Bill Harris.

The steam tug *Hardback* operating from Seaham Harbour. The crew in 1939 were Skipper Jack Moffat, Engineer Mat Wears, Fireman Wilf Doust, Mate Bob Kirby and Boy Joe Henry.

Photo courtesy of Steve Doust.

Crew of the Seaham tug *Hardback* – Wilf Doust centre, with sandwich, mid-1930s.

"A little about Wilf: He was born Wilfred Ernest Doust on September 24th 1904, so would have been 97 this year. He died on September 11th 1981. He worked almost all of his life in some way connected with the docks, and especially on the tugs; he ended up operating the big engine that opened and closed the dock gates, until his retirement. I always remember he would disappear off to work at the most odd times, and it wasn't until I was a little older that I realised that his life, and that of his family, was ruled by the tides."

Photo and description courtesy of Steve Doust.

The *Henry & Jane* was one of the cobles that went to the rescue when the S.S. *Anglia* went aground on Needle Point, Newbiggin, 9 December 1904. Though most of the crew of the *Anglia* were brought safely ashore, the coble capsized in the rescue attempt, with the loss of seven lives; only John Armstrong ('Long Jack') survived. The coble itself was later recovered.

Photo courtesy of Bill Harris.

Jacky Lisle Robinson and Bobby Dawson fitting the coble *Margaret Lisle* onto wheels, after salmon fishing. Bobby's father was lost at sea.

Photo courtesy of Bill Harris.

View of coble from stern – Hartlepool Marina, 1995, illustrating the slope on the square stern or transom that is special to coble design, and aids with launching and recovery on a sloping beach – both actions undertaken with stern to beach. Note the depth of the rudder, which would be unshipped for launching and recovery.

Photo courtesy of Bill Griffiths.

The *Andrea Jane*, a trawler with forward wheelhouse, entering Seaham Harbour. It was used for trawling for prawns, off the stern, at 5 to 20 miles offshore. The frames at the rear support the (diagonal) derrick. The white 'box' above the wheelhouse is radar; above this, a small aerial (not easily visible) is the GPS satellite navigation; the tall mast carried the VHF ship to shore radio.

From original colour photo by Peter Adamson.

Coquet Star, with Bobby Tuck at the helm, entering Seaham Harbour. This beautiful 38 foot coble was built in Amble in the 1980s, but ended up 'decommissioned' (that is, cut up) as the money offered to decommission exceeded the market value of the boat if sold out of the fishing trade. Note the yellow tag with no.139 – indicating that the coble has been drift-netting for salmon. The wicker emblem at the mast is the symbol of an active fishing vessel.

From original colour photo by Tom Henderson L.R.P.S.

Pilot cutter entering Seaham Harbour, 1990s. The pilot boat took the pilot out to a ship about to enter harbour; conversely, when a ship was leaving harbour, the pilot cutter would follow the ship out and take the pilot off when his job was done. Note markings on prow and flag.

From original colour photo by Tom Henderson L.R.P.S.

The keelboat *Why Not?*, owned by Peter Adamson of Seaham, winching in the cod end of the trawl net. The catch is largely prawns, trawled for in a mud or sand bottom, then winched on board with a derrick; once onboard, the ties at the bottom of the cod end are released and the catch teemed out onto a 'table' (any work surface) on deck. The prawns are then graded by size and put in baskets for the market.

Photo courtesy of Peter Adamson.

The *George Elmy*, provided by money left by his two sisters, was a 'Liverpool' type lifeboat with two screws. It had "a good beam, solid construction... The hull was wooden, 40 foot overall. There was a canopy and watertight compartments; any water on deck ought to clear quickly through the scuppers. We were told that if it did go over, if you all went one side and pulled on the looped rope, it could be righted. But it wasn't self-righting" (Joe Henry). It served at Seaham from 1951 until the disaster of 1962. It was swiftly replaced and after two stop-gap boats, the *Will & Fanny Kirby* arrived in 1963 to serve as Seaham's new lifeboat, and did memorable duty for some 16 years.

After mounting on wheels, the coble is drawn up the beach in a concerted effort!

Photo courtesy of Bill Harris, Newbiggin.

Kinley Tower

This sturdy stone-built 'folly' from the early 19th century stands next to an isolated farmhouse on the coast south of Seaham. Such buildings are conventionally regarded as 'observation towers' from which a privileged view of the sea and its shipping could be had; but it is also likely that many of these unusual buildings were actually signal stations to communicate with smugglers. The isolated beach below the tower would be an ideal dropping off point before ships reached Sunderland.

Photo courtesy of Seaham Archive.

Chapter 3. Coble words

Definition

Coble – 'a very distinctive clinker planked rowing and sailing boat used for fishing, piloting and foying, and on occasion as a pleasure and racing boat along the North-East coast of England' (Mannering & Greenhill, 1997, p.49).

> The Coble is twenty-six feet long and five broad, the floor is wide, and the bottom nearly flat, with a stern remarkably sharp. The burthen is about one ton, and it carries three men who row with each a pair of short oars, and a mast is occasionally stepped, with a lugsail…The Cobles do not go so far to sea as the large boats (in the summer, they go to the inner edge of the scarr, to the distance of three or four miles), nevertheless they take great quantities of the different kinds of fish; and, between the month of December and the beginning of February, frequently meet with abundance of haddocks…
>
> (Hinderwell, 1798, pp.227–28,
> re Scarborough, incorporating footnote)

> Cobles – a boat very common on many parts of our coast, and in a small degree different in shape at different places.
>
> (*Dictionary of Trade,*
> *Commerce and Navigation*, 1844)

Shape and size

The larger boats of about 38 feet in length were mostly used as herring drifters and for trawling. Medium sized cobles about 27 feet (8.2 metres) overall were used for long lining while smaller cobles of about 20 feet (6 metres) in length were mainly used for salmoning. All sizes could be used for lobster and crab potting.

(http://www.twmuseums.org.uk/fishtales)

bull-heed – 'an ugly, wide bow on a coble' (KP, Beadnell).

flare (adj. and noun) – 'widening of coble from stem' (KP, Beadnell). "The forward flare gave lift in heavy seas and buoyancy when heeling" (Mannering & Greenhill, 1997, p.51).

gripe – 'depth of coble at forefoot' (KP, Beadnell) [OED: Du greep 'forefoot'].

kilp, kilt – 'curve of underside of coble aft' (KP, Beadnell); 'kilp – upward curve in the after part of some rams' (Hill & McKee, 1978); kilp –'a rise in the ram aft' (Salmon, 1885, p.15) [ON *kilp-r*, 'bow, handle, loop', i.e. roundness].

laid in – see **tumblehome**.

neeaks – "is neeaks is weel doon," i.e. coble heavily laden; low down in the water (Umpleby, Staithes, 1930s) [nook – corner, probably from ON].

plosher – coble '35ft (LOA, Whitby) and (Staithes, Bradley, I, p.24).

spring (noun) – 'S-shaped curve of top line forrard in a coble' (KP, Beadnell).

skyelled oot – 'description of curve of coble outwards' (KP, Beadnell).

shoother – 'shoulder; also, the width of a coble's bow' (KP, Beadnell).

sheer – 'upward curve of bows of coble' (KP, Beadnell).

storey – 'beamy (Amble): "A storey boat, yon"' (KP, Beadnell).

tumblehome – 'inward curve of upper-part of coble: "She's nicely laid-in"' (KP, Beadnell). The curve is useful in keeping water out when the boat keels over in the wind.

(See also salmon coble, and corf/calf in Chapter 6.)

Hull components

bilge clogs – 'the side runners are called bilge clogs' (Derek Rowell, S'd) [clog ? < log (ON)].

binn, listing – "helps protect a clinker-built boat's vulnerable plank edges (e.g. at exposed tumblehome of a coble)" (AO); listings (N'd), binns (Yx) = rubbing strakes, (Bradley I, p.31); *EDD – listing* as protective edge to cloth, Nth.

chock end – 'the curved end of a coble's drowt' (KP, Beadnell) [NF].

crook – 'one of the timbers which fan out forward in coble' (KP, *WW*, Beadnell) [?ON].

draft – 'runner on coble hull' (BT, Cullercoats);

drowt – 'one of the twin 'keels' which coble stands on aft; also **scorbel**' (KP, Beadnell); "the drafts facilitated beaching, prevented her after end from digging into the sand, and held her upright when ashore" (Mannering & Greenhill, 1997, p.51) [ME draht, MDu dragt, but common Germanic] re scorble see later; (Salmon, 1885, pp.9–10) has also 'bilge strakes'.

forefoot – 'curved 'keel' extending half way aft from bows of coble' (KP, Beadnell); forefeet – 'front of keel of coble' (Umpleby, Staithes, 1930s); forefoot – 'the fore section of the keel' (Derek Rowell, S'd).

foregrip – forefoot (Cunliffe, 2002, vol.2, p.266).

garboard – 'top strake' (BT, Cullercoats) [Du, *gaarboord*].

gunwale – "the top of the skin is normally covered with a horizontal board or rail, which is called a gunwale" (Lethbridge, 1952, p.4).

horn – 'top of stempost of Tweed salmon coble, where it projects above gunwhale' (Sanderson, 1969, p.279).

landin' – 'the landing-plank or first rising plank on a coble. Traditionally painted a different colour from the rest of the boat' (KP, Beadnell).

listins – 'ridge at joinings of planks round the coble' (Umpleby, Staithes, 1930s); 'listin's, not binns' (external strips) (FT, Cullercoats).

plate – 'protective iron covering on coble's forefoot and scorbels' (KP, Beadnell).

quarter-chock – 'protective cover on outside of planking at a coble's stern' (KP, Beadnell).

ram – 'central bottom plank, from which a coble is built (and by which it may be measured)' KP, Beadnell; 'The *ram* denotes the broad central bottom plank in the cobles, which have no keel' (W. Elmer, 1973) per *OED*; ram – 'coble keel' (Umpleby, Staithes, 1930s); 'ramp plank' (Derek Rowell, S'd) [probably from ON *ramm-r* (adjective) 'strong'].

ruther – 'rudder' (KP, Beadnell).

sandstrake – 'that next the keel' (Carle Robinson, Amble); **landplank** (Yx) = sandstrake (N'd) (Bradley I, p.28); *EDD* – N'd only.

scorbles than drafts (side runners) (Carle Robinson, Amble); **skorvels/skirvels** N'd, **draughts** Yx (Bradley I, p.31); **scorbels, scowbels** – 'twin "keels" which coble stands on aft. Also "drowts"' (KP, Beadnell); **skirval** – 'two pieces of wood acting as a keel in cobles' (Heslop);

skorvels – 'made of oak which was then covered with iron' (www.twmuseums.org.uk/fishtales). "The skorvel's function was twofold: to protect the bottom, and to provide a steady platform for the coble to sit level on the sand or stone" (Bradley, I, p.31) [a possible source for this is /s/ + carvel, perhaps because it was fitted flush to the coble hull (compare 'scarbel-built' earlier but also s + corbel 'ornamental or protruding feature' (Fr)]; *EDD* – only *skirval* N'd.

scut – 'stern of coble' (CR, Amble); **scut** – 'wooden planks across the back of salmon coble to hold the net' (JC, Spittal/Berwick); scut – 'top upper cross-plank at coble's stern. 'Skud' in Seahouses' (KP, Beadnell). Scut 'built carvel or cypher fashion with larch planks' (Bradley, I, p.30) [ON *skut-r* 'stern of a vessel']; *EDD* – as removable tailpiece to farmer's cart, Cumbria.

scutbooa'd – transverse timber resting on scut; scut-top not scut-board (FT, Cullercoats).

skeets (Amble/Newbiggin) – 'wooden battons for sliding boat over sand. Called **boat-sticks** at Beadnell' (KP, Beadnell); *EDD* – *skeets* as runners in pit shaft, N'd,D'm [ON skjott? (swift)/ON skið?].

strake – plank in side of coble [ME strake – a Northern form from a number of possible roots]; *EDD* – Ork, Sc, N'd, EA.

sweep – 'curve to planks/strakes' (BT, Cullercoats).

wale – 'a wale, a plank all along the outer timbers along a ship's side' (Whitwell & Johnson, 1926) [ME wala OE *walu*]; *EDD* – 'ridge' – in general use.

watter-nail, **witter-nail** – 'wooden plug through joint in coble's forefoot' (KP, Beadnell).

If we consider words proper to the coble, rather than common to boats in general, though the origin of many of these coble-words is uncertain, some basic terms like 'clog', 'scut', 'ram', 'skeet', 'strake' are specifically Northern, and some of these very likely Old Norse in origin (and below, 'thoft', perhaps 'thole'). Though far from conclusive, this does help to make feasible a Viking role in the design of the coble as we know it – very few words in this group are based on French or Dutch.

Timbers and seats

carlin – first (forard) stretcher or bench; carlin – 'seat nearest head of coble' (Umpleby, Staithes, 1930s) [<?ON, cf. Ice. kerling 'supporting timber']; *EDD* – nYx only.

feeatin'-piece – 'piece of wood fixed between lowsethoft and midshipthoft in sailing cobles: "ti git foot-'o'd"' (Umpleby, Staithes, 1930s) [?foot].

floors – 'cross-members in a coble' (KP, Beadnell); 'the lower transverse member of a complete frame' (AO).

forethoft – 'seat between carlin and midshipthoft' (Umpleby, Staithes, 1930s).

frames – 'the inner timbers of a coble, made of oak' (KP, Beadnell).

futtock – L-shaped support to make deck beams more rigid (FT, Cullercoats) [foot-hook].

gantrees – fore-aft plank between carlin and forethoft [?OFr gantier].

haa'k – 'inside breast timber in coble's bow' (KP, Beadnell).

knee – 'supporting timber in coble, e.g. under thofts or in bows' (KP, Beadnell); "coble uses a grown knee of wood for rib" (BT, Cullercoats). Compare **spoths**.

inwiver – 'inner rail' (FT, Cullercoats); inwiver – 'inner rail, compare toe-rail' (Amble per CKBS);

inwaver – 'inner supporting lateral timber in a coble. 'Inwyer' at Amble' (KP, Beadnell); inwire – 'wooden rail round inside of coble: "thi mittens is i' t'inwire"' (Umpleby, Staithes, 1930s); *EDD* – N'd only. Compare **weyres, woyres** 'possibly the same as Wales' (Whitwell & Johnson, 1926, p.192) [OED *wyer* – obsolete, of obscure origin].

scudbooa'd – 'small seat just inside stern of coble' (Umpleby, Staithes, 1930s).

settin' booa'd – '40 inches in length: initials of fisherman and his wife cut in it' (Umpleby, Staithes, 1930s).

stomach-piece – 'part of the inside of a coble's stem' (KP, Beadnell).

shootin' stick – 'upright stick propped in inwavers of coble, to clear tow when shooting drift nets' (KP, Beadnell).

spoths – 'short supports at end of each coble seat (named 'knees' at Whitby) (Umpleby, Staithes, 1930s); 'knees' (Bradley, I, p.32) re Yx. [not in OED].

thoft – 'thwart, seat in boat' (KP, Beadnell) [ON þofta (supported by distribution) than OE *þofte*]; *EDD* – Sc, N'd, Yx, Linx.

forethoft – second stretcher or bench.

midshipthoft – third stretcher or bench; 'coble seat between forethoft and lowsethoft' (Umpleby, Staithes, 1930s).

lowsethoft – fourth stretcher or bench; 'coble seat between midshipthoft and afterthoft; this is removable, i.e. 'lowse' (loose)' (Umpleby, Staithes, 1930s0.

afterthoft – fifth stretcher or bench; 'seat between scudboard and lowsethoft of coble' (Umpleby, Staithes, 1930s).

timmers – 'timbers; floor timbers of coble' Umpleby, Staithes 1930s; 'ribs of coble' (BT, Cullercoats).

Use of space

amidships – space between midshipthoft and lowsethoft carlin – space forward in coble, beside step for mast. Cf. *carlin-thoft – fore-thoft* (KP, Beadnell); amidships – 'space between midshipthoft and lowsethoft in fishing coble' (Umpleby, Staithes, 1930s).

bogie – 'a cast iron stove common in galleys/quarters of decked fishing vessels but not, I believe, cobles; there, customarily, a **firebox** more likely to be used' (Adrian Osler); booagy – 'coble fire' (used at night) (Umpleby, Staithes, 1930s).

cuddy – 'a sort of cabin, or cook-room, in the fore-part, or near the stern, of a lighter or barge or burden' (Falconer, 1780); 'sheltered section on coble…; a canvas cover on a coble known as a cuddy at Craster, a **hood** at Boulmer and a **dodger** at Amble' (KP) [compare C16th Du. *kaiûte*, mod.Du. *kajuit*, used in same sense].

dodger – 'hud, or sheet, not cuddy (re covered shelter on coble)… **cuddy** might be used for a small locker or the like' (FT, Cullercoats); dodger – 'canopy on coble' (KP, re Amble).

fishroom – 'space amidships in coble. In Yorkshire this is called the **crib**' (KP, Beadnell).

foreroom – 'space between midshipthoft and forethoft' (Umpleby, Staithes, 1930s).

haelin room – 'space between lowsethoft and afterthoft' (Umpleby, Staithes, 1930s) [?hauling].

hud – 'small cabin' (Carle Robinson, Amble); see also **dodger**, and compare **huddock** in keels section of Chapter 6.

scappers – 'scuppers' (KP, Beadnell).

There is a considerable of variety of names for an improvised shelter to the fore of a coble, perhaps because a fairly recent feature, i.e. post-engine:

Cuddy more typical of bigger trawlers. For a coble, if the mast was down, the sail could be draped over the mast to make a shelter or tent. A [bowsprit] projecting forward and use of a jib would make permanent cuddy impractical in a sailing coble.

(Bart Taylor, Cullercoats)

Oars and poles

bang – 'a strong fir pole...a long pole used for guiding or propelling a boat' (Heslop); *EDD* – N'd, C'd. [?ON *banga* 'to drive', etc.].

barlsteead – 'ring that fits on oars' (Umpleby, Staithes, 1930s).

bool – 'an iron plate attached to the oars of keels and wherries... through this the thole pin passes' (Heslop); **bole** – 'ring on oar that sits on thoweld' (KP, Beadnell); *EDD* – 'iron staples on a boat's oar' N'd only [?Du *boghel*; curve or hoop'].

choke-nail – 'metal in front of thoweld on a coble to keep the oar lying at the correct angle' (KP, Beadnell).

oars – "The oars of the coble were made up of 2 parts; the 'loom' and the 'blade' [OE/ON ār]. The loom was usually made of larch and was painted the same colour as the inside of the coble. The blade was usually made of ash and was painted white" (http://www.twmuseums.org.uk/fishtales); "coble oars had an iron ring on one side of the loom which fitted over a thole pin in the sheet so that they should not be lost should the rower let go" (Mannering & Greenhill, 1997, p.51) ['clog and wash' in some areas, see March (1970)].

poy (noun) – 'a boat-stick (Beadnell & Boulmer usage)' (KP, Beadnell); 'pole...with an iron forked point used by keelmen on the Tyne' (OED); *EDD* – **puy** 'long pole with a spike on the end used for propelling a boat', N'd, D'm, Notts, Linx, EA [source unknown].

plies – 'oars' (KP, Beadnell).

rowth irons – 'irons on oars' (Umpleby, Staithes, 1930s); *EDD* – *rowth* 'rowing' Shet, Ork, Sc ["?same root as the *ruth/rooth* that protects the gunwale from oar-wear on Shetland boats, so likely also Norwegian/ON in derivation" (AO)].

sweep – 'a long oar' (KP, Beadnell); **swaape** – 'swape (oar)' (Umpleby, Staithes, 1930s).

thole – pivot for oar; **thowle** – thole-pin (Amble per CKBS); **thowll pins** – 'uprights on coble side for oars to fit on' (Umpleby, Staithes, 1930s); **thoweld** – 'thole pin (for oars)' (KP, Beadnell). "Tholes were made from hickory hammer shafts" (AO) [OE *þol* 'oar-peg', ON *þoll-r*].

thyea (Nth N'd) – 'the thole pin of a boat' (Heslop).

wale – 'the clog or loom of a coble's oar in Yorkshire' (Hill & McKee, 1978).

wheealin' (whaling) – 'iron affixed to strengthen part where thowls are placed on the side of the coble' (Umpleby, Staithes, 1930s).

Mast, sails and tackle

chock – 'wood used to support boat on land; also to support mast in step in a sailing-coble' (KP, Beadnell).

cringles – rings in a sail corresponding to pendants, for reefing.

cutch – 'a brown liquid with which the lugsail was coated. It was made by boiling up oak bark and 'catechu' (an imported resin-like product). The sails were treated with this once a year; it helped make them windproof'.

(http://www. twmuseums.org.uk/fishtales). 'One source quotes it as being a mixture of oak bark and catechu; another as a mixture of Stockholm tar, red oche, sap of a Spanish oak and oil' (Bradley, 2, p.26).

dead wood – blocks of timber to strengthen and reinforce main structural elements.

deed eye – 'block used to stop ropes running on rigging, also called **numb block**' (KP, Beadnell); **deadeye** – 'a block with a hole to help secure and tighten shrouds from mast' (JF, Seaham).

dolls – 'sticks to hold sail to enable the fisherman's hands to be liberated' (Umpleby, Staithes, 1930s) [cf. *dolly* 'a wooden instrument'].

eearin' – 'sails of coble: "lee and weather 'eearin'"' (Umpleby, Staithes, 1930s).

gammon – 'loop of rope at bow of sailing coble to hold bowsprit, or mast and oars, in place' (KP, Beadnell).

gantrees – 'board flush with forethoft and carlin in which mast is fixed' (Umpleby, Staithes, 1930s); reinforcement and support for thofts at mast foot.

gilney – 'hole at coble head through which **gilrope** passes' (Umpleby, Staithes, 1930s) [?eye].

glut – wedge used to fix tilt of coble mast (Bradley, I, Yx, p.32); *EDD* – Sc, N'd, Yx, EA.

jib – supplementary forward sail. 'If a jib was regularly set, an omega shaped iron 'loof', 'cradle' or 'gammon' (Bridlington) was mounted on the breasthook to take the bowsprit' (Bradley, I, p.28).

jib alliotts – 'rope attached to mast to hoist jib' (Umpleby, Staithes, 1930s) [halliards].

leeaf – 'rope that passes through parril' (Umpleby, Staithes, 1930s).

leeaf-heeak – 'hook for the leaf' (Umpleby, Staithes, 1930s).

lugsail – 'so called from the 'lug' or yard from which it hangs…The yard is further so balanced that it hangs at an angle, with one corner of the sail higher than the other. The bottom corners of the sail were made fast by ropes' http://www.twmuseums.org.uk/fishtales; 'a dipping lugsail is one that has to be lowered and re-hoisted on the other side of the mast when 'going about' on the opposite tack… Dipping lugs, though very efficient, require considerable crew skills for safe use' (AO) [source of *lug* uncertain]. On tacking – "when the sail was lowered and hoisted again for tacking, and the sheet hauled aft, she started off like a bird on the wing" (Salmon, 1885, p.14).

mast – "A coble also had 2 masts, one for summer use and a shorter one for winter use and/or heavy weather. These masts were usually made from white pine, which was imported and came to the River Tyne from Riga in Latvia" (http://www.twmuseums.org.uk/fishtales) [OE *mæst* but ON *viða*].

parril – 'that sail hangs upon' (Umpleby, Staithes, 1930s); **parrels** – "hold the yard and sail to the mast" (Landstrom, 1961, p.156).

peak – 'angle of top of sail on sailing coble; this was steeper to the north, hence: "Beadlin men had a right peak on the sail" (KP, Beadnell); "During most of the 19th century coble had quite square-headed sails, easier to handle in a seaway (peaked sails swing around more) and in heavy weather; however, demands for increased performance to windward saw luff lengths grow by giving more peak to the sail – similar trends occurred with lug sailed boats elsewhere" (AO).

ryff – reef (for sail) (*Newc. Noah Play*).

sheffs – 'sheaves' (KP, Beadnell).

skeg – 'slot into which foremast was lowered in herring keelboat' (KP, Beadnell).

tabernacle – 'seat of mast' (BT, Cullercoats).

tack-hyeuk – 'place either side of coble's bows to attach sail' (KP, Beadnell).

traveller – 'iron ring to hoist dipping lug sail up the mast on a coble' (term used beyond Northumberland) (KP, Beadnell).

tye – 'greased rope attached to 'traveller' and running to halliard block on sailing coble' (KP, Beadnell).

yard – 'spar from which lug sail hangs (term used beyond Northumberland)' (KP, Beadnell) [OE].

There are few demonstrable Old Norse-based words in the above; some basic terms are OE: *segl-gyrd* than ON *siglu-rá*, OE *saegl* (sail) than ON *skeg/skegga* (*EDD* – Orkneys, Shetlands). But overall – "the chapter on Masts, Sails and rigging is particularly rich in terms of [later] foreign extraction" (Sandahl, 1951, p.23) in keeping with a later date for the introduction of sail on small fishing vessels; the terms used are then borrowed from wider English. For more on the use of sails, see (Salmon, 1885, pp.19–22).

Mast
Well, it was a standard pole and if you could get a good scotch fir – the only problem with scotch fir was the knots – columbian pine or anything like that made an ideal mast for its true grain and lack of knots, but it would be long way more expensive – but what used to be used was scaffolding poles – that was maistly what they used to use like for their masts, to my memory anyway.

The mast sits in a tabernacle where forefoot joins ram plank. Carlines (running fore and aft) help steady the mast, and the mast would be kept in place by a 'hook' that went round its base. A bowsprit would provide support for a second, lighter sail, as needed.

(Bart Taylor, Cullercoats)

Other elements
booat-'eeak – 'boat hook: "give us 'o'd o' t'booat-'eeak"' (Umpleby, Staithes, 1930s).

breest-hyeuk – 'Y-shaped connection at top of gunwales at stem of coble (Amble). Called a 'haak' at Seahouses' (KP).

freak – 'a ship's chest' (Amble / Newbiggin) (KP, Beadnell).

ginny – 'small rollers in coble for hauling pots' (KP, Beadnell).

gudgeon – 'where the lower pintle of the rudder sits' (KP, Beadnell); 'hole in casting at stern so that hook can be inserted to haul coble' (Umpleby, Staithes, 1930s).

horns – 'protuberances of gunwale either side of coble's stern' (KP, Beadnell).

lanchin' woods – 'woods used to launch coble; they are well greased: "wi' talla eightpence a poond at Jausiph's"' (Umpleby, Staithes, 1930s).

rowell – 'roll; also roller, e.g. rollers on side of coble' (KP, Beadnell).

skeat – 'skid, transverse log or sleeper used for launching' (Hill & McKee, 1978) [?ON skíð].

tap leets – 'coble lantern' (Umpleby, Staithes, 1930s).

If we except common terms and terms for masts and sails, then (as noted above) we find a not unexpected imput – these being maritime matters – from Old Norse. Other terms may be deemed ON by reason of their distribution, especially where this is limited to the East Coast. However, many terms cannot be traced to a root at all, their origin either local or lost – a reminder of how specialist (and personal?) the details of boat construction have always been.

Chapter 4. Building a coble

In coble building, no plans, drawings or moulds were ever used. Instead, the boats were built by eye and long experience was needed in order to produce a fast boat. No two cobles were ever the same and each one was tailored to the needs of the new owner.

(http://www.twmuseums.org.uk/fishtales)

First I make the shell, shallow as a true coble should be, for ease of hauling her up the beach. Then I fit the ribs in.

(Hargrave Hopwood, coble-builder at Flamborough, qu. March, 1970, I, p.113)

Well, the standard way of building would be to get the stem and the forefoot fastened together, along with the ram plank at the base. And then automatically adjust your port and starboard strakes at the same time to help keep the boat even as you built it; and you got planked right up and you never used to put the scut in because that was your way of getting in and out of the boat – that was the last thing that was ever built on a coble.

The first added plank or strake at the base is parallel to the ram, but curves violently at the stem – a valid case for steaming. Steaming is not generally desirable – it knocks the nature of the wood. Older cobles were only six planks a side, so called 'a six-plank coble'. These would be of larch, and the builder would always look for windswept trees or trees with a natural curve, for there was lots of 'sweep' or curve to the top planks. Some, it seemed, needed to be almost 'S' shaped. The top strake or garboard had so much sweep you would usually need to scarf it. The high forefoot was almost a natural function of amount of timber to be carried forward from wide mid-portion of boat – as the boat narrows towards the stem, so the strakes define a rising forefoot.

Once you got all your planking up – they were very flexible still because there weren't any ribs in, which meant that you could make a little bit more tumble-in or open them up, whichever way you wanted. And then once you got them to your satisfaction that way, you started putting your timber in or ribs – they were known as 'timbers' – and you worked from forward to aft with those and you put your floors in which was the follow-on of your timbers right across the boat's bottom. You would need to make templates for the ribs, and fit these to pieces of wood that had grown in a natural curve, called a 'knee'. And then your inwiver went in and your thwarts or thofts, one at a time, until you finally had the boat almost completed and then you put your scut in... and that was it!

There was nothing put between the planks, no point of any preparation because the idea was that once the water hit the wood it swelled and tightened so they were water-tight – which always worked. Additionally, on the underside of the coble, two drafts (runners) would be fitted, contributing to its strength.

(Bart Taylor, Cullercoats, 21 June 2006)

A slightly different, older version is found in John Salmon's book on the coble:

> The order of construction is this. The ram or substitute for the keel of other boats, which is rather more than two-thirds of the extreme length, is nailed down to the floor of the building room or shed, and to this is scarfed the forefoot dead-wood to which will be afterwards fastened the stem. The bottom planks are then placed in position and nailed together and the flooring timbers fitted. This is contrary to the practice in building ships of which the frames are first put together. Then come the side planks and the timbers, and the stem and gunwales. The boat is then turned and the forefoot added. The drafts, or bilge streaks, to protect the bottom when the boat is beached, are then nailed on, and it is turned the second time…The raisings or inwires as they are called, and the thwarts or seats, complete the hull, which is then ready to receive the iron work and other small matters of detail.
>
> (Salmon, 1885, pp.9–10)

Detailed specifications of coble design will be found at (McKee, 1985, pp.114–18, and (Mannering & Greenhill, 1997, p.50).

> The general proportions I have heard reckoned as follows:
>
> Overall length approx 4 times beam
> Bow should rise twice height of stern, viewed on land
> Transom should be half the beam at its widest
> Rudder needs to be long, about quarter length of boat at waterline.
> Mast should be a length so that it fits inside the boat, not longer

Besides Cambridges at Hartlepool:

> The famous boat building firm 'Harrison's' which was established in 1870 in Amble by James and John Harrison made many hundreds of cobles. The firm 'Dawson's' built cobles at Seahouses, but mostly for the smaller villages like Boulmer and Craster further down the coast.
>
> (www.twmuseums.org.uk/fishtales)

The Tyne & Wear Museums collection includes the Fulmar, by Cambridge, also the half-decker *Glad Tidings* by Harrisons. George Cambridge retired in 1920, to the advantage of J. & J. Harrison. Another example of a coble by Harrisons is on display at Hartlepool Museum, built in 1921 at Amble, and named the *Three Brothers Grant*. This once had an engine, but is now presented as a sailing coble. It is slightly over 30 foot in length. A shorter example, about 20 feet, from around 1900, is held by the Sunderland Maritime Trust and viewable on application. In the nineteenth century, Robert Hopwood (born 1836) and his son Hargrave were noted coble builders in Scarborough, credited with building many hundred boats. Other local builders of the time included Hodgson of Sunderland, the Lee family on the Tweed, and firms around the Coble Dean on the Tyne [via OA].

Though one or two capable of building a coble may remain, attention has shifted to conserving and renovating such examples as survive. Several members of the Coble and Keelboat Society have undertaken such work, and one has contributed the following account for this book:

Renovation of the *Joan Dixon* (Mel Deighton)

The coble *Joan Dixon* was built by Harrisons of Amble in 1946 for Bill Dixon and named after his year-old daughter. When John Dixon (Bill's son) retired from fishing he sailed her from Beadnell to Seahouses where it was to form part of the museum (Sealife Centre). At Seahouses it was craned onto a lorry, driven to the back of the museum and craned down into the back yard – the museum was then extended over it!

The new viewing gallery was a fairly simple construction with a corrugated roof. The coble was set diagonally in the space in a plaster sea, with mannikins aboard to crew it, and the odd stuffed seagull. Nearby was a video presentation on a TV screen.

In time, the coble exhibit was reckoned not much of an attraction any more and it was decided to replace it with a trout pond. Peter Weightman of the Coble & Keelboat Society told me it was available, so I came to look over it, climbed aboard, tapped it, checked the hull (the boat was raised on wooden blocks). I expressed an interest in her, and was told I had four weeks to get it out before a chainsaw was taken to it.

Extricating it from the museum was to be no easy matter. Taking the roof off was one possibility, but a hefty deposit was asked for that option. Since the walls were built in sections, it was easier to take part of the back wall out and access the coble that way. In November 2003 – possibly the wettest November ever – Peter and me, with the help of Gordon Brown, set about removing 12 foot of wall, rough stone below and corrugated asbestos cement board above. It took us 3 days, including inserting the occasional prop to support the roof. Then we hired a flatbed lorry with 35 ton hi-ab to get her out. As the arm of the lorry was at full stretch to reach the coble as it was, there was not enough lifting power; also there was not much headroom to lift and manoeuvre the boat properly. Instead, the boat was pulled gradually towards the gap in the wall, and pivotted round from diagonal to straight on, then slid out of the housing and lifted onto the lorry.

I was to work on it on a slipway at Ouseburn on the Tyne. The hull was in very good condition – being under cover so long; the only problem there was a few holes where electric cables had been inserted to light the boat up from inside. But during the move, there were a fair few 'cracking noises' – the long storage may have led to sagging; and the strain of moving cannot have helped, especially the bit when we had to twist her round to line her up with the hole in the museum wall. Consequently some fittings gave; for example, the doors on the half deck wouldn't shut for a long time after.

It needed a lot of cleaning. In the bottom, under the boards of the deck, was a good inch of old shells, dry seaweed and mummified starfish left from the days she was on active service – a memory of a marine atmosphere. A main problem was the engine – a 1965 Kelvin 4-cylinder marine diesel. The museum had considered it would never be used again, so had left it just as it was without draining the fuel, oil or water. The chain connecting the reversing wheel and gearbox had rusted solid; the valves in the cylinder had jammed shut; the starting motor was seized. It was necessary to strip the whole engine down from the top – fortunately it has a fairly simple design – and clean it out. The water channels and all the pipes were blocked with sludge and had to be blown through or poked clear with welding rods. The fuel tank had only slime where diesel once had been and the sump contained no longer oil but a tarry black stuff. And most of this had to be worked on in situ, lying flat in the bottom of the boat and straining to get the right purchase.

The coble was out of the water November 2002 to March 2003 for these basic repairs; when we eased it down the slipway into the water – for the first time in 16 years – it sank, of course. Clinker-built boats like this have no caulking, so the long time on land had led to some drying and movement of the timbers, and inevitable gaps. We pulled her a little way back up the slipway, let the tide wash over her – then pumped her out and brought her to stand clear of the water. This cycle had to repeated over 3 months to get her sea-worthy.

(While that is going on, it is worth explaining that similar problems often affected the salmon boats at Bambrough. Rather than pay for moorings all year round, it was cheaper to store them on land when unused for duing the winter. When the new season came round, they used to sink the boats in the sea for about a week to get them sea-worthy again. It works.)

Back on the *Joan Dixon*, there was further delay of nearly 3 months finishing the work on the engine and getting a replacement starter motor. The first time we took her out on a proper sea voyage – in 2004 – was for the Cullercoats Lifeboat Day, and that under power all the way.

Her real debut as a renovated and fully functioning coble was in June 2005 for the Mouth of the Tyne River Festival. I had fitted a new mast, made from a telegraph pole. The great square brown sail was bought secondhand. The sides were freshly painted blue, with the top strake white. (Incidentally, painting her is a non-stop job: the outside needs painting every 2 years, the rest every year.) Anyway, there she was at last, at sea, under sail, just as she been, long before.

Chapter 5. Handling a coble

Tow a Cow

'Tie the halter to the coble,' said Tresham; 'we'll try if she'll tow over.'

'I'm feared the coble wunna steer wi' her.' said Hamish, 'but any way we'll try;' and having fixed her halter onto the broad clumsy stern, away they pulled.

While the boat continued in the dead water, the cow, with a docility which proved her sense of danger, swam after, and nearly as fast as the coble pulled, so as scarcely to impede its course. But when the stream took both the cow and the boat in flank, the former became terrified and restive, and pulled against the latter, so as to embarrass the efforts of the rowers. It was with difficulty they reached mid channel, having lost much way; when a sudden jerk of the animal's head almost overset the coble, and she shipped a great deal of water. 'Cut the tow, cut the tow, and let the coo drift, or we're lost!' cried Hamish, and Ronald sprung up to undo the knot. But the struggling of the beast, and his own irregular movement, precipitated the catastrophe he sought to prevent, for a violent jerk tore out a plank from the stern, and pitched Ronald quite overboard, while at the same moment, the coble filled and upset, and Tresham and Hamish were also left floundering in the stream.

(James Bailie Fraser, *The Highland Smugglers*, 1832, p.77)

(Of interest also as indicating a Scots wooden coble with apparently a square stern.)

The following description is based on conversation with Bart Taylor – direct quotations, unless otherwise marked, are from him:

The smaller coble, "an open boat with a broad beam" was suited for inshore work, seldom venturing out of sight of land, or staying at sea longer than a short working day.

Fisherman could have 2 boats, 1 for summer (drift netting against pier), 1 for winter (using lines – winter coble tougher, in better condition for winter weather).

Though designed for storage on a beach between ventures, the coble was adaptable to a stone or concrete landing slope (especially Yorkshire), or could ride to a mooring post in a harbour.

Many features of the coble related to launching and recovery and seaworthiness. The tall stem was equally useful while launching bow-first, keeping the prow above water; and for facing a high sea with breaking waves. (If attempting to beach bow-first, the stem would dig into the sand, and the rest of the boat swing round...)

The lack of a projecting keel was essential if drawing up onto a beach; but risked the boat drifting to leeward when sailing. The forefoot, projecting below the hull, only partially compensated for this. A deep rudder was the main counter. "Rudder must be deep to compensate for high forefoot, and go 18" to 2' into water – the hull of a coble only draws about 8" of water – area underwater of rudder should equal area underwater of forefoot. Or coble will tend to spin round…"

[Stability depended in some measure on the use of ballast – "It was also important that the cobles had ballast which was placed onboard. Ballast could be any dense material which was used to stabilise a vessel… Sand, stones or shingle were the most common form of ballast used aboard fishermen's cobles as it was in plentiful supply. Bags of it were filled by the women before every trip" (http://www.twmuseums.org.uk/fishtales) – "some could be discarded if sufficient weight of fish caught!" (AO)]

The tilt of the square stern gave assisted during recovery onto a sloping beach (e.g. for "getting your shoulder under to lift onto wheels etc."). It provided a practical housing for the rudder, and later a propeller. In a following sea, its tilt meant it tended to rise with the waves, avoiding waves breaking over the stern.

The tumble-home gave more options for boat to be leant over sideways, e.g. when working nets over side ("always shot to starboard").

The basically square (lug) sail was economical and effective, but like all sails can only take advantage of wind from favourable quarters. However, a coble could "practically go into a wind – gave you a grip on the water – you didn't sheer off to port or starboard."

But it could be dangerous in a strong following wind: "if head digs in too deep you can broach [go sideways to waves] – one solution to add weight at back of boat – or run in on jib alone.

The mast was adaptable. It could be set "a bit raked backwards," e.g. in storm, when the crew would "reef mainsail to a scrap" and "run with it". Alternatively, in high weather a short 'bowsprit' mast could be used in place of main mast.

"You had the main mast and then you had a short mast which was used if it was bad weather when you had to put 4 or 5 reefs in the mains', and cocked it [with] a bit taper aft and you just used to run with that.

"Danger points were running before a sea and wind: you could, if you weren't careful, broach to, so what they used to do was bring all your ballast aft and sometimes just run on a jib and with it being angled well aft, it acted like a glorified parachute – you lifted up on a sea; as you were coming down it used to fill with air and you used to lower yourself down like – it were pretty good that way."

More exact navigation could be achieved if the mast were taken down and the coble rowed.

Oars were long and overlapped inboard, extra inboard length giving more leverage. Also would be rowed cross-armed… If it needed to be, a coble would be towed stern first – that way the forefoot acts as rudder. "Also you could have a big hook to the stern for tractors to haul the coble up on a beach. At Bridlington, where you have a rocky base, a coble needs big draughts underneath; for any hard bottom, the draughts would need to be reinforced with iron."

An engine became a useful addition to the coble, from the 1930s on. To begin with, 'Kelvin' engines were often used, and the Austin 7 car engine was popular in smaller cobles. The engine would be added in middle of boat – as forwards as practical, to leave room for fishing operation. The engine gave the coble a measure of independence of wind and tide, and should have made fishing quicker and safer.* But there was the problem that engines encouraged the building of bigger cobles; bigger cobles needed more powerful engines, and so on. Whereas the coble was a very specialised craft for sailing, the engine was not entirely suited to the coble's design e.g. a vertical stem would have been better for an engine-driven boat. "Once you stopped sailing, a coble shape wasn't necessary."

(Based on interview with Bart Taylor, Cullercoats, 21 June 2006)

---

* The engine gave ideal energy-saving over rowing, independence of the wind (though a sail could still be used to save fuel) and greater manoeuvrability. Saving time on reaching the fishing ground, a longer time could be devoted to fishing rather than reaching the fishing ground, and a larger number of fishing days possible since it was no longer necessary to be quite as cautious regarding wind and weather. Though the engine should have provided extra safety (one need no longer be caught on a rocky lee shore), it can never quite match the force of the sea: the tragedy of 1962 at Seaham resulted in the loss of nine lives, when the lifeboat, sent out to rescue a coble caught in a sudden storm, itself capsized, caught broadside to the wind, turning to manoeuvre its approach to the harbour entrance. It is a brutal reminder that however good the design of boat, all vessels are subject to the forces of the sea and wind, and in the North Sea those forces can be very changeable and very severe.

Chapter 6. Other boats

A brief survey of the some of the main types of boats associated with the North East.

Collier or **collier brig** – the sturdy sailing ship favoured for the carriage of coal to London and elsewhere. In fact collier can cover 'any vessel used exclusivley in the coal trade' (JF, Seaham). In the days of the sail, this was likely a **brig** or **brigantine** – "a merchant-ship with two masts… [with] her mainsail set nearly in the plane of her keel" (Falconer, 1780).

half-marrow – 'a crew member on a collier who was rated (and paid) between an apprentice and an able-seaman' (AO, re Runciman, 1924, p.92) [after pit term].

stick – 'the tiller of an old-style (pre-wheel steering) collier' (AO, re Runciman, 1924, p.208). About 1850 on, "the development of iron shipbuilding and advances in the screw propeller and suitable steam engines to drive it, opened the way for successful steam colliers to be built" (MacRae & Wayne, 1990, p.12).

Description of a Voyage in the Coal Trade with other poems, published for the benefit of the widow and orphans of the author (late a sailor of North Shields) (1835).

Our ship's now load, the deck's all clear,	
But still lays moored in the <u>tier</u>.	row of mooring buoys (AO)
The Captain, he then comes on board,	
With all the dignity of a lord –	
"Well, John, you are all load I see,	
But she looks very <u>bold</u> to me.	high in the water
I think the <u>measure</u> still grows worse,	weight of coal filling a cauldron or wagon
The coal trade won't be worth a curse –	
Did she take in all <u>two and twenty</u>?"	i.e. keels of coal
"Yes, sir,- all and there was plenty!"	
"John, have you got on board the ale and beer?	
I'll change our brewer, if I live, next year;	
His beer he makes so very <u>small</u>,	weak
His ale I'm sure won't keep at all.	

I expect you will all ready be.
For, at high water, she must go to sea,
If wind or steam can take her out,
And go, she must, there's not a doubt."

"Oh, the ———— ohoy!" the pilot cries,
As under the ship's bow he lies:
The captain then looks o'er the nows
When the following dialogue ensues:

"Well, sir,- all ready for sea?
Tully can't get, so has sent me;
If you think of going, let's begin,
It's time you had your stern rope in –

She won't sail out the wind's too shy,
But we must heave her out and try;
The wind looks as if it would be
All from the north-east at sea.

So come my lads and let's be at her,
We'll have a <u>steamboat</u>, where's the [m]atter?"   paddle tug
"Sea! certainly, pilot, there's no doubt,
We won't lay here if we can get out."

Our ship now hove out of the tier,
At single anchor lays all clear;
The steam-boat, she then comes a-head
And by a <u>warp</u> the ship doth lead.   tow rope

Our anchor, then, hove to the bow,
With <u>catt and fish</u> the same we stow;   the anchor raised, hangs from the brig's 'cat (AO)
"Come, lay aloft my lads, hurro,
Your yard-arm <u>gaskets</u> too let go!   rope ties securing furled sails (AO)

Hold fast your bunts, let go your gear,
For sheeting home see all things clear.
With rapid pace the vessel goes,
Nor cares which way the wind it blows.

The wind at north a pleasant gale,
Below the Middens we make sail;
"Steam-boat, ahoy! Let go the warp.
Come, haul it in, my lads, look sharp!"

The ship, now safely out at sea,
The pilot, the, discharged must be;
"Now, sir, I'll thank you for my <u>note</u>,   authorising the pilot's fee
Brace the yards by, haul up the boat.

You know, sir, what you mostly pay,
You'll make it <u>square money</u> I dare say."   rounded up
The pilot now has got his note,
With haste he steps into his boat.

"I wish you a good passage, sir,- goodbye!"
"Thank you pilot" they reply;
The captain, then, takes the command,
And on the quarter-deck does stand.

"Square away your yards, my lads, right square,
and all your steering sail gear prepare;
Look sharp, my lads come bear a-hand,
Set every steering sail that will, stand…"

corf – "one or two of these small cobles (22–24ft. length) were commonly carried on deck and despatched at sea as the principle long-lining/herring fishery tools of 'five man boats' (luggers) and, the later, 'Scarborough Yawls'; these decked boats acting as mother ships to receive and process the corfs' catches (thus, corfs were rather more than 'a tender')" (AO). "Calf – 10–15ft LOA, rowed only; flat stern, carried on Yorkshire and Bridlington cobles" (Bradley, I, p.24).

fifie – see keelboat.

Five man boat
A robust three masted, lug rigged herring drifter and line fishing vessel used primarily by Yorkshire fishermen… so named because five shareholders were involved and usually sailed in her… From March to September five-man boats went line fishing… on the edge of the Dogger Bank or even further afield, usually sailing on Monday and returning on Friday. In the autumn the five-man boats took part in the Yarmouth herring fishery and were then laid up for the winter… Fishing was done from two square sterned cobles which the bigger boat had carried to sea on deck.
(Mannering & Greenhill, 1997, p.53)

The Five-Men Boats, during the winter. do not go to sea; but, at the beginning of Lent they fit out for the fishery on the edge of the Dogger. In the month of September they go to Yarmouth, where they are employed in the Herring Fishery, until the latter end of November.

These boats generally take great quantities of cod and ling, which, in the months of July and August, are salted, for exportation...

(Hinderwell, Scarborough, 1798 p.228)

The five-men-boat is forty feet long, fifteen broad, and twenty-five tons burden. It is so called, though navigated by six men and a boy, because one of the men is hired to cook, and does not share in the profits of the other five. All our able fishermen go in these boats to the herring-fishery at Yarmouth, the latter end of September; and return about the middle of November.

The boats are then laid up until the beginning of Lent, at which time they go off in them to the edge of the Dogger, and other places, to fish for turbot, cod, ling, skate, &c. They always take two cobles on board, and when they come upon their ground, anchor the boat, throw out the cobles, and fish in the sea in the same manner as those do who go from the shore in a coble...

(Goldsmith, 1824, p.189)

Also known as Yorkshire Lugger, and:

farm – 'herring coble' (Yx) (Godfrey, 1974, p.11).

In 1614 re Yarmouth: "the fishermen of the north countries beyond Scarborough and Robin Hood's Bay, and some as far as the Bishoprick of Durham, do hither resort yearly in poor little boats called five-men cobles..." (qu. *Journal of the Coble & Keelboat Society*, 27, 2006). This type had declined in use by early 1900s.

Foy boat

foy – 'fee for piloting a boat into harbour: "what's the foy to be?"' (John Green, S'd, 1879, p.24); 'foy – a fee' (Heslop) [*OED* properly derives *foy* from Dutch *fooi* 'a parting present... given by or to one setting out on a journey']. The Dutch source suggests the act of assisting a ship out of harbour or rivermouth – compare the poem under 'Collier', previous. The foyboat and pilot boat seem to overlap in function, to a degree, but it is unlikely the foyboat would range far out to sea to obtain a customer; their function as I understand it was to assist at the point a sailing boat could no longer proceed under its own power; *EDD – foy* as hauling fee, East coast, N'd to EA, plus Kt; in Scotland, closer to Dutch sense of parting gift.

click – 'to make a click is the act of 'hooking' a ship from an open boat in order to tow alongside and render services; by association, to contract at sea to provide pilotage or mooring (foyboat) services to a ship' (AO).

swivvy or **snivvy** – a short-handled hook used for caching hold of a buoy (after AO) [?swivel].

Tyne foyboat – "a stalwart, manoeuvrable, two manned rowing, sculling and sailing boat, employed in mooring and unmooring ships" (Mannering & Greenhill, 1997, p.47).

Before the advent of steam tugs, the prime function of foyboats and foyboatmen was to tow or kedge-haul ships to/from sea, and to 'make fast'/loose their mooring warps… Early Wear foyboats were well-manned, fine-lined rowing gigs, but in the steam era Wear foyboatmen adopted small (c.19 feet) common, two-manned (harbour) cobles for mooring purposes. Meanwhile, Tyne foyboats became regularised into strongly built, conventional transom sterned, clench-built, rowing/sailing boats some 15-17 feet in length, manned by a crew of two, with specialised internal features to suit their work.

(Adrian Osler)

The late 19th century… became the heyday of the foy men, who sensible concentrated on mooring services for ever-expanding steam shipping" (Cunliffe, 2002, vol.2, pp.271–72). In the age of steam, Sunderland foyboatmen forsook their traditional man-o-war's gig for the local coble.

In foying a ship the foymen moved ahead in a small boat, and at warp's length dropped a small kedge [anchor], which, being being hove upon by the ship's windlass, brought her up to a position nearly over it. The kedge was then…weighed, carried ahead again, dropped and hauled upon, the process being repeated until sufficient sea-way had been attained by the vessel.

(Haswell, 1895, p.39, re Tyne)

A foy coble would help moor a ship: the (line) would run from the stern of the coble, and the coble would row ahead to take the line to a buoy." Derek Rowell (Sunderland) "Foy boats – would fasten colliers' lines to shore or buoys" Bart Taylor (Cullercoats) "Foyboat oars were **pulled** (not, rowed) between pairs of carefully fashioned (hand-whittled) hardwood thole pins which, when not in use, were tucked in the owner's top pocket – both to discourage others using the boat and as a badge of office/occupation.

(Adrian Osler, re South Shields)

Foy boat men – they would never take a dead body aboard the boat, they would tow it along side the boat, fasten it, and take it to the police station, because if they took it in the boat, they got the job to bury it, it was a thing on the river, never take a body on the boat cos then its your job to look after it, it could have been a family or a squabble so there's inquests and dear knows what. So they say we found it in Jarrow staithes, something like that, rowed the boat and took it to the police.

(Ernie Keedy, Beamish, 2005/84)

Easily identified, foyboats were conventionally painted black with a white topstrake.

Geordies and *Jamies* – *collier brigs from Tyne and Wear respectively*
"Towards the end of the 18th century the three-masted collier barques began to give way to the two-masted collier brigs which were often called 'Geordies'" (G.S. Laird Clowes, *The story of sail*, 1936) via Johnson, p.49.

"South county people…gave all north country vessels the name of Geordies" (Walter Runciman, *Collier brigs and their sailors*, 1926) re c.1860.

"You thought of the channel aswarm with just such vessels as she – Geordies deep with coal" (WC Russell, *Jack's courtship*, 1884) via *Johnson*, p.48.

"A North-country 'Geordie' that was coolly snuggling down and outweathering the fierce squall" (*Daily Mail*, 13 Oct 1897, p.7).

"A writer in a recent periodical supplies us with the curious information that 'Mariners term a vessel from the Tyne a Geordie, and from the Wear a Jamie" (William Fordyce, *History of...the County Palatine of Durham*, 1857, vol.2, p.509, fn.

There was rivalry also between the foyboatmen of the two rivers: "vocalised in the Tynesiders' derogation of the Wear's men as mere river 'mowrahs' (i.e. moorers) whilst, convervsely, the Tynesiders were held to be rather foolhardy 'hobblers' or 'sculler-men'" (AO).

Keels

Keels (and the keelmen who operated them) were needed on the rivers of coal ports to assist the movement of coal to the colliers – the ships that carried coal to London and Europe.

> Though technically unsophisticated, keels were by no means as clumsy and as inefficient as is often portrayed, especially if taking into account the fact that their main constraint was a statutory one – by King's acts they were not allowed to carry any more than 21 tons of coal.
>
> (Osler & Barrow, 1993, p.24)

The railways that brought the coal from inland pits to the Tyne originally stopped west of the Tyne bridge; but the exporting collier brigs were limited to the deeper water east of the Tyne bridge whose low arches blocked access upriver; and so they tended to collect at Shields and the river's lower stretches. The keelmen supplied the missing link, collecting the coal from the staithes, moving it downriver in keels of shallow draught, on the tide, and then 'casting' it aboard the colliers' holds.

The development of 'staithes' with 'spouts' meant coal from pits east of Newcastle could be poured direct from above into the ship's holds, a saving of manual effort that led the keelmen to risk a major strike in 1822 (see article by Stanley Mitcalfe, 1937). Though they lost the strike, there was work enough for some decades to come. It was in the 1860s railways brought the coal to convenient downriver staiths and "virtually eliminated the keels" (MacRae, 1990, p.22); and in the 1870s, the dredging of the river, the removal of the old bridge and the building of the Swing Bridge, opened more of the Tyne to colliers and other craft. Keelmen finally became redundant. (Further information at www.sunnisidelocalhistorysociety.co.uk/keelboats.html, and Roger Finch, *Coals from Newcastle*, 1973.)

Tyne keel – 'a beamy double-ended, shallow rowing, sailing and poling lighter' (Mannering & Greenhill, 1997, p.47).

keel – 'a low, flat, clumsy-looking vessel or barge...in which coals are carried from the colliery-staiths to the ships in the Tyne and Wear... In the Chartulary of Tynemouth Monastery, the servants of the Prior who wrought in the barges (1378), are called **kelers**... In a writ of Bishop Neville (1440) the craft in which coals were brought from the upper to the lower part of the Wear are denominated **keeles**' Brockett; 'a large cargo-carrying boat' (Heslop); 'boat transferring coal locally: "went in the keels" (took employment in...)' (John Green, S'd, 1879, p.34).

keel – 'a vessel on the River Tyne about 50 feet long and 20 feet broad and carries 8 Newcastle or 15 London chaldrons of coal, or 21 tons 13 cwt. [It] is navigated by a skipper, 3 men and a boy, who is called the **Pee dee**... Keels are navigated three different ways on the Tyne, viz by sail, by rowing [with oar and swape] [and] by putting which is done with a **puuy** or **puvy**, a pole about 25 feet long with an iron fork on the end. [The] Pee dee, the boy, takes care of the huddock or cabin of the keel, or fetches and carries as the keelmen and skipper direct' (*Bell-White MS 12*). [Note – 'the *Bell MS* gives rather large size, other sources suggest somewhat smaller' (AO).]

The word *keel* is a Northern pronounciation of the Old English word 'ceol' (pronounced cheyol) meaning any boat. In the North-East it retained the meaning of 'boat', but an alternative word from Old Norse gave the more general meaning of 'the spine of a boat'.

caster – 'a shoveller or caster of coal from a keel to a ship, e.g. Wearside, Blyth' Heslop; **casting** –

shovelling: "casting the coals from the keels into the ships" (John Green, S'd, 1879); "he and his 'marra' had to 'cast' – that is, shovel – [the coal] from the keel into the hold of the vessel being loaded" (*The Maister*, p.35); "coal was carried almost at deck level, keeping the difference in working levels between keel and collier to a minimum" (Mannering & Greenhill, 1997, p.47) ['cast' as Northern alternative to southern 'throw'].

huddock – 'the cabin of the keels on the River Tyne' (*Bell-White MS 12*); **huddick**, or huddock – (Brockett, 1829; Heslop, 1880s); *EDD* – N'd, D'm.

jells – 'vertical components of the structure which contained the cargo of coals on a keel' (AO); [deal, as wood].

keel-bullies – 'the keelmen, or crew of the keel - the partners or comrades in the vessel; keel-brothers' Brockett; 'keel-bully – a mate or comrade on board a keel' (Heslop, 1880s). keelmen – 'the watermen who navigate the keels; an exceedingly hardy and striking race of men' (Brockett, 1829).

teemer – 'the teemer at the docks is the worker who empties the wagons' (JS, Newbiggin) [teem – 'to empty'].

A race almost equally distinct at an early period were the Keelmen. On the Tyne the coals were formerly almost entirely conveyed from the staithes to the ships in oval boats designated 'keels', and containing 8 Newcastle chaldrons. These were managed and navigated in a peculiar manner by the keelmen, but the necessity for these keels is now generally obviated by the erection at the staithes, of spouts or frames for lowering....the coals.

(*Parliamentary Papers*, 1842, Commissioners Reports, vol.16, p.517)

When about six or seven years old I went with my Father in the keels, summer and winter, night and day; in winter nights he always carried me on his back, at the time I had neither stocking or shoes on; my Father being skipper of the keel under Tempest and Blakestone, Mr Tempest was the first master I had, I knew him and his son well, I have seen them many times upon Painshaw Staiths, they have had hold of my little cold hands and have given me many a sixpence and shilling…

(Douglas 1848, p.32 re 1780s)

On Tyneside in 1792, an estimate of the workforce (excluding pitmen) gives:

fitters and runners 113
keelmen, boys, boatmen, etc. 1547
trimmers, ballast heavers, etc. 1000
pilots and foymen 500
seamen and boys 8000
shipwrights, keel-builders, etc. 946
purveyors of ships' keels 1,100
coal factors, clerks, etc. 2000

(Holmes, 1816, pp.234–5)

keel dighter – 'a woman who scrape[s] or clean[s] out the floor of the keels, and get what small coals may have been left after the delivery of the keel' (*Bell-White MS 12*); 'keel-deeter / keel-dighter – a keel tidier or cleaner [female]' (Heslop, 1829).

to kep – 'the act of swiftly lowering a keel's mast from its tabernacle when passing under Newcastle bridge' (AO).

lyin-tide – 'overtime or extra time occupied in discharging a loaded keel, and on which demurrage is-due' (Heslop, 1829).

pea-jacket – 'a loose rough jacket or short covering with conical buttons of a small size, termed pea-jacket – a jacket worn by the old

Keelmen on the River Tyne' (*Bell-White MS 12*); 'the outer holiday dress of a keelman' Wilson/*Pitman's Pay* [Du pij-jakker].

[I'll be a sailor]
and I'll have a New Brown <u>Pee</u>   short jacket
I'll have a new Blue Jacket
and I'll be a Sailor te.

(after Harker, 1985)

pe-de – 'a boy employed on board the keel'; pee-dee – 'a young lad in a keel, who has charge of the rudder' (Brockett); **pee-dee** – 'a miniature marble; on the Tyne…a small boy' (Luckley/Alnwick, 1870s); "[The] Pee dee, the boy, takes care of the huddock or cabin of the keel, or fetches and carries as the keelmen and skipper direct" (*Bell-White MS 12*) [Fr *pedier* or *petit*?].

puoy – 'a long pole with an iron fork at the end, use by keelmen on the Tyne to puoy or push their keels' (*Bell-White MS 12*); puoy, puy or pouie – 'a long pole, with an iron spike or spikes, at the end; used in propelling keels in shallow water, or when it is inconvenient to use sails or oars' (Brockett); puoying – 'punting: "Bobby Gowlan' comes puoying his keel up"' (John Green, S'd, 1879, p.14); "puoys (poles) for setting (punting) through the shallows at low-water or catching favourable marginal eddies" (Osler & Barrow, 1993, p.24); 'thirty foot punting poles' (Mannering & Greenhill, 1997, p.47); *EDD* – N'd, D'm, Linx, EA.

put – to push, to propel; 'putting a keel' (Brockett, 1829).

set – 'to propel, to push forward: "setting a keel"' (Brockett, 1829).

skipper – captain of a keel or coal barge (Brockett, 1829).

staith – 'often pronounced steeth or steith, a place

to lay up and to load coals at… The word occurs in a demise from the Prior of Tynemouth, AD 1338' (Brockett, 1829); staith – 'a quay, a permanent stage or platform by the water-side to facilitate shipping or landing goods; an enbankment or sea-wall' (Atkinson, 1868, Cleveland); staithes – 'jetties for transferring coal into keels to take it downriver to ships' (John Green, S'd, 1879, p.13); staith (pronounced steeth) – 'an elevated platform at the waterside from which coals are shipped by a spout or a drop' (Heslop, 1829) [OE stæð 'shore' ON stoð]; *EDD* – East coast, Scotland to EA.

swape – 'a long oar or sweep used in working a keel on the Tyne, that at the stern acting as a rudder' (Brockett, 1829); 'the long oar formerly used at the stern of a keel on the Tyne' (re 1789) (Heslop, 1829); "steered by a huge oar or 'swape'" (Mannering & Greenhill, 1997, p.47).

Great use of the tides was made in getting down and up the river, down on the ebb laden and back on the flood empty, and the keelmen worked hard to get their loads off in one tide. One evening down at Shields an empty keel managed to get foul of the moorings of a man-of-war. Hearing a commotion the officer of the watch looked over and observed, 'Do you know, my man, the consequences of interfering with one of Her Majesty's ships?' Back came the reply, 'D'ye knaa, mistor, the conseques of wor missin' this bloody tide?'

(H.R. Viall, 'Notes',
Mariner's Mirror, 28, 1942, 162)

The Little P.D.

'Twas between <u>Hebbron</u> an' Jarrow	Hebburn
The cam' on a varry strang gale;	
The skipper luik'd oot o' the <u>huddock</u>,	shelter aft
Crying, "Smash, man! lower the sail!	
Smash, man! lower the sail!	
Or else to the bottom we'll go!"	
The keel an' <u>a</u>' hands wad been lost,	all
Had it not been for Jemmy Munro.	

The gale blew <u>stranger</u> an' stranger;	stronger
When they cam' beside the Muck Hoose,	
The skipper cry'd oot, "Jemmy, <u>swing 'er</u>!"	onto a mooring or anchor (AO)
But still wes as fear'd as a <u>moose</u>.	mouse
P.D. ran to clear the anchor,	
"It's <u>raffled</u>," right loudly he roar'd;	tangled up
They a' said the gale wad sink her	
If it wasn't seun thrawn owerbord.	

The laddy ran sweaten, ran sweaten,
  The laddy ran sweaten aboot,
Till the keel went bump 'gainst Jarrow,
  An' three o' th' bullies lap oot.   leapt
Three o' th' bullies lap oot,
  An' left nyen in but little P.D.,   none
Who ran aboot, stampin' and cryin',
  "How, smash! Skipper, what mun a' dee?"   must I do?

The all shooted oot frae the Kee –   quayside
  "Steer her close in by th' shore,
An' then thraw th' painter t' me,
  Thou cat-faced son of a whore!"
The lad threw the painter ashore,
  They fastened her up to th' Kee;
But whe knaws how far she might gane   who knows... out to sea perhaps?
  Had it not been for little P.D.?

Then into th' huddock they gat,
  And th' flesh they began to fry;
They talked o' th' gale as they sat,
  An' how a' hands were lost (very-nigh).
Th' Skipper roored oot for a drink;
  P.D. ran to bring him th' can,
But, odsmash! mun, what d'ye think!
  He coup'd a' th' flesh out o' th' pan.   tipped? spilt?

(from Angus's, *Newcastle Garland*, 1805, Allan, pp.27–28)

keelboat – 'term used to distinguish a herring drifter of Scottish 'Fifie' type, used in Northumberland in 19th and early 20th century. Also applied in 20th century to trawlers and seine-net boats' (KP, Beadnell). Keelboats were larger wooden vessels designed for deepsea trawler fishing, e.g. the 'Fifie' (1850s), the 'Zulu' (1879), and the single masted 'Holy Island Keelboat'. Thus **fifie** – 'a straight-stemmed, double-ended, C19th, sailing fishing craft of the Scottish east coast held, by some, to originate from the Fife coast; once used in all areas of the east coast herring fishery...built on a conventional vertical-section keel' (AO); 'wooden, heavily built, with a single pole mast and lug sail, and perhaps a Kelvin engine' (JF, Seaham).

iron man – 'a hand-capstan used to haul nets and raise sails on sailing keelboat' (KP, Beadnell).

mule – 'a double-ended coble. Also applied to Scottish double-enders used in Seahouses between the Wars' (KP, Beadnell); "a mule has coble head and body but pointy stern – can be up to 50–60' foot and used for herring fishing, e.g. round Flambrough" (BT, Cullercoats); "a mule is of coble typology, built up from a flat 'ram' plank…. Favoured in the late C19th by pilots for its speed and, in its larger form, for the capacity it afforded fishermen for herring drift nets" (AO); "In place of the square stern she had a part-keel aft, a pointed and raked sternpost" (Mannering & Greenhill, 1997, p.52).

Some fishermen preferred the 'mule coble'. Northumberland mules were usually 40 feet (about 12 metres) in length and had a double-ended hull (bow at each end). It is thought one reason why the mule was sometimes favoured over the coble was because it was more manoeuvrable. This is why it was favoured for particular jobs like drifting for herring.
(http://www.twmuseums.org.uk/fishtales)

The term 'mule', implying a composite form, could well mean a merging of coble and double-ended traditions, or perhaps more generally "the case where a specific boat description has become varied (degraded?) over time" (AO). (It would be handy, but tricky, to invoke the rare Scottish word 'mule' meaning 'something pointed'.) The design fitted a harbour context rather than beach. Two types are recognised: sharp sterned coble – 'Scarborough Mule', also at Filey, Hartlepool; round sterned type (herring mule) Scarborough, Whitby, Bridlington (see Bradley, I, p.24).

salmon coble – From Berwick north, the Tweed salmon coble – same 'tumble-home' as a coble – more of a platform at stern of boat. "Tweed salmon coble has less pronounced forefoot and stem, but flat bottom, clinker build and transom stern, in common with other cobles. Generally 14' if operating in river, 18' if in harbour" (Sanderson, 1969); "Tweed salmon boats more a Scots design" (BT, Cullercoats); 'Scottish Salmon Coble … 15–22ft LOA, rowed only, no rudder, flat upright stern' (Bradley I, p.23).

townie – 'small boat used to ferry herring from keelboat or for salmon fishing. Called a 'towie' at Boulmer' (KP, Beadnell) ["from 'to tow'? a small boat towed behind a larger vessel" (AO)].

trawler – Sailing trawlers were usually keel boats about 32 feet long (9.7 metres), with a wooden hull. The net which was used was a drift net hung down some 10 feet from the surface and could be up to 600 yards (548 metres) in length. (http://www.twmuseums.org.uk/fishtales)

Steam trawlers came to dominate the North Sea fishing industry from their introduction about 1877 – originally paddle steamers – and trawler ports like North Shields and North Sunderland prospered at the expense of smaller traditional fishing villages. By 1885 steam trawling had come to dominate over sail (Hedges 1989, p.20) – by around 1900 the paddle steamer gave way to the screw steamer.

"Screw trawlers were normally outside the pocket of individual fishermen, and so steam fishing companies were set up in major fishing ports" (Godfrey, 1974 p.30). "Steam tugs originally assisted sailing drifters, then Purdy's of Shields used steam tugs to do the actual trawling" (BT Cullercoats).

"Each boat had a crew of ten: the skipper, the mate, third hand, three deckies, the cook, the fireman, two lads… Each trip to sea lasted eight to ten days" (Brook, 2005, p.65, re North Shields).

drifter – 'a small trawler, either team or motor' (FK, Berwick). A twentieth century trawler is likely to be 120–130 ft long, with metal hull and diesel engine. "Some '**rock-hoppers**' – trawlers – can bounce off rocks" (Eric King, Seahouses). "Though steam-powered beam trawling was specifically a North-East 'invention', steam trawling as such was an activity common to most East Coast ports…Sailing trawling was largely a Yorkshire Coast activity" (AO). (For more on trawling, see Part Three.

Trow

A sort of platform boat, with two narrow hulls in "a 'V' plan, paired-boat arrangement", used for salmon fishing on the North Tyne, up to the early nineteenth century. Of the crew, one punted with a **bang**, the other speared salmon with a **leister** [after *The Mariner's Mirror*, 71, 1985, p.337] [< trough – implying origin as log-boats?].

Tugs

"Tyne was the first port to employ steam towage for ships leaving and entering: common there by 1820s" (AO).

There were the tug boats – Lawson-Batey, Frans Fenwick; the Anchor Line, who moored at North Shields; Ridley's tugs, black funnel with three red bands. Joffre, the biggest tug on the Tyne. There was dozens. They used to lie off Tyne Dock Engineering, and Shields, off the buoys there. You'd get tons of stories from the tugboat men, if there's any left. They've all got diesel engines, they were [formerly] steam, coal. Coal was the fuel – all these – where you've got a chimney, you've got a coal fired boiler. Somewhere there would be a heap of coal. But I've never known of a fire on board a one.

(Ernie Keedy, Beamish, 2005/127)

The following account relates to a steam tug, with paddle-wheels, serving in Seaham Harbour:

In March 1939 when I was 16, I started work as 'boy' on the tug *Hardback*, one of two tugs working at the time, the other being *The Seaham*. The *Hardback* (skipper Jack Moffat) was the head tug, *The Seaham* (skipper Tom Smith) the stern tug, for the colliers would be led in by lines at fore and aft. The crew was skipper, mate, engineer, fireman and boy. The engine was a coal-powered steam engine, which drove two paddlewheels: this made the tug very manoeuvrable – it could turn on its own circle. The tug was steel hulled, with the paddles cased in wood. Each paddle could be worked independently, by engaging a lever – but it wasn't that simple, for the direction the paddle would turn depended on where the crank was in its cycle. That defeated most seamen for a start.

The job of the ship's boy was to keep the fo'castle clean, clean the skipper's cabin, to fill the paraffin lamps that served as port and starboard lights etc. (there was no electrics on these tugboats), and to shovel the coal into the stokehole ready for the fireman. I had to help fix the tow-rope and secure it with a clip and a pin, when we picked up a boat. And if nothing else was on hand, I would be set to chip the boat and paint it!

The days of sail were already past, and we did not concern ourselves with small craft: the job of the tugs was to aid the coal-ships to their berths. These colliers were large craft, called **flatties**, and loaded to only 6 inches of freeboard on their journey out. Returning, they would be ballasted with water – how much depended on the expected state of the sea – the water could be pumped out in harbour. Previously, great disks of a black material – a melted iron slag – was often used as ballast, and so ended up on the local beaches here.

When a collier was about 2 miles off Seaham, the pilot cutter would take a pilot out to it. In 1939 there two pilot cutters, *Astarte* and *Lady Romain* (which had a cabin). The pilot would remain in charge during the rest of the approach, and give orders to the tugs. The tugs would take up the tow at about one mile out, and bring the collier through the outer piers, through the tidal gates (sea-gates) on the South Dock, and so on to its very berth. The mechanic for the pilot cutters was pretty well automatically appointed mechanic for the lifeboat, as was Lenny Brown.

The process would be reversed on the collier setting to sea, with the pilot being taken off by the cutter when the collier was well clear.

The Harbour could be entered about 3 hours before high tide and about 1 hour after (or maybe a bit later if a ship was close enough). This meant the tugmen had to work shifts of 4 hours on and 8 hours off, round the clock, for of course there were 2 tides a day – and those changed slightly as each day passed. The job could truly be called 'tidal work'. The tugs would assist as many as 20 boats on each tide, and it was not unknown for a collier to come in, load, and depart, all on the one tide – though that was not very popular with the collier's crew who missed their shore-leave.

The boilers of the tug were filled with fresh water from the quay, but also needed topping up continually, and salt water would be used for that. Accordingly, the boilers needed a good cleaning every 5 or 6 weeks (you could test the water with a salonometer, to check how dense it was getting). This cleaning meant drawing the fire, blowing the water out, and putting fresh water in. It had to be done between tides, so you could end up working a 4 hour shift, followed by 8 hours on the boiler, then another 4 hour shift, straight off.

During the War, big guns were mounted on the top of the bank to defend the docks; it meant moving the old lighthouse. Not that we were a special target. One day a row of bombs fell along the line of the North Pier – but outside it. Three spitfires came up and shot down the German bomber. The lifeboat went out, but could find no trace, not even an oil-slick.

One day, a pilot went aboard a ship that was ready to sail. As he thought, he blew the whistle to give a signal – but pulled on the wire of a parachute flare by mistake. And to everyone's amazement, suddenly a great flare went flying round the dock. Unexpected, that.

Well, I worked on the tugs throughout the 1940s, for 11 years in all. But in the end the strange patterns of the tidal work was too much, considering the pay, and I joined the pits.

The paddle-tugs lasted till the 1950s, when the present type of twin-screw tug took over."

(Based on the words of Joe Henry)

wherry/whurry – 'wherry, large boat; a sort of barge or lighter' (Brockett); 'a wherry is a light sharp boat, used in a river or harbour for carrying passengers from place to place' (Falconer, 1780). "NE (especially Tyne-) wherries were normally of clinker-built (overlapping plank) construction and were general purpose river carriers shifting goods and passengers" (AO).

The wherries took over from the keels, the keels were on the river, it wasn't navigational, the sailing ships had to moor down the lower reaches and the keels used to go into Newcastle to load the coal and come down the Tyne, cast the coal aboard the colliers that went to London or wherever. The wherries had a deeper hold – they've got some in the Museum of

Discovery, the hold is deeper – the keel has a shallow hold, from the gunnels, it's got a high floor to enable the men to cast coal. The hold of a wherry could be that deep – six or seven foot. The keels had a high hold, they were small – I think thirty ton was round about the quantity of coal it carried, so you could cast on to the – it was all manual you know, shovel it off. The wherries were more of a big lift thing, they would make things at Vickers Armstrongs, engine bed, boiler, or something – they were deeper. We had a fleet of wherries, but there was the Newcastle Wherry Company, the Tyne Wherry Company – they worked at the Newcastle end of the river, where the ships used to go to discharge and load, and we did this end of the river.

The work we did, we carried coal, timber and sand in our wherries. And of course these wherries were made of English oak, copper fastened. What used to happen, the yard that used to build wherries, a way before my time, was a firm called Wood Skinners, round about Bill Quay near Richardson's slipway. There was a train service used to go from North Shields to Newcastle and under one of the viaducts there was two men there, the Lindsey brothers, who actually owned part of an oak forest or plantation, they used to plant trees and watch them grow, and trees that had boughs shaped like ribs, they used to grow their trees to as near as they could to the shape of – the ribs being what you called cross grained, the natural growth of the bough…They used to build and repair wherries, they had their place underneath one of the arches, people used to take their boats there if they wanted to repair.

(Ernie Keedy, Beamish, 2005/84)

The descendants of the keelmen looked after the handling of the wherries, but the increase in size and towing by tugs meant the employment of many less men, and these hardy fellow drifted gradually into other employment.

(H.R. Viall, 'Notes', *Mariner's Mirror*, 28, 1942, p.162)

Chapter 7. Navigation

back fu' – 'wind on the wrong side of the sail, a dangerous situation' (KP, Beadnell).

the back o' – 'on the seaward, or far, side of some natural feature or man-made structure, e.g. the ship was driven ashore at the back o' the North Pier' (AO).

brander – 'bollard on pier for mooring ropes' (KP, Beadnell).

broach – 'to be knocked sideways by a sea' (KP, Beadnell).

burning off – 'warning boats not to attempt to enter harbour during bad weather at night by lighting a beacon' (Scarborough) (Godfrey, 1974, p.20).

cadge – 'a small anchor, used for warping a boat' (KP, Beadnell) [cadge/kedge 'to fasten'].

coower – 'to cower or duck the head; of a boat whose bows are too low in the water: "She cowers hor heed"' (KP, Beadnell).

draugs – 'sea anchors: "T'draugs slit reet atweea as wa war cumin' ower a gert sea"' (Umpleby, Staithes, 1930s); **dreg** – 'a sea-anchor, trailed behind boat to slow it down' (KP, Beadnell) [drag].

drive – 'pushing too hard ahead: "He'll end by drivin' under" – he is too forceful, he will wreck himself' (Amble, Newbiggin) (KP).

dunsh [in'], dunch[in'] – "descriptive of a boat's 'slamming' [common nautical term] hard into a head sea, especially when towing alongside a steamer" (AO).

heed-rope – 'mooring rope from bows of boat' (KP, Beadnell).

kenned grund – 'familiar surroundings' (AR, Seahouses).

laggers – 'name given to men who assist with Iaunch of cobles' (Umpleby, Staithes, 1930s).

lanch – '[to] launch' (Umpleby, Staithes, 1930s); **lynch** – 'to launch, usually with 'doon'. 'Lynch up' – to haul a boat up' (KP, Beadnell).

marks – 'landmarks lined up for navigation' (KP, Beadnell).

owil – 'boat requiring assistance' (Umpleby, Staithes, 1930s).

ratch – 'to tack (of a boat, verb and noun)' (KP, Beadnell); ratch = "to reach [verb] or 'ratch', was to sail into or across the wind (modern usage, 'to reach', or 'to be on a reach'); 'ratching', the act of going about (i.e. tacking) through the wind" (AO).

ride – '(of a bow) to stand up in the water. (Of a boat) to lie at anchor' (KP, Beadnell).

run – '(sailing) to sail before the wind' (KP, Beadnell).

run up – 'rope caught round the propeller: "He's run up aboot the Carrs"' (KP, Beadnell).

sea-gate – access by sea: "we have a great sea-gate in a storme" (Scarborough, 1565). Raine from Egerton MS [ON gata means 'way', 'road' not the modern 'gate'].

swat – 'a deeply-laden boat was "gey swat"' (AR, Seahouses) [?squat].

off – 'to or at sea: "gan off' – to go to sea;" "tyek him off' – take him to sea"' (KP, Beadnell).

Suthart – 'south (opp. **Norrard**)' (KP, Beadnell).

tack taakle – 'gear for tacking' (Umpleby, Staithes, 1930s).

tripped – '"A'e sha tripped?", i.e., Has the anchor become liberated ?' (Umpleby, Staithes, 1930s).

trot – 'presumably the same derivation as a common mooring trot: a line, or lines, which are well anchored to the sea/river bottom in open water; vessels mooring to these through a secondary system of fixed lines' (AO).

wetter in – 'enough water to get into harbour: "If ye divvin't get a move on, ee'll no get wetter in"' (KP, Beadnell).

There is not room here to give a proper study of navigation or sailing skills at sea for sailing ships in any form, though a few points about handling a coble are noted above (section 5). One practice, that of lining up 'marks' to recognise a good fishing spot or a safe approach to a harbour, is demonstrated in the following advice on how to find moorings at Coquet Island:

Being to the southward and eastward of the island, and not able to weather it, I should bring the old tower to bear N. ½ W. and steer directly for it until the centre of Warkworth castle come on with the chimney of the old ruin at Amble pans. I should run on with these marks until the old tower bear S.E. by E., at the same time observing not to approach the island nearer than 1¼ cable's length – then anchor.

(Baharie, 1849, p.6)

Away from the coast, the risks were of a different kind – indeed almost anything could befall the unprepared…

A Voyage to Hamburg

In 1835, I joined the Albion brig, of Sunderland, Captain Kirkham, a borther-in-law of mine. We sailed from Seaham Harbour for Hamburh, and when on the Dogger Banks was overtaken with very bad weather, the vessel…sprung a leak, and before we were aware there was about 2 foot of water in the hold. The crew, all told, consisted of the Captain; J.Monkford, mate; W.Errington, able seaman; Atez Keer, cook: myself, shipwright; and two German apprentices; and the captain's wife and daughter. In this predicament, the pumps choked up with small coal, which formed part of her cargo – having drawn the lower boxes and fresh leathered the spear box forty times, using sorts of appliances that my ingenuity could invent, without success. I took the pumps out, lowering the mate, a smart young fellow, head-first down, when he discovered that one of the deals was off the pump well, which was full of coals. Having got the dimensions of the hole, I managed to get it stopped up, when with a dinner plate and buckets we got the coals out, then placing a basket down the well we lowered the pumps and managed to carry the ship in our arms, so to speak, for several days and nights, in awfully tempestuous weather, arriving sadly jaded at Hamburg, where we delivered our cargo…

(Thomas Sanderson, 1873, pp.15–17)

Chapter 8. Pilots

At the end of a voyage, for larger ships nearing harbour, direction would be handed over to a pilot, whose status was enviable enough, if he made no mistakes. Pilots were licensed by Trinity House in Newcastle, and often came to regard the post as virtually hereditary. After a shake-up in the 1860s, the supervision of pilots was transferred to the Board of Trade.

A 'pilot boat' signified a function rather than a specific type. A pilot coble would be typically 25–28 ft LOA; but "mule cobles achieved great popularity with pilots in the 19th century and early 20th century. The already industrialised port of Hartlepool was their spiritual home..." (Cunliffe, 2002, vol.2, p.269). "One of the advantages for pilotage was that mules towed astern of the host vessel more readily than a square-sterned coble; conversely, they didn't beach so easily" (AO).

John Green's *Tales & Ballads of Wearside* (1879) has some interesting dialect material to present on Sunderland. Here, for example, from p.235, is an almost religiously zealous discussion of pilotage fees. The pilot boats would row out from harbour when an incoming vessel was spotted, but there remained the problem of arranging the fee...

Dialogue

Pilot: Now, ye're a man <u>Aw'se</u> proud to see!   I'm
    Mister Gowdy, what's the <u>foy</u> to be?   pilotage fee
Skipper: Well, pilot, if you had your way,
    What would your conscience let you say?
Pilot: <u>One pund one</u> is all Aw wish,   1 guinea
    An' a bit o' beef iv the cobbel dish.
Skipper: Fifteen shillings, you'll understand,
    Is all I give for Sunderland.
Pilot: Fifteen shillings! Disn't thou think sham
    When we've rowed see monny miles frae hyem?
Skipper: Fifteen shillings; I'll pay no more;
    If you don't like it, go ashore.
Pilot: Haul up the cobbel; we <u>winnot</u> stop,   won't

But we'll row tiv Suth'ard till our hands they drop.
Skipper: You'd better change your mind, old boy,
    And take the fifteen shillings foy.
Pilot: Eff others likes ti <u>tak't</u> they may,   take it
    <u>Aw'se</u> off ti Suth'ard, so good day;   I'm
    Aw'se nut like Esau, Mister Gowdy,
    Ti sell my buthreet for a <u>crowdie</u>.   a mess of pottage!

North sea pilots – mottle-faced men in pea-jackets, standing no nonsense from owner or skipper, and brooking contradiction from no man, standing back to back when conversing, and keeping their keen puckered-up eyes always upon 'the offing.'

                                        (Haswell, 1895, p.37)

The authority and infallibility of the pilot inevitably led to some satire. To the following two passages (the second of which is also available in Cunliffe (2002, vol.2, pp.254–55) I have added 'dramatic directions' to the scant text, in the hope you will come to appreciate them as much as they deserve to be.

The Crew by John Stobbs
(in this the pilot is in charge on a sailing vessel entering harbour…)

[everyday orders, shouted to crew on ship he is piloting]
Claw your foretop-garnsail up and stow it: you boys, jump up and stow it.
[notices a slacker, sternly]
Look sharp, lad, what are ye gawn crawlin' up the riggin' that way for?
[confidential, to man at helm, regret over good old days, etc]
Aw shoor aw dinnot knaw what the lads are gettin' to now…
[sarcastically]
…Where do ye get your lads? –
[interrupted]
2nd voice: It's the owner's son. –
[to himself, realising blunder]
O… … … it's the owner's son.
[thinking it over, then to helmsman, jocular, explaining]
Aw didn't knaw it was the owner's son.
[comments loudly and cheerily, to helmsman, but for general consumption]
There's a canny little lad gawn up the riggin look'e. Aw shoor but he is a clever little lad that, gans up like a rat.
[shouting, pleasantly, to lad in rigging]

Mind, dinnot be in ower great a hurry, maw canny little fellow –
[continues, concerned]
mind...! ... keep haud...!
[followed by a little scream and a loud thump?]

The Bear by John Stobbs
(in this, the pilot is attempting to moor a ship, after bringing it safely up the Tyne...)

[loud – orders shouted to distance...]
Pull away there, my lads –
[short pause]
jump aboard of that offside ship and make the end of that line fast for'd –
[to nearby, ordinary level, curious]
Whe's that awd man coming for'd to interfere wi' the men?
[shouted across, superior tone, giving reasonable order]
I say, you awd fellow, cannot you let them make the line fast?
[pause to see effect – no effect – so shouts over to his own men]
Never mind the awd fyul, my clever fellows –
[to nearby, ordinary level, amazed]
I wonder to see two young fellows run away up the riggin' for an awd man like that –
[shouted across, as a challenge]
You obstinate awd fyul ye, if I come aboard to you I'll pull that hairy cap off your head.
[to nearby, exasperated]
I've seen a vast of obstinate awd men like you, but I never saw such an obstinate awd man as that before.
[shouted across]
Cannot you let the men make the line fast now?
[shouted across, losing his temper]
If you'll put off that hairy coat of yours, I'll come aboard and fight you in your shirt-sleeves like a man –
[interrupted by]
2nd voice: Whisht, pilot, pilot; don't you see it's a bear? –
[pause – puts telescope to eye?...]
[astonished]
O! it's a bear, is't!
[excusing himself]
I never thowt a bear was owt like that.
[small pause, is he being made a fool of?]
Are you sure it's a bear?
[2nd character shakes head in assurance; small pause, then acceptance]
Oh! then I warrant you it is a bear.

Part Three: Fishing

Hi Billy
Trawl for Drift for
salmon
Whiteings T netting
monk fish Salmon & grisle
cod
Plaice The salmon season lasts 3 months
Haddock
prawns
Hope this little to you billy
cheers

(Carle Robinson, fisherman)
(In response to my permutational text
'Trawler Race' at www.acknowledgedland.com)

Chapter 1. The fishing calendar

The sort of fish to be caught varies with type of ground, season of year, and long-term variations of stock. One crew would need to tackle different tasks through the year, to keep income up.

A typical traditional fishing year would mean a summer largely spent drifting for herring: shoals of herring would migrate down the east coast of Britain from Shetland southwards, starting as early as the end of May or as late as August, remaining available through to mid October.

Over winter the boats could long-line for cod and other fish till Christmas. Then they could line-fish or go crabbing in smaller cobles, or perhaps go away as crew on the trawlers till Easter. An alternative for middle-sized cobles was to continue long-lining through to February or March then work lobster pots to May. Salmon and trout could be caught from about May to August as they moved inland up the main rivers to breed. Older men, it was reckoned, would stick to working lines or pots from smaller cobles, making use of sites close inshore and easy to reach.

Yet another option was to drag the coble high ashore in the late autumn and sit the winter out... If a family had two cobles, the stronger one would be brought into use for winter work, and the lesser laid up till Spring.

The use of the trawler eclipsed commercial fishing with long lines; while refrigeration and modern rail and road connections have meant a better market for deep sea catch. Chances of catching the cod, haddock and flat fish typical of deep water are considerably improved by echo scanners that identify shoals of fish. Only occasionally do such fish venture into the inshore zone, during the colder months – when storms have stirred the sea-floor and exposed the tiny crustaceans cod feed on.

Trawling brings a more rewarding catch, but implies a bigger vessel, more capital investment, longer trips, etc. so that by a spiral of logic even the sophisticated modern-day trawler is likely to be overtaken by 'fish factory' ships financed by larger companies. Such efficiency has led to the depletion of fish stocks, and it is sad to think that small-scale fishing from the traditional coble has also suffered from this crisis, though it has been innocent of grosser offence.

Cobles and smaller boats have concentrated in recent years on crabs and lobsters, found on the rocky seabeds common off the North-East coast, and fishing with pots now features largely in local agendas.

Chapter 2. Some basic techniques

Methods of fishing have taken many varied forms over the centuries...

The simplest way is to scan rockpools as the tide recedes, and see if fish have been stranded there. They sometimes are.

An equivalent, artificial barrier was a weir, or **yare**, a kind of obstruction across a river; not so much to back water up as hinder fish going downstream. Collected above the weir, such fish could then be speared or netted. This strategy is believed to have been in place since Anglo-Norman times (e.g. from the evidence of place-names in the *Boldon Book*) or earlier.

A substantial and sophisticated man-made weir has been excavated at Hemington Quarry on the River Trent. It takes the form of a submerged dam of oak piles, wattle sheeting and stone blocks. The weir is angled and at the apex the relics of a cone-shaped basket was found to trap the fish (or eels?).

> Higher up the rivers, weirs are formed, by building a dyke across the stream, generally of small size; in this dyke are several apertures, leading to enclosures of different kinds, called **cruives** into which the fish enter, and are taken out at convenience, being unable to find an opening through which to escape.
>
> (Bushnan, 1840, p.181)

Tickling a salmon

I have heard this described as used in streams in North Yorkshire. When a salmon is found in the shade of a stream-bank, a hand is gently introduced to the water to tickle or stroke the fish from below. This seems to pleasure the fish so that it remains still while the hand howks it out onto the bank:

> Tommy was laying on his stomach his head overlooking the bank of the river.
> Just below him in the shade of the bank was the largest Salmon he had ever seen.
> 'What is he doing'?' asked his father.
> 'He is just sort of hovering there,' said Tommy.
> 'Alright lad, let me roll up your sleeve while you keep an eye on our next meal' His dad rolled up Tommy's right sleeve. 'Now lad, gently lower your hand into the water so that it comes alongside the fish, but do not touch it, not yet'.

Tommy did as he was told and the chill of the water ran up his arm.

'Now very gently touch his belly with your finger tips', encouraged his dad. Tommy did so and the fish moved slightly away from his fingers.

'Just follow him keeping your fingers on his belly, he will get used to them. Now lad stroke him ever so gently along his belly, let him think that your fingers are weed'. Tommy was surprised that the fish stayed where it was, and a thrill went through his whole body.

'Now lad lift up your thumb as far as you can so that it comes across his back. 'But dad my hand is to small' whispered Tommy 'It wont go that far".

'All right lad, now bring your fingers together gently so as not to spook him and bring your hand just below his gills'. Tommy did as he was told.

'Now this is the tricky part, when I say now, bring up your hand and toss him onto the bank'.

Tommy's heart was pounding, suppose he made a mess of it, what would his dad think? 'Now' 'said his dad. Tommy lifted the fish with all his might, up and over towards the bank. Dad said not a word, and poor Tommy who had his eyes closed could only guess that he had failed to land the fish. He felt his dad's large hand come down upon his shoulder. Tommy opened his eyes, and there in front of them was the Salmon. He had done it; he had tickled his first Salmon and landed it.

(Robert Harrison on: https://authorsden.com)

trots – a bar or stick of wood with snood (short line) and hook attached:

tratt – 'fishing line used by youths and old men. They bait a line and anchor it to the rocks at low water and at the succeeding low water reclaim it' (Umpleby, Staithes, 1930s).

To put the trots in – a method of fishing from the beach. A trot was placed on the sand at low tide; the suction of the sand buried and held the trot secure; at the next low tide, the trot could be checked to see if a fish was hooked.

(Joe Henry, Seaham)

However, the lazy fisherman might leave trotts in place from tide to tide, forming a risk to paddlers and bathers – so this as a form of fishing has been discouraged.

booler – an iron hoop or perhaps the metal rim of a bicycle wheel, covered with net. A piece of bait would be put in the centre, and cords attached to permit the booler to the lowered and raised in a horizontal plane. The idea was: the unsuspecting lobster would come for his snack; the fisherman would raise the booler from time to time, hoping to catch a lobster in the act.

or:

A simpler trap was made with a square of net raised by lines at each corner, or by a similar 'bag' of netting fitted into the rim of a bicycle wheel. A piece of wood from rim to rim would hold the bait, and the 'booler' would be raised every 20 minutes or so, by lines attached to the wheel rim, to check. Any lobster caught on the thin bit of wood holding the bait would fall into the net as the wheel was raised to the surface.

(Katrina Porteous, 2006)

Lights

"I have heard the way to get to catch salmon was to go out at night and light a brazier on board the coble – to attract the fish to the light"

(JH, Seaham).

blaze – 'to take salmon by striking them at night, by torchlight, with a three-pronged and barbed dart' (Brockett, 1829). This is well recorded as a Borders river practice; EDD – N'd, Yx.

Anglers often used to build fires on the beach when fishing overnight, though surely these were to keep themselves warm.

Even with a simple miner's helmet lamp for company, lone night fishing could be a tadge cheerless. One Easington angler recounted his feelings about fishing on the beach below the cliffs at night: there were always tiny sounds behind him – probably bits of dirt or pebbles slipping from the cliff – but he would spin round and point his helmet lamp, never catching anything moving. In the end, the invisible stirrings unnerved him so much he packed himself off home. Indeed, he would only recount the story on the beach in full daylight.

Snigglin'

snig – 'an eel; hence, to sniggle, to fish for eels' (Brockett, 1829); *EDD* – general.

A primitive method of catching an eel with bait on a bent pin on a line or stick, reaching the eels that shelter during daylight. "There was other catch... Eels could be caught in the South Dock, round the wheels of the paddle-steamers."

(Joe Henry, Seaham)

Other

taum – 'piece of stick with twine and hook used by boys for catching pennock, etc.' (Umpleby, Staithes, 1930s) [strictly *tawm* equals fishing line – ON *taumr* 'cord'].

hyeukkin' – 'hand-lining without bait. Also **jiggin'**, **rippin''** (KP, Beadnell).

cleek – 'long stick with a barbed hook, used by poachers' (Jim Cromarty, Spittal/Berwick); *EDD* – Sc, N'd.

Chapter 3. Hand line

The word angler derives, of course, from the 'angle' or hook at the end of the line...

croon – 'the top end of the hyeuk, where it was tied to the sneyd' (KP, Beadnell).

gaad – 'a fishing rod' (AR, Seahouses); gaa'd – 'rod, as of fishing rod' (KP, Beadnell) [goad].

gib a the hyeuk – 'barb on hook which stops the fish from getting away' (KP, Beadnell).

hemp on – 'to unfasten snoods on lines' (KP re Amble/Newbiggin).

hyeuk – 'hook, noun and verb' (KP, Beadnell); **heeak** – 'hook' (Umpleby, Staithes, 1930s); compare **yuck**.

hyeutter – 'the barb on a fish-hook: "hyeuk ower the hyeutter"' (KP, Beadnell).

jiggin' – 'hooking for fish with hand-line; cf. **hyeukin**', **rippin**', etc.' (KP, Beadnell); *EDD* re jig – N.I.

ripper – 'a metal lure/spinner' (NJ, re Tyneside).

sneyd, sneed – '**snood**, attaching hook to line' (KP, Beadnell); snood 'short extension of fishing line' (GR, Amble); **sneud/snud/snood** – 'the short piece of twisted hair or cord to which the hooks are attached in a fisherman's line' (Heslop) [OE sn d 'item made of hair']; *EDD* – Sc.

sprowl – 'wire on a hand-line sinker' (KP, Beadnell).

taum – 'fishing line' (Dinsdale, 1849, Tees); tawm – 'a line, especially a fishing line' (Atkinson, 1868, Cleveland); **taam/tawm/towm** – 'a rod line of hair for fishing' (Heslop, 1880s); **tam** – 'a fishing line' (*Bell-White MS 12*); **tawm, tome, tam** – 'a fishing line: "a long twine tam"' (Brockett, 1829); **taw** – fishing line: "i taw pro piscaria" (Scarborough, 1452 via York, *BL MS Egerton 2868*); tawm – 'a fishing line made of hair' (Bailey, 1810, D'm); tome – 'a hair line for fishing' (Cumberland) (Grose, 1787) [ON *taumr* 'cord, line'].

whither – 'the small bent part at end of a fishing hook' (Umpleby, Staithes, 1930s).

yucker – 'hooker of fish, angler'; **yucking boat** 'anglers' boat' (MS, Cullercoats).

The traditional fishing line, prior to the manufacture of synthetic twines, was made of horse hair, if you dared...

B'd Ah finnd ed Ah's wandther'n' fra mi subject, ez oor Peter sed te Jack Featherston's gallowa' [pony] when it streaik em ower twee dykes 'n' o lonnen [struck him over two hedges and a lane], ez t'say'n' is, 'n' he fell belly-flowght on t'grund like a spanghew'd frosk [tossed frog], when he wes pull'n' horse-hairs oot ed tail te mak fish'n' towms [lines] on, b'd he dudn't plet [plait] ony towms that summer, Ah can tell ye, fer that kick knock'd a' his fish'n' idees oot ov his heed, if he iver had ony, 'n' he ga' [gave] his plett'n' sticks te Tommy's Joe's lad te lake [play] wuth. B'd let's te mi knitt'n'...

(Egglestone, Letter to the Queen, 1877)

The hand line, with rod, is the badge of the angler who decorates many a beach or pier around the region. The following word list is from Norman Conn of the Seaham Angling Club:

ripper – 'a large metal lure with two or more single hooks attached'.

spinner – 'a small metal lure with treble hook attached'.

jigger – 'similar to 'ripper' but with large treble hook attached'.

yeuk – 'hook'.

cat-gut – 'monofilament fishing line (today)'.

pennel – 'a hook used above another hook on a length of line'.

sneddin – 'a length of line to attach hook'.

plunder – 'a lead weight for end of main fishing line'.

sinker – as above.

spider – 'a lead weight that incorporates 3" wires (spider's legs?) to hold sandy bottom'.

back-lash – 'a run of line from reel that goes back under the reel causing tangle problems'.

bird's nest – 'a tangle of line on reel whether a 'back-lash' or other cause'.

fast – 'end gear of fishing line stuck in rocks or other obstruction' [OE *fæst* 'secure, fixed'].

snagged – as above.

cast – 'throw line out using rod' [Northern word preference to 'throw'].

shocker – 'a length of strong line attached to main line to assist casting'.

knock – 'a fish bite registering on rod tip (tap, tap, tap)'.

a take – 'a fish swallowing the bait'.

doubler – 'two fish on a single line using two hooks'.

Chapter 4. Long line

back – 'a fishing line used for haddock, etc. at sea... the principal line to which snoods are spliced, each snood being attached to a hook by a hair line' (Heslop, 1829).

balk, baulk or bawk – 'fishermen's line before hooks are affixed. Called *line-balk* when hooks have been attached. *Baited line* when hooks are baited. *Ceeav'd line*' when old bait has been removed' (Umpleby, Staithes, 1930s).

beeat – 'prepare' [sic]: "The've gone ti beeat a line"' (Umpleby, Staithes, 1930s) [bait].

ceeav'd line – 'line from which old bait has been removed' (Umpleby, Staithes, 1930s) [either from cave 'to empty' or cave 'to separate out'].

dog-'eeads – 'dog-heads. Repairs to fishing line that are not spliced' (Umpleby, Staithes, 1930s) [head in sense of projecting out?].

feeak – 'miss. Also steal. When the fisherman is fastening the snuds (with hook) to baulk (22 score and ten hooks to a new line), he measures the distance between each hook thus: heeak, heeak, feeak, i.e. miss one; i.e. tweea an' a feeak; "ther's nut monny 'es a heeak an 'a feeak."' (Umpleby, Staithes, 1930s) [?fake].

graith – 'horsehair used as part of sneyd on long-lines' (KP, re Holy Island); *EDD* – Sc, 'thread'.

grutlins – 'great lines, baited with herring and used in earlier times to catch cod, skate and ling' (KP, Beadnell).

hau'f-piece – 'standard length of fishing line (30 fathoms); 13 half-pieces to the line' (Umpleby, Staithes, 1930s).

kelkin' – 'the knot fastening the snud to the fishing line: "hing it i' t'kelkin'"' (Umpleby, Staithes, 1930s).

key – 'to fasten up hooks on sneyds of long line to make them safe when finished for the year' (KP, Beadnell).

kidged – 'twisted round the snud' (Umpleby, Staithes, 1930s).

lines – 'usually refers to long-lines, baited with mussels and limpets in winter-time to catch white fish. Cf. 'summer lines', baited with ragworm (KP, Beadnell).

middle fleets – 'anchors every two lines on fleets of long lines at Newbiggin. Not used at Beadnell' (KP).

owerlie – 'placing baited hooks on neb of skep' (Umpleby, Staithes, 1930s).

ower heeaks, ower-'eeaks – 'large hooks, i.e. cod hooks as distinct from haddock hooks (40 used to line)' (Umpleby, Staithes, 1930s).

pap lines – 'lines baited with rock anemones (sookers)' (Umpleby, Staithes, 1930s).

perrin – 'a bobbin, such as was used to fasten hooks onto snoods for long lines. "A perrin a threed"' (KP, Beadnell) [cotton-reel].

piece – 'a length of a long-line carrying 100 hooks' (KP, Beadnell).

riddy ricknors – 'ready reckoners; snuds with hooks affixed: "if wa ax'd for a heeak an' a sneead the' wadn't knaw what wa wanted, but if wa a for a riddy-ricknor the' knaw what wa want" (Umpleby, Staithes, 1930s).

ripper – 'cross-pole carrying double hand-line' (KP, *WW*, Beadnell) [C20th Scots for the fishing line itself].

settin' a line – 'fixing sneeads to baulk; preparing a line' (Umpleby, Staithes, 1930s).

skep – 'willow pallet on which a baited long line was coiled' (Hill & McKee, 1978) [ON *skeppa*].

snuds, sneeads (formerly of horse-hair.) – 'short lengths of line with hook attached which are affixed to the fishing line proper (baulk)' (Umpleby, Staithes, 1930s) [OE *snædan* 'to cut'].

stilshon – 'knot used to tie sneyds onto grutlins, i.e. a clove hitch, twisted with an ordinary knot' (KP, Beadnell)

strunt – 'cutting snuds off fishing line' Umpleby, (Umpleby, Staithes, 1930s) [to dock or cut short].

swill not **skep** 'frame for winding baited line' (FT, Cullercoats); **swull** – 'shallow basket, flat at one end, used to hold long line and also herring' (KP, Beadnell); **swole** – box or frame for lines (GR, Amble); 'lines were carefully coiled on to a flat wicker work or wooden tray called a **swill** or skip (Yx + Nd), or *rip* (Hartlepool)' (Bradley, 2, p.31) [OED *swill*, C14 N and EA]; *EDD* – *swill* Nth, EA.

tin man – 'protection for arm when shooting lines (also a Scottish term)' (KP, Beadnell).

waa'-knot – 'wall knot, used to fasten pieces of long line' (KP, Beadnell).

wants – (noun) 'a hook missing on long line. Also "a back wants" – both for a hook missing off a long line, and for something missing intellectually' (KP, Beadnell).

whippin' – 'affixing hooks to snuds' (Umpleby, Staithes, 1930s).

Long line fishing was conducted from boats, as a more commercial version of simple angling with a rod. Its drawback is the time and trouble preparing the lines, and the technique has been little used since the 1950s, due to the time and effort needed for baiting and recovering the lines and the more effective fishing of trawler nets.

Or if your were using them [the cobles] for lines, well you shot your lines out of them and you hauled your lines in with them and that was it. If you were clever enough you shot on a jib: you just used to run and let your lines go out at the same time, which was pretty skillful; you had to be very careful what you were doing [so] you didn't get hooked up.

(Bart Taylor, Cullercoats)

There would be about 600 hooks on a line. When the boat was off-shore, the fishing line with a lead weight (sinker) would be played out, and allowed to lie on the sea bed for about half an hour, before being pulled in.

(Jim Cromarty, Spittal)

…It was winter and the men were long-line fishing, my dad out for the day in his coble with my brother Daniel and coming back in after dark, his beard gone to ice and my job to bring him a bowl by the fire, and he'd hunch over while I held it and watched the ice melt, drip, drip, drip, till the bowl had a puddle.

(F. Shaw, 2003, per *OED*)

The following fuller account is reconstructed from the words of Joe Henry, a Seaham fisherman:

I started fishing with my Dad in 1936 or 1937, when I would have been 13 year old. He had moved to Seaham from Harwich where his Dad had been coxswain of the lifeboat. In the 1930s there would have been about 32 fishing boats in the North Dock, but not all of them professional fishermen: Sammy Wright and his son, Jackie Jobling, and Pop Noble and Alan Noble from Easington – they were full-time fishermen I recall. There would have been about 13 pilots as well, working their boats out of the South Dock.

My Dad bought an ex-pilot boat, called *The Thankful*; he renamed it *The Amble*. It had no engine at that time, just mainsail and jib; and oars of course. It was a 29 foot 6 inch mule, with a 10 foot beam; copper-fastened up to the waterline. The rudder was 10 foot 6 inches; an extra extension to the tiller had to be put on when an engine was installed, so that one person could handle the tiller and engine controls while the second attended to fishing. The first engines came out of secondhand cars, so were petrol engines, but we didn't fit one of them ourselves until 1938 or so. We also reused the car-horn (as a fog signal)! The first fishing boats in Seaham to have engines were the *Expert* and the *Black Wagon*; they had Kelvin engines. There was a special ration of pink petrol during the war – strictly for the boats only.

Long lines would have to be prepared beforehand. We would send away (collectively) for bags of mussels from Boston; they would be delivered to Seaham Station, and cost 6/9d for a bag weighing about 8 stone. We would use maybe three bags a month. The mussels would have to be shelled with a knife and fitted onto the hooks, then the hooks and line were wound round and round on a flat wooden tray for carrying down to the boat. We would set off about 2 or 3 am in the morning, from Viceroy Street, with the trays holding the line balanced on our heads, and you had to be careful not to get them snagged on anything. I remember my Dad setting off once with his boots tied round his neck, bare-footed, in the snow - maybe he thought he got a better grip that way.

Our boat was moored at the south-east corner of the North Dock; we got down to it by a set of steps – you can still see them on the cliff above the old tunnel, they're not used now at all. Then the lines would be lowered carefully into the boat. The harbour was not so silted up then as it is now; and there was more water over the bar. That meant you could work longer each side of the tide, and cross the bar in rougher weather, for even in big swells the waves were less likely to break over the bar given the greater depth of water. As soon as we could, we would hoist the sails and use wind-power to move us to our fishing-ground.

Everyone had their own favourite spots. It depended a bit what fish you were after. Haddock could be found almost anywhere; cod liked a rocky bottom; ling could be found by deep holes like those just south of Sunderland, by the gasometers; local landmarks could be used to fix special sites, like the gates of Seaham Hall, or you might line up Well Rocks with some chimney inland, or Caterpillar Wood with the towers of Dawdon Colliery, and so on.

We would fish with long line in the winter, for cod, haddock, jumbo whities; in those days a north-east wind predominated in the winter; the cod would come in close to the shore in cold spells, they liked to feed off the stuff that was stirred up off the bottom by the rough weather. In the summer, it was mackerel, whities, gurnads (red or black), colies, dew fish (I think they are the same as bream, red or green, with thick 'lips'), maybe a bit cod, some ling – the herring was generally not worth bothering with. The summer gear did not need much preparation, but in winter, you understand, there was a lot to get ready. For a start there was the hemp, that had to be stiffened a little by submerging in a bath of water in which bark had been steeped (the process was called 'barking'). The long line itself was made up of so many 'pieces'. Each piece held 125 hooks, size 18 haddock hooks to be exact, on a snood (that's a short line of cotton) 18 inches long, spaced 40 inches apart, so they could not foul each other. A long line could contain some six pieces joined together; there would be a dhan-end or buoy at each end, and next to that a 'watcher' made of corks where the long line dipped. Two or three 'anchors' kept the baited length of the line near the sea-bed for bottom-feeders like cod.

Paying the line out was called 'shooting', recovering the line 'hauling in'. This was done with a jerk so the fish would come free of the hook and land in the boat, all with the one movement. Well, if you had a reasonable catch, the next thing was get back sharpish to the dock, say by about 9am to be first in the market, in the prime of the morning. The fish was all sold locally, you just displayed it along the rails at the top of the dock.

Mode of Fishing at Scarborough

When the fishermen go out to fish in the Cobles, each person is provided with three lines. Each man's lines are fairly coiled upon a flat oblong piece of wicker-work, the hooks being baited, and placed very regularly in the centre of the coil. Every line is furnished with 280 hooks, at the distance of six feet two inches from each other. The hooks are fastened to the lines upon sneads of twisted horse hair, 27 inches in length.

When fishing, there are always three men in each coble, and consequently nine of these lines are fastened together and used as one line, extending in length near three miles, and furnished with 2,520 hooks. An anchor and a buoy fixed at the first end of the line, and the same at the end of each man's lines; in all, four anchors, which are commonly perforated stones, and four buoys made of leather or cork. The line is always streched across the current. The tides of flood and ebb continue an equal time upon our coast, and when undisturbed by winds, run each way about six hours. They are so rapid, that the fishermen can only shoot and haul their lines at the turn of the tide; therefore the lines always remain upon the ground about six hours. As the same rapidity of tide prevents their using hand-lines, two of the people commonly wrap themselves in the sail, and sleep while the other keeps a vigilant watch, for fear of being run down by ships, and to observe the weather, for storms often rise so suddenly, that it is with extreme difficulty they escape to the shore, often leaving their nets behind...

(Hinderwell, 1798, pp.227–28)

Chapter 5. Bait

arseband – 'band attached to rear of fishermen's skep' (Umpleby, Staithes, 1930s).

back beean –'main hazel of a skep' (Umpleby, Staithes, 1930s) [backbone].

baities – 'fisher girls who gather bait' (Heslop, 1880s).

bullet – 'a crab that is in the first stage of peeling but still too hard to use as bait' (NC, Seaham).

doggers – 'green crabs' (Umpleby, Staithes, 1930s); dogger – 'small crab, or tab end, cigarette end' (Alf Sterling/H'pool); 'small inedible shore crab' (H'pool, 2005); 'small crab for bait when fishing' (Alan Geggie/Ashington); 'dogger – green crab (Beadnell); **Tommy dogger** (Holy Island) (KP).

flithers – 'limpets or anything similar used for bait' (GR, Amble); flithers – 'limpets. Flither gatherers used to all dress alike and travel as far as Saltburn and Robin Hood's Bay, in the early davs afoot and later by train, returning on the rocks gathering flithers on the way' (Umpleby, Staithes, 1930s); *EDD* – Yx; *flitters*, I.o.M.

gingers – 'a specie of lugworm, small and light brown in colour' (NC, Seaham).

howk – 'dig' (KP, *WW*, Beadnell).

latney – 'a crab that has peeled and starting to turn hard' (NC, Seaham).

lug / lug-worm – 'the thick, hairy sand worm, *Lumbricus marinus*, used for bait...for white fish' (Heslop, 1880s) [source uncertain].

maddie – 'a small wriggling ragworm' (NC, Seaham).

muck (verb) – 'to remove stinking bait from lines' (KP, Beadnell).

neb-band – 'band at neb (head) of skep' (Umpleby, Staithes, 1930s) [neb 'nose'].

peeliers [sic] – 'tiny young crabs with immature shell that can he peeled off. Used for bait' (Umpleby, Staithes, 1930s); **peelers** – (Seaham); 'peelers or doggers – bait crabs' (Eric King, Seahouses); **pillan** – 'small green-coloured sea crab, used as bait' (Heslop, 1880s); **pillin** – 'a green crab when soft or peeling (Beadnell); **pullin** (Holy Island)' (KP, Beadnell); *EDD* – *peeler*, Sc, Ire.

picker – 'sharp iron blade used to remove limpets from rocks for bait' (KP, Beadnell).

raggy – 'ragworm, used for bait on summer lines' (KP, Beadnell); (Seaham per BG) [ON rogg 'strip of fur or hair'].

runny-down – 'large black lug, gutted and usually frozen down for winter bait' (NC, Seaham)

skaning – 'cleaning limpets for use as bait' (GR, Amble); **skenning** than **skaning** – re knife on mussels (BT, Cullercoats); **skeyn** – 'to shell (of mussels and limpets for bait)' (KP, Beadnell); **skane** – 'taking mussels out of shells' (Umpleby, Staithes, 1930s); *EDD* – nYx only, but see *OED* s.v. *skene* where Scots Gaelic links. Plus: "[the women] had to skairn (open) the mussels" (Brook, 2005, p.58).

red, **rehd**, **reed** – 'clear, tidy, unravel. "Red the lines" – clear the hooks' (KP, Beadnell).

shale – 'to peel, to shell' (Brockett); **sheel** – 'to shell' (Heslop); **skeel** – 'to shell' (Heslop).

shiftin' mussels up – 'changing the water that mussels are kept in' (Umpleby, Staithes, 1930s).

slavverlinin' – 'baiting with flithers (limpets)' (Umpleby, Staithes, 1930s).

softies – 'tiny crabs before shell appear' (Umpleby, Staithes, 1930s).

swill – 'wicker basket used by flither pickers' (Umpleby, Staithes, 1930s).

whites – 'a species of ragworm but white in colour and very scarce, excellent bait' (NC, Seaham).

yellow tail – 'a species of black lugworm with yellow tail, a prize bait' (NC, Seaham).

And did she used to have to go out and dig bait, you know, get bait for the lines? Fishing lines?

Oh it was brought in, from different places, it was the mussels but if you had to get the limpets for to go with the mussel's, you had to go to the rocks and pick them. You had to take the little picks with you and they used to have handles on them, little steel picks. You used to go and pick them off the rocks and put them into baskets, fetch them back and get them all shelled up, see you could take a teaspoon, a teaspoon and take them out of the shell that way, you get them out and bait the lines and the mussels, mix them through with the mussels and bait your lines with that.

(Mrs Libby Grant, Eyemouth, Beamish, 1980/192)

My father was born in 1902 into a fishing family in Spittal. As a boy, he had to dig for lug worms on the shore, also limpets and mussels to bait the fishing lines. He used to tell me, in the winter, it was so cold, he used to pee on his hands to thaw them. My grandmother would bait the lines into a **swull** (an open basket). Grass was used to separate the layers of line. There would be about 600 hooks on a line.

(Jim Cromarty, Spittal)

The baited [long-] lines had to be carefully laid in **swills** which were baskets rounded at one end where the main line was coiled, and flattened at the other where the baited lines were laid either on a bed of sand or grass to prevent the hooks getting snagged when the line was being paid out from the boat. The swills were made with willow twigs but later on men got lazy and made them out of wood. My father [born 1849] used to make two swills every winter for the next season…

(Jack Stewart, b. Alnmouth, 1889)

(and see earlier, under *Long Line* – Joe Henry)

Chapter 6. Nets

General

bab-net – 'a net used on the N'd coast: "in fishing for sea trout off rock ends they use a bab-net of 5 inch mesh"' (Heslop, 1832).

bark – (verb) 'to preserve with tannin from oak bark (noun) or cutch. Bark-pots – boiling pots with fireplaces for barking. Adj: barky' – (KP); **barking** – 'tanning fishing gear and nets' (Umpleby, Staithes, 1930s).

clauve – 'placing of line hooks between two short hazels to prevent snuds or sneeads being barked (tanned)' (Umpleby, Staithes, 1930s).

cutch – 'bark (from Indonesia), formerly used to preserve ropes and nets' (KP, Beadnell). See also under Sails.

fest'ner – 'obstacle which snags nets and ropes on sea-bed (often a wreck)' (KP, Beadnell).

flew –'a kind of fishing net: "flew cum warrap and flot"' (Scarborough, 1391 via York in *BL MS Egerton 2868*).

gaxon – 'a line with alternate corks and stones, used to zig-zag up and down from sea bed in nineteenth century' (KP, Beadnell).

heckwases – [?nets]: "rawe webbes [or] woven netts [or] hekwases" (c.1490, Ripon per *BL MS Egerton 2868*).

hingin's – (noun) 'twine attaching net to tow (south of Beadnell). Called a 'hoppin' at Beadnell, 'norsel' or 'ossel' in East Anglia' (KP, Beadnell).

lap – 'to overlap ends of nets, tying rather than sewing them, so that they can be removed easily' (KP, Beadnell).

lint – 'main part of net' (KP, Beadnell).

nussel – 'norsel, a short rope attaching a net to its head rope, whereby the net is set to its proper length and depth' (Hill & McKee, 1978) [OE *nostle* 'band'].

slump – 'plankton on nets (Cullercoats, not north Northumberland)' (KP, Beadnell).

hand-barra – 'a tray with two long handles, used by two men to carry heavy gear such as nets' (KP, Beadnell).

needle, netting-needle – 'a flat piece of wood, bone or plastic with an eye and tongue cut into it, used with shuttle to knit nets' (KP, Beadnell).

shoot (of pots, lines or nets) – 'to set' (KP, Beadnell).

shuttle – 'flat stick used to make 'mash' when knitting nets' (KP, Beadnell).

trammell – "a fishing nett called a tramell" (Hollinedge/Bradfield, 1667 in *BL MS Egerton 2868*); "net with strong sides, useful trawling for cod" (PA, Seaham)

wus (noun) – 'dregs, left-overs from last boiling of bark pot' (KP, Beadnell).

Beach nets

back metal – 'one of the anchors on the beach-nets' (KP, Beadnell).

beach, on the – 'fishing for sea-trout and salmon with anchored 'hyeuk' or 'T' net on the shore. **Beach-nets** – the nets used for this' (KP, Beadnell).

black net – 'straight part of salmon beach net running from shore; also **runnin' net'** (KP, Beadnell).

hyeuk-net – 'L-shaped net with trap or 'hyeuk' in one end, used for trout-fishing on the beach at Beadnell; essentially half a T-net' (KP, Beadnell).

runnin' net – 'straight part of salmon beach-net running from shore. Also known as the black net' (KP, Beadnell).

stell – 'fishing stations at the mouth of the Tweed, e.g. Hallowstell, Sandstell' (Jim Cromarty, Spittal/Berwick); 'a place in a river provided with arrangements for spreading salmon-nets' (*OED*); stell – "until recently, large numbers of salmon were also caught in hand-hauled nets from 'stells' or fishing stations on the river Tweed and at its mouth at Spirral" (KP, 2005); stell – 'artificial mound of rocks for fishing' (FK, Berwick) [ONorthumbrian *staello*].

T-net – 'T-shaped salmon beach net with both a flood and an ebb-tide 'hyeuk', as used at Boulmer and Amble' (KP, Beadnell).

At Amble a traditional method, believed to go back at least to the sixteenth century, was employed by one or more boats to encircle a catch of fish: "A boat took one end of the net out into the sea in a wide arc then back to the beach. The nets worked most successfully when set a long way out but their feet weighted so they touched the bottom and their head buoyed at the surface" (Hutchinson, 1994, p.133).

Drift and trawl nets

booy – 'buoy' (Umpleby, Staithes, 1930s).

cod-end – 'bag of a trawl net' (KP, Beadnell).

dan – 'buoy'; **dan-leet** – 'buoy.light' (Umpleby, Staithes, 1930s); **dand** – 'a buoy...an inflated bag of tanned skin [dogskin?] through which a light pole was passed...' (March, 1970, I, 96).

to drive – 'drivin' (the) drift-netting' (KP, Beadnell).

hummock – 'buoy for nets' (Umpleby, Staithes, 1930s).

leed-rope – 'lead-weighted rope on bottom of net. Also **sole-rope'** (KP, Beadnell).

mash – 'mesh; "stolen mashes" – attenuated meshes, made to narrow a trawl net to the cod end' (KP, Beadnell).

messenger – 'bottom rope on fleet of herring drift nets (term used beyond Northumberland)' (KP, Beadnell).

powl nett – 'pole net: the first net shot'; compare 'bowl start – bowl to mark commencement of sheeting' (shooting) (Umpleby, Staithes, 1930s).

shot – 'the catch; each attempt at drift-netting: 'w' got six the forst shot' (KP, Beadnell).

sole-rope – 'weighted bottom rope on net' (KP, Beadnell).

swing – 'end of messenger rope, mooring drift-nets to boat' (KP, Beadnell).

taadin' – 'tiding. Resting at sea: waiting period between shooting lines and hauling them in' (Umpleby, Staithes, 1930s).

tow (verb) – 'to trawl' (KP, re Amble).

monk – 'funnel-shaped trap sewn into bag of salmon-net at Boulmer' (KP, Beadnell).

winkie – 'a wooden float with a light on the end used to mark salmon nets at the night driving' (KP, Beadnell).

And they had nets as well didn't they and she would have to knit nets?

Mend the nets, yes, er what they called the drift nets. And er sometimes they got them torn and you used to have to mend them, you know, put them up and I used to give my mother and them a hand with that. I was'nt very old when one day I says to her, I wonder if I could learn to do that now and she says "well have a try". And I was quite pleased because I could do it and I think I was on all day fair pleased with myself, sitting with the needle and the scissors on my, on my fingers like this and just kept it flat like that and the needle and then nicked it off at the end when you was finished, fair pleased because I could do that, I thought that was great.

(Mrs Libby Grant, Eyemouth, Beamish, 1980/192)

Drift nets have been in use in the salmon and herring fishery from at least the fourteenth century (see Hutchinson, 1994, p.133). In the modern era they were favoured for surface (pelagic) fish (herring, mackerel, sprats, pilchards, salmon):

The nets are usually 'shot' in the evening, and the ship then rides at her nets. Herrings generally feed and become active at night. They swim in shoals, strike the net and catch their gills in the meshes. About dawn next morning the net or 'fleet' is hauled in, and the drifter steams back to port.

(Coulthard, 1934, p.124)

For bottom (demersal) fish like cod, haddock and the flat fishes a trawl net is used: the trawl funnels the fish into a 'bag' and is drawn along behind the boat. (See Chapter 16 Trawling.)

Chapter 7. Ropes

becket – a loop of rope, such as that attached to pot (also known as bridle) (KP, Beadnell).

beckets – 'any thing used to confine loose ropes, tackles, oars, or spars, in a convenient place…beckets are either large or short pieces of rope, with a knot on one end and an eye in the other, or formed like a circular wreath' (Falconer, 1780).

bend (verb) – 'to tie or fasten, of ropes, etc. Also 'bend on'. "Bend on thon creeve", "The lines is bent t'gither" (KP, Beadnell).

bite – 'a loop in a rope' (KP, Beadnell).

bridle – 'a loop of rope, such as that attached to pot (see 'becket')' (KP, Beadnell).

fake, fyek – 'a coil, loop or hank of rope. Also verb, to fyek it – to take a loop in it' (KP, Beadnell); **fake/flake** a rope or line, 'i.e. to lay it out in coils or set pattern in order that it will run freely' (AO); hence **arsefyek** – 'a coil that comes out of line' (KP, WW, Beadnell); 'an arse-about fake' (AO); *EDD* – *faik* 'to fold or tuck up', Sc,Yx.

fid – 'spike used for splicing rope' (KP, Beadnell).

fool – 'foul, tangled, caught (of rope). 'Fool tows'. 'Fool groond' is rough ground on which ropes catch' (KP, Beadnell).

gash – 'slack (in a rope)' (Craster) (KP).

hitch – 'clove-hitch, the most commonly-used knot, cf. half-hitch, rollin' hitch' (KP, Beadnell).

jinny, jeanny – 'a rope-roller' (KP, Beadnell).

plet – 'plaited up, twisted, ravelled (as with lines). "Tows [ropes] was aa' plet up"' (KP, Beadnell) [plaited].

string-knott – 'knotts to indicate which part of the line is in hand, e.g. 'string knott,' 'half-piece string knot,' etc. (Umpleby, Staithes, 1930s).

strop – 'short rope tied to pot-tow' (Umpleby, Staithes, 1930s).

swings – 'forrud ropes of coble' (Umpleby, Staithes, 1930s).

tagareen – marine stores (Heslop, 1880s); *EDD* – N'd,Yx.

tow (noun, rhymes with now) – 'a rope' (KP, Beadnell) [C14 tow – fibre or strand of a rope, cf. NE tarry towt].

waps – 'rough flannel with thumb-hole for maintaining grip of lines. These are named **dog-cleeats** at Filey' (Umpleby, Staithes, 1930s).

whup (verb) – 'whip, lash, fasten. **Whuppin's** (noun) – fastenings, bindings' (KP, Beadnell).

Chapter 8. Lobster and crab pots

BeadnDookas – 'large floats'; corky dookas' (KP, Beadnell).

becket – 'a loop of rope, such as that attached to pot (also known as bridle)' (KP, Beadnell).

brailor – 'net on a long pole for scooping fish aboard. See also: didle, fish-stop, kep-net' (KP, Beadnell).

breeadin' – 'making a crab-pot' (Umpleby, Staithes, 1930s).

bridle – 'a loop of rope, such as that attached to pot (see 'becket')' (KP, Beadnell); bridle – 'string attached to crab-pot to steady it' (Umpleby, Staithes, 1930s).

Bob an' Wully – 'a lobster pot with a soft flap entrance to act as a trap; called after Bob and Willy Liddell' (KP, Beadnell); Bob n Wally – 'dual purpose net' (EK, re Beadnell).

bow (rhymes with 'now') – pot-buoy. "Bows is doon." **Steeky-bow** – small version of dan, making end of single fleet of creeves' (KP, Beadnell).

bow (rhymes with 'now') – 'curved frame of crab or lobster pot. "A fower-bowed string-eyed creeve"' (KP, Beadnell).

bull – 'supporting piece of wood in bottom of a creeve' (KP, Beadnell).

bunches – 'foul tows and pots jumbled up after heavy seas' (KP, Beadnell).

cover – 'net which covers crab or lobster pot. "Stephen's i' the hut, knittin' covers"' (KP, Beadnell).

corrk bunches – 'corks used as guides to pots' (Umpleby, Staithes, 1930s).

crab eye – 'for crabs, the creive has a 'crab eye' i.e. simple pattern for entry, as aim to catch as many as possible' (EK, Seahouses).

crab-creeves – pots for crabs (EK, Seahouses).

crab-sticks – 'sticks to measure size of crabs' (Umpleby, Staithes, 1930s).

creel – 'crab or lobster pot, Holy Island only. Elsewhere, a basket carried on the back' (KP, Beadnell) [?OFr *greille* 'wickerwork'].

creeve, creuve – 'a crab or lobster trap; **crab-creeves** – pots for crabs (Heslop, N'd, 1890s)

creeve – 'crab or lobster pot (Seahouses, Beadnell, Boulmer and Amble only)' (KP); creives – 'actual pots for crabs/lobsters' (EK, Seahouses); *EDD* – N'd.

creeve-stone – 'stone with waist cut into it, tied into creeve as a weight to sink it' (KP, Beadnell).

dhan – 'float for line of lobster pots' (FT, Cullercoats; BG Seaham); "At Cullercoats, a **dand** or buoy, marked the place where nets or lines were cast" (March, 1970, I, p.96); dan – 'a large marker buoy at the end of several fleets of pots' (KP) (OED) 1685+ (*dann*).

door –' laced opening in crab or lobster pot through which catch is removed' (KP, Beadnell).

end-styen – 'weight at end of fleet of pots' (KP, Beadnell).

eye – 'way in to crab or lobster pot, as opposed to 'door', through which catch is removed' (KP, Beadnell); 'eyes rather than spouts' (GD, Parkside).

flaggy-bow – 'buoy with flag marking end of fleet of pots' (KP, Beadnell).

fleet – 'a string of pots or drift nets' (KP, Beadnell); fleet – '52 crab pots: "wa've lost tweea fleet o' pots this summer up ti noo"' (Umpleby, Staithes, 1930s).

hummel (noun) – 'a float (Holy Island)' (KP).

lat – 'a lath or strip of wood. Cross-wise strips on base of creeve' (KP, Beadnell).

leet'nins – 'corked line affixed to tows for potting and fishing' (Umpleby, Staithes, 1930s).

markin'-iron – 'iron brand with initials used to identify pots' (KP, Beadnell).

monk not spout – 'entry to crab pot' (FT, Cullercoats).

o'erhaal, owerhaal – 'to shoot crab pots one by one as they are hauled, rather than stowing the fleet aboard the boat before shooting them' (KP, Beadnell).

parlour pot – 'for lobsters - has dead-end trap as only expect to catch one' (EK, Seahouses).

pellet – 'a small float. Variant: **pennant**' (KP, re Amble/Newbiggin; Cullercoats, 2004, AO).

pots – 'crab pots. they contain: 4 bows, 4 side sticks, 1 top stick, 2 end sticks, 2 deear sticks, 2 bait bands, 1 slip band, 2 deear bands, 2 spoots or smoots' (Umpleby, Staithes, 1930s).

pot-tows – '[ropes] used with crab pots' (Umpleby, Staithes, 1930s); **pot strings** – d[itt]o (Umpleby, Staithes, 1930s).

rail – 'lengthwise part of frame of crab or lobster pot' (KP, Beadnell).

sheeat blocks – 'blocks used in sheeting' (shooting) (Umpleby, Staithes, 1930s).

sheeated – 'shot; act of casting lines or pots: "the've gitten sheeated;" pots are shot 9 fathoms apart' (Umpleby, Staithes, 1930s).

skowbs – 'cut sticks for pot rails' (KP, *WW*, Beadnell); *EDD* – *scob* Sc, Ire, N'd.

spout – 'way into a Flamborough pot for a crab' (Hill & McKee, 1978).

strop – 'rope attaching each pot to main tow. Any rope attaching one thing to another' (KP, Beadnell).

styen-piece – 'one of the anchor-tows at the end of a fleet of creeves; runs between chain and end-stone' (KP, Beadnell).

sweel – 'swell. Also a swivel or pivot, used by some fishermen to attach buoy to pots' (KP, Beadnell).

tier – 'a fleet of pots (Holy Island only)' (KP, Beadnell).

tingal – 'a patch of wood... small hoop nets for lobster fishing' (Heslop, 1880s).

top-stick – 'rail of crab or lobster pot' (KP, re Craster).

top-tow – 'small rope fastening strop of pellet to thicker tow' (KP, Beadnell).

trunk – 'a metal hoop covered in net, baited and used to catch crabs and lobsters in nineteenth century' (KP, Beadnell).

under-running – 'hauling pots for examination and afterwards returning them to sea without hauling them aboard' (Umpleby, Staithes, 1930s).

wadge – 'a wedge, used at bottom of bow in creeve, intended to swell in water and hold bow in place' (KP, Beadnell).

And then the other thing was crab pots and lobster pots – you used the boat for carrying them once again from place to place and just dumped them over the side with bait in and left them there and came back to them later on. That was a very simple mode of fishing that was usually done by old-timers.

(Bart Taylor, Cullercoats)

The standard lobster 'pot' is handmade by the fisherman with some spare wood, flexible piping and netting. The lobster would enter a one-way tunnel of netting to secure a piece of bait, like raw mussel or junior crab, and so be trapped. Bait could also be fishheads and fish fillets ("bits of undersize fish or a slice off waste whiting, rest discarded" – GD, Parkside). Pots could be laid in a relay of up to thirty in a row, connected with rope, and hauled back on board for checking maybe on a daily basis. The string of pots would then be relaid on new ground, a 'step' further along, as it were.

Older-type lobster pots had a frame of ¾" drilled cane with plank base. Metal plates would be put in the base as ballast (near Whitby sash weights from old windows were used). Today, plastic tubing of the sort provided (inadvertently) by phone companies and others, is favoured.

Associated with lobsters are octopuses, that feed on them. These often come up in nets, accidentally, and though not favoured as a food in this country, are skilled performers, changing colour according to the background you put them on, and, on return to the sea, cover their get-away with a cloud of ink. One fisherman used to amuse himself (and possibly the squid or octopus) by clagging it onto his bright orange overalls for the sport of seeing it change colour... (JP). Not much eaten in this country, yet the tentacles of the octopus make an appetising dish, pressure-cooked with a little liquor; served with salt and pepper, and (to give a meaty flavour) some walnut oil (GD).

Chapter 9. Bringing the fish onboard

This is only a problem with the large, deep sea nets, which are power-winched back on-board, the fish being pulled from the net by hand as it rolls in, or released onto the deck from the bag of the trawl.

back-finner – 'fish that is nearly through the net, caught by back fin' (KP, Beadnell).

brailor – 'net on long pole for scooping fish aboard' (KP, *WW*, Beadnell) [Fr *brail*, 'belt', etc.].

davy – 'a wooden or metal roller…for hauling the pots' (N'd, Bradley, 2, p.31).

didle – 'net on a long pole for scooping fish aboard, especially salmon and trout' (KP, re Craster).

fish-stop – 'net on a long pole for scooping fish aboard' (KP, re Amble).

ginny – 'small rollers in coble for hauling pots' (KP, Beadnell) [OF, engin].

gog – 'to stick fingers down throat of fish which has swallowed a hook. Also, 'Gog-stick', stick with notch in end used for same purpose (Craster)' (KP) [?gag].

holly – 'to leave lobsters in boxes in sea for a period; 'holly-boxes' – fish boxes fitted with lids to keep lobsters in water' (KP, Beadnell); 'to keep catch alive – holly boxes usually laid on sea-floor' (FT, Cullercoats).

kep-net – 'net on a long pole for scooping fish aboard' (Craster, Amble) (KP).

picket – 'a boat-hook or gaff' (KP, Beadnell) [Fr for pointed stake].

priest – 'a baton of wood, used to kill salmon' (JC, Spittal/Berwick); **dolly knocker** 'wooden stick, kills red fish' (MS, Cullercoats).

sned – 'is a Hartlepool word for to catch – "Aw've snedded twee at a band"' (two fish on one line) (Brockett) [OE *snædan*].

strike – 'to take the net' (KP, Beadnell).

watter! – 'warning of a big sea approaching, while men working on deck' (Yx) (Godfrey, 1974, p.19).

Chapter 10.
Landing, processing and distribution

bad-weather-geordy – 'a name by which the cockle-seller is known' (Heslop, 1880s; Briscoe 2003).

bell (the) – 'name given to the Seahouses fish auction' (KP, Beadnell).

cadger – 'tinker, someone who hawks fish from door to door' (KP, Beadnell).

clean (verb) – 'to gut a fish or shell a crab' (KP, Beadnell).

cran – 'measure of herring, 28 stone. (Used all over Britain, not just in Northumberland)' (KP, Beadnell) [?Gaelic]; *EDD* – SC, I.o.M.

creel – 'a basket or pannier, especially for...fish' (Atkinson, Cleveland) [OFr *greille* or OIr *criol*]; EDD – Sc, Ire, Nth, Linx. "Local man Cuthbert (Cud) Simpson was an expert creel and basket weaver. The canes came from Norfolk" (JP, Cullercoats).

gallusses – 'lifting gear on a trawler' (KP, Beadnell) [?gallows].

gyte – 'fish-slime' (KP, Beadnell); EDD – 'herring spawn', N'd.

swil – 'a sort of flat wide basket used by flesh carriers and fish wives in Newcastle' (*Bell-White MS 12*).

The major fish markets like North Shields sold wholesale, and "Most lobsters caught went straight to London hotels" (JP, Cullercoats). At smaller centres like the former Sunderland Fish Quay restauranteurs and public alike could buy as much or as little they liked from a quite bewildering range of fish – one I swear had a sort of tartan check on its side...

Helen Hemingway sent this about North Shields:

North Shields Fish Quay
In about 1971 and a bit earlier there used to be large 'Hoover' type machines that were about 15ft high that dropped off the quayside into the holds of the fishing boats. They were for unloading the small wet fish that get sold in tins as whitebait/sild. They were always called Sprats... Kids used to go down and pick up the ones that dropped out of the sides of the machines and sell them on to fishermen or take them home for the cat! It was a vivid memory of North Shields fish quay in the 1970s and probably much earlier too. Along with the cod laps (cheeks) that you could get from the filleters who slid them off the end of the benches into big wooden fish boxes."

(The area is now nominated for a major refurbishment grant.)

When the market is over the trawlers are loaded with coal at the staiths and with ice from the ice factory. After they have taken on board provision, they will steam out again and fish for six or seven nights in various parts of the North Sea east and north of Shields. Many of these trawlers were built at smith's dock in Middlesbrough.

(Coulthard, 1934, p.127)

Inland
Once a week on a Friday a lady would travel by train to Annfield Plain with a 'creel' of fish. She set up a stall near the station and did a roaring business. Her name was Polly Donkin...

(Jack Gair, re 1920s)

A lot of food was delivered, by local sellers coming to the back door. There was a lady from Sunderland who carried a basket of crabs, and sometimes a lobster or two, on her head. She had a persil-white apron and a black shawl. Then there were men with a small pony and trap selling herrings. Six a penny, they would call out; but as the day wore on, you would often hear 'twelve a penny', as they needed to sell the catch that day. There was also a vegetable seller, but he had a more substantial cart and bigger horse: there was a large set of scales to weigh the produce. And fish vans, and milk and so on...

(Margaret Reed, Seaham)

At that time fresh fish was collected by 'Hartlepool Fish Wives' in old prams stocked with either ice or dry ice then brought to Blackhall – a distance of over 5 miles walked and then hawked around the colliery rows and scheme houses. I still remember the cry of 'FRESH FISH' and the various prices – cod being the cheapest and crab or lobster being the most expensive.

(Jack Leger)

You had a sort of a local market you know where I mean there was lots, we had a chap at Boulmer who had a little pony and trap and used to go round selling one to one in Alnwick, we had a fish shop in Alnwick as well, so we had quite a local market for things, but we also used to – I'm talking about quite a while beer the war this – a lot of kippers from Craster went to the London market. After that it sort of retracted a little bit and a lot of the kippers were distributed locally in Northumberland. During the War what happened was the Ministry took over, the Ministry of Agricultural Fisheries took over and what happened was we were classed as a sort of wholesaler/supplier, whatever fish we got in was a percentage, it was worked on a percentage we got before the war, there was a percentage of the fish that was landed in each port was bought from you. The Ministry gave you customers you had to supply and I remember my father telling me we had one in Newcastle, a shop in Hexham, a shop in Durham and a shop in Alnwick. That was our sort of retail outlet that we had the rest had to go to wholesale markets and of course we had Leeds, Manchester and London, they were the markets we had to supply with fish …you know before the war it was a case of having too much stuff and you couldn't sell it, it was the opposite way round. Of course during the war it was the opposite way round.

Then after the war there was a keen demand for it and these people had got our products and one thing and another and they kept on wanting them. Then in later years the whole thing changed completely, you know over the years. Naturally a lot of fish was landed after the war because the grounds hadn't been fished for a number of years, and we used to send fish to Glasgow, Newgate markets, Grimsby, London, we used to send fish to all of these markets because there was a lot of fish demanded; but then it got over fished and we were back to square one. You've got a demand for kippers and you can't get herring, decent herring you know. You've got a demand for fish and you can't get fish. What happens with crabs and lobsters and there was salmon of course, we got all farmed salmon, but again this is we're getting an enormous supply of salmon for the demand so that puts the price down considerably, you know. Crabs and lobsters, lobsters are not too bad but if you get a lot of crabs – we had good outing with crabs – we used to send crabs to Leeds, to a customer in Leeds in the wholesale, he would take 50 or 60 stone of crabs every day. We had one at Hull, we used to supply him with a wagon at least 200–250 stone of crabs. What happened was the crabs got over fished and the people couldn't keep their businesses. The one in Hull had to pack up and diverse into something else. The one in Leeds unfortunately got stopped for boiling in Leeds market, you know new regulations, they weren't allowed to have steam flying all over the place so he had to finish…

We get a few crabs in here now, not the quantity we used to get but I wonder what we would do with them if we did get a large quantity. These markets have now been lost…

(Alan Robson, Beamish, 1992/50)

Chapter 11. Fisherman's duds

baa'mskin – 'fisherman's oilskin apron, tied at the front' (KP, Beadnell).

byits – 'boots; **sea-byit stockin's** – sea-boot stockings' (KP, Beadnell).

cheese-cutter – 'peaked cap worn by fishermen' (KP, Beadnell).

dopper – 'oilskin' (KP, Beadnell); **dapper** (MS, Amble) [perhaps after *dopper* 'a diving bird'].

dungarees – 'work-trousers traditionally worn by fishermen over breeks' (KP, Beadnell).

dut – "Many older [foyboatmen] favoured a 'dut' (bowler hat) afloat" (AO).

dyeg(s) – 'mittens, fingerless gloves worn at sea (cf. 'Daag', Shetland)' (KP, Beadnell).

gallusses – 'a pair of braces to hold up trousers' (KP, Beadnell) [?gallows].

gansey – 'fisherman's traditional woollen sweater, usually navy-blue and patterned. Designs varied from family to family' (KP, Beadnell); 'seamless garments, knitted on five needles with a tight weave to 'turn water'' (KP, 2005) [Guernsey – but compare Norw. *genser*]; *EDD* – Shet, Yx, Suf.

gravit – 'silk scarf worn by fishermen with collarless shirt, under gansey' (KP, Beadnell) [Fr *cravate*].

jumper– 'fisherman's smock (Seahouses)' (KP, Beadnell).

piggons – 'ties for oilskin sleeves' (KP, Beadnell).

slowp – 'fisherman's smock, worn over gansey' (KP, Beadnell); *EDD* – general.

sprag – 'small nail used to mend sea-boots' (KP, re Holy Island).

stocking hat – long knitted hat, not now used (Cullercoats).

You see, in a lot of places they say you can recognise where someone's come from by the pattern on their jersey.

So you could. You see some of them knits different, now the North people, way up in the North of Scotland, they knit different to here and the Fisher Row people knit different to the Eyemouth people. I think I told you before about the shoulder heads with the buttons, you know, so many buttons up to the neck, from the shoulder head up. Now you see we knit the shoulder head and just put the two buttons, that you put on the ones with the buttons. But the most of them likes the Polo-Neck, the younger ones now, but the older ones like the buttons.

(Mrs Libby Grant, Eyemouth, Beamish 1980/192)

Pilots were very experienced in the art of keeping warm. They wore thick woollen trousers topped by a navy blue donkey jacket, underneath were thick woollen jerseys (ganseys). To stay dry the pilots wore thick oilskins made of stiff calico that had been waterproofed by applying boiled linseed oil.

(Journal of the Coble & Keelboat Society, 27, 2006)

(One ex-fisherman swore the warmest lining was a borrowed pair of his wife's panti-hose – BG.)

Chapter 12. Food at sea

piece – 'a packed lunch, usually bread; alternative to 'bait' in Seahouses and Scottish East Coast' (KP, Beadnell).

Q: You took food with you and kept it in the boats?

No, you just had it at home, you know. You didn't have any... I'll tell you what we had, you'll not remember the pitman's bottles, there used to be flat ones, there used to be flat ones you carried on the hip, and they had lugs on that you put a lanyard in, that had a little top on, you could drink out the bottle. We used to make our tea in the morning, and we used to carry one of them, and sandwiches, depending where we went if we had sandwiches. And I still like cold tea! You can buy iced tea... You had nowhere to heat it up, the barges we had, you couldn't pop ashore to have a cup of tea, there wasn't any.

(Ernie Keedy, Beamish, 2005/84)

Out on the trawler – breakfast was bacon, dinner, cornbeef and onion sandwiches, tea ditto – as we were there for days it got a bit monotonous – prepared by the lad – there was only the owner and his son, so the son served as cook – so it went on day after day – one day he noticed a rat on boat helping itself to cod ends exposed on deck – cook said, "Dad, why has that rat just jumped o'erboard and committed suicide?" "Because it's sick of cornbeef and onion sandwiches."

(Anon.)

Chapter 13. Salmon fishing

bailey – 'bailiff; usually a water bailiff overseeing salmon fishing regulations' (KP, Beadnell).

blash, plash – 'to hit the water with an oar (or similar) in order to disturb and drive fish when inshore netting for salmon' (AO); **ploshing** – 'the act of beating the bows of a coble with a rope at the waterline to drive the fish [salmon] into a net' (Bradley, I, p.24).

cables – 'lots, as in drawing lots for salmon berths: "Draa'in' cables"' (KP, re Amble, Newbiggin) [kyevils, cavils, from ON *kafli* 'bits'].

driving – 'fishing for salmon from open boats' (EK, Seahouses).

Born in fresh water, the salmon migrate to the sea to feed, and return to their particular river to breed in successive years. This has led to a number of terms to distinguish the various stages of the salmon's life cycle (see Part One). Naturally the best chance of catching quality salmon was as they returned to spawn. River fisheries are recorded in the Medieval period; from the mid-nineteenth century drift nets were used, at the estuary or out at sea (see Osler, 2004). According to John Robinson of Newbiggin the introduction of (transparent) nylon nets from about 1966 meant a much improved rate of catch if you fished by day.

Fishing? They [cobles] were mostly used for salmon fishing, just for carrying the nets and standing by them; while the nets were fishing you just rigged yourself a little shelter... you used to lie the mast on an angle, aft, and then put the sail itself over it like a tent and did your drifting (drift-netting) like that.

If you were fishing from the riverbank, then boards were put side-to-side at stern of the coble; net was placed on boards ready for shooting; as more and more of the net was paid out, the net would begin to shoot itself. You made a big half-circle – half width of river – and after the net was all shot, you would take the rope ashore – both ends of the net would now be ashore for when you wanted to pull in.

A salmon licence ran from end February to September – an annual licence costing £10 in 1935. Covered sea trout as well. Anglers objected to anyone drifting for salmon! At Whitby, they used mules for salmon fishing. A small coble was stowed inside – used later to help manage nets. In Scotland, they would also fish for salmon from the beach with T-netting.

(Bart Taylor, Cullercoats)

…But perhaps more salmon are taken by what is called the coble and net fishery, than by any other method. This is carried on in large streams, such as the Tay and Tweed, in the following manner: A small boat of a peculiar construction, called a coble, managed by a single man, and carrying at the stern a long net, one end of which is fastened to the shore, is rowed out into the stream; the net, which is heavily weighted, sinks to the bottom, and is kept neatly perpendicular by means of huge floats in its upper margin; and, as the boat proceeds, the net continues dropping into the water, describing, by the time the coble reaches the shore, a complete semicircle. The whole net is then dragged to the bank, sometimes by the means of a windlass.

(Bushnan, 1840, p.181)

In the summer, that is 1 June to end August, the catch is salmon and sea-trout, which means paying a special license. The idea is to catch the fish off Seaham as they are heading north to enter the River Wear to spawn. This means going out anything from a half mile to two miles or so, and setting the net East-West to intercept the fish. The net used is a drift net that hangs down some 10 feet from the surface. It is up to 600 yards long, and made of monofilament (a bit like fishing-line). We shoot the nets in a East-West line, by the compass, then let them drift with the tide for about an hour. The boat is at one end of the long net, ideally at the seaward end to ward off any passing boats, and at the other is a dhan-end or buoy. After perhaps an hour we bring the net back onboard using a net-hauler, which is powered rollers, and pick the fish out. That's when you have to be wary of the seals. Catch like salmon and sea-trout don't need gutting. We land them whole. Nor is it worth refrigerating. We just keep them wet. So, we shoot the net seven or eight times in a working day of maybe 12 hours, lining it up on an East-West axis each time. Then we make back to harbour; a van comes and picks up the fish at the quayside; and it is selled at Sunderland Fish Market.

(Peter Adamson, Seaham)

Salmon fishing took on a new lease of life in the 1960s on the Wear when improvement in water quality and the clearing of barriers to fish movement saw it reborn as a salmon river.

In the last decade, breeding or 'farming' salmon for the table has come to rival netting for wild salmon, and driven the price (and some would say, the flavour) down.

Chapter 14. Herring

In spring, a plankton bloom provides food for the herring, which move from deep to shallower waters to feed and spawn. There is also a daily cycle in which the herring feed in deep water by day, near the surface at night.

> When the herring starts to spawn it loses its oil content and therefore they're no good to us; you know you can't make a good kipper out of a poor herring; it's no good at all and we don't do it, we just stop: whenever the quality of the herring deteriorates we stop curing.
>
> (Alan Robson, Craster, Beamish, 1992/50)

Catching the herring

The herring migrate in shoals, according to season, and on more or less predictable routes, that can change, nonetheless, over the centuries – to the benefit or loss of various nations. For a comprehensive account see Mike Smylie's (2004) book on the herring: *A history of the silver darlings*. There is an assumption that the route of migration favoured the North Sea from the mid-fifteenth century on, when "The North Sea became the new focus of the herring industry" (Hutchinson, 1994, p.143) – but it may simply be that the North Sea nations woke up to the potential of the herring, and began to build specialised craft to harvest the fish. In Holland this was the 'herring buss'; in England, the 'five-man-boat' or 'Yorkshire lugger'; and in the second half of the nineteenth century the 'Scarborough yawl'. The coble was also used, perhaps when a shoal came more inshore: "The coble's main occupation was fishing… they worked drift nets for herring, and long lines for cod, halibut, ling, haddock and skate" (Mannering & Greenhill, 1997, p.51); certainly small cobles were used as auxiliaries carried on board larger boats; but with the advent of motor trawlers, the herring fishery became too commercial for the coble, a boat based on personal or partner finance.

> The signs the men looked for when trying to identify a rising shoal [of herring] at nightfall, before the invention of the echo-sounder, included diving gannets, blowing whales, and the memorable sight of 'fire' or phosphorescence on the water.
>
> (Katrina Porteous, 2006, p.69)

For herring, [there] were ports all the way around coast, from North Shields, Whitby, Scarborough, Lowestoft, Dover, up the Welsh coast... [names various places in Scotland, down to Berwick, Seahouses, and Shields again.]...

> Shields was best June–August. Then the season moved on down: Whitby, Scarborough. Yarmouth was October–December. From December we usually moved to Oban and Ullapool, etc., top west of Scotland. Spring herring were from Ayre or off Fraserburgh, Peterhead, Aberdeen...
>
> Fishing boats would go out specifically for white fish or herring. White fish boats would be either inshore, mid, or deep – further out, bigger the boats were. Herring boats stayed within sight of land, not deep water. Apart from Yarmouth/ Lowestoft, where company owned, most were family owned, with a crew of 5–12 men.
>
> In my day they were coal burners, later diesel – father's day were sailboats.
>
> "Drifter" – drift nets, for herring, drifts with the tide, nets not anchored – hangs like a curtain, weights at bottom, floats on top. This catches the big ones and smaller get through, as swim through it.
>
> Nowadays herring fishing done with purse netting, encircles them and everything brought out.
>
> (Fred Ballard, Beamish, 2005/74)

In the twenty-first century, herring is hardly worth pursuing; what is caught goes into animal feed. Frozen herring from Norway or Iceland is imported to sustain the production of kippers. Mackerel, that come close inshore in shoals in the autumn, provide much sport for the angler, and could form a commercial catch, though the quota is currently used up by the Scots.

Curing the herring
From c.1400, the Scandinavian method of curing herring was adopted, i.e. "...gutting the fish, packing it between layers of salt in wooden casks, and later re-packing it in fresh brine – made preserving them up to a year possible, as opposed to the few days afforded by light salting without gutting" (Starkey *et al.*, 2000 p.22). Light salting could also be a preliminary to smoking the fish.

> The process of it, well what they used to do was the herring used to come in and they used to what they called rough salt them. As the herring were being brought off the boat they used to salt them with a coarse salt and put them into barrels, and then the barrels were brought up here [with horses] and the herring were tipped on to a long bench; and when they were on the bench they were again salted as they were tipped in. Then what used to happen was, they had a wooden shovel similar to what they use in the hops and the maltings you know where they used to turn them at one time with a wooden shovel, and they used to turn the herring and salt them again. Then the women used to be there along the bench and they used to take the gills out of the herring to gut them, it was called gutting. They took the gills and the long gut out leaving the roe in the herring and then they used to have various baskets in front of them and they had to select them usually into three different baskets. They worked in a crew, you would have possibly two women... or maybe three who would be gutting, there would be two women

packing. They used to take them to the barrels and pack them in the barrels, and they laid the herring up with the belly sticking up over, and each row was salted and then turned and they would lay one row like that and one row like that, and they did that till they got the barrel filled. When the barrel was full they used to leave them and the Cooper used to come and put the lid on the top of the barrel, after it had stood for two or three days to let the herring settle. Then they used to put the barrels on their side and fill them, there was a little plug on the side, fill it full of brine, salt and water, there was already salt in because as the herring were in the barrel and the salt dissolved it did make a brine but they used to have it completely topped up with the salt and water and that preserved them for many, many months; and that was the main thing that happened to herring in those days.

(Alan Robson, Craster, Beamish, 1992/50)

An earlier slightly more poetic picture of the herring season, comes from Craster in 1875:

The herring fishery was the harvest of the fisherfolk; on summer evenings it was a joy to watch the fleets of herring boats putting out to sea with their great brown sails. Some of the men would follow the shoals of herring with their boats to other parts of the coast, and be away for weeks at a time. During the herring fishery those who wished to see the people had to pursue them to the curing yards, where the heaps of silvery fish brought in carts from the boats were quickly cleaned, salted, and packed in barrels to be off to Italy and Spain for the consumption of the peasants in Lent. The cleaning and packing were done by the women, dressed for the purpose in oilskin jackets and petticoats. If herrings were sufficiently plentiful, a clever worker could earn as much as ten shillings in the day, and women collected from the country round to help in the curing. To the remark that it was dirty work, the ready rejoinder came at once, "Aye, but the money's clean".

(Creighton, 1904, 1/153–4)

…a comment which translates aptly into verse:

Oh what'll we dee wi; the herrin's heed?
Oh what'll we dee wi; the herrin's heed?
We'll mak it into loaves of breed, and all manner of things.

A flavoursome developing of plain salting was the smoking process, to produce kippers:

Boat arrives in with herring – try to fish through the night and arrive in around 6 am. Oarsman brought a sample of the herring to the herring ring, put on a sample tray, all the buyers would examine, salesman would tell the buyers how many cran the boat has to sell – this is a measure, four baskets – average weight of 28 stone, but based on baskets. Recently sold by the unit, around 16 stone, as majority are boxed at sea – my day they were just put into hold then shovelled into baskets. Auction, then pulled by boat with a load of quarter cran boxes, swung from baskets and tipped into boxes.

Then transported to the smokehouse, where women waiting to hand or machine split them. Split and washed, put in pickles – vats holding two gallons of water and 5 hundredweight dissolved salt – in brine for 30 minutes –

transferred into trows with trestles, kipper stick had hooks in, pricked them onto the sticks, then into kilns, smoking rooms, hung on racks and allowed to drip. Then men would get up and the herring was handed up from one to the next and laid out along the lums five inches apart till house is full. Oak wood chips laid, traps set, and doors set, by smokers – drafting or backdrafting. Get fires blazing, dampened down with oak sawdust – could adjust to smoulder and smoke all night, and in the morning kippers probably cured. Struck from kiln back onto racks, packed in boxes by women.

Smoking kippers – prolong herring life, fresh one only has 2 or 3 days, a kipper will last a week. So preservative, and also for the taste – flavour altered by type of curing and brining. Both processes preserve it but major reason for former is flavour. Oak is good for this, and produces good smoke, and much better flavour than from pine.

(Fred Ballard, Beamish, 2005/74)

As I say now we've got the machines that split the herring; it's still pretty labour intensified because you still have to put them on to the hooks and put them into the smoke house and again they have to be smoked: because we still smoke them in the way they were smoked many years ago. We don't do quite as many as they did years ago, but it's still talking about working a sixteen or eighteen hour day in the busy season.

(Alan Robson, Craster, Beamish, 1992/50)

A further firsthand account of salting, by May Telfer, is transcribed in Maureen Brook's *Herring girls and hiring fairs* (2005, p.70).

The herring 'crew'

…a lot of Scotch girls used to follow the herring down the coast. These girls used to follow the herring, they were known as 'crews' and they used to follow them and cure them at different places, they used to come here. As I say my father and grandfather and grandmother and some of my father's sisters used to all go as a crew down to Yarmouth after the herring finished here and they would work down at Yarmouth doing the herring.

(Alan Robson, Craster, Beamish, 1992/50)

Q. Did you used to move around for the fishing? Because you've mentioned going to other places.
Well my mother used to go to Stornoway and Frazerborough and [Lostiff?] and she came home in the winter to do the fishing nets, she never went to Hull but my auntie used to go to Hull.
Q. Was this for the herring that they used to go?
For the herring, aye.
Q. And was that before you were born?
Yes that was before she was married. I used to go to the fishing an' all. Frazerborough I used to go to and Girvan, St. Ives…

(Mrs Libby Grant, Eyemouth, Beamish, 1980/192)

Q. Now you, you tell me you left school at fourteen at Eyemouth. Well, what was your first job?

My first job was kippering the herring.

Q. You cut the herring.

Aye, I split them for to make kippers.

Q. So it was just a case of splitting them. There was no . . .

Splitting them and then you had to clean them and they had to be washed and after they were washed, they were put into what we called, drying. For to pickle, pickle. And put into the brine, taken out and we'd prick them on and then they went into the smokehouse… and after they went in we handed up the herring to the man that was putting them along in the kiln. For to be smoked.

We went out, we went out in the morning and started at… eight o'clock and we went right on until six.

I think I started to travel when I was… nineteen… and I went to, as I say, I went to Yarmouth. We had to go into lodgings. When we were in Stornoway, we were in the huts. And the same with Mallaig. We were in the wooden huts at Mallaig. And then, when we went to Yarmouth, we went into lodgings.

Q. How did you travel? Did you go on the train?

Train. By train.

Q. Well, who, how did you take your, all your clothing, because you'd be away for months?

Well you see, we had a box. We called it a kist.

A kist we called it and we took that with all our clothes in and we took that both to Mallaig and Stornoway and the same with Yarmouth, in the lodgings in Yarmouth you see? And… we'd be there maybe about seven, eight or nine weeks.

It's still the herring, and it was still kippering you see. But, when I was in Lowestoft it was gutting but I was a packer. I used to do the packing the herring in the barrel. I packed the herring for the two gutters you see. Well, the other two were two gutters, you see and they asked me if I would go as a packer. Like a crew. They called it a crew. So, in fact there's a, there's a crew working together. If you don't pack them fast enough, the gutters…

Well they, they came to help you when they were finished. We did, when the herring was finished. The gutting you see. They came and helped you to pack the rest of the herring into the barrels. You packed them and packed up. Salt all the way. Put the salt in each tier you were packing, till you got to the top and then the cooper, he put the lid on. Now, they were left for a wee while, in the barrel and then the, the cooper came with a can to put brine in. that's from Yarmouth and Lowestoft.

Q. You were talking about packing these in crans?

That's a cran of herring.

Q. Is that a, is a cran something peculiar to Eyemouth?

Well it is that. They call that in Eyemouth a cran of herring you see… well… you see, there was a lot of women travelled. A lot of fishing. And I used to go, the first year that I went away, I went with my sister. My oldest sister. And she aye, she would travel the fishings as well. All the way round, for Woodgers just the same.

Mmm huh! Well… you went there when you were nineteen so we're talking about 1928…

Now then just when, when you were working on with the herring, it always seemed to me when I've seen the pictures, that you had, like you had a um, a sort of uniform you wore.

Well, it was the oilskin coat we called it, and an apron, a yellow apron. The, what they called bratts – they called them long ago, you know, in the Eyemouth (…).
Aye. Well, of course, what, what the listener wouldn't hear is, Miss Angus has just demonstrated and it, it surprises me how they didn't get their faces and, their faces cut with the knives you know, the knives . . .
No. No, no. You see it was right down and they were bent and we called the[m] farlins….
The farlins?
It was a big wooden box and the herring was all heaped up in there. And they're all salted, you see?

(Sean Angus, Bewick, Beamish, 1998)

Update

Some were married to fishermen whose boats came down to do the fishing, so they moved down as well, and some of them were single, just young girls who wanted the jobs in those day. I can remember when I was working in here and that was after the war and we had about ten women from the village who worked, but things have completely changed nowadays – it's very difficult to get someone to do our type of work. This was because it's seasonal and they quite prepared to come out and make a little bit of money during the season; and their husbands were possibly working at quarries and things like that and they'd come here during the day and work and then get back for five o'clock to make their husbands' meals. In them days women had done it from being girls, nowadays girls tend to go to work in offices or shops and things and they get the job straight away so they don't have to look for something.

(Alan Robson, Craster, Beamish, 1992/50)

Amble was a great place, I used to drop them off to a lady in Amble who used to push a pram around Broomhill selling kippers, an old pram, four wheeled pram, she used to push it around and sell kippers; she could sell kippers as well, I'll tell you, a great old dear she was, she emigrated to New Zealand in her later years. I heard they had a little pony and trap and sell them in Warkworth and she used to sell them in Red Row and Broomhill. Later on she did learn to drive a van. She came back from New Zealand to visit her sister… and she came along to see us and she chatted to me for quite a while and she said, "I'm thinking of getting a van just to sell a few kippers while I'm here, I can't sit in the house doing nothing. Will you let us have some?" I said "Of course I will". So she stayed for about six weeks and just before she went back she came to see us and she said "I'm off on Monday". I said "You've had a very busy time". She said "I've thoroughly enjoyed it, I've seen all my old friends that I used to see before on top of that I bought the van, I've sold it and made a profit on that and I've paid for the holiday with the kippers".

(Alan Robson, Beamish, 1992/50)

Eating the herring

This can be done two ways:

– as "fresh herring...hanging out to dry, among the newly-washed 'duds' which bellied out in the wind" (Haswell, 1895, p.34).

caller – fresh, cool: 'Here's yor caller harrin', here's yor bonny fresh harrin!'" (Heslop, 1880s); 'cool, refreshing: "Caller herrings'" (Brockett, 1829); 'The cry of fishwives is still, "Caller hair'n (herring)! Fresh, caller hair'n'" (Palgrave, 1896, Hetton).

...to be toasted or baked...

...or cured (and reheated to taste). Obvious. Delicious.

Open fires also made good toast and fried kippers to a turn. Every Monday a man used to bring round boxes of the latter on a flat cart and they provided a welcome tea, even though we suffered constant thirst all that evening.

(Fred Stainthorpe, p.24)

My maternal granddad worked [in the Yorkshire fishing industry] during his early years whilst he ended his days as a labourer in the steel industry. I have only two things that I can recall that may be of interest to you.
(a) He always insisted that the only way to eat kippers was to use your fingers. Knives and forks were not to be used and here he had a disagreement with my mother who was trying to instill some table manners into me!
(b) He would never eat mackerel as he believed that they fed on the corpses of drowned fishermen and sailors.

(Peter Kendal)

Lamenting the herring

Gold age of herring from turn of century, when coal boats didn't have to rely on the wind – but died off from the 1950s, caught less and less.

Decline through over fishing by the British fishermen and also the continental ones in the North Sea and around the ports, which they still do. There's only so many, have to allow them to reproduce.

(Fred Ballard, Beamish, 2005/74)

...the salting of the herring and that side of the business had gone, because of the War, and that had been finished and it never really came back after the War, the herring curing.
Q. Why was that?
Well for two reasons I think. One of the reasons was just after the War a lot of these countries where herring was exported began to have their own fishing fleets.

(Alan Robson, Craster, Beamish, 1992/50)

In fact, herring catches were good 1945–50, but by 1960 low yields were "directly attributable to the overfishing of the southern North Sea herring... The collapse of the herring fisheries was due to the collective failure of states in the region to commit themselves to solving a common problem" (Starkey *et al.*, 2000, pp.194–5).

> Factory ships go to sea for six or nine months, freezing on board. Big wholesalers need a huge deep freeze. Family business – kippering but [they use] also vast stocks of frozen herring from Iceland and Norway as can't rely on fresh herring, would be only seasonal work – and only a couple of months in the year, not ten months as in my day. What can be done to improve British fishing? – government are doing some by enforcing quotas, but I think we should have done what Iceland did ten years ago – made a limit and kept them all out. We had the best fishing grounds in Europe, but everyone is fishing it. We're supposed to have patrols, but foreign commercial boats come up, fishing the waters clean or all size fish – can only do that so many times, no future in it.
>
> (Fred Ballard, Sunderland, Beamish, 2005/74)

From 1977 to 1981 a total prohibition was declared on fishing herring in the North Sea; when fishing was resumed the English herring industry no longer existed (Starkey *et al.*, 2000, p.195; Smylie, 2004, pp.142, 196).

> ...it's the same with the herring, when we had the ban of herring fishing for seven years on this coast we weren't allowed to catch herring. We're now allowed to catch them, but if we were getting any quantity of herring we wouldn't be able to handle them, we wouldn't be able to market them anywhere you see and for one thing at North Shields: I used to go to North Shields every day to buy herring and in North Shields when I was there, there was people up from Yarmouth to buy herring and the one I mentioned in Yarmouth – Suttons is now closed because it couldn't continue with the ban on herrings they couldn't get the supply so they went out of business and the same thing happened in North Shields. There was about nine people who kippered in North Shields I think there's two now.
>
> (Alan Robson, Beamish, 1992/50)

Chapter 15. Trawling

Trawling covers a number of techniques, in which a net is actively moved through the water to maximise the fish catch.

Deep sea fish include the famous cod and haddock; sea floor fish are the flat fish, and also prawns, that live in the mud bottom e.g. the Farne Deeps – up to 60 fathoms deep.

Most boats now have an echofinder, but still the eye has to recognise the image on the screen, distinguish fish from sea bottom.

When people caught white fish, most skippers could do perfectly well without them (echo sounders). White fish is sandy bottom, edge of. Trawl round edges of hard ground (rock/sand boundary), trawl as close to rock as safely can go.

(Eric King, Seahouses)

'Winter Trawling'

Written up from a conversation with Peter Adamson, whose father fished from Seaham in the 1960s in a coble, but himself owned a small trawler:

The trawler – a keelboat – is 32 foot long, a wooden hull, oak on oak, with a 6 foot draught: that's fairly substantial. The wheelhouse is aft, and the remaining space decked over to give maximum working room. She was French-built, in the 1960s. The engine is a six cylinder diesel giving 120 horse-power. There are two masts for communications, plus a derrick. If she needs lifting out then that has to be done at Hartlepool Marina, there aren't the facilities at Seaham.

In the summer, that is 1 June to end August, the catch is salmon and sea-trout... In the winter months, we are ready to go trawling on a daily basis, perhaps working 12-14 hours a day. There are limits on the number of hours you can work, but ultimately these tend to be set by the weather rather than by regulations – there are just so many winter days it's not worth setting out on because of the weather. The winter trawling is for prawns and can take place anything from 5 to 20 mile out. Prawns live in mud and sand, and that sort of smooth bottom is ideal for trawling: a net is carried on a loop of wire (cable) – ending up with two wires running out over the stern of the boat ready for the tow – while the mouth of the net is kept open by trawl-boards – and so the main net scrapes along over the sea-bed.

A trawl may last for up to 4 hours, and it's here the navigation gear comes into use. A 'Nav-Star' gives exact latitude-longitude position, based on accurate satelite signals; we can compare that with a chart and trawl up and down corridors or tracks, covering areas we reckon to be suitable. Also we have to be careful to avoid obstructions on the sea-bed that might snag the net: like rocks or even wrecks. After the trawl the net is brought back on board using a winch and the prawns and other fish tumbled out onto the deck. Though prawns are the main catch, there are also some flat fish like whiting, and some cod and monkfish. The prawns are then shovelled up onto a table to be graded – they have to be sorted as they are paid for by size. You need to wear good gloves then, because prawns can nip you, you know. The whitefish is kept and gutted provided it's of a certain size. You aren't allowed to land undersize fish: those have to be returned to the sea, even if they don't stand too much a chance of surviving.

A day's fishing will usually mean two trawls; the first catch is processed while the second trawl is under way, so the boat needs a few extra crew for winter work. The catch is collected, as before, at the quayside, so we don't have anything to do with the marketing. Well, the work fishing is hard enough – and getting harder – though there's still a living to be made at it. It's not an easy skill to come by – people don't understand that. It's not just a job; it's a way of life."

Fishing Fleets

By the end of the nineteenth century, fishing was dominated by steam trawlers, especially from Hull and North Shields. This tilted the balance of the fisheries against small boats and small boat owners in favour of large commercial enterprises, to the ultimate disadvantage of all (especially the fish).

Q: Big fishing fleets going out from South Shields?
"There was Irving. Purdeys, they used to have steam trawlers, they went to Iceland. It was possible to get fresher fish off the Norwegian mail boats than off the local trawlers. There was no refrigeration, only ice... they would steam out towards Iceland for a couple of days – could be wrong with this but took a long time to get to the deep sea cod – the first days catch, it was iced, they would fish for a few days and each day's catch was iced one on top of another, they could be away for a few days, so if you bought fish that was the first days catch it was the last one out the hold so it was a few days old. But there's deep sea cod just off the coast of Norway and it only takes nineteen hours to get across from there. Now they're all motor or diesel...

The fishing fleet from North Shields, the prime fish, lemon sole, halibut, turbot, it was very expensive because it all went away to London on passenger train to the top hotels, where the money was, so it was dearer than it should have been if you wanted it here. You used to see halibut in the shops; it's a thick coarse fish, and turbot, and lemon sole steak, thick as that, now they're skinny little things...

You had the big steam drifters to travel the distances, they used to bunker in the Tyne at the commissioners' staithes that we called the Flankers. That was where the big passenger ships land now."

Ernie Keedy (Beamish 2005/127)

John Green's account of Sunderland in the early and middle nineteenth century includes several references to the Quebec fishing – for cod that would have to be brought back salted or iced.

"Holloa!" exclaimed the skipper, "how did ye come here?" "Why," replied the youth, "Aw stowed mysell away at Sunderland." "An' div ye think for a single moment," pursued the master, "that Aw's gawn ti find ye wi' grub all the way tiv Quebec? What hae ye been?" "Aw've been a carpenter wi' Jacky [Hutchinson] varry near three years." "Can ye caulk onney?" "Yis, Aw can caulk a buth. [?cow-shed]" "Then Aw'll just tell what it is – Aw've plenty oakum an' plenty o' pitch, an' a new set o' second-hand caulking irons Aw bowt iv the Law Street, an' a good caulking mellet; so ye can gan ti wark an' caulk the decks frev the watter-way seam o' both sides right in tiv the hatch combin's; an' biv the time ye get that dune, ye'll hae wrought for yer passage."

(Green Tales of Sunderland, 1879)

Chapter 16. Whaling

This now thoroughly unpopular branch of the fishing industry flourished in the early decades of the nineteenth century, from ports like Hull, Whitby, Sunderland, Tyne, Berwick and Dundee, the blubber of the whale being rendered down to produce whale oil, a major fuel for lamps and lighting; to a lesser extent 'whalebone' was marketed for its plastic quality. A whale needs to surface every so often to breathe air, at which time it becomes a sitting target for harpoonists. So 'successful' was the whaling trade, that several species were hunted to near-extinction in the nineteeth century, a sober forewarning of the risks of over-fishing.

The trade declined from the 1840s on, due to the introduction of gas for lighting; a few whalers from Dundee continued till World War I. Twentieth century whaling has concentrated upon the Antarctic:

Last whalers I saw just after the war – *Southern Venturer, Southern Harvester* – went whaling in the Antarctic – just like a glorified trawler, with a hell of a spring on the deck… and a platform from the bridge to the forecastle – that was where the harpoon gun was. They took a lot of the local lads with them – the wages was the attraction. The whalers themselves were strongly built – but the ancilliary boats were small – could be stowed nested inside each other.

(Bart Taylor, Cullercoats)

For more on the tradition of whaling, you are referred to A. Barrow *The Whaling Trade of North East England*, Sunderland, 2001.

Earlier, in Part One, we mentioned a reference to whaling in Anglo-Saxon times. A precious eighth century Northumbrian relic called the Franks Casket bears, among its many intricate carvings, a short verse in runes that transcribes as follows:

Fisc flodu ahof   on fergenberig
(this-fish the-tide   onto mountain-mound
raised (i.e. stranded)   (i.e. ashore);

warþ gasric grorn   þær he on greut giswom
was ocean-beast   when he on the-grit
mournful   (i.e. shingly beach) swam (i.e. ended-up.)

followed by the words "hronæs ban" (whales bone) as though in solution to the riddle – for that is what the casket is made of.

Notes

Cod, as well as other species of roundfish (whiting, haddock, etc.), come inshore to feed during and after storms. The storms disturb the sediments and rocks, washing out worms, crabs, molluscs, sandeel, shrimps, etc. which are otherwise safely hidden away or buried during calm conditions. Cod also come inshore to help clean themselves of parasites, rubbing those off their skin on the rocks and shingle. Another reason why they come inshore is to feed on certain sea anemone (we call it "paup" – a green anemone which sticks to rocks in the intertidal zone), the reason for this is that it is believed to clean their stomach and aid digestion. And the most obvious reason is that at certain times of the year shoaling sprats and sandeels move inshore, followed by everything else that feeds on them (Norman Conn, Seaham).

Part Four: Communities and the sea

Term: Integrated Coastal Zone Management

Description: A multisectoral approach with involvement of stakeholders to managing the coastal zone

(*glossary*; www.durhamheritagecoast.org)

Chapter 1. Communities at the start

Coastal settlements have been a feature of our social geography since retreating glaciers and rising seas at the end of the last Ice Age defined our modern island. It is presumed that scant vegetation on the coastal strip made new colonisation that much simpler (see *An historical atlas of County Durham*, 1992, p.8). After waves of pre-Celt and Celt, the Anglian settlement began via the Humber and its tributaries, in the mid-fifth century; it was not until 547 AD that Ida captured Bamburgh and set up the kingdom of Bernicia; and about 560 Aelle founded Deira to the south, with York at its heart.

An in-depth study of settlement names is not feasible here, and attempts to relate such place-names to a sequence of Anglian settlement remain a topic of hopeful research (see www.yorksj.ac.uk/dialect/Angset.htm for a useful introduction; also E.V. Watts' recent *Dictionary of County Durham place-names*, 2002). Jackson (1953, ch.6) gives an interesting older view of the settlement (from the British point of view); and for the latest speculations, see Stephen Oppenheimer's The Origins of the British: A Genetic Detective Story (Carroll & Graf, 2006) and Bryan Sykes' Blood of the Isles (Oxford, 2006).

Here we have space only to record briefly the main second elements in coastal settlement names…

Borough – OE burh –'a town with municipal organisation, a large town'; exx.: Bamburgh (N'd), Dunstanburh (N'd), Goldsborough (nYx), Flamborough (nYx), Scarborough (nYx).

The differences here are basically of spelling: the more recent form *–borough* sometimes obscuring an older *–burh*: thus Goldsborough in the Domesday Survey of 1086 is spelt 'Godenesburh'. Curiously the Old Norse (ON) sense of 'a fortress', discounted by the OED, would be applicable to several examples above. Scarborough is recorded in Viking sagas as Skarthabork (< ON borg 'fortress'): it was founded as late as 966–67 AD and received royal charters in 1135 and 1163.

by – ON *byr* and perhaps OE by 'a farm'. Used in the *Lindisfarne Gospel Gloss* of the mid-tenth century: "hus vel lytelo by" (a house or small 'by') *Mark* 5:3; exx.: Boulby (nYx), Whitby (nYx), Scalby (nYx), Osgodby (nYx), etc. A practical, though not infallible, marker of Viking settlement.

ham – Usually from OE *h'm*, 'hamlet'; exx.: Coldingham (N'd), Seaham (D'm), Coatham (Teesside). The list, in coastal terms, is surprisingly short; 'Sea-ham' is the only use of that combination of terms in the UK (for a second, you would need to go, as some local folk surely did, to Australia).

mouth – i.e. rivermouth; exx.: Tweedmouth (N'd), Burnmouth (N'd), Eyemouth (N'd), Lynemouth (N'd), Alnmouth (N'd) and Tynemouth.

shiel(d) – From ON *skále* in a Northumbrianised form. 'Temporary lodgings', "...from April to August [they] lie in little huts (which they call sheals and shealings) here and there among their several flocks" (Camden, sixteenth century); "such turf houses as shepherds build to watch their flocks on the moors, also fishermen's houses" (*Bell-White MS 12*). In the case of North and South Shields this came about from an agreement of 1279 to limit permanent built fishing stations in competition with Newcastle. **Shiel** – 'salmon fishers' house along the Tweed' (FK, Berwick).

ton – Usually OE *ton* 'an enclosed or demarcated settlement'; exx.: Easington, Widdrington, High Buston, High Newton, Scremerston, Lamberton, Buckton, Reighton, Speeton and Bempton.

tun/–ton – is the commonest termination in Durham place-names. Watts (2002, p.xiii) suggests "ham is generally thought to have been an element belonging to the early period while *tun* was productive throughout." Second elements *–ing*, *–ham* and *–tun* can be seen at typical of low land rather than later settled higher land.

A special case here is the frequency of Seaton place-names: North Seaton (N'd), Seaton Sluice (N'd), Seaton Delaval (N'd), Seaton Burn (N'Tyne), Seaton (D'm), Seaton Carew (D'm)...If we include Seaham (D'm), Seaburn (Sunderland) and Seahouses (N'd) the North East coast has nine out of the thirty UK place-names begining in Sea- that I have been able to trace. This high frequency is unlikely to be coincidental. Is it reasonable to speculate this chain of names tells us something of the conformity, organisation and speed of the Anglian settlement?

wick – Northern pronunciation of OE wîc 'a house, a hamlet', ultimately from Latin vicus 'a village'. Sometimes implies a work settlement, e.g. Saltwick, where salt would be obtained from sea water, Berwick, a barley town; exx.: Berwick-upon-Tweed, Cheswick, Howick, Saltwick, Elwick, Fenwick and Goswick.

There are two note-worthy anomalies, showing word use outside the expected settlement patterns: Newbiggin-by-the-Sea (N'd), which derives ultimately from the ON verb *byggja* 'to dwell'; and Saltburn, nYx, which includes the OE *burna* 'stream'. A whole series of Anglian place-names would have applied along the Yorkshire coast before the arrival of the Vikings, then being 'overwritten' – Bede mentions 'Streoneshalh' as the original name of Whitby, for example. Later additions and modifications are by no means ruled out – it is worth remembering that the initial cultural assertion of place-naming does not serve as a guide to later population distribution or language patterns.

Apart from providing footholds for incomers, coastal settlements have had a variety of functions – fishing, fish-curing, salt-making, boat-building, and a key role in communications and transport, inland, along coast and overseas (when Keats in 1818 visited Scotland, he set off by boat to Liverpool, and returned by boat from Cromarty). Until turnpike roads were established, and subsequently railways, it was arguably easier to travel by sea than land, and the number of monasteries dotted along the coast, and up rivers, reflected the ancient need for seaborne organisation and comunication, of personnel, ideas, foodstuffs and the interchange of other products.

The role of the Church would have been important in sustaining as well as exploiting seaside settlements (and transport) in the Medieval period. The exception could be Newcastle, originally a strategic point on the Tyne and the main route north, but increasingly important in the Middle Ages for ship building and export (e.g. of millstones). In 1295 it was sending two Members to Parliament. By the seventeenth century it had become the centre of administration and export for the coal industry, and attained a status in the North East that challenged the old order and the priority of Durham City.

Chapter 2. The progress of fishing communities

Fishing, for herring and salmon, and latterly for crabs and lobsters, was important in sustaining smaller coastal villages, but even here apparent independence could conceal aristocratic patronage: thus the Duke of Northumberland built cottages to rent to fishermen; the Londonderry family supervised the building and planning of Seaham, etc. Society, in a sense, is always 'managed'.

The fisherman's world was nonetheless a special one, regulated more by the needs of the sea than landlords:

> The fishing communities were insular, seldom travelling far from their own environment. They were not articulate; indeed some older folk could neither read nor write. Their meagre livelihood was hard-gained from the sea. I grew up among some wonderful characters, big men with big hearts. They were extremely hard working and when ashore, hard drinking, though seldom mixing the two pursuits. I thought this was a normal background, that everyone lived in a world such as mine. I couldn't have been more wrong: this way of life was unique."
>
> (Fred Normandale, 2006, re Scarborough)

A description of Craster, Northumberland, from the point of view of the vicar's family, gives a similar if less affectionate picture, going back to 1875:

> The Crasters, one of the oldest familes in Northumberland, have exercised a beneficent influence upon the inhabitants of the village, a sturdy, high-minded race of fisherfolk, many of whom have built their own cottages on land obtained from the squire. Like other fishermen, they had a strong tendency to Methodism, and used to hold open air services on the beach and even in the neighbouring villages...
>
> The fisherfolk kept much to themselves, and seldom married outside the village of some two hundred inhabitants; there were old women there who had never been in a train, and knew and cared nothing about the outer world. There was hardly a soul in the village who was not called either Archbold or Simpson, so that it was difficult to distinguish between them.
>
> (Creighton, 1904, 1/153)

This is surely overstated: the general pattern for the North East in the nineteenth century is one of population mobility – at least in the coal industry. Yet something of the practicalities of early wooing are reflected in a well-known song:

The Fisher Laddie
On Bamboroughshire's rocky shore,
  Just as you enter Bowmer Raw,
There lives the bonny fisher lad,
  The fisher lad that <u>bangs</u> them <u>a</u>'.   beats/exceeds… all
O the bonny fisher lad,
  That brings the fishes fra' the sea;
O the bonny fisher lad,
  The fisher lad <u>gat had</u> of me.   got hold

My mother sent me out one day,
  To gather cockles fra' the sea;
But I had not been long away,
  When the fisher lad gat had of me…

A sailor I will never marry,
  Nor soldier, for he's got no <u>brass</u>;   money
But I will have a fisher lad
  Because I am a fisher's lass…

(Bell, ed., Harker, p.161)

The relative stability of the small coastal settlements had much to do with the complexity of the skills needed for local navigation and fishing: such skills had to be learnt from an early age and this long process of maturity encouraged a common identity built on shared skills and risks that made for unity and continuity. Moreover with boats in family or joint ownership there were good practical reasons to make fishing a traditional way of life that passed from generation to generation.

My father, was a poor keelman on the River Wear, Sunderland, at which place I was born, and I may say principally brought up on the River, in the keel, which was mostly my home, and all the school I had; schooled to the water was the only education my poor parents could bestow on me.

(*Life of Martin Douglas*, 1848, preface)

Even when schools provided some choice, there was little expectation among the young other than to become a proper fisherman:

> Now I was born in 1916 and I was born into a fishing family. Now in those days all young fisher lads – their only ambition in life was to get left school and be a fisherman. What I mean… we didn't go to school regular, and we didn't pay as much attention [as] we ought to have done for eddication. When you're looking back, what I mean, some of us might have made better o' worsell's, if we'd putten more effort into it. We didn't put effort into it. Our main [aim] was get left school to be a fisherman. That was our aim in life and mostly all young fishermen was of that same opinion – to be a fisherman… However, to be a fisherman you've got to look back and remember it has its risks. There's lots of dangers attached, and occasionally there's tragedies…
>
> (From a tape of John Lisle Robinson, Newbiggin fisherman,
> issued by the Healthy Living Centre, Newbiggin)

This sense of local purpose and identity survived well into the twentieth century, and fishing communities, like Cullercoats, are remembered as a fine place to grow up, between the Wars:

> You could call ours a close community because most in this part were fisher folk – one or two worked in shipyards, or on the railways – a few on the buildings – but most owned cobles or were partners in cobles.
>
> I remember it as a safe community too. The front door was always left open and you took care the passage inside would be neat – with flowers and a mat. You never knocked when visiting friends, just walked in and shouted 'Hello!'
>
> We had a fine local school. When very small our mothers would walk us there – the nice caretaker, Josh Bell, would shepherd us all in. Then mothers would bring extra food at playtime – a banana or some Fry's chocolate – they were insistent we needed to eat: 'Have you had enough to eat?'
>
> Lessons included English, History, Geography; and once a week we had 'Housewifery' at North Shields – this included how to light a 'pot fire' (for the home laundry), how to bath a baby, how to cook… perhaps rock cakes with apricot jam, but I used to eat everything before I got home. Boys had their own lessons, in a separate part of the school. The lady teachers were all single; if they married, it was considered they had to give up their jobs.
>
> After school we would all play together in the streets – games, or skipping ropes, or a top n whip. Mothers would gossip on the steps at dusk. When the lamplighter came he would scatter us and send us home.
>
> In the summer, Newcastle folk would come to Cullercoats for a holiday, 'to catch the sea breezes'. People here would rent out rooms by the day – with an evening meal. Not much for visitors to do, but then they liked it as a quiet resort, one safe for children. Once a year there was lifeboat day: men would dress up, with their stocking hats, and drag the lifeboat to Whitley Bay on a wheeled ramp – the aim was to collect money. And there were pubs, but many of the locals were Methodist and therefore teetotal.
>
> You wouldn't necessarily marry a local person: you might meet someone on the beach; or you could go to the Plaza in Tynemouth, where they did teas and dancing, and served ice cream in silver dishes! But there was a sense of 'Cullercoats Village' – if you went over the railway bridge that was a different world – new housing for office workers and considered very genteel. If you made good, you might move and buy a smart new house in West Monkseaton.

The Second World War changed things. Civil service jobs came into the area. The fine stone fishermen's cottages on the front were pulled down. New estates were built. Women went out to work. There's still a community spirit, and a clear sense that people have to do things for themselves – conservation, for example. And of course the fishing tradition is fading away...

(From an interview with Joan Taylor Philips, Cullercoats)

The tight-knit fishing communities that have endured and evolved from not long after Noah landed have faced radical change in the recent half-century. Admittedly, the increased used of steam trawlers in the nineteenth century must have begun to erode the local fishing community's scope at sea, but there seemed plenty of catch for all until... Well, some attribute it to the failure of the UK government to maintain exclusive fishing rights in territorial waters... In 1971 the Common Fisheries Policy announced the principle of 'equal access to each other's waters'. The implications of this soon became apparent, and there was a campaign to impose a 50-mile exclusive UK fishing zone in 1972:

In the next few weeks Britain could be forced to hand over one of her most valuable food supplies, part of the nation's birthright, to foreign nations. Britain's fish, the fish in her own maritime waters, could be given, free of charge to the European Economic Community to be shared out among the member states...

(Poster illus., Whitmarsh, 2000, p.232)

Unexpectedly, it was Iceland that took the initiative in 1976, with a 200-mile ban on fishing by other nations round its coast. Belatedly, the UK declared a 12 mile limit round its own coast in 1987, to be ruled in contravention of EU Law. There seems no immediate prospect of reversing the decline the British fishing industry experienced in the last three decades: "the decisive factors have been the loss of access to traditional distant-water fishing grounds, increased competition from foreign vessels on grounds nearer to home, and a diminishing natural resource base caused by overfishing" (Whitmarsh, 2000, p.234).

There is "something wrong with the sea," confided one fisherman to Katrina Porteous (2006 p.73) – but of course it is mostly our own fault, whether as catchers or consumers. It means that communities that once regarded themselves as primarily fishing folk have seen the number of fishing cobles decline from encouraging numbers in the 1950s to a handfull of craft; there may soon be no new generation of North East fishermen.

Chapter 3. Sharing the load

While the brunt of danger was borne by the menfolk (as in the mining industry), there was certainly a full share of the work for the womenfolk. Although woman was taboo onboard a boat, she was by no means relegated to housework, but was regarded as more a partner in fishing – in olden times helping with launching and recovering the boats; and on shore in baiting the long lines, and in the complex curing and packing processes of the fish caught.

> The wives and daughters search for bait, sand worms, in muddy sand at the mouth of the Coble-dean at head of North Shields, gathering mussels in the Scalp, near Clifford's Fort, or limpets and dog-crabs among rocks near Tynemouth. They assist in baiting hooks… carry caught fish to North Shields in large wicker baskets called creels and sit in the market to sell them.
>
> (1838, qu. March 1970, I, p.96)

A more elaborate assessment of the woman's role was penned by Sir Walter Scott:

> 'A wheen [I think] poor drudges ye are,' answered the nymph of the land to the nymph of the sea – 'As sune as the keel o' the coble touches the sand, de'il [devil] a bit mair will the fisher loons work, but the wives maun [must] kilt their coats, and wade into the surf to tak the fish ashore. And then the man casts off the wat [wet] and puts on the dry, and sits down wi' his pipe and his gill-stoup [?can o' lager] ahint the ingle [by the fire] like ony auld houdie [old midwife], and ne'er a turn will he do till the coble's afloat again! – And the wife, she maun get the scull [basket] on her back, and awa wi' the fish to the next burrows-town [market town], and scauld and ban [argue and curse] wi' ilka wife [each woman] that will scauld and ban wi' her till it's sauld [sold] – and tha's the gate [way] fisher-wives live, puir slaving bodies.'
>
> 'Slaves? gae wa', lass! – Ca' [call] the head o' the house slaves? little ye ken about it, lass – Show me a word my Saunders daur speak, or a torn he daur do about the house, without it be just te tak his meat, and his drink, and his diversion like ony o' the weans [children]. He has mair sense than to ca' ony thing about the bigging [building] his ain, frae the rooftree down to a crackit trencher on the bink [bench, table]. He kens weel enough, wha [who] feeds him, and cleeds [clothes] him, and keeps a' tight, thack and rape [thatch and rope], when his coble is jowing [rocking] awa in the Firth, puir fallow. Na, na, lass – them that sell the goods guide the purse – them that guide the purse rule the house – Show me ane o' your bits o' farmer-bodies that wad let their wife drive the stock to the market, and ca' in the debts. Na, na.'
>
> (Sir Walter Scott, *Antiq*, ch. 26)

Some indirect testimony to their hard work comes indirectly from Umpleby's list of Staithes words (1930s):

rowler – roller. An apron or duster rolled up to protect the head when carrying coal, wood, etc. The Staithes women can carry great weights upon their heads.

skeel – wooden tub: formerly used for carrying water when each household had its own 'skeel' painted inside and out and bearing initials of the owner. They were carried on the heads of the womenfolk.

If fishermen knitted nets, fisherwomen from early on aimed to learn how to make fishermen's jumpers:

Now then how old were you when you first learned to knit?
When I first learned to knit? Oh, when I was at the school, I couldn't be very old. Maybe about eight or nine? Maybe nine year old I would think. You see, when I first went to school, I had to stay away from school, I could'ne do with it and I'd be sitting in a huff before I went. Yes I think I would be nine when I started learning.
And how old were you when you – first of all did your Mother teach you to knit? Your Mum? Did your Mum teach you to knit?
They teached us at the school and then my mother used to and then I asked her for to how to do the patterns for the jerseys, learn to do a jersey. And then she showed us you see and then-you were showed but you were left for to find out for yourself and then ask if it was right and then you just got on with it.
And what sort of patterns did you learn first?
I started with the plain diamond and the closed diamond.
And were they quite easy ones to knit, or?
They was the easiest ones for to do first.
And then did you move onto more adventurous things, just as you learned them?
It was that diamond that's on that jersey and then the purl stitch like what we call the closed diamond and that and then there were a plain and purl all the way up but it was very nice after it was finished.
Did you find it difficult to knit the jerseys at first?
No, we just thought it was great because we could knit a jersey.

(Mrs Libby Grant, Eyemouth, Beamish, 1980/192)

More detail of local designs will be found in Mike (M.R.R.) Pearson's Fisher-Gansey Patterns of North East England (1979), including detailed patterns.

The women also had their preferred dress:

Did the fisher ladies of Eyemouth used to wear shawls when they were going about.
That's right, yes. They always had their shawls about their shoulders.
Was there a traditional sort of dress that they wore? I mean a skirt and blouse or what? Did they all wear more or less the same things?
Jumpers and that. Do you mean knitting jumpers?

Yes and did they ever wear hats?
No the shawls was always put on their head. They just had hats for Sunday when they went to church.

(Mrs Libby Grant, Eyemouth, Beamish, 1980/192)

In the humbler days of Sunderland in the early nineteenth century:

> You might have walked down High-Street and scarcely have seen a woman with a gown on, except Sundays. Their habiliment being a calamenkey [calamanco] petticoat, a cotton jacket, and linen blue and white checked apron, with a bib. These native women might have been seen wending their way to work in the fields, with children on their backs.

(Sanderson, 1873, p.9)

This thrifty way of life (you may recall the use of the thrift plant as a national emblem on the old threppenny piece) relaxed with the consumer boom of the later twentieth century; choice of careers and partners has opened up, far exceeding the promise of the local colliery's or Co-op's dance.

Chapter 4. The luck of fishing

The risk involved in fishing on the North East coast led to a meticulous carefulness in the matter of navigation and boat-handling, but also gave rise to a body of superstitions meant to protect against bad luck – by which is meant the reality of loss at sea, and to a certain degree the disappointment of poor catches (that a woman on board might result in disappointing trawling is a theme of Tom Hadaway's film *In Fading Light* (Amber Films, 1989); on the use of fire to purify, you might want to see Henderson, 1879, pp.134–46.]

Courage and skill a fisherman must have, but this did not preclude the occasional rational or irrational fear. These could range from lurid fantasies like "the 'Giant Wrath' who would lurk in the caves, [to lure] the passing ships to their doom, always ready and waiting to catch ship-wrecked sailors for his meals" (Wright, 1874, p.33) – to the more commonplace.

One of these was the word P-I-G, which was not to be uttered. A replacement word might be used, or the dialect equivalent 'guissie', ('guff' at Eyemouth, 'guffie' on Holy Island, 'grumphy', 'guffy' or 'grecian' at Berwick), but never the P-word. This is also found among coal miners, but makes more sense in a maritime context, as P-I-G-S have been associated with strong winds for centuries. Perhaps this arises from the way the animals continually sniff and snort at the air, as though with a special knowledge or control of how the winds work?

Taboos included: "…meeting a pig on way to sail – also a parson – also anyone cross-eyed ["skelly-eyed"]. You would avoid them! Some Scots – if even the word 'pig' was mentioned – would grab a lump of iron to neutralise bad luck" (Bart Taylor, Cullercoats). "Fisherman would turn back if they met a cross-eyed woman or clergyman or pig en route – especially on a Friday. And never wore green or brown" (Joan Phillips, Cullercoats). "Friday morning was an especially unlucky time to use the word P-I-G" (Eyemouth).

At Flamborough:

One of the strictest taboos concerned the humble goat, any mention of which in working hours was considered most unlucky and could be relied on to rouse the gentlest fisherman to offensive action. The same applied to a pig, fox, cat, hare, or rabbit, the reason being that there is nothing easier to bewitch than a boat and that a witch can just as easily assume any of these animal forms. To name them was an open invitation to her to bewitch not only your boat and gear but you as well…

(www.wiles.family.btinternet.co.uk/flamborough_ghosts.htm)

In *Flamborough Village and Headland*, the story is told of an enterprising poultry and game dealer who went into a fisherman's cottage to ask if he wanted to buy any rabbits. Receiving an emphatic "Neea", the poulterer hopefully suggested a hare instead. On which the fisherman lost his temper completely and roared out, 'Noo thoo's gan far eeneaf, TAK THI 'OOK' [Clear off]" (*ibid.*).

Lethbridge (1952) is in agreement that these animal superstitions arose from the fear of a witch taking animal form and using the disguise to get close and cast a bad spell on a boat. His two examples concern a woman and a herd of goats:

> We were finally becalmed off the coast of Jutland and the Dutch woman could bear the inactivity no longer. A Danish fisherman came alongside and she was taken ashore. No sooner was she over the side than one of the Finnish crew wetted his finger and held it up. 'See,' he said triumphantly, 'the wind comes.' It did not come, as a matter of fact, and we drifted so close to the shore of the skaw that we had to be towed off by a motor fisherman…
>
> (Lethbridge, 1952, p.74)

> At that time a Cornish fisherman was working lobtser-pots off the shore. Many goats had run more or less wild on the cliffs and the fisherman's boy happened to see some. 'Look at those up on the cliff,' he said. The fisherman immediately picked up a stretcher from the bottom of the boat and hit him over the head.
>
> (*Ibid.*, p.90)

Chapter 5. In peril on the sea

The dangers of the North Sea have been keenly appreciated since human first set out upon it; even in an estuary, a boat could only too easily be caught in contrary tide and wind. In the following passage from a 15th century Life of St Cuthbert, only the saint's intervention can serve to avoid a tragedy, while pagan Angles, on the river bank, were more than content to see the hapless monks swept away…

Cuthbert and the Storm
(þ equals 'th')

Certayn <u>brethir</u> of þis abbay	brethren
Went forthe <u>be</u> water on a day	by
Trees and <u>fowel</u> for to gett.	fuel
In <u>slike</u> peryle <u>þai</u> were sett	such/they
Þat when þai <u>wend</u> to row to lande	meant
A west winde was <u>rysande</u>	rising
And bare þe <u>botes</u> nere to þe <u>se</u> –	boats/sea
Þai were likly lost to be.	
Þair brethir brathely wer aboute	swiftly
To save <u>þaim</u>, and sent <u>bates</u> oute.	them/boats
Bot þai war <u>lett</u> be wynd and <u>flode</u>	hinder'd/tide
So þat þai myght do na <u>gode</u>;	good
Bot <u>syn</u> mannes myght moght helpe noght	since
Of Goddis help þai all besoght...	
By þis þe fyve <u>bates</u> on þe <u>fame</u>	boats/foam
Þai were dryven so farr fra hame,	
Þat þai semed fyve litil <u>briddes</u>	birds
<u>Welterand</u> þe waves <u>in</u> <u>myddes</u>.	rolling/amid

On þe north water banke	
Stode many men, were <u>noght to thanke</u>,	unsympathetic
For þai had na compassioun	
Of þair neghburs confusioun;	
Þai scorned þair maner of <u>lovyng</u>,	worship
For it accorded to thairs na thing	
And saide þat þai were worthy	
To have þat harme and <u>vylany</u>.	disgrace
Þan Cuthbert curtasly þaim <u>blame</u>,	reproved
And saide, brethir, <u>leeves</u> for schame;	cease
It es mare <u>manhede</u> þaim to <u>mene</u>	humane/pity
And beseke God þair <u>bote to bene</u>	help to be
Þan <u>outhir</u> for to curse or scorne,	either
When þair lyves <u>er nere forlorne</u>.	are nearly lost
Þai ansuerd <u>heynosly</u> in haste:	nastily
To pray for þaim we <u>halde</u> it waste,	hold
Þai have <u>fordone</u> our <u>alde lawes</u>	destroyed/old customs
And broght in newe þat na man <u>knawes</u>;	knows
Were þai all <u>deede</u> it war na <u>charge</u>:	dead/shame
Þan myght we <u>leve</u> all at our <u>large</u>.	live/liberty
...When þus he þaire <u>countenance</u> sees	attitude
He kneles doune on <u>bathe</u> his knees	both
And bowed his <u>heved</u> in to þe erthe,	head
Prayed God to <u>gif</u> þaim better <u>werde</u>.	give/fate
Þan þe wynd it chaunged <u>belyue</u>	quickly
And all þe bates agayne dryve	
With all þair <u>charge</u>: whare þai walde be	load
Come þe batemen with <u>gamen</u> and gle.	mirth

(*The Metrical Life of Cuthbert*, Surtees Society, vol.87,1891, Bk.II)

The risks multiplied as fishing and coastal trade became major industries in the modern period. There have been many great examples of heroic work by local lifeboats – and some disasters – and these all need to be seen in the context of the overwhelming risk to sailing vessels, if a contrary gale drove them toward the rocky coast:

"Dominating easterly gales turn the coast into a treacherous lee shore with heavy breakers and surf sometimes well out to sea, preventing safe entry to many harbours" (Mannering & Greenhill, 1997, p.45).

Some were saved, but many, many more perished: a House of Commons Committee 1857–58 reported 850 lives and property to value of £1.5 million to £2 million lost *annually* by shipwreck on British coasts (Cortis, 1871, p.3), while specific to the North East region, "The loss of from 50 to 100 vessels and from 20 to 50 or 60 lives in a single day on this line of coast, was shown to be a far too frequent occurrence" (*ibid*. p.5).

The following examples give some idea of the scope of the problem – not only bad weather but unseaworthy vessels kept at sea by their owners for reasons of false economy – and the various consequences – examples drawn unnecessarily from round where I live at Seaham for I take them to be typical of much of the North East coast:

Seaham Harbour – Severe Gale, Shipwreck and Loss of 1 Life

Late on Saturday night and early Sunday morning last 29th November, a very sudden gale from the South-East was experienced here. At daylight and for some time afterwards, it was impossible to distinguish anything at sea, the clouds and driving torrents of rain, and the raging sea seemed to blend together.

About 8.45am the weather slightly cleared up and a vessel was seen exactly opposite and very near to the entrance to the Harbour. When first seen she was standing to the North, but immediately afterwards her head was turned towards the harbour and she ran rapidly in: she was however carried by the force of the wind and sea past the entrance and North Pier on to a bed of rocks and sloping breakwater at the base of the lighthouse.

By this time the crew, four in number, had taken to the rigging, the sea making a clear breach over the vessel. At the first appearance of the vessel the harbour bell had been rung and the alarm given. A crowd of men including many sailors from vessels in port assembled to render what help they could. The lifeboat Sisters Carter was launched and manned but it was found impossible to make any use of it as the distressed ship was on the rocks within 15 minutes after she was first seen.

The Coastguard under Mr R. Ching were promptly in attendance with rocket apparatus and line but the vessel was so near the North Pier that a line could be thrown on board by hand. The first line was hauled on board by the crew with the intention of fixing a hawser line to the Bowsprit and getting the men on shore with the 'cradle'.

The next swell of the sea carried away both masts and bowsprit and the men had to be hauled ashore by lines. One of the men had a narrow escape, the line attached to him slipped and he fell into the raging sea. Seeing the danger a man named [Anthony] Hedworth employed by the Londonderry Engine Works jumped in to save him and both men were helped out.

The captain, an elderly man named Ranson, was still on board and although several lines were thrown and fell close to him, he seemed to make no effort to save himself. Seeing this, a pilot named John Marshall volunteered to get on board with a rope round his waist. He succeeded in doing so, but before he could reach the Captain, a hungry sea broke over the ship carrying him away with the portion of the rigging to which he was lashed, it also washed Marshall overboard but by means of the line he was drawn ashore. Although only a few minutes had elapsed, the ship was now a complete wreck. She proved to be the *Lady Ann* of Wells, Norfolk, for where she had sailed on Friday with a load of wheat from Stockton on Tees. She had been overtaken by the storm when off the Yorkshire coast and was unable to make the land until she reached Seaham.

The Captain's body was found on Monday on the beach opposite the Vicarage, Seaham, quite naked and mutilated. The *Lady Ann* was about 80 tons and owned by the Captain.

(Durham Advertiser, Friday 4 Dec., 1874)

On Oct. 9th, 1823, during a great storm, a vessel came ashore a little south of Castle Eden dene, and lay over at a considerable angle some distance from the beach. The occupants of a farmhouse in the vicinity were speedily on the beach to render aid, if possible. It was soon seen that there was someone in the roundtop of one of the masts, and the farmer's son, George Gray, offered to swim through the space of water between the ship and the shore. He did so, and got on board by means of the wreckage which was hanging over the ship's side. On ascending the mast he found a poor boy who had been lashed there for about six hours, and who was so benumbed with cold that he could not render himself any assistance. Gray cut the lashings which bound him, but the boy was so utterly helpless that he took him in his arms and jumped overboard with him, and managed to reach the shore, when those on the beach took him in charge. Gray then swam back to the ship to assist the remaining crew, who were sheltering as best they could. The tide was rising, and the spray covering them. It was quite dark before the last of them got on shore, and it was quite certain that if they had not been thus rescued they would all have perished before the next morning's light.

(Baharie, 1887, p.133)

Though the examples above involve commercial vessels, terrible disasters also befell the fishing boats of the North East, and were felt the more keenly in the effect loss of life could have on a small community...

On the morning of the Tuesday 18th March 1851 a fishing fleet of 23 cobles manned by 92 men and boys went out to sea to go line fishing. During the late morning the weather worsened and the wind became gale force. Many of the fishing boats cut their lines and hurried for home. Some boats landed at Creswell and one landed at East Sea Sands. One coble manned by brothers Robert and Henry Brown and brother-in-law William Armstrong attempted to land at East Sea Sands but the boat was overturned. The 2 brothers were seen clinging to the upturned coble but the sea washed them away; they then clung to an oar and a buoy...

In total 9 fishermen from 3 vessels drowned during both disasters on that day in 1851. The loss of the 3 cobles and their crew devastated the community of Newbiggin-by-the-Sea and every fishing family suffered a loss of some sort. In fact the 18th March was a day to be remembered for years to come – some families would not go out fishing on that day, and this day was avoided for arranging weddings or baptisms.

(www.twmuseums.org.uk/fishtales)

Well-designed harbours to provide shelter, the chain of lighthouses, the efforts of life-savers did what they could to reduce the terrible annual loss of life, but it was, in the long term, the fitting of engines to the majority of boats that gave the crew a somewhat better chance of a safe voyage – with the provisos that, for fishermen, "it's still the most dangerous of businesses and, today, machinery is the cause of some of the danger" (Adrian Osler).

Chapter 6. Life-saving, lifeboats and lighthouses

Communities of fishermen, well aware of the dangers attending their work on a moody sea in vulnerable cobles, had a brave sense of looking after their own and helping when they could. This is expressed in twentieth century form here:

> If a motorcar breaks down on the road, someone will come put it right or tow you away. But if a boat breaks down on the river, you've got the wind and the tide, you cannot control it. If it's a falling tide, you don't want to blow onto the bank side. You cannot control the elements. You waited, and if someone happened to pass, 'hey, you alright?' – there was a great camaraderie, everybody waved to each other. The foy boat men used to have a great big hook, they've got one in the Museum of Discovery, it would hook on to the ship's rail anyway they could, when a ship came in, if the ship was going onto the river, to Pelaw or something like that, to the buoys, they used to hook onto the ship and the ship would tow them out. If you were drifting and someone saw you they'd always say do you want a tow – 'Aye, you can give us a tow, just tow us to Mill Dam, or Ferry landing' or somewhere. It did happen, but you generally managed. You didn't want to break down.
>
> (Ernie Keedy, Beamish, 2005/130)

But if it was a case – only too frequent – of some alien commercial vessel in distress, the motivation was not always so strong. In former centuries there was a certain indifference to life-saving, perhaps stemming from a belief that one should not interfere in the darker workings of the Deity, and if He had preordained drowning for some or many, it was not up to humans to interfere with His judgement. It was in this tradition, likely, that most sailors did not bother to learn how to swim.

An even more negative influence was the common law on salvage, which allowed that private individuals could not claim contents of a shipwreck if any of the crew survived alive to assert the original title to the cargo. Though such assertions were set aside by statute in 1771, the Law continued to regard the salvage of cargo and the rights of property above and against the saving of life: attitudes that had, in effect, to be unlearned during the nineteenth century.

A particular role in this was taken by Christian philanthropists who encouraged the sense of Christian mission that came to imbue the work of the lifeboat. An early example, the initiative of Canon Sharpe, was a 'benevolent insitution' based at Bamburgh Castle. It provided that: "in every great storm, two men on horseback are sent from the castle to patrol along the coast, from sun-set to sun-rise, that in case of an accident, one may remain by the ship, and the other return to alarm the castle". In the castle itself:

> ...rooms, beds, and support are provided for shipwrecked seamen [and] cellars and storehouses for depositing their goods saved from the wreck. Screws for raising ships, chains for weighing vessels, blocks, tackle cables, handspikes, ropes and every necessary is ready for the relief of ships in distress or wrecked, and when any dead bodies are cast on shore, coffins and funeral expences are furnished gratis.
>
> (Baharie, 1849, p.12, fn)

There were many factors informing the new enthusiasm for lifeboats: a mix of "a favourable social framework of humanitarian ideals, maritime awareness and upper-class 'interest'" (Osler, 1990, p.82) – not least from boat owners and insurers. The promotional work of Henry Greathead is covered admirably in Osler's *Mr Greathead's Lifeboats* (1990) – a boat builder, he pioneered early lifeboat design in South Shields around 1800.

An early lifeboat station was established at Seahouses in 1827 by the National Lifeboat Institution (forerunner of the RNLI); and it was from Seahouses in 1838 that Grace Darling and her father achieved the memorable rescue of members of the crew of the *Forfarshire*, wrecked on the rocks of the Farne Islands. By the end of 1839 there were thirty lifeboat stations round the British coast. These were often set up by local initiative, as for example after the gale in March 1851 mentioned above, the Duke of Northumberland was moved to provide the town with a lifeboat. At Seaham, fishermen and townsfolk joined to raise funds to finance their own lifeboat. An unusual contribution to this project came from the publishing of a small booklet *The beacon: A poem in 3 cantos by Thomas Moore* (printed and published by David Atkinson, Seaham, in 1854) – of which a copy survives in the British Library. A short introduction, headed 'Life Boat for Seaham Harbour', explains:

> The exposed position of the Port of Seaham, and there not being an efficient Life Boat attached to the Harbour to communicate with vessels in the Offing in distress, or cast on the Coast by gales, renders it important that efforts should be forthwith made to supply the Port with a Life Boat.
>
> The Board of Trade is disposed to assist Voluntary Subscriptions, but it requires near upon £163;400 to supply a Boat, Boat-house, and Carriage, with all suitable Gear.
>
> The heavy Gales, Snow Storms, and Loss of Life during the severe Winter of 1853–4, has led the Seamen of Seaham to remedy, if possible, this defect. They have therefore appointed a Committee... to endeavour to raised the necessary funds...
>
> The Boat, if the necessary funds are forthcoming, will be under the super-intendence of the Seamen's United Friendly Association of Seaham, and manned on emergency by Volunteers, experience proving that regular crews are not always at their post in the hour of danger. The Government are about to offer rewards to persons saving life at sea, which would act as an additional stimulus to pilots, fishermen, or seamen, to render help when needed. As a means of assisting in raising the requisite amount, the President of the Seamen's United Friendly Association has placed this POEM at the service of the Committee, and the profit on the sale of the copies will be carried to the LIFE BOAT FUND.

Watching for the lifeboat

The Tynemouth Volunteer Life Brigade Watch House was built above the treacherous Black Middens, rocks on the north side of the mouth of the Tyne (away to the left of the watch house in this photo); the observation towers of the building face out to sea as well as towards the Tyne. From the grounds of the watch house a rocket could shoot a line out a ship aground on the rocks to enable a 'breeches buoy' to be set up between ship and shore.

Photo courtesy of Bill Griffiths.

Crew of *Will and Fanny Kirby* (Seaham lifeboat) ca.1974 – left to right: John Foreman, Dan Cave, Arthur Farrington, Malcolm McConnachie, Harry Sayes, Dick Thornton, Ray Riddle, Ronnie Leng; in black jumpers: Jeff Fox, Billy Black, Maurice(?) Bruce, Jimmy Cougle.

Photo courtesy of Story of Seaham Archive.

45lb salmon, the largest ever caught at Newbiggin. The two Newbiggin fishermen are Bob Robinson and George Robinson is the one with the big salmon.

Photo courtesy of Bill Harris.

"My mother Margaret Dawson nee Robinson... As a young girl my mother would go selling fish to help with the income; as the family grew older she also helped with lines, etc.

Years later my mother married Robert Dawson and had four children but my father who was a fisherman was lost at sea in 1940, so to bring her children up she had to start selling fish again. There was no pension, family credit or financial help as they have today, only the Parish, but my mother was a proud woman and brought us up on her own" (Mary Dickman).

Photo courtesy of Bill Harris.

"Cullercoats fisherwoman Mrs Storey (née Elizabeth Taylor) with a customer in Eltringham (near Prudhoe in the Tyne Valley) and three feline admirers looking for titbits. The creel on her back and the 'white handed' baskets appear empty so perhaps she is heading for home from Prudhoe railway station.

Little is left of Eltringham but the cottage in the background is an interesting item from the early 1900s.

Mrs Story was a familiar figure as she plied her trade in all weathers along the Tyne Valley for many years, working well into her 70s. She was a wonderful woman."

Photo and description courtesy of Joan Taylor Philips.

The older lady centre is Mary Smith. "The baskets were used by the women of the village to sell fish: they carried a creel on their backs and a basket on their arms and walked miles selling fish" (Mary Dickman).

Photo courtesy of Bill Harris.

Mr Robert Dawson and his wife Mary Dawson, of Newbiggin.

Photo courtesy of Bill Harris.

George Robinson of Newbiggin, 'reddin' the line'. "In fine weather the fishermen would bait and clean their lines at their front door" (Mary Dickman).

Photo courtesy of Bill Harris.

Cullercoats fisherman John Matthew Scott is sitting in the backyard of No.9 Promontory Terrace mending lobster pots. By his side is his wife Jane (néeTaylor) who is calling their black labrador, 'Rover'. John is wearing his Cullercoats gansey. The couple had a daughter Elizabeth Jane (Betty) who ran a wet fish business with a shop in Ryton; son John Heddon worked alongside his dad in the family coble *Silver Spray*.

They were a loving compact family but sad times lay ahead. John Heddon was drowned when the fill-fated Cullercoats lifeboat, the *Richard Silver Oliver*, capsized when out on exercise on 22nd April 1939; six others drowned including a 16-year-old naval cadet. John Matthew died of a broken heart 5 months later."

Photo and description courtesy of Joan Taylor Philips.

John Lisle Robinson and Robert (Bobby) Dawson of Newbiggin, with their catch – a box of salmon.
Photo courtesy of Bill Harris.

May Black née Kennedy, centre; Norman Kennedy to the right; old Mrs Kennedy left. The scene of the beach party is Dawdon, the year c.1938.

Billy Kennedy and friends at the beach party. To his left, Norman Kennedy, to his right the young Olive Newton. You may just be able to make out an indispensable Co-op pack to the fore.

Margaret Storey and Bella Arkle unloading the *Margaret Lisle*, returned from long line fishing (ca. 1932). "This was the women's job when the cobles landed – to carry lines and fish from the boats, then help pull the boats up the beach" (Mary Dickman).

Photo courtesy of Bill Harris.

Unemployed young men from Bishop Auckland JIC [Juvenile Instruction Centre] in camp at Seaham Harbour, 1936.

"In 1934 the Government made a law compelling all young persons between the ages 14 and 18 years to attend specially set up Juvenile Instruction Centres, (JICs). School leaving age was then 14 years, for those attending the Elementary Schools. These JICs were quickly called 'Dole Schools' by the youngsters who attended.

Many charitable and social organisations were worried about the debilitating nature of youth unemployment and organised activities for 14–18-year-olds. The then Duke of York (Later King George VI) had a charity fund which organised camps for unemployed youth. I helped run these camps at Seaham Harbour on the Durham Coast and I do know the youths enjoyed their 'breaks' at the camps. Trips to factories, shipyards, and fishing ports were arranged. One of the factories we visited was making meat pies and how the lads enjoyed the samples! Cricket and soccer matches were arranged with grammar schools. Results were immaterial – it was the well stocked tables of refreshments that won the games. During Coronation Year (1937) some of the youths helped to construct bonfires. They slept in tents beside the bonfire until the actual Coronation Day itself. Many took part in displays, parades and athletic competitions…"

Photo and description courtesy of Jack Gair.

The poem was, predictably?, a rhyming work in praise of Grace Darling. Properly classic in its diction, the narrative emphasises at every point the danger of the rescue attempt, perhaps with an element of adventure to the fore, but with undisguised admiration of the heroine's role in sallying forth "boldly amid the eddy's foam…"

Among the many other poets tempted to immortalise Grace Darling in verse are William Wordsworth and William McGonagall, whose plainer account opens:

> As the night was beginning to close in one rough September day
> In the year of 1838, a steamer passed through the Fairway
> Between the Farne Islands and the coast, on her passage northwards;
> But the wind was against her, and the steamer laboured hard…

Having seen the 'frail boat' whilst in temporary storage at Beamish Museum (you can now see the boat at the Grace Darling Museum in Bamburgh), I was struck indeed by her modest dimensions – and relieved at her state of preservation. I made her length overall 21 ft; six planks (or 'strakes') per side to the fore, tapering to 3 planks at the stern.

The nobility and heroism of risking one's life to save others' caught the popular imagination, and ensured that there was no lack of volunteers when it came to manning a lifeboat: in place of reluctance or indifference (and lack of practical means), we now see a positive competitiveness to take part in the privilege of assisting strangers at risk of their lives on the coast:

> Down on the 'Sand end', near the Narrows, is a curious busy, striving crowd, from which, in strange contrast with the solemn sense of danger and peril oppressing all other groups, the jarring discord of a wrangling disputation arises. There are brawny pilots in great sea-boots, oil-skins, and sou' westers; huge fishermen in thick jerseys and woolcaps; riverside hands and steamboat-men in heavy pilot coats and moleskins, gaunt keelmen and giant ship-carpenters – all shouting, gesticulating, and, at times, even threatening each other with upraised arm, expostulating, or denouncing in fierce earnestness something that is said to be 'not fai-or'. Strong-faced, herculean men, most of them, but no stronger in a certain dauntlessness of visage than other quieter and slighter-framed individuals whose dress denotes the ordinary non-seafaring townsman, possibly young doctor, or under-viewer of a colliery, or manager of an anchor works. The clamour is fitful but unending; its burly tones mingled with the voices of anxious, tearful women, clinging to or pulling at the arms of the unnoticing, contentious men. A few hand-lanthorns cast a flickering light upon the scene, and a dull ruddy glow from the rude cresset standing by the doors of the lifeboat-house fitfully tints the rolling masses of vapour blowing in from the offing, the wind now and then carrying a whirling column of red sparks away over the top of the Look-out House.
>
> These are volunteers for death, and the deep-voiced struggle is for the precious right to a place in the forlorn hope. Shields is the birthplace of the life-boat, and this fierce wrangle for a place in the very ark of God is one of the most precious heritages of her sons. Men who were scarce strong enough to ship one of the big heavy oars, won by strenuous fight a seat in the devoted bark, and only when in the crux of a struggle with unimaginable

billows, showed by lack of strength – never by want of courage – that it had been better they'd not been there... Men were drowned or killed at their oars, thrown out of their places as they struggled through some frantic confusion of waters, and sometimes the whole crew was overwhelmed by the upsetting of the boat, and drowned in sight of the people on shore, whom they had just shaken loose from.

But in the terrible jaws of the Tyne, the greater peril of a cast-away ship lay in the fact that she could not be reached by the life-boat when in the sharpest stress of danger. The shoals of the Herd and ridge of the Middens were accessible only in certain states of the tide, hence men chafed and fretted as they saw lives lost while the life-boat floated uselessly at the foot of the slips. When however, some battered craft passed through the iron portals of the estuary, and came to grief on a point that might by some lucky chance be reached, then with a rush the boat was crowded by a struggling mass of men, beating off frantic assailants, and angrily bidding their women and bairns to 'be quiet' – palpitating with a great fear that the south-side boat* might be first – towed as far as the venturesome tug dared, and then cast loose in the face of a sea that would appal the soul of any man not born within the sight and common experience of it.

Through the day and through the night these men await their chance, and when it comes, hang by hours on the skirts of death, trying to get 'longside the shivering wreck and picking up now and then the man or two who have not already been swept off by the rushing mounds of live water which follow each other so swiftly over the broken hull...

(Haswell, *The Maister*, pp.150–52)

* "An equally devoted band was carrying on the same scene on the south side of the river" (*Original footnote*).

While there is a definite feel of Romantic heightening in this account, it was true enough that a terrible risk to vessels was posed by the 'Black Middens', a partially covered reef off the north shore. The Tynemouth Volunteer Life Brigade was set up in 1864 specifically to aid ships foundering on these rocks, by use of a rocket shooting a line to enable a 'breeches buoy' to be set up between ship and shore. The TVLB headquarters had less of a role to play once extensive breakwaters were built at the mouth of the Tyne, but the clinker-built brigade house endures, a unique living 'museum', its history magnificently fictionalised in Robert Westall's book *The Watch House* (London, Macmillan, 1977).

Remarkable examples of the lengths local crews would go to launch the lifeboat in case of need are recorded. On New Year's Day 1861 the *Lovely Nelly* from Seaham was driven onto rocks at Briadene in a blizzard. The women of Cullercoats (assisted, it is said, by horses and some menfolk) hauled the lifeboat over the headland to launch it from where they could reach the wreck, saving all but the cabin boy, Tommy, who clung unhappily to the wreck. This great endeavour was recorded in a painting by John Charlton now hanging in the Laing Art Gallery, Newcastle, and in 1993 by an opera, *Cullercoats Tommy*, by Michael Wilcox and Edward McGuire, performed with the Northern Sinfonia, Northern Stage, Folkworks and Dance City as part of the Tall Ships Race celebrations that year. And:

It is recorded that, at times, as many as 100 ships a day were entering Seaham Harbour, the local pilots being expert at ship handling. They were also prepared to risk their lives in attempting to save the crews of vessels in distress, such as the occasion on January 1st, 1835, when, with the help of a large number of people, they hauled a coble overland to Hawthorn Hythe where the brig Rainbow had been driven ashore in heavy seas and driving snows. Manned by four Seaham pilots, Taylor, Ellemor, Appleby and Dobson, the coble was launched and, in two trips, brought ashore the brig's crew, plus the body of the Captain's wife.

(Jeff Morris, 1988, p.1)

It only remained for proper organisation to direct willing effort. In 1824 Sir William Hillary co-ordinated the first lifeboat service. His appeal to the nation led to the National Institution for the preservation of Life from Shipwreck (later to become the RNLI).

Lifeboats

In 1849–51 a competition was held by the Duke of Northumberland for an ideal design for a lifeboat, though opinions on this continued to vary, and well into the twentieth century there was no one standard lifeboat design. As a local crewman in Seaham recollected, on arrival in Cowes to select a new lifeboat, why they chose a Liverpool class over a 'self-righter':

> In the 1930s, the lifeboat was an open boat, called the Elliot Galer. This was replaced in 1936 by the *Elizabeth Wills Allen* (boats usually named in memoriam). That had a canopy, was steered by wheel and had a watertight compartment for the engine, aft. The hull was wooden, and there were both sails and a single screw worked by a petrol engine, on special high octane fuel. It was a 36–38 footer. The crew was a Coxswain, Second Coxswain, Mechanic, Second Mechanic, two Signallers and a Bowman. The First Signalman would do the morse (with a shutter on an electric light – this stopped the beam being visible from above in line with war-time precautions) and semaphore. The signallers would be expected to help with the sails. The Bowman looked after ropes, etc. The area chief was Commander Wheeler – a real corker – an ex-R.N. man and used to makingyoudowhatyouweretold... The worst night we had on the *Wills Allen* was when we were sent out to rescue a motorship called the *Crescence* that was like to get blown ashore near Dawdon Pit. There was a strong (onshore) north-east wind. Her engine broke down and she started dragging her anchors. Then they sent rockets up. The tugs couldn't get out of Seaham Harbour because of the adverse tide, so a signal was sent to Sunderland for a tow; we were to help them link up. The tug was a screw tug, but had difficulty getting near enough to get a line across to the *Crescence* because the weather was so bad. It set the ships rolling too much. So we went between and fired a line to the motor vessel and got the other end to the tug ready to tow out to sea clear of the shore. They towed her back to Sunderland and we accompanied them in case the line broke, which it did off Seaham Hall before we reached Sunderland. Then we came back under sail – with the wind behind us, we went like a flash, flew down from there. But it was a long night that, and hard work.
>
> Anyway a new lifeboat was to be brought back, and the crew and Commander Wheeler went down to Cowes. The mechanic, Lenny Brown, had been there for a week or two learning about the engine. The rest of us, Coxswain, Bowman, me as Second Signaller, came down a day before sailing; two of us were billeted in the 'Robin Hood' overnight. We had had a choice of lifeboats, and went for a Liverpool type, because that was what we were

familiar with. There were self-righters too – one was under construction for Brixham at that very time – but it looked too narrow in the beam. It seemed that once that got overset, it would just go on and on rolling over and over. Whereas the Liverpool type had a good beam, solid construction and was proven in bad weather – as best we knew. Anyway, the boat selected was the George Elmy, provided by money left by his two sisters. This was a much improved model with two screws which did away with the need for sails. The hull was wooden, 40 foot overall. There was a canopy and watertight compartments; any water on deck ought to clear quickly through the scuppers. We were told that if it did go over, if you all went one side and pulled on the looped rope, it could be righted. But it wasn't self-righting.

We set off home on the 7th January 1951 and reached Seaham on the 13th. That was a good run, really, considering the choppy seas. Commander Wheeler – the Chief Inspector for North East lifeboats – was in charge on the first cruise of the *George Elmy*, and plotted the course. His friend and Chief Mechanic, Harry Horder, was along. The Coxswain was Bill Tracey from Seaham, the Mechanic Lenny Brown, Second Signaller Joe Henry, and Frank Page, Bowman.

The daily routine was, we breakfasted before we set out – about 6 am – we were dressed for the cold in oilskins and a lifebelt (which helps keep you warm). During the day we could have self-heating tins of soup, some chocolate, and ship's biscuits. Otherwise we had to wait for dinner until we made landfall for the night. The journey was made in six stages. The first day we went from Cowes to Newhaven, and stopped overnight at a hotel. (There was no room to sleep onboard, of course.) The second day we made Newhaven to Ramsgate, and again slept ashore. Then Ramsgate to Gorlston near Yarmouth; Gorlston to Spurn Head (we slept in the lifeboat-men's houses at Spurn – that was a long day: we sighted Spurn at 6pm but didn't reach shore till 2am because of the strong tide against us); then Spurn to Whitby; Whitby to Seaham.

Generally we kept to the shore – except going outside of the Goodwin Sands – then we were way way offshore. One day we witnessed a minesweeper blowing up a World War Two mine – we felt the shock onboard, though the explosion was 2 or 3 mile away.

The lifeboat house at Seaham was a shed with a ramp down from the east wall of the south Dock, in behind the South Pier. It could be launched any time, but risked hitting the bottom in a neap tide. There had been a radio since the Wills Allen; it connected to Cullercoats (the main radio station for the coastguard).

(Joe Henry, Story of Seaham Archive)

It was the ill-fated *George Elmy*, on the 17 November 1962, overturned at the very entrance to Seaham Harbour, after rescuing a coble crew caught in sudden bad weather. All but one life were lost (for a fuller account, go to www.story-of-seaham.com).

While life-saving round the coast continues to involve a number of public initiatives such as the Coastguard and Emergency Services, the RNLI with its lifeboat stations remains the core practical resource. The number of these stations has been reduced in recent years with the advent of faster lifeboats, better equipment and hi-tech communications and detection gear – yet something of the romance and Christian crusade of the work remains, and will always be present.

Lighthouses

Early assistance with navigation came in the form of local church towers, and is probably why St Mary's at Easington is set back a mile or more from the coast – but on the skyline as viewed from sea. Later on, look-out points and beacons are recorded on the coast, but these may have had more to do with defence than life-saving. Indeed "in the nineteenth century, such 'accidental' light sources were often regarded as a danger. In Co. Durham ordinances were issued to screen coastal lime-kilns from seaward view as their intense fires were confusing seamen over the proper lights" (Adrian Osler). Less confusingly, the coastal pits – until recently brilliantly lit up at night – served as excellent seamarks.

Lighthouses proper started to be used along the North East coast in the seventeenth century when the Farne lighthouse was established in 1673. The Trinity House of Newcastle-upon-Tyne was founded by charter in 1584; in 1606 it was given supervision of the coast from Whitby to Holy Island, principally dealing with the licensing of pilots. It took over the provision of lighthouses in the eighteenth century, and early examples in the North East included Berwick-upon-Tweed, Bamburgh, Farne, Coquet Island, Amble, Blyth, Souter Point and North and South Shields. These served not only as warnings of hazards but continued the tradition of providing useful seamarks – so it was important each could be identified visually by day or night

Tynemouth lighthouse, for example, showed at night:

> …a revolving light, which is constantly kept there, exhibiting a light in its brightest state, once every minute, like a star of the first magnitude; but gradually declining, and becoming less luminous, until it is quite eclipsed… [The] lantern is elevated 148 feet above the level of the sea, and may be seen 6 leagues off.
>
> (Baharie, 1849, p.2, fn)

At Bamborough, in fog, a bell was rung, and a small canon fired every 15 minutes (ibid., p.12, fn). Some lighthouses served as 'leading lights', signalling a safe passage for local fishermen:

> Eight miles north from the pier of Berwick is the small harbour of Eyemouth, formed by the outfall of the river Eye, and subordinate to the customs of Dunbar. The lights have been erected for the benefit of the fishermen frequenting the port of Eyemouth during the herring season. The brightest of the two lights is erected on a post about 28 feet form the ground, and is seen at a distance of more than 6 miles. The smaller light is placed at the pier-head, and whilst it indicates the entrance to the harbour it is in such a position relative to the other light as to afford a leading mark when the lights are brought into one line for the best passage into Eyemouth bay.
>
> (Barharie, 1849, p.33, fn)

Topics like wrecks and life-saving are dour enough but could be treated locally with a certain dark humour. The 'yearly box' referred to below was a mutual insurance club: after any pay-outs for loss of life and accident, what remained was distributed between contributing members at the end of the year, hence the rescuers' concern:

Many years ago, when the antiquated yearly box was more the rule than the exception, a mason and a shipwright went off into the roads in a small boat to fish. Returning to the harbour, they encountered two or three rollers on the bar, and the boat unfortunately getting athwart, was upset, and the two piscatorial adventurers* were thrown into the water.

Having a slight theoretical knowledge of swimming, they struck out in opposite directions.

A pilot standing on the pier hailed a pilot coble just coming to the bar, and directed the attention of the man on board to the men in the water. He began to pull vigorously towards the mason, when he was hailed by his friend on the pier with – 'Nut him. Geodie, nut him: Save the tother one fust.'

Geodie rested on is oars for an instant, and looking up to the pier, exclaimed – 'What matter dis't mak' which one aw save fust?'

'What matter!' shouted the other almost frantically – 'it mak's all the matter iv the wurld – divn't ye knaw that carpenter chap's iv our box!'

(Green, 1879, pp.30–31)

(**Note**: *fishermen!)

The bitter humour must have appealed for very much the same joke turns up in Seaham over a century later:

The North Pier at Seaham is a slippy place for anglers to fish from. It is not unknown for someone to fall in the sea and need speedy rescuing. On one occasion (after the pits had all shut) just such an accident occurred on the pier. Several ran round shouting for a lifebuoy to hoy to the man in the water, but another called out, 'Nivvor mind aal that, ax [ask] the man wheer he warks!' [works].

Chapter 7. The navy and big ships

The Tyne in particular became an important base of operations for the Royal Navy in the Napoleonic War era, and with it came the dreaded press gang. Sailors on the colliers were prime targets, and even those who obtained substitutes or exemptions were not respected – George Haswell opens his account of nineteenth century Shields with the shooting of a seaman by the press gang, apparently from sheer resentment that he had exemption.

The case of the *Blenheim* of Hull is extraordinary in that after defending herself successfully and bloodily against a boarding party from the press gang, the crew were brought to trial and acquitted (the full story can be found in Tyneside: *A Christmas annual for Tynemouth, North & South Shields and district*, printed in South Shields in 1890).

The loss by the press-ganging of the family breadwinner must have had serious consequences for the wives and children. Here, for example, is a description of the level of poverty in Sunderland in the 1810s:

> Sunderland about this time was in a wretched condition, wages for shipwrights employed about 15s per week, most of whom were cutting away Haughton-le-Spring embankment at about 1s 6d per day. The keelmen in arms, setting fire to and pulling down the staithes and railway bridge across Galleys Gill... No gas, no flagging, no policemen, no market place, a few sentry boxes, and a few old men as watchmen, who patrolled the streets, calling the hour and the state of the weather.
>
> (Sanderson, 1873, p.9)

The author, Thomas Sanderson, himself recollected going without food for one or more days as a child, before and after his father left the army. The resentment against the dominating role of the military in the North East is expressed in various satirical songs (e.g. by John Shield), but most poignantly in the following short verse:

> Where hez t' been, maa canny hinny,
> Where hez t' been, maa winsome man?
> Aw's been ti th' nor'ward, cruisin' back an' for'ard
> Aw's been ti th' nor'ward, cruisin' sair an' lang,
> Aw's been ti th' nor'ward, cruisin' back an' for'ard,
> But durna come ashore for Bover* an' his Gang.
>
> (from Haswell, 1895)

(*leader of the pressgang, 1770s)

On the lighter side, Heslop in the 1880s noted the word press gang as meaning 'a group of romping children'.

Several of the Navy's men-of-war ended up as training ships. *The Industrial Schools Act* (1866) permitted a magistrate to commit for training "homeless and destitute boys unconvicted of crime" of under 14 years of age (Baynham, 1904, p.5), in order "to have a constant supply of good, intelligent, and well conducted boys for both the Royal and merchantile marine" (*The Diana*, 1868, p.7).

> Boys typically joined the ships at the age of eleven or twelve and stayed until they were fifteen or sixteen. Discipline aboard the ships was strict and the birch often used to enforce it. Food was limited in quantity and variety — biscuit, potatoes, and meat were the staples, with occasional green vegetables... Sleeping accommodation was usually in hammocks which could be comfortable in the summer but icy-cold in winter.
> (http://users.ox.ac.uk/~peter/workhouse/trainingships/trainingships.shtml)

On the Tyne at North Shields, the Diana was replaced by HMS Boscawen (built 1844), renamed *TS Wellesley*, which trained boys aged 12–16 (a shore-based establishment took in children as young as seven). The *Wellesley* was destroyed by fire in 1914 and the school moved ashore becoming the Wellesley Nautical School. The *Trincomalee*, now berthed at Hartlepool, owed its preservation during the nineteenth century to its role as a training ship.

During the nineteenth century, Tyneside was at the forefront of technological developments in ship-building – the iron hull, the screw propeller, the turbine engine (1894). By the early twentieth century, Tyneside shipbuilders were constructing not only many cargo ships and the occasional liner, but dreadnoughts; armaments formed a massive industry on Tyneside.

In many respects, Sunderland and Wearside shared the good fortune of Tyneside as a major ship-building centre in the nineteenth and twentieth centuries – for an account based on the Austin and Pickersgill shipyard, see Tom Pickard's *We make ships* (1989). The term 'Makem' for a Wearsider is thought to come from the phrase "we mak 'em, ye tak 'em" referring to their reputation for fast and reliable ship-building.

A late-comer, Middlesbrough only developed as an industrial centre after the exploitation of iron ore deposits in neighbouring North Yorkshire in the 1870s. Not being dependent on ship-building, it has fared rather better than most over recent years, with Corus (the steel plant), a major oil refinery (Petroplus) at Port Clarence and up the coast, ICI at Billingham (until 1998).

Detailed coverage of the large-scale ship-building industry is beyond the scope of this book, and indeed occupied the banks of the rivers rather than the coast itself, but the reader is referred to J.F. Clarke's *Building Ships on the North East Coast* (2 vols, Whiltey Bay: Bewick, 1997).

Chapter 8. Development of ports

During the nineteenth century the main role for many coastal settlements became the export of coal: "…it was soon evident that if steam colliers were to achieve their full potential then harbours and loading facilities would need to show the same degree of improvement as the steam collier was to the collier brig" (MacRae & Waine, 1990, p.21). Considerable wooden structures (staiths and spouts) that carried coal wagons over the ships' holds to discharge their contents became main features of coal ports like Blyth and Seaham; Hendon Dock was constructed 1868, West Hartlepool's facilities expanded in the 1870s. The distinction between small fishing villages and well-funded coal ports became marked by the end of the nineteenth century, for the coal trade brought with it the need for hostelries for sailors, marine stores and victuallers, homes for dock workers, etc.

The following summary of port development is based on MacRae & Waine, 1990. Amble at the mouth of the Coquet "served the northenmost part of the Northumberland Coalfields" (MacRae & Waine 1990, p.32). The harbour here was consolidated in 1847. It remains as a busy fishing port.

Blyth lies some 8 miles north of the Tyne. The original quays and breakwater from 1765 were improved by John Rennie in the 1810s, and again when the port became a public company in 1854. The main problem is the lack of depth of water provided by the River Blyth.

Seaton Sluice also played a role in coal export. Here the river made an awkward 90° turn just before entering the sea, and an artificial cut was made, offering a straighter route and acting to scour the river it connected to.

The Tyne itself had been a major focus for shipping out coal and boat building from the late Middle Ages. Major facilities were the Albert Edward Dock at North Shields and the Tyne Dock at South Shields. The large piers at the mouth of the Tyne were completed in 1895.

The Sunderland Dock Company was established in 1846 by Act of Parliament, and the main piers at the mouth of the Wear were built in the late nineteenth century. Hendon Dock (the South Dock) was built in 1868 – with links by rail from Seaham, but is now empty, unused except by a few cargo vessels. The North Dock at Roker is now a marina.

Seaham Harbour was built specifically for coal export in the 1820s, and much expanded around 1900 with a large South Dock to cope with the new output from Dawdon Colliery. In the mid-1990s its warehousing was relocated and storage and distribution services are now as important as seaborne trade. The historic North Dock, once a thriving base for fishing cobles, awaits grants to re-form as a small marina and water sports centre.

West Hartlepool, like the Tyne, was a traditional shipping point – "the navigation in and out was quick and easy" (MacRae & Waine, 1990, p.44). New docks were built here in the 1840s and 1850s, to serve the East Durham coalfield. The docks were bought by the North East Railway in 1864, and the building of the Newcastle-Middlesbrough coastal railway c.1900 further advanced coal export opportunities, with new coastal pits opening shortly afterwards.

Much coal was destined to serve power stations, which accordingly were positioned on the coast (e.g. Fawley/Southampton) or on the River Thames (e.g. Battersea). To access the Thames west of the main bridges, a special type of collier was built, called a flat iron – with no superstructure to talk of, and funnels that could be lowered.

In the 1960s, transport of coal increasingly switched to the road system, which was speedier, cheaper, and capable of delivering coal to any destination. The decline of North East ports therefore predates the final closure of our coastal pits in the early 1990s.

Coal and the beaches

From about 1900 improvements in the technology of sinking shafts meant the deep-level coal along the coast of East Durham and out under the sea-bed could be accessed, and a number of collieries (Dawdon, Easington, etc.) started production. The spoil, in the tradition of ship's ballast, was cast on the beaches, particularly the Blast Beach at Dawdon and the foreshore around Easington.

In those days [1930s] the beach at Blackhall was a long stretch of golden sands before the effect of slag tipping despoiled the coast. We had no need to visit any of the local resorts having the sea and sand on our doorstep. Cost was another factor as no bus or train fares needed to be found out of the miner's small wages.

Towards the end of the 1930's slag and sea coal were being washed up on the beach and unemployed men from Hartlepool cycled to Blackhall beach and collected two or three bags of sea coal before facing the stiff climb up the access road to level ground. We kids 'helped' with the heavy load from the beach to the top for the going rate of one Woodbine between two of us – not a very good turn as it worked out!

As a special treat we were taken on foot to Crimdon Dene Lido where the beach remained spoil free until long after the war so far as I remember. Alas, we moved inland to Bowburn when I lost contact with the coast but have many happy memories of learning to swim, fishing for cod and fires on the beach and baked potatoes acquired from the nearby allotments.

(Jack Ledger)

The switch to automatic cutters for ripping out the coal meant a major increase in the amount of spoil to be disposed of, and ramps of shale were built to allow tankers with liquid slurry from the washeries to access the beaches. The load of spoil soon became more than the tide could scour away, and lurid layers of spoil built up, greys, greens, yellows... The Blast Beach, Dawdon, where the high tide could reach the cliffs in the 1930s, grew a wide new foreshore, with its own ecology of hazels and rabbits, a recreational facility in its own right.

(Incidentally, miners were often keen part-time fishermen with their own boats. As late as the 1970s it is rumoured that the DOSCO 1 team at Easington Colliery, who had purchased a fishing boat for recreation, found they could do better from their catch – during the Cod War with Iceland – and took a prolonged leave of absence to make the best of this windfall – to the exasperation of their formal employers.)

With the closure of the pits in the early 1990s, tipping ceased. A project, 'Turning the Tide', was initiated to deal with the worst of the problem, but in effect it was the tide that cleansed the beaches best, and the colour has faded from black-grey to tawny-sandy in the last 15 years – at the same time that the depth of foreshore has narrowed by perhaps half. Ironically, the tipping of spoil protected the foreshore and cliffs from erosion.

In terms of public enjoyment of the Durham coastline, the presence of collieries often blocked access to the beaches and cliff tops, so that the coastal zone of East Durham remained 'wild' in the sense of little visited. Now a cliff-top path is in place that links the denes and gives splendid views of this little-known stretch of coast. Sadly, new factory development has been encouraged between Dawdon and Hawthorn Dene that dominates the skyline and is beginning to eat up open farmland. It is a return to 'Victorian values' we could do without.

Chapter 9. Smuggling

It may seem that given that given the blessing of a beautiful coastline, nothing has so much occupied us as finding pernicious uses for it. Nonethless, I hope you will agree that smuggling is a proper topic to include in this survey, if only to counterbalance the view that Cornwall holds a monopoly on the dubious practice and the considerable income its ghostly reputation generates today. Whether any county or town should parade its black past in order to sell cream teas is a reasonable question; it leaves me speechless with envy that Whitby can capitalise on Count Dracula.

Such considerations aside, you may like to know that it was in the reign of Charles II that smuggling took off, that king having realised that a small import duty on a large number of popular goods provided him with an excellent non-parliamentary income. The operators who sought to avoid paying duty in order to supply people with goods at a lower price were from this time known as smugglers (from the Dutch… previously, 'owlers' had aimed to smuggle wool *out* of England. Some also used the term 'moon-rakers').

From 1668, there was a 5% levy on imports of tea, coffee, tobacco, spirits and fine fabrics. (It is difficult to object to taxes on luxuries or what some would consider vices.) By the mid- eighteenth century rates had risen steeply: tea cost 7 shillings a pound in England, of which 5 shillings was duty. By the end of the century, whisky costing 1 shilling per gallon to make would have to sell for 2/9d to cover duty, while brandy that was worth 5 shillings in France would command 32 shilling in England (or about 25 shillings if smuggled in). (Figures *via* Morley, 1993, pp.44, 48; and Nicholls, 1973.)

The main items that attracted import duty around 1800 would have been spirits, tobacco and tea, "but any article that could show a reasonable return was smuggled, for instance books, candles, dice, sailcloth, salt, soap, and sugar" (Smith, 1994, p.77). Morley further mentions chocolate, spices and precious metals. Moreover, during the war with France (1793–1815), "Customs duties rose sharply to pay for the materials of war and the importation of all French goods was totally forbidden." In short, the ideal conditions for smuggling.

In 1821, it was noted here in the North East that:

Geneva [gin] may be bought in Holland for 1s 8d per gallon and the selling price in England is 19s 6d. This enormous difference resulting from the duty upon the importation of foreign spirituous liquors. The consequence is that smuggling holds out such temptations that the greatest exertions are used to carry it on.

(Losh, 1821, p.128)

Clearly the difference between the taxed and the smuggled item was sufficient to make it worth while braving detection and secretly importing the goods to resell. The public benefited from lower prices, greater availability and a frisson of glee in outwitting the authorities; the smugglers benefited financially in a higher degree, though they risked higher penalties. Those that lost out were the government, through reduced revenue, and legitimate traders, whose more highly priced goods became suspiciously unpopular.

However, popular sympathy is almost always with the smuggler, and it might well be said, in this case, that the Law creates the crime. "Excessive duties present a temptation to evade them; and the law loses a part of its moral force, when it first tempts to a violation of it and then punishes the offender" (Banks, 1871, p.4). This element made it particularly hard to suppress smuggling: it was seldom seen as a serious offence in public eyes, even when the war with Napoleon made any contact with France virtually treasonable. It was just a traditional local industry much as tourism now is, or playing the planning permission regulations.

A faint echo of North East involvement in smuggling may survive in place-names like: Brandy Lake (north of Amble, N'd); Frenchman's Bay (Marsden, D'm); Fenchies' Creek (Blast Beach, Dawdon, D'm); Gin Cave (Blackhall, D'm); Wine Haven (Robin Hood's Bay, nYx)… but more direct testimony is not to hard to find: the diary of James Losh records, for Northumberland, in 1821:

> I went to Boomer…I never saw any thing more striking than the state of that village, as shewing the miserable effects of over taxation, and excessive duties…
>
> The consequence is that smuggling holds out such temptation that the greatest exertions are made to carry it on. A large capital is embarked in it and regular arrangements made not only for avoiding the duties, but for protecting the persons employed in that illicit commerce…
>
> The worst consequences of all are, however, the profligate habits and utter disregard of morality, of most of those concerned in this traffic. Boomer is a small fishing village, well situated both for catching and selling fish, and the inhabitants who are all tenants of the Duke of Northumberland have their cottages and each a garden and a small piece of ground upon very moderate terms, but with the true spirit of gamblers or desperate speculators, they neglect their ordinary affairs, seduced by the hope of immense profits from smuggling…
>
> (Losh, p.128)

In the words of a modern writer:

> Cobles were in use in all the recognised fishing villages along the coast and because of their design and sturdy adaptability they were able to turn any stretch of sand into a fishing and therefore a smuggling harbour… During the heyday of smuggling there were literally hundreds of them sailing the inshore waters of the Yorkshire coast… Indeed they were so suited to smuggling that one could imagine they had been specially designed for the trade.
>
> (Smith, 1994, p.43)

In Cleveland:

> It was generally reckoned inside revenue circles [in the 18th century] that practically the whole populations of Redcar, Saltburn, Marske, Staithes, Runswick and Robin Hood's Bay were concerned with smuggling, many of the inhabitants having no other occupation.
>
> (Dykes, 1978, p.30)

At Saltburn:

> Continuing past the miniature railway station, you'll pass the boats beached on the shingle before arriving at the Ship Inn, a beach side pub... Next to this is a little museum dedicated to Saltburn's illustrious past as a smuggler's haven with tales of illicit spirits, tobacco and other contraband, set in original fishermen's cottages next to the pub which can provide an interesting half-hour's entertainment...
>
> (From a webite of day-trips from Chester-le-Street)

At Seaham:

> Smuggling was carried on to some extent, and the farm buildings afforded convenient hiding places for stowing the goods. Smuggling went on until comparatively recent times. The last capture was said to have taken place on a dark night by information laid by one of the agents of the estate, who had himself profited by the trade. However this may be, it was noticed that from the time of the capture this same agent never dared to be abroad after nightfall, no doubt fearing the threats of his victims.
>
> (R.A. Aird, 1909)

And oral accounts... such as that of the cave at the foot the cliff near Seaton Sluice – a beacon would be lit above to indicate when it was safe to land.

While direct contact between Newcastle and Amsterdam could account for a good trade in illicit gin, this sort of import would be better conducted through the less supervised fishing villages of the coast. Colliers returning in ballast from London would make especially useful carriers; when they reached the North East what easier than for local fishing cobles to sail out and unload the gin or brandy? A curious piece of circumstantial evidence for this is the tower on Kinley Hill, south of Hawthorn Hive (D'm) – a ruin, built as a ruin. A harmless folly? But consider the following...

> On a much larger scale were the smugglers' towers, which today are usually dismissed as being follies or eye-catching features built by landowners to enhance the interest of their estates.
>
> (Morley, 1994, p.61)

In practical terms, such towers were ideal look-out posts, from which both the sea (for approaching appropriate vessels) and the land (for encroaching Coastguards) could be readily scanned. A signal could be sent to assure a vessel of the readiness of those on shore; indeed, without any signal, the tower itself could serve as a sea-mark where colliers could haul to and expect to get contraband unloaded by local cobles.

As the merchandise reached land, a pair of tubs, ready roped together, would be placed over a man's shoulders (one tub in front, one behind) for carrying to the stashing place. (This initial journey might well be up paths too steep or tricky to permit the use of animal transport, especially at night.)

> Although the actual landing and storing of contraband was largely the responsibility of the seafaring folk, the job of transporting inland eventually fell to organised groups of horse owners from the farming community or the gentry.
>
> (Labistour, 1996, p.51)

Again:

> Especially in the northern part of the county [Yorkshire], farmers and fishermen, normally poles apart, had a strong common interest when it came to contraband. The fishermen carried, the farmers consumed and stored. Many must have had mini-warehouses…
>
> (Dykes, 1978, p.35)

– which we call 'barns'. (Cellars and caves might play a similar role.) The contraband would then be transported, probably by donkey (hence the need for a code-name like 'cuddies'?) or on carts (farm-wagons), to the nearest town, or to individual inns or purchasers in the neighbourhood. It is unlikely that contraband goods would be sold, at least openly, in shops or markets.

Countermeasures in the eighteenth century were somewhat haphazard. By the 1800s, with maximum income needed for the war with France, a Preventive Waterguard was establish in 1809 under the Customs Board. In 1816, with the war over, the Waterguard was adsorbed into the English Navy and the Navy employed to blockade its own coast. The combined power of the smaller, more agile fighting ships was used to intercept contraband in transit across the sea. The target was principally the South East coast, where the blockade was in effect by 1817; it is uncertain how far this would have been the case in the North East, though James Losh (1821, p.128) noted:

> In addition to a whole host of Custom House and Excise officers, they [the government] have armed cutters at sea and armed men ashore stationed along the whole coast, under the command of officers of the Navy…

In 1822 the Coast Guard was formed under the direction of the Customs Board, to form a land force to co-operate with the naval blockade. The reasons for all this activity are clear. The sums at stake were stupendous: in 1832, £15,892,792 worth of tobacco was imported into England, producing £2,428,532 worth of revenue for the government at a rate of 2/9d or 3 shillings per pound weight.

By combining land and naval forces, it seemed that the government was winning the war against smuggling by the 1830s. But the final victory came with a much simpler solution. In his budgets of 1842 and 1845, Peel lowered all duties, and abolished duty altogether on some 600 commodities. It signalled the end of smuggling as a trade. Peel argued that not only would his measures encourage free trade, and counter the lawlessness of smuggling, but encourage people at last to buy the legitimate taxed goods (as prices went down). In its place he revived income tax, but that is another story.

Some North East statistics
The main Parliamentary record of smuggling offences forms part of their *Papers* for 1825 (vol.XXIII, p.505). This is useful as recording by county the total committals to jail between 5 April 1814 and 5 April 1824 "for illegally vending, or attempting to introduce FOREIGN GOODS."

For Co. Durham, year by year, they are *(numbers in prison)*:

2 in 1817	1 in 1818	1 in 1821	13 in 1822	10 in 1823
9 in 1824				

For comparison, in Northumberland, the figures were:

1 in 1815	5 in 1816	4 in 1817	2 in 1818	6 in 1819	7 in 1821
2 in 1822	3 in 1823				

But in Kent:

13 in 1815	10 in 1816	34 in 1817	27 in 1818	60 in 1819	67 in 1820
50 in 1821	65 in 1822	46 in 1823	24 in 1824		

These show either:

(i) that smuggling activity was less in the North East than in the South East
(ii) that smugglers in the North East were better at evading capture than their Southern brethren or
(iii) that efforts to capture smugglers were concentrated on the South East.

As is often the case when you are presented with tricky options, all are in some measure correct. The devotion to smuggling in the South can readily be explained by the fact that smugglers there had the almost insatiable market of London to supply. An enquiry ordered by Pitt the Younger in the 1780s confirmed that smuggling west of the Tamar and north of the Humber supplied only local demand; the bit in-between had the plum job of supplying London.

Further records from 1833 (*Parliamentary Papers*, vol.XXXIII, p.269, ff) give detail of individual cases:

- a vessel at Hull was fined £100 "Knowing 66 lbs of foreign manufactured tobacco to be on board on vessel in port, in illegal packages."
- at Grimsby: "Found on board a vessel laden with 6,623 lbs foreign manufactured tobacco, in illegal packages."
- at Newcastle, in 1832, Charles Redwood was fined £100 and spent 1 month 1 day in gaol after he was "Taken on board a vessel laden with 954 gallons of foreign brandy, 648 gallons of geneva (gin), and 28 bales of tea, in illegal casks and packages."
- in Durham Jail 1831–1832 there were five prisoners guilty on charges relating to illicit spirits. They included: Peter Hallowday, sentenced to a £25 fine and 3 months in gaol, for "having illicit spirits in [his] possession," and Edward Gorman, sentenced on 14 January 1832 to a £50 fine and 9 months in gaol, but remaining in custody in 1832 "till payment of penalty".

The problem of dealing with prisoners who could not pay their fines was tackled at Newcastle Jail "by employing the prisoners in breaking stones for the highway; a great saving is likely soon to be effected in the expense of maintaining them" (*Parliamentary Papers*, 1831, vol.XXXIII, p.521).

Even more practically, of 1827 persons convicted of smuggling in 1833, 596 were "sent to serve on Board His Majesty's Ships" (*Parliamentary Papers*, 1833, vol.XXIX, p.403).

Not everyone at that time condoned smuggling:

John Wesley was bitterly opposed to smuggling – he had spoken out strongly against it just up the coast in Sunderland. On 16 Jun 1751, he recorded in his journal that he had 'told them plain, none can stop with us unless he part with all sin, particularly robbing the King, selling or buying run goods, which I could no more suffer than robbery on the highway.'

(Labistour, 1996, p.53)

It seems that an unrepentant sector of his congregation stood up, no doubt with some regret, and left.

Helping oneself

It can be tempting (after the Cornish model) to attribute the custom of wrecking to our region, with, I think, little justification. The following testimony from a visitor to Holy Island in 1643 shows the islanders expressing an interest in ships miscarrying on the coast – but one can surely detect an unhealthy cynicism on the part of the informer:

The Governor tould us how the common people ther do pray for shippes which they sie in danger. They al sit downe upon their knees and hold up their handes and say very devotely: 'Lord send her to us: God send her to us.' You, seeing them upon their knees and their hands joyned, do think that they are praying for your sauveties [safeties], but their myndes are far from that. They pray not God to sauve you, or send you to the port, but to send you to them by shipwrack that they may gette the spoil of her.

(qu. *Journal of the Coble & Keelboat Society*, 27, 2006)

A little 'light looting' has certainly been common enough:

It seems that a Danish ship laden with kegs of butter ran aground opposite Hendon Paper Mills, or was it Ryhope? At any rate a large proportion of the cargo was washed up at Seaham and people hastened to the beach with all manner of conveyances to get a supply of 'free butter or bacon'.

Most of the cargo was eventually sold by auction in Messrs Elgey's timber yard in Foundry Road, and the police were kept busy examining prams which were seen leaving the beach, for in several instances the so-called 'sleeping babby' turned out to be a nice fat keg of butter carefully covered with sheet or shawl. I have myself seen a faded picture of the butter kegs strewn along the shore...

(C.A. Smith in *Sunderland Echo*, 13 May, 1965)

This event is known locally as 'The Butter Boat', alias the *Niord*, that ran aground on the last day of 1899. The cargo was casks of butter and other edibles, safe from spoiling by the sea, and in number so plentiful that nigh on everyone turned out to take a share, at least until the police collared a few.

The agents of looting were not always human. When the *West Hyka* ran aground on the Blast Beach, Dawdon, 1936, it ended up a total right-off. However its cargo was millions of those little rubber rings used to seal the tops of old-fashioned pop bottles. Fishermen reported that for years after, it was unusual to land a cod without one of these in its belly.

Chapter 10. Shanties and sea songs

Half way between the worlds of work and recreation, true shanties are proper to sailing ships on the main trade routes, e.g. between America and Liverpool. Yet in terms of structure, they share the use of short repeated lines not unlike the refrain in some Border Ballads. Consider for example the following verse:

> There was a ladie of the north country
> (Lay the bent to the bonny broom)
> And she had lovely daughters three
> (Lay the bent to the bonny broom)…

(Borderers' Table Book, vol.7,1846, p. 85)

Here, as in a shanty, the 'refrain' gives the company a chance to join in, while the soloist takes the narrative lead. However, no shanties come to mind that have been composed in our region, though Terry recorded his version of the Liverpool shanty *We're all bound to go* in Newcastle. The reference to 'Winchester Street' in his version of *Blow the Man Down* could well refer to Sunderland, though the shanty itself ends at 'Liverpool Town'. *Good Morning, Ladies All*, we are told, was popular on Blyth and Tyne ships. The well-known *Billy Boy* may have served as a capstan shanty – here the structure is question and answer in lovely mockery of the border ballad *Edward*. *The Drummer and the Cook* was also a North East favourite: "I learnt it from Capt. John Runciman, who in turn had it from the cook of the Blyth brig *Northumberland*, in which vessel it was used as a shanty," says Terry (1926, p.ix).

More sea songs, as practised in the North East were published by Terry in his Salt sea ballads (1931) "old favourites…of the forecastle" if not necessarily work shanties. One of the most beautiful of the songs, *Blow the Wind Southerly*, is attributed to John Stobbs (not necessarily the same man who wrote the texts about pilots in the nineteenth century.) The diction of the song has something an eighteenth century stamp.

Lest there is any doubt, the song anticipates the collier ships returning home to the north (viz. "As the wind became southerly…these [ships] proceeded north" (Cortis, 1871, p.9).

Blow the Wind Southerly

Blow the wind southerly, southerly, southerly
Blow the wind south o'er the bonny blue sea.
Blow the wind southerly, southerly, southerly
Blow bonny breeze, my lover to me.
They told me last night there are ships in the offing
And I hurried down to the deep rolling sea
But my eye could not see it where'er it might be
The barque that is bearing my lover to me.
Blow the wind southerly ...
Blow the wind south that my lover may come,
Blow the wind southerly ...
Blow bonny breeze and bring him safe home.
I stood by the lighthouse that last time we parted
Till darkness came o'er the deep rolling sea
And I no longer saw the bright barque of my lover
Blow bonny breeze and bring him to me.
Blow the wind southerly ...
Blow the wind south o'er the bonny blue sea
Blow the wind southerly ...
Blow bonny breeze my lover to me.
It is sweet to hear the breeze singing
As lightly it comes o'er the deep rolling sea
But sweeter and dearer by far when 'tis bringing
The barque of my true love in safety to me.

My thanks to Johnny Handle for bringing these to my attention. There is much more to be made of sea music, hornpipes, the songs of William Shield, Charles Dibdin, etc. but it is time for a little relaxation and recreation...

Chapter 11. Leisure

'Pleasuring' or the provision of boat trips for the holiday-maker is an entirely honest way of celebrating the world of water, and has a long tradition in the North East. By 1820, for example, you could spend a fun day on:

Jemmy Joneson's Whurry

<u>Whei</u> cowers biv the chimlay-<u>reek</u>,	who, smoke
Begox! it's all a <u>horney</u>;	game
For thro' the world aw wisht to <u>keek</u>,	look
<u>Yen</u> day when aw was <u>corney</u>;	one, ?tipsy
Sae, wiv some varry canny <u>chiels</u>,	guys
All <u>on the hop</u>, an' murry,	?on the drink
Aaw thowt aw'd myek a voyage to Shields,	
<u>Iv</u> Jemmy Jonesons' Whurry.	in
Ye niver see'd the church sae <u>scrudg'd</u>,	packed
As we wur there thegither,	
An' gentle, semple, throughways nudg'd,	
Like burdies of a feather;	
<u>Blind Willie</u> a' wor joys to <u>croon</u>,	(the fiddler), crown
Struck up a hey-down-derry,	
An' <u>crouse</u> we left wor canny toon,	merry
Iv Jemmy Jonesons' Whurry.	
As we push'd off, loak! a' the Key	
To me seem'd <u>shuggy-shooin'</u>,	swaying/swinging
An' tho' aw'd niver been at sea,	
Aw stuid her like a new-on.	
And when the <u>malls</u> began their reels,	girls
Aw kick'd maw heels reet murry;	
For faix! aw liked the voyge to Shiels,	
Iv Jemmy Jonesons' Whurry.	

Quick went wor heels, quick went the oars,
   An' where me eyes wur <u>cassin</u>,   casting (looking)
It seem'd as if the bizzy shores
   Cheer'd cannyTyne i' passin.
What! hes Newcassel now nae end?
   Thinks aw, it's wondrous, vurry;
Aw thowt aw'd like me life to spend
   Iv Jemmy Joneson's Whurry.

Tyne-side seem'd clad wiv bonny <u>ha's</u>,   halls
   An' furnaces sae <u>dunny</u>;   dark
Wey, this <u>mun</u> be what Bible <u>ca's</u>   must / calls
   'The land ov milk and honey'!
If a' thor things belang'd tiv I,   to
   Aw'd myek the poor reet murry,
An' cheer the folks i' <u>gannin-by</u>   going past
   Iv Jemmy Jonesons' Whurry.

Then on we went, as nice as <u>owse</u>,   anything
   Till 'nenst au'd Lizzy Moody's,   opposite
A whirlwind cam', and' myed <u>a' souse</u>,   ?all fall over
   Like heaps o' <u>babby</u> <u>boodies</u>.   broken china
The <u>heykin</u> myed me vurry <u>wauf</u>,   up-n-down, wobbly
   Me heed turn'd duzzy, vurry;
Me <u>leuks</u>, aw'm sure wad <u>spyen'd</u> <u>a</u> <u>cauf</u>, looks, spaned a calf
   Iv Jemmy Jonesons' Whurry.

For <u>hyem</u> an' bairns, an' maw wife Nan,   home
   Aw <u>yool'd</u> oot like a <u>lubbart</u>;   howled, fool
An' when aw thowt we a' shud <u>gan</u>   go
   To Davy Jones's cubbart,
The wind <u>bee-baw'd</u>, aw <u>whish'd</u> me squeels, ?changed, quieted
   An' <u>yence</u> <u>mair</u> a' was murry,   once more
For seun we gat a seet o' Shields,
   Frev Jemmy Jonesons' Whurry.

Wor <u>geordies</u> now we <u>thrimmel'd</u> oot,   guineas, trickled
 An' tread a' Shiels, sae <u>dinny</u>;   loud
Maw faix! it seems a canny <u>sprout</u>,   youngster
 As big <u>maist</u> as its <u>minny</u>:   almost, mother
Aw <u>smack'd</u> thir <u>yell</u>, aw clim'd thir <u>bree</u>, tasted, ale, hill
 The seet was wondrous, vurry;
Aw <u>lowp'd</u> sec gallant ships to see   jumped (for joy)
 Biv Jemmy Jonesons' Whurry.

To Tynmouth then aw thowt aw'd trudge,
 To see the folks a' <u>duckin</u>;   bathing
Loak! men an' wives together <u>pludg'd</u>,   paddled
 While hundreds stud by, luikin.
Amang the rest, aw <u>cowp'd</u> <u>me</u> <u>creels</u>, danced
 Eh, gox! 'twas funny, vurry;
An' so aw end me voyge te Shiels,
 Iv Jemmy Jonesons' Whurry."

(Marshall, *Chap-book*, 1823, Allan, pp.50–53)

Note by Allan: "The song relates to a time when steamboats were unknown. Then the conveyance on the Tyne was by wherries, and Jemmy Joneson, whose wherry is here celebrated, was well known to all passengers on the river, but the fame of Jemmy and his wherry was soon to be eclipsed. The *Tyne Steam Packet*, the first steamer of the Tyne, commenced plying on Ascension Day, May 19, 1814."

More strenuous participation was possible in the sport of rowing, and races on the Tyne attracted great attention in the nineteenth century, with popular heroes like Harry Clasper and Robert Chambers (see Dillon, *The Tyne Rowers*, Jesmond, 1993). From small work-boats like **foy-fours** on the river, the idea caught on as coble races: a Blyth versus Whitby coble race, for a silver cup, is said to have been instituted 1866. In 1876 John Salmon formed a Racing Club "by a coalition of a few gentlemen of boating minds, residing on or near to, the North-East coast" (Salmon, 1885, p.29). They enjoyed excursions, day cruises, flotilla processions and especially races:

> The hour next arrived, and the competing boats were placed in line according to drawn lots, and started by the Commander by the firing of a gun. Up went all their sails together like magic, and as they sailed away before a favouring breeze with their [white] wings glittering in the sun, they looked extremely pretty. They gradually grew smaller and smaller as they reached along in a southerly direction, and kept well together till they [rounded] the first mark. In their running they displayed about an equal amount of speed, but when they hauled their wind they began to separate, and there was soon a great distance between the first and last boats. The usual features of a race presented themselves, each boat in its turn getting a breeze or a calm, and after all had exhausted the well-known sailing dodges, and exercised the usual manoeuvres of a racing match, so industriously rehearsed by the crews, the first boat at length passed the goal, 'mid acclamations, and her name was Hydra.
>
> (Salmon, 1885, p.31)

Salmon notes that the fishermen of Cullercoats and pilots of the Tyne were so impressed, they resolved to have an annual ocean race of their own. In time, the craze spread to trawler races, seriously competitive events, though increasingly with a festival tinge…

> *You mentioned the fish quay festival…?*
> When it first started it was great. I was at the first one, the trawlers had taken it on themselves to have a run up to Newcastle quay, they had their flags out and the bunting, they had their families on board. But they were sponsored by the breweries, and they had cases of beer. By the time they got back to the fish quay they were half drunk, and they couldn't get up the ladders to get ashore, and the language – 'hey, dint ye gan in that berth, that's the berth I had!' They were all drunk. I cannot remember what year that was. It was a mistake, the brewery sponsoring them, crates and crates of brown ale, and the language was nobody's business, 'you're in my bloody berth there!' 'aw, shut up!'. To me that was great. (Later fish quay festivals not the same.)
>
> (Ernie Keedy, Beamish, 2005/130)

Some fascinating videos of fishing boats and trawler races at Amble have been produced recently by Carle Robinson of the Coble & Keelboat Society – there is surely much scope here for the amateur 'film-maker'….

Chapter 12. Angling

Something between a sport and a primeval hunting obsession, angling has appealed to generations of coast visitors. The equipment can be relatively inexpensive, the skills not too hard to learn (with some guidance), the rewards often tangible and edible.

Angling is free from the foreshore, and not unreasonably priced from a private jetty or harbour wall, or even from a hired boat at sea. Not only does the sport take diverse forms, but each venue, each day and type of weather adds variety, and the fish to be caught change with the season and require different strategies. If a shoal of mackerel venture inshore in the late summer, there sometimes seems not time enough to take one fish off the lure before another presents itself.

An impressive success in angling organisation is the Seaham Angling Club, who pioneered…

Angling competitions

Records show that angling competitions in the North East, at Seaham, were arranged as far back as 1919 when members of clubs 'put their money where their mouth was' with their/our natural instinct of competitiveness. The winner of this first 1919 event was awarded a prize of a hand stitched cushion, very much appreciated in those days.

The 'invention' of the big Open Angling Competitions really began on the North East coast in the 1960s. 'Open' meaning that any angler could enter these events rather than just the locals or club members. Seaham Angling Club were one of the first to introduce large prize incentives for the successful competitors, anything from a radio to a car were on offer in some of the bigger events. The biggest open angling competition was held by Seaham SAC in 1971, in which 2,002 anglers turned out from all over the UK – this competition still holds the European record for entries into a single day's sea angling competition.

The old open competitions of the North East are still being arranged annually to this day, those are Shiremoor Open, Tynemouth Open, South Shields Open, Newbiggin Open and Seaham Open. However the entries have decreased from an average of over 1,000 to 450 entries due to many more 'new' opens arranged by recently established clubs.

(Norman Conn, Seaham)

Some fishing stories…

Two aud fishermen arguin the size o' fish they'd catched ower th' years… One was exaggerating so much the other said, 'Noo haad on! Aa was oot fishin in th' Atlantic one time – gorra bite – wound in the line – and thor, at varry end ovit was a ship's lantern – an what's mare, it was still aleet!' 'That's owermuch!' 'Weel, chop the heed n tail off yor last fish, an Aa'll blaa th' cannel oot.'

(Gordon Patrickson, Seaham)

An old story that keeps repeating itself as true, is the day a load of lads went out rod and line fishing in a boat from Seaham Harbour. There was a bit of a swell on and an older bloke was sea sick and whilst leaning over the gunnels, hoying up, he lost his false teeth in the water. About half an hour later one of his mates pulls a big cod in and guts the fish, only to find a pair of false teeth in its stomach. The older bloke was ower the moon and couldn't believe his luck to get his expensive false teeth back; however when he washed the teeth and tried them, they were not his and threw them back in the water!

(Norman Conn, Seaham)

Chapter 13. Holidays

Saturday afternoons off (1850s onwards) led to the rise of amateur football in the first instance, but in the longer term, increasing free weekends for factory workers, and the traditional summer week's holiday when factories shut and workers set out on holiday together (a 'waysgoose') encouraged the leisure use of the seaside. The appeal of the sea was fostered in Regency England by the belief that sea air was good for you, plus bathing in the sea, and even drinking sea water. For a country seized with this health craze, there is an entertaining satire in Jane Austen's last unfinished book *Sanditon* (1817). The association of sea and health soon caught on:

> The village of Filey is seated in a small and beautiful bay. The settled inhabitants depend chiefly on the fishery, which is carried on with success to a considerable extent, although of late years a few good houses have been built, and several respectable families have resorted thither during the season, for the purpose of sea-bathing, for which the beach is well adapted.
>
> (William Hone, 1837, p.638).

Modest bathing soon turned into swimming, and swimming clubs were popular on the coast in the early twentieth century – in an age when people were content to use the chilly sea in bays and small harbours (later in the pleasantly warm 'cooling pools' of the big collieries).

Meanwhile the appeal of the day out at the seaside had spread to all classes of the populace, and coastal towns soon found it profitable to cater for this enthusiasm. There were the smart facilities of Tynemouth, the easy-going donkey rides of Seaton Carew, the sands of Redcar and Marske, the annual motorcycle race on the beach at Druridge Bay, lifeboat days at Staithes, Cullercoats, etc. local miners' galas at Ashington and Bedlington, or the dancehalls and funfair of Whitley Bay...

The 'townies' used to come to Tynemouth on the train and I am certain that they had a funny word for candyfloss when they asked for it... I'm sure it was related to hair/sugar but I can't remember. On this topic... Slot machines – slotters! Always used! Never 'bandits' as a contraction of 'one-arm-bandits'. The Spanish City at Whitley Bay – The Spanna – Hence – 'ha'way let's gan and feed the slotters at the Spanna!' (Helen Hemmingway)

When I was young a few years back
My father used to say
Behave yourself and wash your face
And we'll go to Whitley Bay

Looking back I see myself
Sixpence clutched in hand
Drinking in the wonder
Of that seaside fairyland

With multi-coloured deck chairs
Donkeys on the sands
Music from the carousels
And the local colliery bands

Candy floss and shuggy boats
And plodging in the sea
Yes, Whitley was a magic place
For little lads like me…

(Jack Davitt, from '*When I was a lad …
Whitley Bay*, 1934')

In due course the day out developed into a week's holiday or even better, the 'Scotch fortnight', and the coast (in good weather) remains a major draw. In a mini-survey accompanying this project, popular destinations (if we exclude Blackpool and Scarborough) were South Shields (for its beaches and entertainment), Tynemouth (for its clean beach, surf, good coffee shops and waterfront parking), Seahouses and Holy Island (for history and birds), and Whitby (for its boats and happy atmosphere); while declining in popularity was raucous Whitley Bay. Factors that attracted visitors included a clean beach, reasonably priced accommodation, 'atmosphere' and places of interest to visit locally. Heading the list for holiday pursuits were not the more active diving and sailing (my participants being mostly of mature age), but walking and visiting historic sites. As to how North East resorts could be improved: there was a call for better transport links, better facilities (cafés, toilets), more beach activities, less inappropriate development, and a general call for cleanliness and smartness.

Inevitably, the whole concept of coastal holidays suffered with the rise of 'package holidays' abroad in the 1960s, so that it is hard sometimes to realise how little an older generation expected from their holiday at the seaside (and how inventive they were at entertaining themselves!). The naïve appeal of the sands for children in the 1930s is exampled in the following account by Fred Short:

Oh ah do like to be beside the seaside!

Ey lad, them was good days! We thought we had gone miles and miles, them days we took two double decker's to the seaside…

[Me mother'd] make sure her housework was either done, or could be left, just so's she could take us bairns to the sands when we were on school holidays. She'd pack sarnies, usually either mashed up hard boiled egg and tomato or spam, or maybe 'sandwich spread'.

Excitedly we would walk down to the bus-stop, the first of the two-bus-trip to get from West Hartlepool to the beach at 'Old Hartlepool'. For some reason, it was called the Fish Sands!…

And of course, all the busses in them days were "Double-Decker's!" We used to love going upstairs, cos you could sit at the front and have a fantastic view, with no driver blocking it!

The Fish Sands was only a very small area of sand, sorta in a corner with the Town Wall as the backdrop. Needless to say, the sand area got increasingly smaller as the tide came in! Folks used to have to shuffle back and shuffle back to keep dry! What was a lovely beach with folks spread all over, ended up with folks sitting like sardines!

We could never get stripped and into our cossie quick enough! Off with our clobber, on with the cossie and race down to the water for a plodge! Hey, if we were really lucky, some enterprising fisherman would bring his boat to the beach and give rides out to sea for a small charge!

Comes the time to eat (and it never came quick enough) my mother would leave us sat on the beach, and go back through the tunnel in the town wall, up the steps and over the road to the hut! The hut did a thriving business with us day trippers! My mother used to go up for a jug of boiling water to make a mashing of tea for us!

When she got back, we'd settle down to sand sandwiches! Well, no matter how hard we tried, the sand got everywhere! Sand-sarnies and tea! Oh, and my mother had her favourite little knife, handed down through the generations with which to cut the sarnies. A little miniature knife in a soft leather pouch!

If the tide was out, we'd go looking for crabs! Tiny, tiny crabs under the rocks! Or, or, we would collect winkles! Hey, we loved them! We'd take them home, my dad would boil them, then we would pick them out with a pin and eat them. We became very adept at the twisting action in order to get them out. Weird how something like that never leaves you. Just the other day, some fifty years since the last time I had winkles I bought some and was amazed just how the twist action came so natural.

Isn't it strange how folks are creatures of habit? Well, it seemed no matter what day we went to the Fish Sands, the same folks would be there.

At the end of the day, or when the incoming tide dictated, we would take our cossies off, TRY to get as much sand off our bodies in the water as we could before our mother dried us down with a towel that felt like sandpaper! NO WAY could we ever get ALL the sand off our feet, so we went home with sand filled socks in our shoes! Two busses back home, maybe a lucky ticket on one of them (hey, we even searched the tickets chucked away on the floor! You never knew your luck!) Back home, in the tub, then off to bed! Tomorrow was always going to be another day!

Many a supportive text has been received:

Whenever I peel a banana, I remember our annual trips to Hart Sands. We never used to 'go away' on holidays (very few people in Shotton did this in the '30s) and the highlight of my father's week off was often the visit to the seaside. Mother made us banana sandwiches and the sand often made its way into them...

[On the beach] we boys busied ourselves in making sand castles and playing 'pot-pie-lady'. This involved making sand pies with the buckets and spades which were de rigueur in those days. Damp sand was best. When we up-ended them, we used to smite the bottoms of the buckets with the spades, chanting 'pot-pie lady, pot-pie lady!' (the origin of this phrase escapes me) before arranging them round the base of a sand castle. The ice-cream man did good business. If we were lucky, he occasionally had a Walls 'Sno-fruit' for sale – a forerunner of today's iced lollies, but sometimes we had to make do with a 'Sno-Cream' which was not quite so nice.

Once a year we ventured further afield when the Sunday School made its annual trip to Seaton Carew by special train. Everybody had to take their own food but the Church supplied us with tea! The donkeys carried us uncomplainingly along the sands and there were some swings and probably a small roundabout but not much else...

(Fred Stainthorpe)

...it occurred to me that in the 1930s I had the same experience as my father in his childhood and his father in his – and it's still available today. That was and is, the Cliff Railway at Saltburn. I saw it at Christmas. It has the same cars, the same cast iron turnstiles, and I dare say the same attendants. It was a real adventure, especially going up. The car descended from some hidden height – it was awesome and a bit frightening. The ride up was spectacular as the view of the pier, Huntcliffe, and the sea opened up. Unforgettable then as now.

(Bill Thomas)

My Mother loved the beach and when we got the big Wolsey about 1935 she bought a square tent which folded up and was carried along the side of the car, resting on the dashboard. When it was rigged up the family was set for the day no matter what the weather.

She preferred the Cullercoats end of the long sands as all the swings, etc. were at the other end and it was 'common'. My Dad came from the golf course with some friends (all in plus fours) and sat on the sands sharing our sandwiches, pies, etc. My brother never took his cap off and I can't remember him in a bathing costume, though he had one; mine was knitted and went twice as long when it was wet. We were joined by various aunts and uncles at different times; we all loved it.

'Hot Rice' was a game we played – as popular as beach cricket but quicker, and everyone having a turn if there was time. Played with an old tennis racket and ball. One person defended herself with the raquet while everyone tried to hit her/him on the body with the ball. (If hit, the defender and the successful thrower changed roles.)

Later the beach was closed because of landmines. After the Second World War, it resumed its central place in social life:

Meeting everyone after work was commonplace. The local lads were into weight-lifting, gymnastics, body building, and 'did their dickers' [dares] as my Mother would say – climbing up on shoulders and making pyramids, including some of the girls with handstands, and anything they could invent. 'Catching the saliers' was North Shields lads catching the waves in the wake of any of the boats in the river...

(Meg Stephenson, North Shields)

The Second World War affected fishermen considerably: at Cullercoats 30 cobles were requisitioned by the Royal Navy – probably to help practice marine commando landing techniques – the boats were never returned, though owners were paid £250 compensation per boat (Bart Taylor). And: "After the Second World War, aided by government grants, many North East fishermen invested in bigger boats. Line-fishing was superceded by seine-netting, then by trawling" (Katina Porteous, 2005).

Growing up in Spittal during World War Two, the coast was a no-go area. The beach was cordoned off with barbed wire. The Royal Artillery had a large gun emplacement facing out to sea. It was just yards away from the local gas works...

During the war, at Spittal fish quay, the Royal Air Force had two very powerful air sea rescue launches which would put to sea at night to rescue air crews who had ditched in the sea after bombing raids. The boat crews and support personnel lived in Nissan huts on land next to the fish quay. They had a cookhouse and a mess hall, etc. After the war, a local business man turned the base into a mini holiday camp. It catered for families. The beach was re-opened, it had a programme of entertainment. Families came for Newcastle 'race week', 'Glasgow Fair' and 'Borders Hoidays', etc. Many families returned in subsequent years; the camp finally closed in the early 1950s.

(Jim Cromarty, Spittal)

Lewis Carroll in the North East

Although a stuffed walrus, held in Sunderland Museum, has been discredited as the source of Lewis Carroll's poem *The Walrus and the Carpenter*, Carroll (Lewis Dodgson) had undoubtedly strong links with the North East, and stayed with relatives at both Whitburn and Southwick as well as visiting Whitby. The rector of St Mary's, Easington, the Rev. H.G. Liddell, whom Carroll first met in 1856, was grandfather of the Alice who inspired the children's stories.

Most of his famous poem 'Jabberwocky'... was written on a visit to his Wilcox cousins in Whitburn, near Sunderland in 1855. The word 'beamish' in the line: "Come to my arms my beamish boy" is assumed to be taken from the Durham village. Carroll also probably composed 'The Walrus and the Carpenter' – "who wept like anything to see / Such quantities of sand" – while walking on Whitburn and Seaburn beaches. The distinctive headgear of a ship's carpenter was a common sight in a great ship-building centre like Sunderland.

(www.myersnorth.co.uk)

The Walrus and the Carpenter and *The Lobster Quadrille* are arguably two of the wickedest, funniest, most thought-provoking poems in English, and would undoubtedly be included in our beach survey if they were not readily available elsewhere, and rather long for our purpose. But there must be room to sample a less well-known verse of Carroll's that gives the classic symptoms of shore fatigue:

> …For I have friends who dwell by the coast–
>   Pleasant friends they are to me!
> It is when I am with them I wonder most
>   That anyone likes the Sea.
>
> They take me a walk: though tired and stiff,
>   To climb the heights I madly agree;
> And, after a tumble or so from the cliff,
>   They kindly suggest the Sea.
>
> I try the rocks, and I think it cool
>   That they laugh with such an excess of glee,
> As I heavily slip into every pool
>   That skirts the cold cold Sea.

(from the *Sea Dirge*)

Of course, the poem belies Lewis Carroll's own pleasure in the seaside, and has failed to affect the general devotion to the coast. In the course of which, Carroll was not the only one to take a tumble from a cliff:

> During the summer months, we seemed to spend most of our free time playing on the Blast Beach to the south of Seaham.
>
> This beach, and others on the same coastline, was used as a dumping ground for the stone and other rubble discarded by the National Coal Board. In later years, the degeneration of the area had reached a level of desolation, whereby a film company found it ideal for use as an alien landscape in a sci-fi movie (Alien 3).
>
> Cud, Arty, Jaimsie, and Nian (all nicknames), were fooling about on the cliff top at the Blast beach. It is not known what happened, but Arty slipped and fell over the edge of the cliff. He tumbled down the side of the cliff to the beach below, a broken drop of some ten or fifteen metres.
>
> Jaimsie immediately set off for home at a quick trot. He entered 'The Wide Back' street shouting at the top of his voice, 'Artie's deed, Artie's deed' (dead)!
>
> With the amount of people running in the direction of the Blast Beach it would seem that half of Dawdon had set off on a rescue mission. It was just as well, Cud and Nian had already clambered down the footpath to the beach below.
>
> They discovered Artie lying on his back, spread-eagled over the top of a large boulder and softly moaning.

A twelve-year-old's view of circumstances can, at times, be very basic. Nian turning to Cud cried, 'Oh no Cud, look, Artie's in agony. Go on, put him out of his misery, smash his head in with a rock!' Fortunately, Artie's mother arrived on the scene before they had time to 'Put Artie out of his misery'.

(Tom Moreland)

Sometimes, in generous mood, the coast could reward casual strollers, rather than afflict them or empty their pockets:

Beach combing

(From Maureen Anderson, *Bygone Seaton Carew*, Ch 11, 'Flotsam & Jetsam'):

In *Bell's Guide to Sunken Treasure*, it is recorded that on 4 June 1669 a vessel, believed to be a Spanish galleon, sank in Seaton Bay. The vessel was named the *Little Duck* and had sailed from the Netherlands carrying £300,000 worth of gold and silver specie. Two hundred years later the villagers were given the opportunity to live in luxury for a time. On a Saturday might in March 1867 a severe storm with high winds blew the sand from the beach revealing the clay and peat beneath. The following day dawned fine and clear. Two men were walking across the sands on their way to Middlesbrough to seek work. The tide was out, and as they were passing close to the Longscar rocks, one of them dropped his pipe. As he bent to pick it up he spied something curious in amongst the seaweed. On picking the object up and cleaning the black muck from it he realised it was a silver coin. A quirk search of the immediate area revealed hundreds more coins, both of silver and gold. The two men picked up what they could carry and, returning to the village, sold the lot. They then headed straight into the public house for a good drinking session. The news of the find spread around Seaton like wildfire. The rest of that clay and all through the night the beach was lit up by the lanterns of crowds of people riddling the sand to try and find every last coin. The Lord of the Manor tried to claim the treasure, but he was too late, the villagers, with lightning speed, had changed everything they had picked up into currency they could spend. The following letter was sent to a local newspaper shortly after the treasure had been found:

Tawkin' fornent lock-oots an' torn-oots, what de ye think o' the Hartlepeul Torn Ups, mistor? A varry *doolar-is* iccount has been forridid te me biv a Hertlepeul Toon Coonsillor, and too iv his chums, that's Mistor Richard Varlow, Captin MacKarthy, an' Benjymin Roome, the Sporrit Rappor, o' Hartlepeul, consarnin' the goold an' silver mine thit's been fund on the beech thair, sor. Too half-rockt layborrors gan dandorrin' illang be the sea side, the tuthor day, happind te drop on tiv a peety reef o' rocks, an' the doddil o' won o' the cheps pipes teuk intiv it's heed te fawl on te this seaweed gardin. Tommy stoopt down te pick the doddil up, when he seed what te him leukt like a black penny lyin' close te the reekin' baccy.

Tommy picks her up, rubs her a bit, finds oot she's silvor, an' cawls on his meyt that was wawkin' on iffore him te cum back. Annuther, an' annuther, an' still lots iv uthors, torns up thor black bellies fra the peet. 'What's te be deun noo, Tommy?' says reed haired Dick Man. 'Thore croon peeses, but thor nut iv onny king's rain that aw naw on. Heer's Carrillis; but whe Carrilles was aw naw nowt, xsept it wis Jowlyis Seesor.' Se te the Joo they gans an' sells thor prizis for too or three bob a peece, an away they gans an' gets bleezin' drunk, blaws the gaff, an' lets the cat oot o' the poke. Next day thor's hundords o' foaks seekin' the doolar-is trisshor an' putten black munny in thor pockits. Fond feuls; them layborrors mite hae gethort a little fortin had they oney kep the lucky spot te thorsils, but, like the cats, they cuddent fare weel an' had thor gobs. It's thowt thit a ship hid geyn doon heer loded wi' silvor an' goold munny, is [=as] the price iv a cargo o' niggers, an' the silvor coins, nawin' the unholy porchise o' yewmin flesh, hid torned black in the feyce, an' cum te the sorfis o' the sea, like pigs in Paddy's land wiv a nife an' a fork in thor gobs, skweekin' oot, 'Whe'll find me?' ...

Retiort Keelmin
(*South Durham Herald*, 23 March 1867)

The leisure future

Coastal settlements in the North East are already adjusting to new roles, based in some measure on the sea itself, or at least the scenic appeal of the coast and sea.

Still actively linked to the water are pursuits like angling, diving and leisure craft sailing; they will tend to be weekend pursuits and to accommodate them the everyday harbour has to subtly convert itself to a marina, that is high-security moorings often with additional facilities like a club-house and marine stores. Thus at Hartlepool, Roker and (at planning stage) Seaham North Dock.

On the side of entertainment, the great Whitley Bay fairground ('Spanish City') has shut; and though the link between drinking and the coast remains strong, a new emphasis has been placed on informative, educational facilities – the Historic Quay at Hartlepool, the Blue Reef Aquarium at Tynemouth, plans to regenerate the North Shields Fish Quay...

Expanding also is the use of coastal sites for housing – foreshadowed by the elegant Edwardian seafront terrace and equally the thrifty caravan site as at Newbiggin, Whitley Bay ('Feathers'), Blyth (some converted to housing), Seaton Sluice ('Crag Caravan Site'), Crimdon Dene (curtailed in the 1990s), etc. Traditionally, too, it is not unusual to find an enterprising old people's home on a seafront – reassuringly called 'The Haven' from our Anglo-Saxon word-pool. But it is typically new estates on or overlooking the coast have proved super-attractive to developers and buyers, though residents' jobs will be unattached to sea skills, for the work that feeds the mortgage will likelier be based in one or other of the main cities. Here the sea and coast are scenic attractions, to be viewed and enjoyed from your own property – and yet paradoxically a scene that too much development can itself detract from. Examples of new sea-estates include the former Vane Tempest pit site at Seaham ('East Shore Village'), and the north bank of the mouth of the Wear.

Accordingly, the culture of the coast is becoming higher-cost and higher-status; its traditional cottages (when evading demolition) no longer a practicality so much as a symbolic accessory. Terrace housing is 'out', smart detached maisonettes with space for cars are 'in'... It is the culmination of a century and more of regarding the seaside as a leisure and health resource - but new communities take time to cohere, and the long process may well see the loss of any coastal dialect.

Chapter 14. Conclusion

One question remains to be considered – do (or did) the settlements of the North Sea coast form a coherent culture, linked north-south? And if so, how does this coastal culture relate to the opposite coast in Europe?

It is difficult for us now to conceive a time when the whole east coast was an Anglian and then a Viking 'communications highway'. Indeed, we tend to overemphasise the difference between Anglian and Viking. Some clues, such as the early use of the word 'till' (Old Norse for 'to') in the *Old English Bede*, suggest that the Anglians who settled on this coast maintained relations with North Germanic cousins across the sea; and the difficulty in attributing word origins to either Old English or Old Norse may be a problem we make for ourselves. Certain it is, the Anglo-Saxon sense of identity resided in their pride in their historical Continental origins – the whole of the action of *Beowulf*, for example, is set in Denmark and Sweden. Later the Vikings figure as raiders and invaders, but their targets are the high-level monastic organisation, not the commoner; their purpose to shake loose the Church estates for their own use. In time, an accommodation between Pagan and Christian is necessarily reached; and the final resting place of St Cuthbert at Durham could hardly have been arranged without Viking compliance. To many Anglians in the North, the Vikings may have appeared more sympathetic to their interests than Saxon or Norman overlords from the South. In this sense, we should not be surprised that coastal feature names show signs of interepenetration between Anglian and Viking zones; indeed the influence of coastal dialect speakers could have promoted the use of Old Norse based words in a Common Northern English.

A charter of 1155 from Seaham has as witnesses the names Eilwin de Saham, his son Raven de Slinglawe, *John* son of Herebert de Saham, *Roger* Dreng, Radulf de Hassewelle, Ailmar de Daltune, plus the aristocratic Reinald Escolland, and many others (Surtees, 1816, pp.2 and 273). Interestingly, in these names, Anglo-Saxon, Norse and *French* elements are all present and while names do not necessarily indicate ethnic origin, there is the implication that the different strands of Anglian, Viking and Norman-French culture were not so rigidly maintained as we glibly assume.

A crude assessment of Viking influence is provided by surnames:

> Very often different forms of name are revealing of naming practices in different regions of the country. When we map the geographical distribution of people with patronymic names ending in '–son' we find highest concentrations along the North Sea coast, from the Humber to the Shetlands...
>
> (http://www.spatial-literacy.org/UCLnames)

...the form '-son' could be reckoned a Viking tradition.

Given that for centuries before and after their arrival in the North East, Vikings remained major seafarers, dominating the North Sea, unity along our coast would surely depend on their influence, and the ubiquity of the coble may well be an example.

Some old words are even restricted to North and West Germanic. For these, Kluge 1975 uses the term *Nordseewort* 'North Sea word'… This phenomenon fits well into the context of a North Sea culture defined by North and West Germanic people.

(Their, 2002, p.117)

Not only words: interchange would have included goods, technical terms and ideas, practical knowledge and skills, as well as a fluidity of population. The orbit of North East contacts ranged widely overseas: "There was a significant export trade in the later Middle Ages from Newcastle to the ports of Flanders, Holland, Zeeland, France, and the Baltic, where coal served to dry madder and smoke fish, as well as to burn lime and work iron" (Hatcher, 1992, p.26). In the North Sea, the Hanseatic League maintained Scandinavian primacy, but faltered in the seventeenth century to be replaced by the Dutch as the major international carriers (a role they maintained till about 1800), while from England the Eastland Company (1578 on) opened trade routes with the Baltic, importing timber (we lacked soft woods), pitch, tar, ropes, and flax (for sails).

It must be borne in mind that intercourse between Scandinavia and Britain on the sea did not cease with the Norman invasion. Up to the end of the 14th century there was a flourishing timber trade between Norway (and other parts of Scandinavia) and the east coast of England. The leading towns were Ipswich, Boston, Lynn, Grimsby, Hull, Ravensere, Scarborough and Newcastle.

(Sandahl, 1951, p.21)

One of the implications of this is that loan-words from Norse languages need not be limited to the eigth–eleventh centuries, but could well have continued to be adopted throughout the Middle Ages. A sense of insularity was slow to develop…

Castles along the coast need not presage war at sea – Tynemouth started as a Norman motte and bailey and would have had as much to do with internal control as external defence; Dunstanburgh was built for the War of the Roses. Rather, trade typified the interests of the Medieval North East, especially the ports of Tyne and Hartlepool. Coal dominated the trade increasingly, while fishing and boat-building sustained other coastal communities.

With regard to the Dutch:

…the great influx of Low German and Dutch terms started early: since the beginning of the Middle Ages English and Low Dutch intercourse on the sea has been unbroken. Up to the end of the 16th century the mercantile contact at sea between England and the continent was close, and the sailors of the two races met and mingled not only in the sea ports of Holland and England but also in other ports at which they both traded... Later on, in the 17th century, the naval wars and maritime trading of England and the Netherlands brought them into prolonged contact with each other, and a steady borrowing of Dutch terms has been going on till the present day.

(Sandahl, 1951, p.22)

And again: "about 1,100 Britons worked in the Dutch [herring] fisheries in the mid-eighteenth century, though most, if not all, were unskilled landsmen employed casually" (Starkey *et al.*, 2000, ch.7, p.65).

The 'national fisheries' of herring, cod and whale and the work of smuggling not only reinforced a sense of coastal cohesion and identity but must have financed the building of many small craft on the North East coast. The informal links across the sea may not have had the intimacy that connected one fishing village to its neighbour, but it is valid to speak of a North Sea Community in the sense that events on one coast often influenced the opposite coast as vividly as the affairs of the hinterland did. In Lethbridge's summary: "they [fishing and farming comunities] were standing back to back and not face to face. The one looked outward to the far horizon over the glittering sea; the other inward over the fruitful plain" (1952, p.27)

Many words (of whatever source) were shared along the Eastern coast of England, but were not in use elsewhere, attesting to a cohesion that can only be maritime based. Examples noted earlier include *gare, ness, pule, piner, acker, lipper, hag, dowly,* (sea)*fret, caller, baggit, brat, lofting, scare* ('scarf'), *blare, strake, thoft, puy, rowth, glut* ('wedge') and with extended occurrence (via *EDD*): *finner* 'whale' (Shetlands, Orkney and Northumberland), and *sea-pie* for 'oyster catcher' (Shetlands, Orkney to East Anglia).

In the post-Reformation centuries, individual initiative and private ownership have been to the fore and each coastal community has, to a degree, its own story and a measure of rivalry with its neighbours. It is not surprising in this context to find considerable variation developing between the vocabularies of fishing villages along the coast, like varying patterns within a common tradition of *gansies* (jerseys).

From this time of individuated development will date many of the interesting nicknames coastal folk have devised for each other, and still do: *Gull* – 'sometimes used in a derogatory sense for a Holy Islander' (FK, Berwick); *Jowel* – 'a native of Spittal' (FK, Berwick); *Twempie* – native of Tweedmouth (FK, Berwick); *Monkey-hanger* – unfortunate inhabitant of Hartlepool; *Cod-heed* – coastal dweller in general, e.g. Seaham; *Steeas-yacker* – Staithes person; *Poolie* – Hartlepudlian; *Geordie* – Novacastrian; *Jamie* and *Makem* – Sunderlander...

Immigration to the region by Scots and Irish in the nineteenth century should have challenged traditional loyalties: in fact, North East dialect survived significantly, albeit in gradations along the coast, and fishing communities maintained much of their integrity well into the twentieth century. The developing technology of fishing vessels, and the success at fishing it made possible, has itself, arguably, brought about the dwindling of the fishing industry. As in the case of coal mining and ship-building, modernisation followed by closure has rendered a wide range of technical terms redundant; the attendant social upheaval has queried the relevance of dialect.

The advance of national and international English has put dialect further on the defensive, and dialect loss is in itself a marker of change that has not received due attention. The post-War re-shaping of our lives is as near a revolution as we are likely to experience: how it has been conducted remains a mystery. The sense of participation and a say in our community's future has sadly declined in the face of ever more efficient local, national and supernatural regulation; somehow we have lost the sense of the inclusiveness of society and perhaps the best evidence for this comes from the fragmentation of spoken language.

Of course, the future remains just as exciting whatever it holds, but planning for the future would work better, I feel, the more awareness it shows of the past and the more respect it accords the communities it holds in balance. The image of 'turning the tide' may serve as all too real a metaphor of social cleansing.

As regards history, there could not be a stranger or more colourful succession of realities to cherish than can be encountered on the North East coast... like images of when "Dutch fishing boats came to Blyth – I remember in the 1950s all the Dutch fishermen clunking through Blyth wearing their clogs – an impressive sight!" (BA, Seaton Sluice).

Appendix 1

Katrina Porteous: words used by north Northumbrian fishermen and their families

This list of north Northumbrian fishing words is a work-in-progress. It is extracted from notes collected between 1989 and 1996 from fishermen and women, most of whom were born in Beadnell in the first two decades of the twentieth century. Over this 7-year period, I recorded the stories and working life of the community; and I am still writing up these notes into a book. At the time of collection, most of the words were still in use, either in a working context, or in the context of stories which were part of the fishing community's everyday life. For example, although sailing cobles and herring keelboats were already obsolete in Beadnell by the end of World War I, they were remembered in stories passed down from parents and grandparents. Words connected to other obsolete practices, such as long line fishing and the preservation of hemp and manilla gear, had been in use well within living memory, and likewise formed a natural part of everyday conversation.

Rather than setting out on my research formally with specific questions, I was lucky enough to spend part of each day for 5 or 6 years listening to conversations in the Beadnell fishermen's huts, where gear was made and mended, and stories told. I also spent time aboard boats, crab and lobster fishing, and observed salmon and sea-trout netting in Beadnell Bay. I took notes constantly, and corroborated specific words and their pronunciation afterwards. A few conversations were also taped or filmed.

While concentrating on Beadnell, I also spent time with fishermen of the same generation from other villages, including Holy Island, Seahouses, Craster, Boulmer and Amble (where my contacts were Newbiggin-born). I have indicated the geographical source of their words in this list. In many cases, these men and women were relatives of my Beadnell contacts: fishermen tended to marry within the community, especially when women were heavily involved in the preparation of long lines. In many ways, the culture of north Northumberland fishing communities had more in common with Scottish east coast villages than with villages a few miles inland. This was especially true during the years of the herring industry before World War I, when small villages like Beadnell were caught up in the traffic following migrating shoals from the north of Scotland down to Yarmouth. My contacts remembered local lasses and boat crews – often their own parents – who had 'travelled the fishin's'; and, in Seahouses, itinerant herring lasses had been part of village life until the middle of the twentieth century.

While the cultural continuity of the small area I studied was striking, equally striking was the linguistic variety. In the first place, the women's language was often quite different from the men's, not only in vocabulary, but in pronunciation, rhythm and inflection, all of which tended to be less 'broad'. Secondly, there were significant differences between villages; not only between Beadnell, recently a more rural community, and Amble, with its mining and coal-port history; but also between what appear to be similar and contiguous communities, such as Beadnell and Seahouses, or Beadnell and Craster. Why should a crab or lobster pot be a 'creeve' in Beadnell, Seahouses and Amble, a 'creel' on Holy Island and a 'net' in Craster? Why is that commonly-seen bird, a tern, a 'pickie' in Beadnell, a 'teerum' in Seahouses and a 'taree' in Craster? Constructions and pronunciations varied, too. Why do Beadnell people say 'come wi' us' and Seahouses 'come wi' w'? Why is 'red' 'rehd' in Beadnell and 'reed' in Seahouses? And why is the inflection of the Beadnell dialect more 'spiky' than elsewhere, and north Northumberland coastal speech much quicker than speech in the Coquet valley or elsewhere inland?

Among the many things which impressed me about the fishing community's speech was its expressiveness – the way the sounds of the words and their rhythm give you a feeling for what they are about. It is easy, for example, to distinguish between the swift, light 'pickie' and the darker, less agile 'gormer' simply by sound. Similarly, between a 'hobbly' and a 'gurrelly' sea, it is not difficult to tell which is a light, surface roll and which a deeper, more powerful swell. The dialect also abounds with picture-language, often drawn from nature: 'Gaa'n back like snaa' off a dyke' is a wonderful image of someone dwindling with disease; 'big seas on!' vividly describes an argument; and the by-names given to particular individuals, such as 'Cuddylugs' or 'Tarbrush', often depict each one through a visual characteristic.

The intensive period of my research came to an end with the death of several of my key contacts. I then spent a period as writer-in-residence in Shetland, where, in the heavily Norse-influenced dialect of the fishermen, I found many similarities to Northumberland. I have included some examples in the notes to these Northumbrian words.

My Northumbrian contributors were too many to thank individually; but in particular I am grateful to Andrew Rutter of Seahouses, a writer himself, who kept, in a notebook which he lent to me, his own list of words used by the fishing community among whom he lived all his life. I have included many of his words in my list, but only when I myself have heard them in use among fishermen. The others I have attached as an appendix, together with some additional words which Andrew Rutter collected for his friend and publisher, Mr F.L. Kennington.

I should also like to thank those contacts of mine who, like Andrew, became over time close friends: in Amble, Redford Armstrong and his sister, Cathy; and in Craster, Bill Smailes. In Beadnell, I was especially helped by Maisie (Dixon) Bell, whom I knew from childhood, by May Douglas and, above all, by Charlie Douglas. Through their stories, working lives and language, I was privileged to catch sight of a world that has now almost entirely vanished.

Katrina Porteous, Beadnell

A

a haa'd – a hold; to take hold or keep hold. *'Keep ahaa'd' – a farewell, literally 'keep well'; 'the chimley's ahaa'd' – the chimney's on fire*

aa'd-farrened – old-fashioned

aa'd yeer's neet – Old Year's Night, i.e. New Year's Eve

aa'n – own. *'It'll work it's aa'n cure' – wrong-doings will bring bad results to the perpetrator*

aback a – behind, e.g. *Aback a the Carrs*

abyen / abeen – above

ablow – below

adge – adze, used by coopers making herring barrels

afore – before. *'Afore ma time'*

Agin – against

aheed – ahead. *'Gan straight aheed' – straight on*

ahint – behind. *'Aa'wess ahint, like the coo's tail'*

air – a breeze. *'Come a bit air for the westart'. 'A fine air a wund'*

airt – direction, place. *'What airt's the wund for'?' 'Th' come for' aal airts'*

airm-whurrels – turnstile (Holy Island)

aix – axe

alderberry – elderberry

arles – retainer paid by herring yard to lasses who 'travelled the fishin's', to secure their work for the season

arse above the shovel (to be) – conceited, over-proud, above oneself

arsefyek – a coil that comes out of line

arsle – (of wind) to back. *'Wund's arsellin'* (Boulmer)

article – the p-i-g (alternative to the taboo word)

away – turned, of tide. *'Tide's away' – tide has turned. 'Is the tide away?' – Is it past high tide? 'Hee wetter away?' – Is it past high tide? Also, died: 'Dickie got away, lad'*

ax – ask

B

baa'mskin – fisherman's oilskin apron, tied at the front

baccy boxes – ??spawning crabs

back end – autumn

back-finner – fish that is nearly through the net, caught by back fin

back fu' – wind on the wrong side of the sail, a dangerous situation

back metal – one of the anchors on the 'beach-nets'

backerlie – (adj and noun) late, especially late potatoes. *'Nor' Sea Backerlies'* – Seahouses Over-60s Club

backside yonder (construction) – back there

baggies – immature coal fish

bagie – a swede (red turnip)

bailey – Bailiff; usually a water bailiff overseeing salmon fishing regulations.

bairn – a child

ballacker – a battering, e.g. *'Gie 'im a cross-ballacker' (Spittal and Spittal Folks, George Russell Jackson c1873, quoted in Early Victorian Spittal, Michael Cullin). Also name of rocks off Amble*

ballup – button flies on trousers. *'Festen yer ballup!' From Burlap?*

bank, bank-top – edge of land, small cliff or sand-dune above sea. *'Mother was shootin' for' the bank-heed'*

banty – bantum hen

barber – a frost. *'A black barber' – a black frost*

bark – (verb) to preserve with tannin from oak bark (noun) or cutch. *Bark-pots – boiling pots with fireplaces for barking. Adj: barky. 'Barky slowp' – smock which has been barked*

barnitickle – barnacle

barr'l – the barrel or main body of a lobster, which is measured for size

barr'l-arse – Squid. Baa'ld-arse at Seahouses. (Also – inkfish)

bat – a light knock. *'Gi' ye a bat on the lug'.*

be' – before. *'Be' Aah'd got wetter in'* – by the time I'd got enough water to get in'

beach, on the – fishing for sea-trout and salmon with anchored 'hyeuk' or 'T' net on the shore

beach-nets – the nets used for this

beadlin – older inhabitants' pronunciation of Beadnell

becket – a loop of rope, such as that attached to pot (also known as bridle)

bedroom fish – the skate (Craster)

beelin' (adj) – swollen and infected, gathering into a boil

beetle – a small prawn (Blyth area, not used in north Northumberland)

belayin'-pin – pin below gunwale forrard in coble, for taking a loop in the halliard when hauling a sail

Bell (the) – name given to the Seahouses fish auction

bellusses (noun) – a pair of bellows

bend (verb) – to tie or fasten, of ropes etc. Also 'bend on'. *'Bend on thon creeve'. 'The lines is bent t'gither'*

bend (noun) – full flow of tide. *'The bend a the tide'*

bents – bent grass. *The Benty is a place name in Beadnell referring to Bent Hall, from bent grass*

berries – eggs on lobster. Berried hen – female lobster carrying eggs

berrel – a whirlpool

berreller – (Holy Island) spindle-weight used to spin horsehair 'graiths' for 'sneyds'. Also 'empstone'

bessie – a mess. *'Ye've med a right Bessie on't'*

bide – to stay. *'Ee should bide at hyem'. 'If ee had bidden'*

big tide – spring tide

bile (noun) – a boil. *'Saa't wetter biles'*

Billy – name of coastguard watch-house at Low Newton; *(possibly from King William IV??)*

bite – a loop in a rope

bittle – to beat or pummel

blaa' – to blow. Also used as a noun to mean a rest: *'Tyek a blaa'*. Also used to mean someone who talks a lot of nonsense: *'He's a right blaa'*

black-back – flat fish found among seaweed

black bowowers – blackberries

black-men's heeds (Craster) – small, black clouds

black net – straight part of salmon beach net running from shore; also 'runnin' net'

black-sitten – of eggs, rotten in the nest. *'Eggs is black-sitten'*

blackjack – fully grown coal-fish

blare (verb) – to low (of a cow)

blare (noun) – mixture of cow-dung and tar used for caulking

bleach (of rain and snow) – to lash, to blow in your face. *'She's bleachin' doon'*

bleary – damp cold

bleb – blister or bubble

bleeze – (noun and verb) fire, blaze. 'Bleezer' – metal cover for hearth to make fire burn up brighter

blethor – chatter

blimmer (Amble / Newbiggin) – blister or bubble. *'Yon compass has a blimmer in hor'*

blue-staa'k – a kind of brown mushroom

boast – breast (of crab) (Newbiggin / Amble). Cf. Brisket

bob an' wully – a lobster pot with a soft flap entrance to act as a trap; called after Bob and Willy Liddell

bogey – a cart

boggle – to peer at (Amble / Newbiggin)

bole – ring on oar that sits on thoweld

bolster – iron spike used with a mallet to split rock

boockie – whelk. Slavvery boockie – whelk shell with snail inside. Craa'lin' boockie – whelk shell with hermit crab inside

boody – broken bits of glazed pottery, usually blue and white

bool – to bowl, to hurry. 'Boolin' alang'

boontree bush – elder bush

born – burn, a stream

bow (rhymes with 'now') – pot-buoy. *'Bows is doon'. Steeky-bow – small version of dan, making end of single fleet of creeves*

bow (rhymes with 'now') – curved frame of crab or lobster pot. *A fower-bowed string-eyed creeve'*

bowelly hyel, boolly hyel – small door or opening for unloading herring or coal into a yard

bowelt – graithing bolt, grappling iron used to drag for lost gear

bowk – to belch

bowlsprit – bowsprit

box bed – bed in wooden cupboard in wall of living room, found in typical nineteenth century fishermen's cottage

brae – a bank

brae – to knock hard: *'Braein' intae a heed sea'*.

brailor – net on a long pole for scooping fish aboard. See also: didle, fish-stop, kep-net

brander – bollard on pier for mooring ropes

brank – to hurry (Holy Island). *Brankin' doon – hurrying down*

brat – turbot 'Brattin' Grund' – *place off Beadnell where turbot were caught*

brattish, brattishy – wicker, lattice

brattle – the noise thunder makes: *'A brattle a thunn'er'*

breeks – trousers

breest-hyeuk – 'Y'-shaped connection at top of gunwales at stem of coble (Amble). Called a 'haak' at Seahouses

bridle – a loop of rope, such as that attached to pot (see 'becket')

the brik – where the sea breaks

boast – breast (of crab) (Newbiggin / Amble). Cf. Brisket

brisket – the main body of a crab (cf. 'boast')

broach – to be knocked sideways by a sea

browtin's-up (noun) – up-bringing. *'It's your browtin's up' – i.e. how you were brought up*

bruff – a ring around the moon. Also, *'a bruff moon' – a moon with a ring around it*

brunt – burnt

brutches – trousers. *'His brutchy-arse' – his trouser-seat*

bubble – to cry. *'He's right bubbly'*

bull – supporting piece of wood in bottom of a creeve

bull-heed – an ugly, wide bow on a coble

bullet – a sweet. *'Taa'k wi' a bullet in hor mooth' – to talk posh*

bumm'ler – bumble bee. Also used for cockchafer beetle

bunches – foul tows and pots jumbled up after heavy seas

bus – seaweed-covered rock; also, ware buses; e.g. *The Bus a the Born, Skyenney's Bus, Falloden Bus, Gapsey Bus. Andrew Rutter suggests also 'bush'*

butt – flounder

by-name – nickname

byennie – blenny

byen – bone

byits – boots. *'Sea-byit stockin's'* – sea-boot stockings

C

caa' – to turn, make go, as in: *'Caa' the handle'*. *'Caa' canny'* – go easy

caa'd – cold

caa'driff – a shiver

caa'l – to call; specifically, to speak badly of someone behind his or her back

caa'l (noun) – a mill dam, a place in a stream where salmon jump

caaldie – rat (especially Beadnell, where 'rat' is a taboo word)

cables – lots, as in drawing lots for salmon berths: *'Draa'in' cables'* (Amble, Newbiggin)

carlin – space forward in coble, beside step for mast. Cf. *carlin-thoft – fore-thoft*

carlins – split peas, as in *Carlin Sunday*

cadge – a small anchor, used for warping a boat

cadger – tinker, someone who hawks fish from door to door. *'The king he lies i' the cadger's way'*

caff – chaff, used to stuff 'teeks' (mattresses)

cahoochey, to be made of – to be strong, signifying endurance

cairen milk – ?butter-milk

can – to be able. A very versatile participle. *Might can, no can* etc. *'Ye wouldn't could remember'*

can-can – a fringe of hair on forehead

canny – good-natured. Also used for emphasis: *'There's a canny bit sea on'*

canvas deck (Beadnell) – canopy on coble, known as a 'cuddy' at Craster, a 'hood' at Boulmer and a 'dodger' at Amble

carr – rock or reef, e.g. *Big Harcar* (Farne Islands), *Braidcarr* (Seahouses), *Comely Carr, Little Carrs and Muckle Carrs* (Beadnell), *Ootcarr* (Embleton Bay)

carra-paa'd, carra-handed – left-handed; also, clumsy

cat o' nine tails – squid or octopus spawn (Craster)

chack – chalk

cheek (of door) – jamb

cheese-cutter – peaked cap worn by fishermen

Chester-le-Street, the right road for – the right direction; used when someone is recovering from illness

chewin' – exhausting. *'It was a chewin' day'*

chiv – cooper's tool for fitting barrel lids

chock – wood used to support boat on land; also to support mast in step in a sailing-coble

chock end – the curved end of a coble's drowt

choke-nail – metal in front of thoweld on a coble to keep the oar lying at the correct angle

chow – to chew, that which is chewed (of tobacco), one who chews; *'He's a dorty chow'* – he makes a mess with his chewing tobacco

claed – covered, cluttered. *'The tyeble was claed wi' dorty dishes'*

clag – (verb) to stick. *'Aah'm claggin'* indicates sweating with heat

claggy – sticky

clarts – (noun) mud. Verb; to clart on – to muck about. Adj; clarty – muddy

clash – to gossip. Noun; gossip – *'What's the clash?'* Also – to throw away; *'Clash it ower the bank'*

clatch – muck

clatt – to claw or scratch. *'Clattin' on ma legs'*

clatter – (noun) chatter

clay cuddy, clay cutty – clay pipe

claypee (to gi' someone) – to knock down, reprove or reprimand strongly. Also: 'get claypee' – to be on receiving end of same

clean (verb) – to gut a fish or shell a crab

Clear, as in: 'to get clear of' – rid, to get rid of

cleckin' – a brood. *'A cleckin' a chickens'*

cled (up) – gathered or hitched up: *'She had hor skort aa' cled up t' gan i' the wetter'*

cleek – a stick. *'Ye bool hor alang wi' a cleek'* Cleekers – *shellfishing using a stick, without bait*

clemmie – big, heavy stone used for a weight

clench – to knock over nails when building coble

clever – fit, well. Generally used in the negative: *'Aah'm not o'er-clever'*

clew – ? a thorn. *'A clew i' yeer arse'* – *a source of irritation*

clinch – a crash

clinkers – clouds rising up from the east, out of the sea; 'a bad-lookin' sky', forecasting easterly winds. Cf. *Andrew Rutter, 'climpers'*

clip – a sight, used derogatively of untidy woman: *'What a clip!'* Also, type (Amble): *'She's the syem clip'*

clock calm – very calm; windless day; smooth sea

clocker – a hen sitting on eggs

clonker – a large prawn (Blyth only)

cloot – a rag. Clooty mat – *a mat made from rags. 'A tongue that wad cut cloots'* – *a sharp tongue*

clumpered – cramped. *'Fair clumpered'*

co – company. *'He got in co wi''* – *kept company with*

coarse – poor, rough, of weather; denotes wind and rain. *'A coarse day'*

cock's comb – a ring around the moon. See also '**bruff**'

cock's comb – a red jelly-like creature found on the sea-bed 5 or 6 miles off Dunstanburgh Castle

cockle – to clear one's throat

cod-end – bag of a trawl net

codlin' – codling: Robbie codlin' (Amble) – small codling; Tommy coddlin' (Amble) – larger codling

coggly – wobbly (Seahouses)

cogs – spikes which blacksmith fitted to boots or horseshoes to grip in snow

collop – a joint of meat

come on, to – used in place of standard English 'get on'. *'Hoo did ee come on?'*

conie – rabbit (Craster only – the word 'rabbit' is unlucky there)

contrive – make out. *'Aah cannot contrive wha that was, noo'* – *I can't remember who that was*

coo-plat – cow-pat

coonter-tide – tide which runs opposite to the normal direction, found around rocks and islands

coower – to cower or duck the head; of a boat whose bows are too low in the water: *'She cowers hor heed'*

corbie, corbie-craa' – the carrion crow

corn flea – harvest fly

corran-dow – scone with currants in it

cover – net which covers crab or lobster pot. *'Stephen's i' the hut, knittin' covers'*

cowble – Coble, pro. from Seahouses to Boulmer [coeble from Amble to Tyne; short /o/ south of Tyne]

cowp – to knock over, upset or fall

craaler, craalin' boockie – hermit crab

crack (noun and verb) – talk. *'Ye're a grand crack, hinny'* – *you're good to talk to*

cracked – mad

cracket – footstool

cramper – mean, eccentric, light-fingered. *'She's a right cramper'*

cran – measure of herring, 28 stone. (Used all over Britain, not just in Northumberland)

crantle – the crown of the head

creel – crab or lobster pot, Holy Island only. Elsewhere, a basket carried on the back

creeve – crab or lobster pot: (Seahouses, Beadnell, Boulmer and Amble only). *In-creeve – those close in, in-bye; oot-creeves – those farther off, oot-bye*

creeve-stone – stone with waist cut into it, tied into creeve as a weight to sink it

crine – to shrink or wizen (e.g. of timber)

cringe – to be battered or bumped, as in expression: *'Crackin' an' cringin'*

crit – the runt, smallest in litter, the weakling

crook – one of the timbers which fan out forward in a coble

croon – the top end of the hyeuk, where it was tied to the sneyd

crop – appetite. *'Aah've nae crop for it'. 'Aah've crop for aal corn'*

croze – cooper's tool for making groove in barrel lid

crum knife – a cooper's knife, used for ??

crummels – crumbs (Newbiggin / Amble). In place-name: *'The Born Crummels'*

cruse – lively, energetic. *'He's gey cruse'*

crutch – the Y-shaped rest into which the mast was lowered on a herring boat

crutchybell – earwig. See also witchy-beetle

cruttelly – crumbly. *'The breed's cruttelly'*

cuddy – donkey. *'Short an' sweet, like the cuddy's canter'*. A cuddy is also a saw-horse (at Beadnell) and a canvas cover on a coble (at Craster)

cuddy duck – eider duck, St Cuthbert's duck. Also, Culbert duck

cundy – conduit, drainage ditch or pipe

cutch – bark (from Indonesia), formerly used to preserve ropes and nets

cut in (to) – draw in, of autumn nights. Conversely, 'Nights is cuttin' oot' – lengthen, as in spring

cushat – the wood-pigeon; *'Gaa'n up Hen Hill t' see if th' was ony cushats'. Place name, Cusha, near Dunstanburgh Castle*

D

dab – the sole (fish)

dabba – a stick with point on end for catching flat fish on sand (children)

dad – to hit, knock or blow. *'A dad a the lug'. 'Daddin' aboot'. 'Smoke's daddin' doon' – a sign a rain*

dae away, to – to get on with something quietly. *'Aah'm just daein' away here, hinny'*

dag (to dag on) – to spit with rain

dale, to be on – to be on loan for a share, as of a boat or gear

dan – a large marker buoy at the end of several fleets of pots

dander – (noun) detritus, like ashes

dander – (verb) to wander; *'She come danderin' doon'*

dandy-lang-legs – cranefly, daddy-long-legs

darkenin' (the) – dusk. Also, *'the duskin'*

darse, darsay – dare say; a widely-used, versatile exclamation. *Rather than say: 'I see,' or 'that's interesting now,' Beadnell fishermen would say, 'Darsay!' or 'Darsay?' It can also be used for emphasis: 'Darsay no!'*

dash – shandy, lemonade with a dash of beer

dat! – an expression of contradiction

deed eye – block used to stop ropes running on rigging, also called 'numb block'

deed tide – dead, small or neep tide

deedmen's fingers – the inedible grey lungs inside a crab

deefie – a dud. Also Douffie, soft, useless ground

deef-nuts, to be – to oppose strongly, to be at loggerheads

dell – to dig; *'get hor delled ower'. Dell Point, Beadnell – a rocky point, mined in the eighteenth century*

derrel (verb) – to hurry, speed. Also noun; *'In a derrel'* – *in a hurry. 'Tyek a derrel'* – *to tumble*

dess bed (Newbigin) – fold away bed

devalve – to relax. *'She nivvor devalved'* – *she never stopped talking*

di'd – do it. *'W' ha't' di' d'* – *we had to do it*

didle – net on a long pole for scooping fish aboard, especially salmon and trout (Craster)

dinky (noun, Amble) – a dinghy

dinna / divvint – don't

dip – deep (adj and noun). Also used to mean crafty

disherlaggy – Coltsfoot, but used locally (Beadnell) for butterbur. *'Doon amang the disherlaggy-leaves'*

dite – to brush or rub in order to clean. To smarten up

divvilment – naughtiness

docken (s) – dock leaves

dode – George

dodger (Amble) – canopy on coble

dog afore its maister (Seahouses) – sea which reaches land before wind which caused it

dogger – green crab. *Tommy dogger* (Holy Island)

dokie – auk, such as guillemot or puffin (Newton). *There was a fisherman from Newton whose by-name was Dokie*

dole – gloomy (Amble/Newbiggin)

donnart – stupid

dook (noun) – a bathe

dookas – large floats; Corky dookas. Also used for breasts (Cf. *Henry VIII, in a letter to Anne Boleyn, praises her fine 'duckies'!!*)

dooket – pigeon loft

door – laced opening in crab or lobster pot through which catch is removed

doot – expect. Properly, doubt, but used to express expectation, as in: *Aah doot it'll be fair the morn'* – *I expect it will be fine tomorrow. 'We'll be oot the night, Aah doot'. Also, 'doot but': Aah doot but he'll be back soon'*

dopper – oilskin

dose – a lot. 'A right dose a folk'. Also, a case: 'A dose a caa'd'

dough – denotes anger. *'She was up t' high dough'* – *she was very angry*

dover ower – to slump over (as in sleep); (Amble/Newbiggin)

draa'-knife – tool used to shape planks when building coble

drak – to mop up or dry. 'Drak it up wi' your cloot'

dreg – a sea-anchor, trailed behind boat to slow it down

drive (to), Drivin' (the) – drift-netting

Also: pushing too hard ahead. *'He'll end by drivin' under'* – *he is too forceful, he will wreck himself* (Amble, Newbiggin)

droomly – cloudy, of liquid. 'Droomly wetter' – muddy water

droothy, drowthy – dry, thirsty. Noun: 'drowth'

drowt – one of the twin 'keels' which coble stands on aft; see 'scorbel'

drukken – drunken

dungarees – work-trousers traditionally worn by fishermen over 'breeks'

dunsh – to shove or nudge roughly. *'Divvin't dunsh us!'* *'Gi' ower dunshin'*

durrel (verb and noun) – to hurry, speed. *'Aal in a durrel'*. *'He come durrellin' doon'*

durna – dare not. Alternative to darsent

duskin', the – dusk

dust (noun) – an uproar

duzzy – dizzy, sleepy, confused, stupid

dyeg(s) – mittens, fingerless gloves worn at sea. (Cf. 'Daag', Shetland)

dyen – done, finished with, worn-out. *'Thon boat's dyen'*

E

earl a hell, black as the – expression used to describe dirtiness

easter – to come round to the east. *'Wund's eastered'*

easy – soft (of ground)

'ee' – you; more intimate than 'Ye'

efternyin – afternoon

empstone – (Holy Island) spindle-weight used to spin horsehair 'graiths' for 'sneyds'. Also 'Berreller'

end-styen – weight at end of fleet of pots

ends, to gan one's – to get excited. *'She was gaa'n hor ends!'*

esh – Ash tree. Ash sticks were bent to make pot bows

ether – adder

ettle – to attempt

eye – way in to crab or lobster pot, as opposed to 'door', through which catch is removed

F

faddom – fathom

fagarrashin – mess, upheaval. *'The hyel fagarrashin'*

fair (adj) – very, very like. *'Ye're fair Wull Carr'.* *'Fair like a cat in paste'* – moving slowly

fake, fyek – a coil, loop or hank of rope. See Arsefyek. Also verb, to fyek it – to take a loop in it

far on – late. *'It's no far on yet?'* – it's not late?

farlins – the troughs at which women stood to sort and gut herring

fash – work (Amble / Newbiggin). *'Aa've haa'den yer fash'* – I've held up your work

fast – caught, snagged (see fest'ner). *'Fast as Jackson'*

femmer, femmel – fragile, shoddy, unsafe. *'By, she looks ower-femmer for me, like'*

fetther – father

fetther-lasher – sea-scorpion, gurnard

featherblaa' – highest dune in Beadnell Bay

ferrier – farrier

ferrier (Amble / Newbiggin) – a small boat used to ferry herring from keelboats. Called a 'towie' or a 'townie' farther north

fest'ner – obstacle which snags nets and ropes on sea-bed (often a wreck)

fetch – to bring. *'Fetch the gully here, lass'*

fettle – to fix, mend, put right. *'Aah'll fettle his hash'* – I'll put him right (Tom). Also noun – mood. *'He's in an aa'ful bad fettle'*

fid – spike used for splicing rope

fieldyfare – the fieldfare

fillies – felloes, spokes of cart-wheel

fine (verb) – to brighten (of weather). *'It's finin' away'* – i.e. getting finer

finish, at the – in the end

finnd – to feel. *'He canna finnd the caa'd'*

finner – Killer, Pilot or Minke whale in Beadnell area. Elsewhere used for dolphin

fire-fanged – description of skin (usually legs) mottled from sitting too close to fire

fishroom – space amidships in coble. In Yorkshire this is called the 'crib'

fish-stop – net on a long pole for scooping fish aboard (Amble)

fit – fought

fit – right, fitting. *Mair fit ye – better for you, more fitting if you… 'Mair fit ye stopped at hyem'*

flaggy-bow – buoy with flag marking end of fleet of pots

flaistered – flustered, in a state

flam – a sudden, light breeze. Cf *'flan', Shetland.* Verb: Flammin' aboot – of wind, variable. *'Wund's flammin' aboot'*

flannen – flannel. Used to make dyegs

flare (adj and noun) – widening of coble from stem

flee – fly (noun and verb)

fleet – a string of pots or drift nets

flig – to fledge. 'Them swallers is fligged'

flincher – cooper's tool for fitting barrel lids

flit – to move house. *Flittin's – annual movement of hired labour on farms*

flite (of rain, snow etc) – to fall lightly, to fall in showers. *'It's flitin'on' – it's showery.* Also noun: *'Flites a rain' – streaks of rain on sky in distance*

floors – cross-members in a coble

flotter – to waste. *'He's flottered it' (of money or goods)*

flow (verb) – to reach high tide. *'Tide flows at haa'f six' – high tide is at half past six*

fluke – a flounder. *The Fluke-Hyel, Seahouses*

fly – Sly, devious. *'He's fly, right enough. He's a blackguard.' 'Fly as Dick's hatband'*

fool – foul, tangled, caught (of rope). *'Fool tows'. 'Fool groond' is rough ground on which ropes catch*

foosh (noun) – enough, plenty, fill. *'Aah've had me foosh'*

foosty – musty

for that (construction) – because

foreby – besides. *'An' others forebye' – and others as well. 'Foreby the others' – as well as the others. 'There was mair foreby them'*

forefoot – curved 'keel' extending half way aft from bows of coble

fornense / fornenst – next to, beside, against, in front of, opposite

forrardsome – cheeky

fozy – shrivelled: 'A fozy tornip'

frames – the inner timbers of a coble, made of oak

frass – sawdust made by woodworm

freak – a ship's chest (Amble / Newbiggin)

fresh (noun) – a spate (Amble)

fret – summer sea mist

frig – fiddle, play with. *Friggin' on – i.e. fiddling on, as with a rope*

frone – starfish. Kyel-frone – sun starfish

frummarty – oatmeal. *'Like frummaty' – brindled*

frush – rotten, as of soft wood

fu' – Full, i.e. adult herring before spawning

fum, as in: 'Gi' him fum' – chastise him

fyece – face; the steep side of a reef, e.g. *Fiddler's Fyece (Beadnell)*

G

ga' – gave

gaa'd – rod, as of fishing rod

gaa'n – going, preference. *'It's no ma gaa'n' – i.e. It's not my cup of tea*

gaa'n folk – gypsies or tinkers

gadgy – the p-i-g (Holy Island). This word is used for a man in south Northumberland

gallics – Scottish Fisherlasses (Seahouses men called them this)

gallusses – a pair of braces to hold up trousers. Also, lifting gear on a trawler

gammon – loop of rope at bow of sailing coble to hold bowsprit, or mast and oars, in place

gan doon, nivvor t' – never to be forgotten. 'That nivvor went doon' – that was always talked about

gansey – fisherman's traditional woollen sweater, usually navy-blue and patterned. Designs varied from family to family

gant – to yawn

gash – slack (in a rope); (Craster). *'The gash a the line'*

gathers – blisters

gau-west, lang-tailed gau-west – The blue-neb or long-tailed duck

gaxon – a line with alternate corks and stones, used to zig-zag up and down from sea bed in nineteenth century

gee (tyek the) – to take offence. Pronounced with hard 'G'

geebaal (pron, with soft 'G') – a scythe

gerrad – hoop of metal worn around the body when carrying pails of water

get – to be called. *'He alwess got Dode'*

get away wi', to (construction) – to begin. *'She never really got away wi' it'*

gey – very

gib (sic) i' the mooth – glib

gib a the hyeuk – barb on hook which stops the fish from getting away

gibby – salmon with 'gib' or barb on its lip

gibby stick – crooked walking stick. In Newbiggin, *'gummy stick'*

gilse – grilse (*Old word for grilse, Wake for the Salmon, Jim Walker, p6*). *#what is it?*

ginny – a skate (fish) (Amble). Also, small rollers in coble for hauling pots

girdle – a griddle

girn – a twisted grin

glaikit – clumsy, stupid

glass – weatherglass, barometer

glasses – binoculars

glaur – mud. Glaury – muddy. *'A glaur hyel'* – a muddy hole or puddle. Origin of 'glory-hole'?

glen welt, to get – to be battered. *'Creeves has got glen welt'*

gliff – (noun and verb) shock, fright. *'Them speedboats gliffs the fish.'* *'Gi' him a gliff'*

gog – to stick fingers down throat of fish which has swallowed a hook. Also, 'Gog-stick', stick with notch in end used for same purpose (Craster)

goller – to talk too much, too loudly. Shouting. *'Gollerin' on'*

gollup – to gobble. *'Divvin't gollup like a guffy!'*

gomeral – a mischievous boy

goonie – nightgown

gormer – cormorant

gowdie (Holy Island only) – squat lobster

gowan – daisy

gowk – apple core. Also used of a thick-headed person

gowlin – possibly a marigold? Used in expression: *'Yella as a gowlin'*

graith – (noun) grade, kin, class, rank, belonging. *'She was of that graith'* – that class. Also (Holy Island) – horsehair used as part of sneyd on long-lines. (verb) to drag for lost gear; grapple: *Graithin' bowlt. Graithin' irons. Graither* – a grapnel

granny loaf – fruit loaf

grape – garden fork

gravit – silk scarf worn by fishermen with collarless shirt, under gansey

green (noun) – cod (Craster)

green b'yened – brittle boned (osteoporosis)

greenbyens, greenhorn – the garfish

greet – to cry. *Greetin' Johnny – by-name of one Seahouses fisherman*

grice – grease, usually bacon fat, used for greasing boat-sticks, thowelds etc.

grice – the p-i-g (alternative to the taboo word)

gripe – depth of coble at forefoot

grumble – to growl (of a dog)

grund – ground, sea-bed that is good for catching

grunt – the p-i-g (alternative to the taboo word). *A pellet med oot'n a grunt's bladder'*

grutlins – great lines, baited with herring and used in earlier times to catch cod, skate and ling

gudgeon – where the lower pintle of the rudder sits

guffy – p-i-g (alternative to the taboo word)

guizers – masked visitors on Old Year's Night (Newbiggin)

gurrelly – rough, gloomy (of sea or hard wind on gloomy day)

gully – a knife. *'The guttin' gully'*

gup – to pick up with the mouth. *'He gupped it up'*

gut – an inlet, especially between rocks, but used for any opening, e.g. an alley between houses. E.g. *Piper Gut (Farne Islands), The Benty Gut (Beadnell)*.

gyte – fish-slime

H

haa'd wetter – to be sound. *'He's thick, man. He winna haa'd wetter'* – he is stupid

haa'dden of – beholden to (someone)

haa'f-share man – hired man with no gear, taken on for herring fishing season on half pay

haa'f waxties – half-grown coal fish

haa'k – inside breast timber in coble's bow

haa'ks – small cuts or keens (in fingers). *'Haa'ks an' cuts'*

haa'k – to hawk or sell. Haa'ker – a peddler who sold small things around the doors

haa'l – to haul

haar – winter mist with frost

hacky – dirty

haddocks: tid haddocks (Amble) – small haddocks. Danny haddocks (Craster, Amble) – middle sized haddocks

haddock bags – sea squirts (haddocks eat them)

hag – a bog, as in *Newham Hag*

hairs on yeer feet, t' hev – to be lucky. Also: Hairy feet. *'She's got hairy feet'* – i.e. treads lightly, gets away with things easily (originally 'airy feet'??)

hairt – heart. Also, courage. *'His hairt's ower-nigh his britchy-arse'* – he is a coward

hairy Hubert, oo'bit – hairy caterpillar. From 'Oo' bit', bit of wool

hammer, claa's of – *'Set it away wi' the claa's a the hammer'* – to exaggerate

hand-barra – a tray with two long handles, used by two men to carry heavy gear such as nets

hank on – to tie; to make friends with, to start to keep company with. *'W' hanked on champion'*

hansel (verb) – to use or sample. *Aah'll hansel it' (of a gift)* – I'll use it. Also of food – Sample it. If you've tasted something before, *'Aah've hanselled it'*. In Shetland *'a hansel' (noun) is a gift*.

hant – to haunt, hang round. Hantin' aboot the place – *hanging round*

hap, hap up – to heap, to cover up, to wrap. *'It's happed up noo wi' sand.' 'Happed up wi' a shaa'l'*

hard, a (noun) – a piece of hard ground, e.g.

Boulmer Sooth Hard, Byre-End Hard

hard (adj) – fast. *He's gaa'n ower-hard*

hard (adj) – often used to denote someone droll, funny: '*Mind she was a hard thing*'

hard-shells – guillemots' eggs

hard up – ill

harrin' – herring

harrin' whale – whale commonly seen around shoals of herring; (probably Pilot and Minke whales)

hash – to mix. '*Hashin' at it*' – mixing, as with paint

hashy – rough, windy. '*She's hashy at the cutter*' – it's a gusty day

haygel – to ease, trundle, or manoeuvre along, inch by inch: '*Aah was haygellin' a box a fish.*' '*Aa the wood he could haygel*'. '*Haygellin' the barra*'. Noun: a struggle. '*He had a right haygel*'

hayn – to spare. '*He wunna hayn hissel*'. '*Th' nivvor hayned theirsels*'

heck – manger in wall

heed-rope – mooring rope from bows of boat

hemmel – cattle-shed with arched entrance

hemp on – to unfasten snoods on lines (Amble / Newbiggin)

herrod – herd, shepherd (Cf. 'herriot'?)

het – hot, heated. *Het wetter – hot water. Het-up – aggravated*

heugh – a rocky outcrop on land

hezzel – hazel, used for rails for pots

hinch – hip

hind – contracted farm-labourer. Generally deprecating

hingin's – (noun) twine attaching net to tow (south of Beadnell). Called a 'hoppin' at Beadnell, 'norsel' or 'ossel' in East Anglia

hinny, hinners – term of affection, usually (but not always) for woman, or children

hippen – nappy. '*The nighest your arse has stolen your hippen*' – those closest to you can play dirty tricks on you

hitch – clove-hitch, the most commonly-used knot, cf. *half-hitch, rollin' hitch*

hobble – short seas, surface ridges on sea caused by wind. '*A bit hobble on*'. Also adj, 'hobbly': '*Hobbly the day*'. On Holy Island this is '*Wabble*', '*wabbly*', in Seahouses '*rabble*'. *A top-rabble*'

hogga – hosepipe

hoik – to shove

hole, hyel – an inlet. '*The Benty Hyel*'. Also used for rockpools. Also: 'wetter-hyels' – rockpools

holly – to leave lobsters in boxes in sea for a period; '*holly-boxes*' – fish boxes fitted with lids to keep lobsters in water

hook – a crook (thief, scoundrel)

hoolet – owl

hootchin' – heaving, teaming, alive, over-run with. Also: hotchin' (Craster)

hoppin's – see hingin's

horns – protuberances of gunwale either side of coble's stern

how – hoe

how! – a greeting

howk – dig

howp – of land, a prominence, or the cut defined by it?? e.g. *Hecla Howp, Seahouses. 'Skeers an' howps*' (hill and hollows??)

howt – to deter, put off. '*Aah couldn't howt hor*'

howway! – Come on!

hoy – to throw. Also noun: '*Gi' hor a hoy*'

hue – widgeon (Holy Island)

hummel (noun) – a float (Holy Island)

hunger-pudden – a person who is always hungry

hunk – to hug. *'Hunk it tae ye'*

hunter – an old pocket watch

hurpel – to hobble, limp

hurrel – to roll or wheel. Also, to hurry. *'Hurrellin' the barra'* – wheeling the barrow

hut – a lot, a heap. *'Sic a hut a cars gaa'n aboot'*

hyem – home

hyeuk – hook, noun and verb. Hyeukkin' – hand-lining without bait. Also 'jiggin', 'rippin'

hyeuk-net – L-shaped net with trap or 'hyeuk' in one end, used for trout-fishing on the beach at Beadnell; essentially half a T-net

hyeutter – the barb on a fish-hook. *'Hyeuk ower the hyeutter'*

hyeven – Haven, sandy landing-place for cobles, e.g. *Beadlin Hyeven, Newton Hyeven, Boulmer Hyeven*

I

idle – fun-loving, humorous. *NOT used to mean lazy; generally approving.* 'He's an idle bugger' – i.e. *He's a good laugh*

in-bye – closest in; *in-bye creeves – those closest to shore; opp. Oot-bye*

ink-fish – squid (Holy Island)

inwaver – inner supporting lateral timber in a coble. 'Inwyer' at Amble

iron man – a hand-capstan used to haul nets and raise sails on sailing keelboat

J

Jack-shine-the-lowe – the moon (expression used when speaking to children)

Jackie Doory – the John Dory

jaloose – work out, detect meaning, understand. *'Aah've jaloosed wha ye are.' 'Aah'll get it jaloosed'*

jantin' – carousing, jaunting. *'Oot jantin' every neet.' Also noun, 'a jant'*

jap – knock (noun). (Cf. jarp, verb – County Durham Easter custom egg-jarping)

jenny groats, john o' groats – cowrie shells

jeesses – joists across ceiling (Amble / Newbiggin)

jib end, to gan off the – go off the deep end, go to extremes (Amble / Newbiggin)

jiggin' – hooking for fish with hand-line; cf. hyeukin', rippin' etc.

jilly – jelly, jellyfish; also used for a sea-anemone

jilly-jar – jam jar

jinked – broken

jinny, jeanny – a rope-roller

John-Alec – the p-i-g (alternative to the taboo word) (Seahouses)

Jonah – someone who brings bad luck at sea

jumper (Seahouses) – fisherman's smock, see slowp

jup – to jump. Past tense: juppen

K

keek – to spy, peep

keek (noun) – pout whiting (Craster)

keekies – Scotch haddocks (Seahouses)

keel, dressed to the – dressed up very smartly (Amble / Newbiggin). *Origin of 'dressed to kill'?*

keelboat – term used to distinguish herring drifter of Scottish 'Fifie' type, used in Northumberland in nineteenth and early twentiethcentury. Also applied in twentiethcentury to trawlers and seine-net boats

ken – to know. *'Pity-but-ye-ken'* – *I'm not telling you!*

kep – catch

kep-net – net on a long pole for scooping fish aboard (Craster, Amble)

kep-shite – skua, so called because it chases other birds until they drop their food, thought by fishermen to be droppings

kets – rubbish, offal; also used for children's sweets

key – to fasten up hooks on sneyds of long line to make them safe when finished for the year

kibble – to beat, pummel. 'Aah'll kibble ee!' 'Gi' him a right kibblin'!'

kick up (a) – a mess. 'A right kick-up'

kilks – haddock rows (eaten as a delicacy)

kill – kiln, as in Beadnell limekilns: 'Kill Corner'

kilp, kilt – curve of underside of coble aft

kilt – to gather up skirt; 'She kilt hor skorts up t' gan i' the wetter'

kist – chest used to house herring lasses' belongings on their travels

kit – a barrel of herring

kittle – nervous, ticklish, restless, sensitive. Also (verb) to tickle. A kittler – a 'character', an amusing person

kittlins – kittens. Also verb: 'The cat's kittlin'

knacks – balls

knee – supporting timber in coble, e.g. under thofts or in bows

knit – to make a net or pot-cover using needle and shuttle

knot (a watter) – a sea (Holy Island, Craster)

knowe – knoll

kyel – Kale. Also, broth

kyel-frone – sun starfish

L

laid in – adj describing inward curve of upper-part of coble, especially sailing coble: 'tumblehome'. 'She's nicely laid-in'

lambin' storm – gale which usually happens in mid-March

land – to arrive. 'She's just landed'

landin' – the landing-plank or first rising plank on a coble. Traditionally painted a different colour from the rest of the boat, hence 'a haa'f red landin'

landsman – someone who is not a fisherman

lantered (adj) – to be made late. Cf Andrew Rutter – exhausted

lap – to overlap ends of nets, tying rather than sewing them, so that they can be removed easily

lat – a lath or strip of wood. Cross-wise strips on base of creeve

lay haa'd to (construction) – believe. 'Ye canna lay haa'd t' aa' she says' – you can't believe everything she says

layger – cover thickly, as with mud. 'Ye're laygered!' 'Laygered wi' glaur'. See also slaegart

lazy wund – a cutting wind, one that 'gans straight through ye'

lead – to carry by horse and cart. 'Th' wore leadin' bagies for' the field'. 'Leadin' lime t' the kill'

leash – (verb) to lash / bind

leashin' (noun) – lashing, that which binds something securely to something else. In Craster: Leaze, leazin's

leash – (adj) lithe, vigourous. A leash lad – a lithe, quick lad

leather – to punish

lee shore, to end up on a – to get nowhere; e.g. to lack success in life through being too meek (Amble / Newbiggin)

leed-rope – lead-weighted rope on bottom of net. Also 'sole-rope'

legs – in net knitting, the four ends of the mesh surrounding the knot

lek – to leak. 'Boat's lekkin like a seeve'

len – advantage, as in *'T' tyek a len of'* – *To take advantage of, to exploit, to make a fool of*

lennart – linnet. *'Catch lennarts'*

lether – ladder

let on – to tell or speak out. *'Aah nivvor let on'*

lick (noun and verb) – denotes speed. *'She was gaa'n at sic a lick…' 'Lickin' alang'*

lift (noun) – a rolling sea. *'Darse, there's a bit lift on the day'*

lisk – groin

limmers – the shafts of a cart, e.g. lifeboat carriage or rocket brigade cart

limmitter – a lobster with one claw missing. (Elsewhere, a disabled person)

lines – usually refers to long-lines, baited with mussels and limpets in winter-time to catch white fish. Cf. 'summer lines', baited with ragworm. See also 'grutlins' ('great lines') with bigger hooks and baited with herring

links – dunes. *'Alang the links'*

lint – main part of net

linty – linnet. *'Fit as a linty'*. See also **lennart**.

lipper – white caps on sea, breaking, choppy, often accompanying southerly wind etc. A confused sea. *'There's a bit lipper on.' Adj 'Lippery':'She's a bit lippery the day'*

lippin' – full to the brim. *'Lippin' full'*

lonnen – lane or road

loo – past tense of to lie (Newbiggin / Amble only)

loozy – lousy, covered in lice

lowe (noun) – glow, light. *Jack shine the lowe – children's name for the moon*

lowes – flames. *Blue lowes – used metaphorically to denote anger or argument*

lowp – to leap

lowse – to loose, set free. *'Lowse hor off!'*

lubbert – cry-baby, stupid person. *'Ye muckle lubbert!'*

lug – ear. Also, a flap. *'Cock yer lugs'*

lum – a chimney, e.g. kipper-shed lum. *A lang-lum hat – a top hat*

lynch – to launch, usually with 'doon'. *'Lynch up'* – *to haul a boat up*

M

maa'ky, maa'ky-rotten – rotten, maggoty

maa'n – must. *'Aah maa'n away'* – *I must go*

mair – more; used with 'nor' rather than 'than'. *'She has far mair brains nor me'. 'Theer's mair nor one'*

man – husband. *'Hor man come in'*

mander (on) – to ramble (in speech)

manners, to mek a hoel in – to behave badly (Amble / Newbiggin).*'She meks a hoel in hor manners'* – *bad manners*

markin'-iron – iron brand with initials used to identify pots

marks – landmarks lined up for navigation

Mary Kramer – denotes hurry: *'She's fair Mary Kramer'*

married on – married to

mash – mesh; *'stolen mashes'* – *attenuated meshes, made to narrow a trawl net to the cod end*

masher – a dandy, an over-dressed man. *'Swinhoe-masher'*

mattie – a fat young herring before roe or milt has developed (this term was used beyond Northumberland)

may tops – brown seaweed that washes ashore when the may is on the trees

maze – herring eggs

med up wi' – made up with, i.e. pleased with. *'Aah'm no med up wi' it'* – *I don't like it*

meddoms – minnows (Craster)

meggie sloper – very untidy in dress. *'Aah'm Meggie Sloper the day!'* Also, Meggie Murphy (for an untidy house)

mek – to make or grow, as in: *'Sea' s mekkin''* – sea is getting rougher; *'Tide's mekkin'* – tide is coming in

mek on – to pretend

mell – mallet

messages (Amble) – errands, especially shopping

messenger – bottom rope on fleet of herring drift nets (term used beyond Northumberland)

middle ends – the two 'steeky bows' between two contiguous fleets of creeves

middle fleets – anchors every two lines on fleets of long lines at Newbiggin. Not used at Beadnell.

miller, to droon the – to make something too watery, e.g. tea

Miller's thumb – properly a kind of fish, but used in Craster for big red starfish

mind – to remember. *'Aah can mind one day...'*

ming-mang – a mixture. Ming-mangin' on – mixing clumsily, as a child playing with food

minister – the p-i-g (alternative to the taboo word)

minnims – minnows

minute, at the – now

mizzle – to go missing

mizzletow – a traditional Christmas decoration made out of two willow hoops covered with crepe paper

monk – funnel-shaped trap sewn into bag of salmon-net at Boulmer

moosh – a cap placed on the head of the dead for burial

morn – morning. *This morn – this morning. The morn – tomorrow. Also: The morra – tomorrow. The morn's morn – tomorrow morning*

moss – bog

mowldie, mowdie – mole. *'Mowldie hillocks'*

muck (verb) – to remove stinking bait from lines

muckle – great, big

mugger – gypsy. *'The Muggers a Yettholm'*

mule – a double-ended coble. Also applied to Scottish double-enders used in Seahouses between the Wars

mullymac – fulmar. Also Mully, very similar to Shetland name, maly

mushel – mussel

musk-shell, musk – cuttlefish

N

nancy – squat lobster

nap – to snap, as of a stick

nearly – almost. *'It wad nearly ha' t' be...'*

neb – beak

neck – impudence. Adjective, necky. *'He had the neck t' say t' me...'*

needle, netting-needle – a flat piece of wood, bone or plastic with an eye and tongue cut into it, used with shuttle to knit nets

neeve – fist

neither wonder – no wonder

net (Craster only) – a crab or lobster pot

nettle, to land on a – to have some bad luck

niggly – in a bad mood

nigh-handed – near

ninepenny man — ??

no can, not can – construction meaning not be able to: *'Ye'll no can mind when...'*

nool – to stun. *He's nooled 'im!* Also 'nailed'

nor – than. *'She's bigger nor ee'*

norr'ard – north; *'Th've been t' the norrard'. Opp. Suthart*

numb – stupid. *'He's that bloody numb!'* Also stiff, inflexible, insensitive: of hooks fastened too stiffly to sneyds on long lines: *'Them hyeuks is numb'*. Also blunt: of claws on lobster: *'The shear claa' an' the numb claa'*

O

o'er, ower – over, widely used to denote place. *'Doon o'er'*, *'up o'er'*, *'back o'er'* – referring to village in relation to harbour. Also to denote 'too much'

o'erhaal, owerhaal – to shoot crab pots one by one as they are hauled, rather than stowing the fleet aboard the boat before shooting them. (See o'errun)

o'errun, owerrun – same as O'erhaal (Amble)

off – to or at sea. *'Gan off'* – to go to sea. *'Tyek him off'* – take him to sea

old maids' laces – long thin strands of sea-weed

on-gaa'ns – goings on

oncen – once, when

oo'bit – a hairy caterpillar. Literally, bit of wool

oot-bye – farthest out; oot-bye creeves – *farthest off-shore*. Opp. In-bye

ootrogue – undercurrent from shore, taking sand out with it (Amble)

or – before, until (like 'ere). *'Be a bloody lang time or Aah gan back'*

owt – anything (opposite of nowt)

oxter – armpit

P

paddle-hoosh – lump-sucker. In Craster, Paddle

paddock – toad. *'Like a muckle paddock'* – swollen, fat

paddock steuls – toadstools

paddy (Eyemouth and Holy Island) – smooth spider crab

paddy's lantr'n – the moon (expression used when speaking to children)

pains (the) – arthritis

palms – pussy willow, used in Church on Palm Sunday

paps (Holy Island) – sea-anemones

pap-styens – soft coral, dead men's fingers

pay – to outdo, to beat at a contest. *'He'll pay ye.'* *'Nae bugger could pay ee'* – you're too sly to get round

peak – angle of top of sail on sailing coble; this was steeper to the north, hence: *'Beadlin men had a right peak on the sail'*

peege, the – in Seahouses, the old non-conformist meeting place and Sunday-school; inland, a lambing-shelter. (Probably introduced by Alexander Ewing, nineteenth century Seahouses herring-merchant, who came from a farming background on the Tweed)

pee'sit, pee'sweep – lapwing or peewit

pellet – a small float. Varient: pennant (Amble / Newbiggin)

perrin – a bobbin, such as was used to fasten hooks onto snoods for long lines. *'A perrin a threed'*

peysey-ware – bladderwrack (Seahouses)

picker – sharp iron blade used to remove limpets from rocks for bait

picket – a boat-hook or gaff. *'Stiff as a picket'*

pickie – a tern

piece – a length of a long-line carrying 100 hooks

piece – a packed lunch, usually bread; alternative to 'bait' in Seahouses and Scottish East Coast

piggons – ties for oilskin sleeves

pike – a haycock

piker – killer whale (Newbiggin)

pillin – a green crab when soft or peeling. (Pullin – Holy Island)

pilot, sea-pilot – oyster-catcher *(from piot, magpie?)*

pinchers – pliers

piner – a penetrating, cold south-easterly wind. *'By, yon's a sooth-east piner, aa'reet!'*

piper – spider crab ('tyed' in Seahouses). Cf. Piper Gut, Farne Islands

pistil – a lobster with no claws

plantin' – a plantation, often used as a landmark

plash – to splash

plasher – a porpoise or dolphin

plate – protective iron covering on coble's forefoot and scorbels

playgen – clay or ware jar. Also used for broken bits of clay pottery

plet – plaited up, twisted, ravelled (as with lines). *'Tows was aa' plet up.'* #wound up for transporting to boat or tangelled?

plenty – enough

plies – oars

ploat – to pluck, as of a bird. Also, to gather. Also, to rob

plodge – paddle, wade. Also: Plode (Seahouses)

plodin' (noun) – a pounding

plook (noun) – a boil or blister

plowt, plowter – potter, struggle (cf. potin') *'He's aa'wess plowtin' aboot'.* Cf. Potin'

podler (Beadnell), podlie (Seahouses), puddler (Holy Island) – small coal-fish

poke (noun) – bag or sack

poke (verb) – to take offence

pokeys – mitts, gloves consisting of thumb and bag for fingers

pollis – a policeman

pomer (noun) – anything big: *'It's a pomer' – it's a biggun*

poother – powder, e.g. *The Poother Hoose at Seahouses*

poos – crabs (Holy Island, also used on Scottish East Coast)

pote – to potter about

poy – to put. *Wheere d' Aah poy it? – Where do I put it?*

poy (Noun) – a boat-stick (Beadnell and Boulmer usage). *'Gi' us yer picket an' yer poy'*

prodder – small hand drill

prog – to prick. Also noun, and diminutive: *'proggles'*, as of prickles on a hedgehog. *'The weever'll gi' ye a nasty prog.' 'He'll prog ye'*

puddens – innards, digestive tract. 'End-pudden's' – bowels. *'Yon fella, strainin' his end-puddens'*

puffy – porpoise (Seahouses)

put up (of tide) – to increase, grow towards spring tide. *'Tides is puttin' up'.* (Opp. of 'tyek off')

Q

quarter-chock – protective cover on outside of planking at a coble's stern

querrel-styen – a stone with a hole through it, carried for luck. *From whurrel, a spindle??*

quick – quick-tempered (Amble / Newbiggin). *'Man, he was aa'ful quick'.* Also: early: *'Tide's quick the morn'*

R

radgy – lustful

raffle (up) – to ravel, tangle

raggy – ragworm, used for bait on summer lines

rail – lengthwise part of frame of crab or lobster pot

ram – central bottom plank, from which a coble is built (and by which it may be measured)

ramage – a mess

randy (noun) – a noisy, showy or annoying person

range – long seas, rollers. 'A bit range on'

rash – energetic, fit, healthy

rashers – rushes, as in *'The Rashers Field', Beadnell*

ratch – to tack (of a boat, verb and noun). *'Ratchin' by the Point'. 'Beadlin t' Amble, yen ratch'. Also 'gan ratchin' aboot' – raking about*

rax – stretch. *'Aah'll rax me legs'. Also over-stretch, strain: 'Divvin't rax ye'rsel'*

reange – to poke, of fire

red, rehd, reed – clear, tidy, unravel. *'Red the lines' – clear the hooks. 'A right red up' – a good tidy up. 'Aah canna red them oot' – I can't unravel how they are related*

reek – (noun and verb) smoke. Also used for steam: *'Aah wadn't gi' 'im the reek off a dumplin''*

reest – to resist, behave badly, be stubborn or recalcitrant. *'The cuddy's reestin'*

reeve – a rivet (used in building a coble)

reive – to tear or snatch

rent – (noun) split which opens up between planks of a wooden boat when left to dry out

reynart, Mr Reynart – the fox

rift – to burp or belch

rickle – a heap. *'Nowt but a rickle a byens' (Amble/Newbiggin)*

ride – (of a bow) to stand up in the water. (Of a boat) to lie at anchor

rindge – to wring, as in *'rindge oot the claes'*

rip – a scoundrel. *'He's a proper rip. A right toucher'*

ripper – cross-pole for carrying a double hand-line for 'hyeukin' (also 'rippin', as in *'rippin' for a codlin'*)

rive – to snatch, tug or tear. Also reive. Past tense: rove, roven

rizzled – aired (Amble / Newbiggin). *'The claes is rizzled'*

roach – little auk

roadster – a tramp

rock pencil – soft red stone for rubbing on steps, gathered at Bamburgh

rockets – rocket brigade lifesaving apparatus. The term 'rocket' was also used for the flares which summoned the lifeboat crew

roondy – (adj and noun) round, as of ungutted fish: *'roondies'*

rowell – roll; also roller, e.g. rollers on side of coble

rowelly – rough, rolling (of sea): *'A right rowelly day'. Also: 'roolly' (Seahouses)*

rowen – row, eggs

Rumshion – a mess

run – swell; the distance seas travel up beach, into harbour etc. *'Theer's a hell of a run on!' Also verb: 'Sea's runnin' – i.e. big swell*

run – (sailing) to sail before the wind

run (of herring) – to spawn

run up – rope caught round the propeller. *'He's run up aboot the Carrs'*

runnin'net – straight part of salmon beach-net running from shore. Also known as the 'black net'

runch – yellow mustard flower, charlock and similar

runch (Holy Island only) – small smooth spider crab

ruther – rudder. *Ruther-pintle: pin for holding rudder in place*

S

sackless – gormless, feckless, useless

sailor's purse – skate's egg-case

sair – hard, sore. *'Toast's ower-sair.' 'Creeves is sair-hammered'.* May also be used to denote someone dry or droll: *'Oh, she was a sair thing.'*

sale – sandeels

sandels – sandeels (Amble / Newbiggin)

sand-hopper – large, woodlouse-like creature which lives on the sea bed (?)

sandy-lowpers – sand-hoppers, small flea-like creatures which live in seaweed on the beach

sang – song, a fuss, as in 'song and dance.' *'Ye're mekkin' sic a sang aboot it'*

sarra – to serve

sark – shirt

scaa'din' – scalding, hot (of weather). Also burning cold

scappers – scuppers

scar – a rock; see 'Carr', e.g. *Scarcar (Farne Islands), Scar Jacky*

scarbel-built – carvel-built, built with smooth planks

scarf – joint on stem of coble (noun and verb)

scarried – scarred

scithers – scissors

scoff – to mock or make fun of. *'He's aa'wess scoffin' ee'*

scoot – (noun and verb) urinate. Noun also used for a guillemot

scorbels, scowbels – twin 'keels' which coble stands on aft. Also 'drowts'

scraffle – to scramble. *'She come scrafflin' doon.'* Cf. *scrapple*

scrape, scraper – used in expressions to have one's tongue scraped – i.e. *to pretend more refined speech.* *'Faa'n o'er the scraper'* – *to talk posh, above one's rank*

scrapple – scramble. *'Aah scrappled ower the fence'*

scrat – scratch. *'Scrattin' aboot'*

scud – a heavy shower

scumfish – to smother, suffocate. Often used metaphorically to mean too hot: *'Aah'm fair scumfished!'*

scunner – to sicken. *'Meat scunners me'*

Scut – top upper cross-plank at coble's stern. 'Skud' in Seahouses. *Scut-iron – iron along edge of scut*

sea – a wave. *'A sea hit him'*. Also used to describe condition of sea when rough, especially in expression 'sea on': *'Plenty sea on the day'; 'a canny bit sea on'*

sea-cat – cat-fish, rock turbot. *'The sea-cat breeze'* – *a gale remembered for bringing many sea-cat ashore at Beadnell*

sea-cock – place in coble where water comes in to cool engine

sea-divvil – the monkfish

sea-mice – small wading birds such as knots or sanderling (usually plural). Also used at Newbiggin for sea-slater

sea-sow – the rock goby

selvedge – salvage

set (ye) **hyem** – to see someone home safely

shaa' – stalk and leaves. *'Titty-shaa's', 'Bagie shaa's'*

shabby – unwell

shad – shoal, shoal water, shallow place or sand-bank, e.g. *Islestone Shad, Glororum Shad (Farne Islands), Tughall Hall Shad*

shade – shed

shake yer feathers – hurry up

sharp – early

shear claa' – sharp claw of lobster (as opposed to numb claa', blunt claw)

sheer – upward curve of bows of coble

sheffs – sheaves

sheiler – a soft crab (Holy Island)

shells – specifically, clams. *'He's at the shells'* – *he's fishing for clams*

shelpy, soft (of crabs); (Seahouses)

shilpit – weak, wan, bloodless. Cf. Shelpy

shite an' sugar – useless, muddy ground (at sea)

shive – a thick slice

shoot (of pots, lines or nets) – to set

shoother – shoulder; also, the width of a coble's bow

shootin' stick – upright stick propped in inwavers of coble, to clear tow when shooting drift nets

shot – the catch; each attempt at drift-netting: *'w' got six the forst shot'*

shuggy-boat – swing-boat (at fair)

shull – shovel (noun and verb)

shuttle – flat stick used to make 'mash' when knitting nets

shy (adj) – poor weather. *'A shy day'* – *a poor day*
Sic – *such*

sic an' so – similar, just the same, just so

sicenlike – such like; such and such. *'Sickenlike man'* – *such and such a man*

simmet – vest worn under sark

sixpenny man – squat lobster (Seahouses)

Skaldeman – what the Holy Islanders call a Seahouses man

skate's egg – the sea-potato, a small white sea-urchin

skeer – rock, exposed reef, e.g. Iron Skeers (Howick). Andrew Rutter suggests a shore-based reef

skeet – to defecate

skeets (Amble / Newbiggin) – wooden battons for sliding boat over sand. Called boat-sticks at Beadnell

skeg – slot into which foremast was lowered in herring keelboat

skeldie – porpoise

skelp – to slap or hit. *'Aah'll skelp yer lug'* – *I'll box your ears.* Also noun: *'A skelp a the lug'*

skemmy (noun or adj) – a lost or thin pidgeon, a racing pigeon that has gone astray. *'Nowt but a skemmy pudgeon'*

skeyn – to shell (of mussels and limpets for bait)

skinner – a cold day

skowb – cut stick for pot rail, barrel hoop etc.

skyell – a scale, e.g. *salmon skyells*

skyelled oot – description of curve of coble outwards

skyul – school

slack (noun) – an inlet

slack (adj) – time at high and low water when tide is not moving, e.g. *slack tide; high-wetter slack*

slackened – mentally unbalanced

slakes – mud-flats e.g. *Waren Slakes*

slaister (Seahouses) – a fuss, carry-on or effort. *'A right slaister'*. Slather in Beadnell. See also slavver and slaeger

slater – woodlouse. Sea-slater – large, woodlouse-like creature found at sea

slather – see slaister, above

slavver – bother, work (noun and verb). *'It's a muckle slavver'*. *'Divvin't slavver on aa' neet'* (as in slave)

slavvery – slimy, slippery: *'slavvery boockie'* – *the whelk*, as opposed to *'craa'lin' boockie'* – *whelk shell containing hermit crab*

slaeger (past tense slaegart) – to cover thickly, spread roughly, splatter, as with mud or paint. *'Slaegart wi' glaur'*. See also 'layger'

slee'in – to sneak, to go about slyly: *'slee'in' aboot'*

slowp – fisherman's smock, worn over gansey

slump – plankton on nets (Cullercoats, NOT north Northumberland)

slunk – thin, as of spent fish

smaa' (noun) – twine

smit (the) – a contagious disease. *'He's gi'en ye the smit.'* Also verb: *'Aah've smitted ee!'*

smooth (a / the) – sandy ground, e.g. *Craister Smooth (Craster), the Benty Smooth (Beadnell)*

snack – to snap, as of a dog

sneck – latch, as on door or gate

sneuk – a point of land which sticks out, as in North Sunderland Sneuk, Ebb's Sneuk Point, Beadnell etc.

sneuk – to sniff about, as a dog. *'He gans sneukin' aboot'*

sneyd, sneed – snood, attaching hook to line

snib – a catch, as on a gate (Amble). See also sneck

snoot – nose

snory-byen – child's spinning toy made out of string and bone (or card)

sole-rope – weighted bottom rope on net

sollan – Gannet or Solan goose

soocker – the lamprey

sorrah – sir; now only in expression, *'Sorra, haa'd yeer tongue!'*

spaa'n – spawn. **spaa'ny** – spawny. *'Ye're like a spaa'ny haddock'* – i.e. thin

speet – spit from which herring were hung on 'tenterhyeuks' to make kippers

spelk – a splinter

spent (noun and adj) – herring which has spawned

speyn – to thwart, prevent, frustrate. Also used agriculturally meaning to wean

split, splet – (of tide) turn?? *'I' the split a the tide'*

spoach – *to snoop. 'Gan spoachin' aboot'*

sprag – small nail used to mend sea-boots (Holy Island)

sprag – large codling (Craster)

spring (noun) – 'S'-shaped curve of top line forrard in a coble. *'Yon boat has mair spring on hor'.* Also (verb) – to open out (of planks of a boat)

sprowl – wire on a hand-line sinker

spuggy – sparrow

spur-dog – dogfish (Craster)

square – typical arrangement of late eighteenth or nineteenth century fishermen's cottages; e.g. Craster Square, Seahouses, Newton Square, Low Newton-by-the-Sea

staapin' – standing

staggart – name of one of the Kyloe hills, used as a landmark. According to Fred Reed, Staggart means a stackyard

stang – a weever fish (sting on the back of his fin) – (Amble / Newbiggin)

starkie – starling

starn – stern (of boat)

starved, starvin' – extreme cold. *'Put the fire on, Aah'm starved'*

steam – to motor. *'W' steamed off for haa'f an hoor'*

steel – a rocky prominence, e.g. *Boulmer Steel, Cusha Steel*

steen – Stephen (both a surname and first name in Beadnell)

Stickle – a state, a predicament, a quandry. *'The world's in sic a stickle'*

sticky-jacks – burrs

stife – smoke, fumes. Also **stithe, stoothe** *'Stoothe him oot'* – to smoke him out, fumigate

stilshon – knot used to tie sneyds onto grutlins, i.e. a clove hitch, twisted with an ordinary knot

stinkin' tom – a kind of thistle

stinkin' wullies – weed that leaves white roots in the soil

stob – a post

stomach-piece – part of the inside of a coble's stem

stook, stookies – bundles of corn sheaves. *'W' wore stooden like stookies'*

stoor – dust. *'A bit stoor fleein'*

stoothin' – plaster

storey – beamy (Amble). *'A storey boat, yon'*

stot – to bounce

stowed oot (wi') – full

stray – straw

strike – to take the net

strop – rope attaching each pot to main tow. Any rope attaching one thing to another

strunts (to take the) – to take the huff. Also strunted – moody, awkward

strup – stepped. *'Aah strup on his tail.'* Also: **struppen** – **stepped**. *'Ye've struppen on ma foot!'* *Strup is also the past tense of 'to strip'*

styen – stone. Styenney – stony. *'Spit on the yen styen'* – spit on one stone, i.e. agree, act in union

styen-piece – one of the anchor-tows at the end of a fleet of creeves; runs between chain and end-stone

suein' nail – sewing nail, copper nail or rivet used to make coble

sun'lan' – Seahouses, literally the south lands of Bamburgh. The 'official' earlier name of Seahouses was North Sunderland. Distinguished from 'sooth Sun'lan,' on the Wear

suthart – south. (Opp. Norrard)

suum – swam

swad – fine green weed which grows on ropes etc. On Holy Island, the term is used for zostra

swath – a small piece of land among rock on the shore (Amble / Newbiggin only)

swatter – jelly-fish

sweel – swell. Also a swivel or pivot, used by some fishermen to attach buoy to pots

sweep – a long oar

Sweet Wulliam (Craster) – male dogfish

swing – end of messenger rope, mooring drift-nets to boat

swull – shallow basket, flat at one end, used to hold long line and also herring

T

t-net – T-shaped salmon beach net with both a flood and an ebb-tide 'hyeuk', as used at Boulmer and Amble

tack-hyeuk – place either side of coble's bows to attach sail

tacketty byits – hobnail boots

taffy – toffee. *'Claggy taffy'*

taggarine-man – tinker (from word for tin??)

tang'el – long seaweed

tappy-lappy – hurriedly. *'Gan tappy-lappy doon the Mally Stairs'*

taree – arctic tern (Craster)

tath (noun), tathy (adjective) – rough grass. *'Tathy grass'*. 'Tath' is used in Holy Island for the feathery brown mossy seaweed that grows on lobster pots

tatty – blustery, of wind or weather. *'A tatty day'*. *In Seahouses, 'tattery'*

teek – a mattress, stuffed with chaff (caff) or similar. *'Aah'm fu' as a teek!'*

teem – to pour. *'Aah'll teem the tea'*

teer – lot, used in derogatory expression, 'aa' the teer', i.e. 'aa' that ee'r', all that ever. *'Aa' the teer th' dae is sit aboot'*

teerum – tern (Seahouses)

tenterhyeuks – hooks which herring hang from on 'speets' while being smoked for kippers

tha' – though

thick – noun; fog ('a thick come on'); adj; *'thick as guts'*, *'thick as tar'*, *'thick as a hedge' (said of fog)*

thick – friendly. *'Them two was aa'ful thick.'* – as in expression *'thick as thieves'*

thick – stupid: *'Thick i' the mooth'*

thicken, thicken on – to become more plentiful

thin – scarce. *'Fish is aa'ful thin'*

thivel – stick used to push clothes into boiler

thoft – thwart, seat in boat

thon – that one there

thonder – there yonder; closer than yonder. *'Somethin's no right thunder'*

thoweld – thole pin (for oars)

thropple – throat. As in place-name: *'Dry-Thropple'*

through w' the – over-hasty, slapdash. *'She's through w' the'*

thrussel – thistle

thunner-splet – a thunder storm

tier – a fleet of pots (Holy Island only)

tight – mean. *'Tight as mustard'*

timm'er – rib of a boat, timber

tin man – protection for arm when shooting lines (also a Scottish term)

tinggel – wooden patch nailed onto boat, doubling planking

tipple – to topple, fall

titty – tatie, potato

toes – claws (of crab)

tommy – small crab, thrown back (Holy Island)

tommy noddy, Tommy – puffin. *Cf. Shetland, Tammy Norrie*

toon – village. Used in Beadnell to distinguish centre of village from harbour. Also for

Seahouses: *'Sun'lan' Toon'*

tooze, toozle – towsle. *'Toozed oot like tows'*

top-coat – overcoat

top-stick – rail of crab or lobster pot (Craster)

top-tow – small rope fastening strop of pellet to thicker tow

touch, toucher – a scoundrel. *'He's a proper rip. A right toucher'* – i.e. *a scoundrel*. *'Toucher'* is used colloquially to mean a storm in Craster

tow (noun, rhymes with now) – a rope

tow (verb) – to trawl (Amble)

townie – small boat used to ferry herring from keelboat or for salmon fishing. Called a 'towie' at Boulmer

trash (verb) – to tire out. Trashy, trashin' (Adj) – tiring. *A trashy journey'*. *'Divvin't trash yersel'*.

travel the fishin's – to follow the herring shoals down the East Coast from Shetland to Yarmouth; especially unmarried women who worked as gutters and packers

traveller – iron ring to hoist dipping lug sail up the mast on a coble; (term used beyond Northumberland).

trimm'lin' – trembling, shivering (Amble / Newbiggin)

trink – gully, trough or deep pool in sand

trow – a trough, such as that which herring are washed in before kippering

trowk – dealings. *'Aah nivvor ha' nae trowk wi' them'*

true tide – north and south flowing tide-flow, unaffected by islands, rocks or land

trunk – a metal hoop covered in net, baited and used to catch crabs and lobsters in nineteenth century

tuck – the miller's thumb (fish)

tudelems – small sea birds, such as knots, dunlin (Seahouses)

tuft – the miller's thumb (fish) – (Craster)

tummel – tumble, fall. *He tummelled his creels – fell head over heels.* Adj 'Tummelly' – rough (at sea): *'He had a right tummelly day'*

twank – to beat (Craster). *'Gi' hor a twankin''*

twist – verb; moan, complain. Noun; In a twist — in a bad mood. Adj; *Twisty-fyeced, twisty*

tye – greased rope attached to 'traveller' and running to halliard block on sailing coble

tyellier (Holy Island only) – smooth spider crab (also 'paddy')

tyed – spider crab (Seahouses). Also tyed-legs – brittle star (Beadnell, Craster). 'Tyed' – toad, although the toad is normally referred to as 'paddock'

tyek off – to diminish (of tides, after spring tides). Opp. of 'put up'

tyek up – close up, of rents in a wooden boat

tyen – past tense of take (Beadnell); cf. Tun – past tense of take (Amble)

U

up aheight – high up

used wi' – used to

V

varnigh, varney – very nearly, almost, probably. *'It'll varnigh gan away through time'*

vex – to annoy. *'Aa'm vexed wi' ye'*

visitors – tourists

W

waa'-knot – wall knot, used to fasten 'pieces' of long line

wacked – dried hard and brittle by the sun: *'Them sheets is wacked'*

wadge – a wedge, used at bottom of bow in creeve, intended to swell in water and hold bow in place

wale – choose. *'Wale the titties'* – sort out the seed potatoes. *'She doesn't wale hor words'* – she doesn't understate things

waller – to waddle, flounder. *'Wallerin' like a muckle seal'*

wallop (of contents of pan) – to boil, simmer. (Cf. 'pot-wallopers' – householders in nineteenth century electoral reform)

waltzers – children's slang for stairs

wang – leather strap, shoe-lace

wank – to pull. *'Gi yon tow a wank'*

wants – (noun) a hook missing on long line. Also used metaphorically: *'He's got a wants, man'* – i.e. lacking brain. Also *'a back wants'* – both for a hook missing off a long line, and for something missing intellectually

ware(s), weir(s) – seaweed. *'Ware-cow': long, thick-shanked seaweed* – *'Cow' meaning clump as in heather-cows? 'Ware-bangs'* – *'bangs' meaning fringe as in American usage? Pillar-wares (pillow?)* (Boulmer). *'Peysey-ware'* – *bladderwrack* (Seahouses)

waregoose – barnacle goose

wasp – a small prawn further south (Blyth?)

watter-nail, witter-nail – wooden plug through joint in coble's forefoot

weathergaa' – a 'sundog' or small patch of rainbow in fine sky, usually presaging weather change or wind from its direction

weatherglass – barometer

weigh – to lift. Also, *'Aah'm weighin' the form up'* – *I'm thinking it over*

well-seen – obvious

wesh, wersh – bland, lacking taste (of baking)

wetter in – enough water to get into harbour. *'If ye divvin't get a move on, ee'll no get wetter in'*

wheesh – to bowl; of a hoop, for example: *'Ye'd wheesh it alang wi' a cleek'*

wheesht! (exclamation) – Be quiet!

whilse – at times. *'It whilse got dyen a bit later'* – *a construction heard more in Coquetdale / Ashington, only occasionally on the coast*

white crab – soft crab, one that has shed its shell

whither – a quandary. *'Aah'm in a whither'*

whullick, whulk – a winkle

whup (verb) – whip, lash, fasten. Whuppin's (noun) – fastenings, bindings

wiggy – name used for squat lobster farther south, Blyth area

winkie – a wooden float with a light on the end used to mark salmon nets at the night driving

winter beef – barrel of salt herring given to women workers as part of payment

witch – a sole (fish)

withoot – unless. *'Withoot he'll come the morn'*

witwhile, every – every so often (Amble / Newbiggin)

wicket – a small gate in a hedge

wideawake hat – hat with wide brim. Also: **'widey-wig hat'**

witchy-beetle – earwig

withoot – unless. *'Withoot Roger brings the milk'. 'Withoot he'll come th' morn'* – *'unless he comes in the morning'*

witter-hen – moorhen or coot

wittery wagtail – pied wagtail

wizenbank fair – extremely untidy. *From Whitson Bank Tryste, or Fair?? 'still important in the 1850s, when old men referred to its great decadence'* (Berwick Advertiser, 23 August 1901)

woomlicks – hemlock or other umbelliferous plants

wawkspring, workspring – a hangnail

wullies – willows

wullymint – guillemot. *'He's like a tarry wullymint gan aboot'*

wund, to be nigh the – to be mean (Amble / Newbiggin)

wundel – machine with four revolving arms, used to take the turns out of long lines

wus (noun) – dregs, left-overs from last boiling of bark pot

Y

yammer – to complain, whine. *'He's elwess yammerin' on'*

yap – to talk energetically, meaninglessly or too much. *'She does yap on'*

yard – spar from which lug sail hangs (term used beyond Northumberland)

yark – to jerk, pull sharply; also beat. *'A right yarkin'* – a beating

yellertops – ragwort

yellm'th – Alnmouth (From Ale-mouth?)

yetlin – three-legged iron pot, used for cooking and also for boiling tar

yet – still. *'Is't theer yet?'*

yett – a gate

yetmul – oatmeal; also used for sleep-dust in corners of eyes

yoll – yawl, a small Scottish double-ended boat

yowe – ewe

Northumbrian words and phrases in common use 60 to 70 years ago. Collected by Andrew Rutter of Seahouses

These words are extracted from two lists, one given to me and the other to Mr F.L. Kennington, publisher of Andrew's book, *A Seahouses Saga*. I have included only words not already listed earlier.

baaf – *'a baaf week'* – a profitless week

begrutten – tearful, near to tears

benesty – *'to be under benesty'* – to be under obligation

birsey – impudent, cheeky

blate – *'gey blate'* – never at a loss about anything

bool – a roundish, fist-sized stone

brizz – *'to brizz doon'* – to shove down

caller – cold, icy, frosty. *(Elsewhere, fresh)*

canch – a ledge of rock

cangle – an acrimonious argument

car-rant – a noisy event. *'Havin' a fine car-rant'*

climpers – cumulous cloud

cruppen – indrawn, doubled over. *'Sair cruppen wi' caa'd'*

deeve – to deafen

dilted – polished; *'Aa' dilted an' dyen'*

dozent – sleepy, stupid. *Cf. duzzy, donnart*

dowfy – dull, damp, mild weather

dwam – a slight faint

either eggs or youngins – one thing or another

ether – a naughty child. *Cf. ether – an adder*

feckless – happy-go-lucky, irresponsible

foumart – a weasel or stoat

gaad – a fishing rod

gar – to make, force, impel – *'That garred him run!'*

glead – avid. *'He was a glead for (money, work, etc.)'*

gizzent – dry, thirsty

harran – jute sackcloth

haa'f-fish – a young cod about 9 to 12 pounds

haggering – distortion of objects by atmospheric refraction

hirsel – a lot, much

hoven – a bleary-eyed person; *'hoven-face'* – *puffy*

jukery-packery – illegal or shady ongaans!

kaims – gravel ridges or banks

kenned grund – familiar surroundings

kythin – worm casts on the beach sand

lang-nebbit – long nosed

lantert – tired, exhausted

lerk, laerk – a pleat or twist in cloth or skin

lippen – to depend (on)

list, nae – no energy or interest in

loppert – curdled; sour milk for example

ma Sartees – my goodness!

maunder on – to ramble in conversation

mense – *'Mair t' yer mense'* – it would be more fitting

myeggs – hands

'neither meal nor seeds' – a delicate person

nethered – very cold

nicker – to snigger

oo – wool *Cf. oo'bit*

owergaffen – heavy, overcast sky

peenge – to whine

reip, reype – to rob (e.g. a bird's nest)

sindry – to pull or tear in pieces (asunder?)

sneesh – sneeze

snotter – snore

spiel – to climb

stound, stoond – to smart, ache

swat – a deeply-laden boat was *'gey swat'*

tagger – unimportant or second-hand belongings. Cf. Taggarine-man

tasterel – a humbug of a child

tewin – exhausting. *'Aa gat a rare tewin'*. Cf. *chewin'*

thole – to put up with, endure

thriveless – unprofitable

'twixt bank and brae – a high tide, spring tide at high water

waffy – poorly, 'under the weather'

what fies! – what reason, who cares, what odds!

wheenge – to whine; cf. peenge

wire in – get on with the job

yell – ale or beer. Cf. *Yellm'th*

yen – an oven

yep – an impudent child

Appendix 2

A Stanley Umpleby: The dialect of Staithes

This is not an easy text. As well as publishing a book of verse in the Cleveland dialect in 1937, Umpleby issued this 'Dialect of Staithes' as a private publication in the 1930s (with a pen endorsement 'to Matt and Jacki Verrill without whose valuable aid this could never have been done'). It abounds with technical terms, only partly explained by his diagram of a coble (here placed at the end). There are also some local, unique words; and the translation offered is not always literal, e.g. to bait (beeat) glossed as 'to prepare'. Some confusion between double-v and w is possible on the printer's part. A few notes have therefore been added in square brackets – more help welcome! (Bill Griffiths)

A

ackruns – acorn

afterthoft – seat between scudboard and lowsethoft of coble

alluns – the Little Auk (alle alle). "The'r leyke Allums efther't"

amell – betwixt, between, in the midst.(Atkinson, 1858) Morris (1892) states: 'The form 'mellum' is or was till lately, used at Staithes, where the fishermen are said to divide the fish 'mellurn yan another.' "Danish, mellem (between). The only sense in which it is used nowadays is when the fishermen sight Roseberry in a certain position, when they say, "T'Cap amell t'moor" (I can see the Cap (Roseberry) in the middle of the moor)

amidships – space between midshipthoft and Iowsethoft in fishing coble

anonsker – eager, very desirous. set upon a thing (Atkinson) This word is only used very rarely nowadays. A child was corning down the street eating an apple, and another said: "Aa, Edie, thoo's sett'n ma anonsker for't"

appron – apron

arseband – band attached to rear of fishermen's skep

assand – in case (Ah'll tak' this 'ere assand as Ah want it)

ass – ashes

atweea – in two. (Ah could 'a'e bitten a naal atweea Ah war that mad)

B

back Beean – (back bone). Main hazel of a skep

backust – bakehouse

backstan – a sheet of iron, sometimes a stone having an iron hoop to enable it to be hung over the fire, used to bake cakes upon. (Backstan-ceeak) (Blakeborough)

badger – starfish

balk, baulk or bawk – fishermen's line before hooks are affixed. Called *line-balk* when hooks have been attached. Baited line when hooks are baited. *Ceeav'd line'* when old bait has been removed

barking – tanning fishing gear and nets

barlsteead – ring that fits on oars

barmskin apron – oilskin apron used by fishermen

beeat – prepare [sic]. (The've gone ti beeat a line)

beeat – boot. (Ther's a hooal i' mi beeat)

beeat-stockin' – stockings used with the sea-boots

bend – fasten. (Bend that bowl on !) [standard maritime?]

birk – birch

bleead – blood. (Blaid at Runswick)

blaid-'oonds – bloodhounds. Runswick men say of Staithes men when they go after coal: "'The'r leyke blaid-'oonds efther't"

bleg – seahen. (**Au'd wife** at Whitby)

blether – bladder. (He's i' t'au'd Allum 'cos [he's] blawin' bletherbowls)

blinnd – blind. (All could sheet blinnd e'e, i.e., without looking)

boorn – born

booat – boat. (Give us 'o'd o' t'booat-'eeak)

booagy – coble fire

booy – buoy

bouns – (which line 'es t'rneeast bouns?, i.e. Which line makes the biggest heap?) That line's bounsy

bowl start – bowl to mark commencement of sheeting

bottery – elderberry

bowlin – type of knot. Running bowlin, etc. [standard maritime]

brat – turbot

breears – briars

breet – bright

breeadin' – making a crab-pot. (Matt and Tich is ower yonder breeadin')

breead winnd – N.N.-W. (Ah thowt t'glass wad a gone up – ther's a breead winnd)

bridle – string attached to crab-pot to steady it

broon leeamers – ripe hazel nuts. (The' tumm'le oot leike broon leeamers)

C

candybout – feast of sweets provided when communally worked clip-rug is completed

carlin – seat nearest head of coble

ceeav'd line – line from which old bait has been removed

chaam'er – bedroom

chawlin' – chewing. (Wa maunt 'a'e them au'd rattens chawlin' this gear)

checkers – periwinkles. (Thoo's browt checkers like mice een)

claggum – Ggeneral term for toffee

chimlas – chimneys

clauve – placing of line hooks between two short hazels to prevent snuds or sneeads being barked (tanned)

clep – stick with a hook on the end for hauling fish aboard. This is named a 'garthangle' at Filey. ("Clep a ling bi t'tail, a cod, butt, an' brat bi t'eead, an' a conger eel bi t'naaval. Y'u deean't allus clep 'ern wheer y'u wad leyke ti clep 'em, bud wheer v'u can git 'o'd")

corrk – cork

corrk bunches – corks used as guides to pots

corrin' – current. ('E wad gan onnywheer for 'auf a corrin'.) [currant]

coulpress – continued breaking of sea (It's breeakin' coulpress ower t'arbour mooth)

crab-sticks – sticks to measure size of crabs

cribs – small compartments at side of coble

cuddy-handed – left-handed

D

dan – buoy

dan-leet – Bbuoy light

deead – dead. ('E scarred 'im ti deead)

deed – work. (Ther's thrang deed)

dog-choups – fruit of dog-rose. Also Dog-jumpers

doggers – green crabs

dog-'eeads – dog-heads. Repairs to fishing line that are not spliced

doldrums – lack of wind. Windjammer held up for wind is said to be in the 'doldrums.' [standard maritime]

draugs – sea anchors. ("T'draugs slit reet atweea as wa war cumin' ower a gert sea")

dot bo'ds – dotteril

dolls – sticks to hold sail to enable the fisherman's hands to be liberated

dubbler – enamel bowl

duck – lamp flare [?]

duck weeakin' – wick for 'duck'

E

eeavun – oven. ('Yuon' generally in Cleveland)

eearin' – sails of coble. (Lee and Weather 'eearin')

een – eyes

ell – pour. (Ell us a cup o' tea out.) [hell]

F

fassen – fasten

feeak – miss. Also steal. When the fisherman is fastening the snuds (with hook) to baulk (22 score and ten hooks to a new line), he measures the distance between each hook thus: heeak, heeak, feeak, i.e. miss one; i.e. tweea an' a feeak: "Ther's nut moony 'es a heeak an 'a feeak"

feeatin'-piece – piece of wood fixed between lowsethoft and midshipthoft in sailing cobles "ti git foot-'o'd"

felties – fieldfares

fewles o' Muck – Bbad weather

flang – flung. ('E flang 'issel doon i' siken a temper)

fleead – flood. ('E teeak t'fleead taade ti Yarmouth - iv a bucket.') ('Flaid' at Runswick)

flayed – afraid

fleet – 52 crab pots. (Wa've lost tweea fleet o' pots this summer up ti noo)

fleeted – grumbled, complained (Walloper fleeted when Ann bowt all that wrangham (small fish))

flithers – limpets. Flither gatherers used to all dress alike and travel as far as Saltburn and Robin Hood's Bay, in the early davs afoot and later by train, returning on the rocks gathering flithers on the way

fettled – prepared. (Bi wi git fettled wa'll 'a'e bin taadin' an 'oor)

fodther – further. (T' 'errin's 'es gone fodther oot)

forefeet – front of keel or coble

foreroom – space between midshipthoft and forethoft

forethoft – seat between carlin and midshipthoft

fond – silly. (Thoo's is fond as leeace)

for ti why? – \Vhy?

foy – a boat requiring assistance. [?offering assistance]

G

gantrees – board flush with forethoft and carlin in which mast is fixed

gar ends – boundary wall of village. End of passages oberlooking sea and beck. (Air see'd 'im o' t'Barber Gar Ends)

gauvin' – gapin[g]. (Wheer's thoo gannin' gauvin' aboot?)

gausarks – exclamation! (Oh, gawsarks! Wheeas this cumin'? T'staation gaffer for 'is mussel bill Ah's think)

gilney – hole at coble head through which gilrope passes

gilrope – (See Gilney)

gildet – hair snare for catching birds. (Y'u caan't cop a sparra' iv a gildet)

gob – mouth

gog – short, stoutish piece of stick for killing fish and removing hook. (Gog a cod bi t'snoot, a ling o' t'back o' t'neck, and a thoornbeck atwixt t'een)

go'nets – gurnets

gowld – gold. (Ah wadn't gan up theer for a gowld coo)

grades – grappling gear for recovering lost lines. (Y'u ma' graade all t'daay an' nut tak' 'o'd)

gudgeon – hole in casting at stern so that hook can be inserted to haul coble

H

haeled – hauled

haelin' room – space between lowsethoft and afterthoft

hairy hats – round sealskin caps worn by fishermen up to five or six years ago

heeak – hook

hau'f-piece – standard length of fishing line (30 fathoms); 13 half-pieces to the line

hooal – hole

hoolibaloos – blowers

hoorn – horn

howsers – scoops

howsumivver – however

hummock – buoy for nets

I

inwire – wooden rail round inside of coble. (Thi mittens is i' t'inwire)

intiv – into. (As seean as t' butt com' Ah war intiv it)

J

jeeat – jet

jib alliotts – rope attached to mast to hoist jib

K

kansh – ridge of rock, sand or other obstacle in a waterway. (Sha's gitten ov a kansh, i.e., coble had run ashore on a ridge in the harbour)

kelk – codfish spawn

kelkin' – the knot fastening the snud to the fishing line. (Hing it i' t'kelkin')

kessen – cast

kidged – twisted round the snud

killation – a fishwife's made word: 'It's killation'

knaps – a local name for a part of the rocks

knott – a bad sea. (Sha teak a nasty knott there)

L

lanch – launch

lanchin' woods – woods used to launch coble. They are well greased "wi' talla eightpence a poond at Jausiph's"

lanthron – lantern

latchets – tabs inside sea-boots to enable them to be pulled on and hung up to dry

lax – cloud. (Sha's (t'sun) gannin' doon intiv a lax)

lazy cod – An ill-fed cod. ('E's neean lazy: 'e warked 'issel ti deead)

leeaf – rope that passes through parril

leeaf-heeak – hook for the leaf

leet'nins – corked line affixed to tows for potting and fishing

leeat – small coal-fish

leear – liar. (Thoo's as big a leear as Tom Pepper)

leeak – Christian name Luke. 'Leeak' White (Luke White)

leks – leaks. (Sha leks leyke a baskit.)

lip ta'en – lip Taken, i.e., a fish hooked by the lip

listins – ridge at joinings of planks round the coble

leyke – like. (It leeuks leyke a lobster wi' yah claw)

litha – look you

lobster Stick – to measure size of lobsters

lowsethoft – coble seat between midshipthoft and afterthoft. This is removable, i.e. 'lowse' (loose)

lonnin' – lane. (Ah see'd 'im up Jooa an' Andra lonnin')

loose – louse (parasitic insect). (Ah could crack a loose o' mi shackles!)

lound – quiet, calm. (It's varra lound ti-neet)

M

mallimawks – guillemots

maft – suffocated. (Ah's fair mafted)

ma'ssy – mercy.(Lawk 'o' ma'ssy)

mally – Molly

meead – went to. (Ah war boorn t' 'eear Talkin' mead Runs'ick wi 'au'f a cran)

meeans – moons

meeat – mate. (Meeat of a ship an' nut t'meeat 'at y'u eeat)

mense – finish. (Th'u wad nobbut ax us for a mense.) [?favour, help]

midshipthoft – coble seat between forethoft and lowsethoft

mirak'lous – remarkable (Wa surntaames git a mirak'lous fish)

N

nantlin' – wandering. (T'au'd wind's nantlin' aboot finndin' a 'ooal ti blaw in)

neea – no. (Wa want neea white pots… It 'es neea good in't)

neeaks – "is neeaks is weel doon," i.e., coble heavily laden; low down in the water. [nook – corner]

neb-band – band at neb (head) of skep

nogglets – Llocal name for part of the rocks

nowthermost – most northerly

O

oilslops – oilskins

o'kkud – awkward

oor – our. (Oor awn wyke)

orgin – young codling

owerlie – placing baited hooks on neb of skep

ower heeaks, ower-'eeaks – large hooks, i.e., cod hooks as distinct from haddock hooks (40 used to line)

owil – boat requiring assistance. (See also 'Foy')

P

pap lines – lines baited with rock anemones (sookers)

parril – that sail hangs upon

peeliers – tiny young crabs with immature shell that can he peeled off Used for bait

petril – petrol

pets – seagulls

pistil – pistol. (Y'u could 'a'e ta'en Steeas wiv a penny pistil)

pot-tows – used with crab pots

pot strings – d[itt]o

potaboilin's – off the end of Cowbar Steel

pooa't – port

'pleean – complain

po'ss – purse

potty hooal an' treeacle – backstan ceeak an' treeacle

Powl nett – pole net: the first net shot

pots – crab pots. They contain: 4 bows, 4 side sticks, 1 top stick, 2 end sticks, 2 deear sticks, 2 bait bands, 1 slip band, 2 deear bands, 2 spoots or smoots

Q

queer-un – 'it's a queer-un if maane 'es ti bi mair 'an 'ers.' 'It war a queer-un when the' brak' a rudder-band iv a gale o' wind'

R

rattens – rats

raxed mi shackles – sprained my wrist

Reck'nins – weekly share out of fishermen. (Ther' neea reck'nins ti-neet (after a blank week))

reekin' – smoking

rewles – rules. (The' 'a'e ti 'a'e rewles, thoo knaws, Billy)

rowler – roller. An apron or duster rolled up to protect the head when carrying coal, wood, etc.

The Staithes women can carry great weights upon their heads (see remarks re 'Flithers')

ram – coble keel

riddy ricknors – ready reckoners; snuds with hooks affixed. (If wa ax'd for a heeak an' a sneead the' wadn't knaw what wa wanted, but if wa a for a riddy-ricknor the' knaw what wa want)

rousby – Roxby. "Ah deean't knaw what wa s'ud deea widoot Rousbv Trees" (as a landmark)

rowth iorons – irons on oars

S

sau't – salt

settin' a line – fixing sneeads to baulk; preparing a line

settin' booa'd – 40 inches in length: initials of fisherman and his Wife cut in it, thus :

W   A

   V

(William and Alice Verrill)

scudbooa'd – small seat just inside stern of coble

Seeat – soot

seeap – soap

scarbers – liver of ling

scawls – clinkers

scrautin' – scratching

shuts – darts. (It war makkin' sike gert shuts)

sheeapsteeanes – sheepstones (rocks near Staithes)

shackles – wrists

sheean – shoes

sholl up – move up

skane – taking mussels out of shells

sheeared – small fish that has been caught on hook and partly eaten off by bigger fish

shooat – catch. (Oh, wa've a middlin' shooat)

sheeat blocks – blocks used in sheeting

sheeated – shot. Act of casting lines or pots. (The've gitten sheeated.) Pots are shot 9 fathoms apart

skeeat – skate (fish)

skeel – wooden tub: formerly used for carrying water when each household had its own 'skeel' painted inside and out and bearing initials of the owner. They were carried on the heads of the womenfolk

skellet – saucepan

skems – pigeons

silverwhips – wild or sea cabbage (Brassica oleracia), which grows in great abundance at Staithes in the clitfs

skinnigryff – Skinningrove

slavverlinin' – baiting with flithers (limpets)

smeead – smooth

smeears – fish spawn

shiftin' Mussels Up – changing the water that mussels are kept in

snuds, Sneeads (formerly of horse-hair) – short lengths of line with hook attached which are affixed to the fishing line proper (baulk)

sookers – sea anemones

softies – tiny crabs before shell appears

soft – general term for fishing grounds with sandy bottom. (Hummersty Soft, Bullfit Soft, etc.)

squids – small herrings

spoths – short supports at end of each coble seat. (Named 'knees' at Whitby)

speean – spoon

slarve – slice. (Give us a slarve o' breead)

speets an' racks – used for roasting fish in front of fire

sprag – codlings

sperrit – spirit

Starn – stern

strop – short rope tied to pot-tow

string-knott – knotts to indicate which part of the line is in hand, eg., 'string knott,' 'half-piece string knot,' etc.

stecked – fastened, closed. (Noo git thi gob stecked)

's'cos'lit'o'th'u – literally 'God's curse light upon you.' An old Staithes woman was going to the polling booth, and one of the party touts asked her number. " 'Scoslitothu !' she replied. "Ah's seventy-three next!"

swill – wicker basket used by flither pickers

swings – Fforrud ropes of coble

T

taade ti Saay – sure to say. [tied, obliged]

taadin' – tiding. Resting at sea: waiting period between shooting lines and hauling them in

tack taakle – gear for tacking

tap leets – coble lantern

teea – tea

teeas – River Tees

tell on't – remember

thrang – busy

thowll pins – uprights on coble side for oars to fit on

thoorns – thorns (starfish)

thorn ears – large dog fish

Timmers – timbers. Floor timbers of coble

U

under-running – hauling pots for examination and afterwards returning them to sea without hauling them aboard.

up-ower, in-ower, doon-ower, oot-ower – directions

V

varmint – vermin

W

wahdni breeches – wide-knee breeches. Fishermen's trousers

waps – rough flannel with thumb-hole for maintaining grip of lines. These are named 'dog-cleeats' at Filev

weeakin' – wick

weather – good weather. (Wa'll gan if it's weather)

wheealin' (Whaling) – Iron affixed to strengthen part where thowls are placed on the side of the coble

whippin' – affixing hooks to snuds

whither – the small bent part at end of a fishing hook

woars – oars

worrurns – worms

wreck, wrack – seaweed

wow-tin – fishermen's lunch tin. [wow = treacle]

wowtin-ceeak – food that is not eaten at sea and returned in wow-tin

wrangham – odd lots of miscellaneous under-sized fish

Y

yallaboys – sovereigns

yat-stoups – gate-posts

yolls – yauls; yawls

Addenda

arden loup – part of the rocks near Staithes

blast, gurnet blast – gurnet's bladder

bo'ddin – burden, bundle

boo – bow

crab cart – empty shell of crab

ceeastrin – cistern

cuvvins – periwinkles

doctor' bottle – term for all medicine. ('A'e y'u browt oor John a doctor' bottle?)

highlaws – name for shoes formerly worn by fishermen. [high-lows]

hod nab – point on cliff near Staithes used as landmark

laggers – name given to men who assist with launch of cobles

moy – mouth

miffy – lobster without large claws

mops – small codlings

nannycocks – undersized lobsters. ('Pawks' and 'linties' at Whitby)

ratch – exaggerate. (That Ridcar man wadn't ratch when 'e war talkin' aboot fishin')

reeasted – roasted. (Backust dinners is allus reeasted at t'top)

swaape – swape (oar)

strunt – cutting snuds off fishing line

smock jackets – fishermen's jerseys

tratt – fishing line used by youths and old men. They bait a line and anchor it to the rocks at low water and at the succeeding low water reclaim it

theet – watertight. (Them beeats is as theet as a bottle) (Used also at Flamborough)

tripped – ('a'e sha tripped?, i.e. Has the anchor become liberated?)

taumed – fallen off to sleep

taum – piece of stick with twine and hook used by boys for catching pennock, etc. [strictly tawn equals fishing line]

weeak – wake. 'White' water left behind moving ship. (Sha's makkin' a despert weeak)

warsit – hill. (Humersty Warsit, Huntcliffe Warsit, etc.)

watther Bo'n – phosphorescence of herrings. (T'watther bo'ns on)

Sources

Admiralty Survey to 1951 – *Flamborough Head to the River Tyne: from Admiralty surveys to 1951*

EDD – *English Dialect Dictionary* ed. J.Wright (used here especially to define distribution c.1900)

MP – Mount & Page *A new chart of the Newcastle Trade* 1760s

LW – Laurie & Whittle *New Hydrographical Survey of the East Coast* (1794)

WL – Whittle & Laurie *Chart of the Coasts of Northumberland & Durham from Sunderland Point to Berwick including the Farn Islands, Holy Island, etc.* (1819)

OED – *The Oxford English Dictionary*, 2nd edition

OS 1850s – first edition, 6" to the mile, surveyed 1855–58

OS 1899 – second edition, 6" to the mile

modOS – current Ordnance Survey maps online at: www.ordnancesurvey.co.uk/oswebsite/getamap

Bibliography

Aird, R.A. (1909) 'Notes on the parish of Seaham', *Antiquities of Sunderland*, vol.10, pp.70–100.

Allan, Thomas (1862) *Allan's Tyneside Songs* (Reprint, with introduction by Dave Harker, Newcastle: Allan, 1972.

Anderson, Maureen (2004) *Bygone Seaton Carew*. Barnsley: Wharncliffe.

Angus's *Newcastle Garland* (1805) Gateshead.

Armstrong W.H. (ed.) (1930) *Song book containing 25 popular songs by the late Tommy Armstrong*. Chester-le-Street: Wilson, 3rd edition.

Atkinson, J.C. (1868) *A glossary of the Cleveland dialect*. London: Smith.

Baharie, Alexander (1849) *The improved coaster's guide*. Sunderland: Vint & Carr.

Baharie, Alexander (1887) *Tales and sketches of Sunderland and neighbourhood.*

Bailey, John (1810) *General view of the agriculture of the County of Durham*. London: Board of Agriculture.

Banks, John (1871) *Smugglers and smuggling*. Reprint, Newcastle: Graham, 1996.

Barrow, A. (2001) *The whaling trade of North East England*. Sunderland University Press.

Cpt Baynham (1904) *An illustrated guide to the Tyne training ship 'Wellesley'*. South Shields: Gazette.

Blackett, Joseph (1811): *The remains of Joseph Blackett*, 2 vols, London.

Bradley, N.C.A. (1978–79) *North East coast sailing cobles* 26 (1978) pp.23–32 and 28 (1979) pp. 25–32.

Brearley, Frank (1971) *A history of Flamborough*. Driffield: Yorkshire Ridings.

Briscoe, Diana (2003) *WIcked Geordie English*. London: O'Mara.

Brockett, J.T. (1829) *A glossary of North Country words*, 2nd edn, Newcastle: Hodgson.

Brook, Maureen (2005) *Herring girls and hiring fairs: memories of Northumberland coast and countryside*. Newcastle: Tyne Bridge.

Bourne, Henry (1735) *History of Newcastle-upon-Tyne*. Reprint, Newcastle: Graham,1980.

Clark, Helena H. (1967) 'More Northumbrian Lore: Extracts from the diaries of a north country naturalist', *Journal of the University of Newcastle Agricultural Society*, 21, pp. 3–7 [re 1880s].

Clarke, J.F. (1997) *Building ships on the North East Coast*. 2 vols, Whiltey Bay: Bewick.

Cortis, W.S. (1871) *Losses of ships and lives on the North-East coast of England, and how to prevent them.* London: Mercer & Gardner.

Coulthard, E.M. (1934) *From Tweed to Tees.* Edinburgh: Johnson.

Creighton, Louise (1904) *Life and letters of Mandel Creighton*, D.D., 2 vols., London: Logmans.

Crocker, Jean (1990) *Northumbrian Words and Ways.* Compiled by Jean Crocker.

Cunliffe, T. (ed.) with Osler, A. (2000) *Pilots of the world, vol. 2: Schooners and open boats of the European pilots and watermen.* London: Chatham.

Cunliffe, T. (under the direction of) (2002) *Pilots, vol.2, Schooners and open boats of the European pilots and watermen.* Le Chasse Marée/Wooden Boat/Chatham Publishing.

Description of a voyage in the coal trade with other poems, published for the benefit of the widow and orphans of the author (late a sailor of North Shields) (1835). London: Pownceby.

The Diana Training Ship for destitute and homeless boys. Report, January 17 1868, to the most worshipful mayor of Newcastle Henry Angus esq. (1868). Newcastle: Carr.

Dinsdale, F.T. (1849) *A Glossary of Provincial Words used in Teesdale in the County of Durham.* London: Smith, Bell.

Dobson, S. (1972) *Aald Geordie's Almanack.* Newcastle: Graham.

Dobson, S. (1973) *A light hearted guide to Geordieland.* Newcastle: Graham.

Douglas, Martin (1848) *The life and adventures of Martin Douglas, Sunderland keelman and celebrated life saver.* Stockton: Firth.

Dykes, Jack (1978) *Smuggling on the Yorkshire coast.* North Yorkshire: Dalesman.

Egglestone, William (1877) *Betty Podkin's Letter ted Queen on Cleopatra's Needle.* Stanhope.

Elgey, J. H. (c.1915) *Star and weather gossip concerning the heaven, the atmosphere, the sea.* London: Simkin.

Falconer, William (1780) *An universal dictionary of the marine.* London: Cadell.

Finch, Roger (1973) *Coals from Newcastle.* Lavenham: Dalton.

Foerster, Max (1941) *Der Fluessname Themse.* Muenchen: Bayarische Akademie.

Fraser, James B. (1832) *The Highland Smugglers.* London.

Friel, Ian (1995) *The good ship: ships, shipbuilding and technology in England 1200–1500.* Baltimore: John Hopkins University

Friel, Ian (2003) *Maritime history of Britain and Ireland c.400–2001.* London: British Museum.

Godfrey, Arthur (1974) *Yorkshire Fishing Fleets.* Clapham: Dalesman.

Oliver Goldsmith (1824) *A History of the Earth.*

Green, John (1879) *Tales and ballads of Wearside.* 5th edn, Leeds: Harrison & Waide, 1897 [re first half 19th century].

Griffiths, Bill (2004) *A Dictionary of North-East Dialect.* Newcastle: Northumbria University Press.

Griffiths, Bill (2006) *Stotty 'n' Spice Cake: A Dictionary of North East Dialect*. Newcastle: Northumbria University Press.

Griffiths, Bill & Osler, Adrian (eds) (2007) *John Stobbs' The South Shields Pilots: an entertainment in speech and song*. Seaham: Durham & Tyneside Dialect Group.

Grose, Francis (1787) *Provincial Glossary*. London.

Harker, Dave (ed.) (1985) *Songs from the Manuscript Collection of John Bell*. Durham: Surtees Society, vol.196.

Haswell, George H. (1895) *The maistor: a century of Tyneside life*. London: Scott.

Hatcher, John (1993) *The history of the British coal industry*. Oxford: Clarendon.

Hedges, A.A.C. (1989) *East coast shipping*. 2nd edn, Aylesbury: Shire.

Henderson, W. (1879) *Folk-Lore of the Northern Counties of England and the Borders*. London: Longman Green & Co.

Herrtage, S.J.H. (ed.) (1881) *Catholicon Anglicum: an English-Latin wordbook dated 1483* (Early English Text Society, vol. 75).

Heslop, R.O. (1880s) *Northumberland Words: A glossary of words used in the County of Northumberland and on the Tyneside*, 2 vols, English Dialect Society, 1893–94.

Hill, H.O. & McKee, J.E.G. (1978) *The English Coble*. Greenwich: National Maritime Museum, Maritime monographs and reports, no.30.

Hinderwell, Thomas (1798) *The history and antiquities of Scarborough*. York: Bayley.

An historical atlas of County Durham (1992) Durham County Local History Society.

Holmes, J.H.H. (1816) *A treatise on the coal mines of Durham & Northumberland*. London: Baldwin.

Hone, William (1837) *The everyday book and table book*. London: Tegg.

Hutchinson, Gillian (1994) *Medieval ships and shipping*. London: Leicester University.

Hutchinson, W. (1778) *A view of Northumberland*, 2 vols, Newcastle: Charnley.

Jackson, Kenneth (1953) *Language and history in Early Britain*. Edinburgh: Edinburgh University Press.

Kemp, Peter (1978) *The history of ships*. London: Orbis.

Kennington, Fred (2006) *As spoken in Berwick*. Stockport: Kennington.

Kurlansky, Mark (1999) *Cod*. London: Vintage.

Labistour, Patricia (1996) *A rum do! Smuggling in and around Robin Hood's Bay*. Robin Hood's Bay: Marine Arts.

Landstöm, Björn (1961) *The ship*. London: Allen & Unwin.

Latham, R.E. (1965) *Revised Medieval Latin word list from British and Irish sources*. London: British Academy.

Life of St Cuthbert in English Verse c. AD 1450 (1891) Durham: Surtees Society, vol.87.

Losh, James (1956) *Diaries of James Losh*, Pt.1, Durham: Surtees Society, vol.171.

Laurie & Whittle (1794) *New hydrographical survey of the East Coast*. Cited as LW.

Lethbridge, T.C. (1952) *Boats and boatmen*. London: Thames & Hudson.

Linsley, Stafford (2005) *Ports and harbours of Northumberland*. Stroud: Tempus.

Litwin, Jerzy (2003) 'The herring fishery and the growth of Britain's Baltic tradition in the 17th and 18th centuries', pp.47-60, in *Britain and the Baltic*, P. Slamon & T. Barrow (eds). Sunderland: Sunderland University Press.

McKee, Eric (1985) *Working boats of Britain*. London: Conway Maritime.

MacRae, J.A. & Waine, C.V. (1990) *The steam collier fleets*. Wolverhampton: Wayne.

Mainwaring (1620s) *The Seaman's Dictionary*, pp.69–260 in The life and works of Sir Henry Mainwaring, vol.2, Publications of the Navy Records Society, vol.56, 1922.

Mannering, J. with Greenhill, B. (1997) *The Chatham directory of inshore craft: traditional working vessels of the British Isles*. London: Chatham.

March. E.J. (1970) *Inshore craft of Britain*, 2 vols. Newton Abbot: David & Charles.

Marsden, Peter R.V. (1964) 'The Walthamstow Boat', *Mariner's Mirror*, 50, pp.2–6.

Mitcalfe, W Stanley (1937) 'The history of the keelmen and their strike in 1822', *Archaeologica Aeliana*, 4th series, vol.14, pp.1–16.

Moore, Thomas (1854) *The beacon: a poem in three cantos by Thomas Moore*. Seaham: Atkinson.

Morley, Geoffrey (1994) *The smuggling war*. Gloucs.: Sutton.

Morris, Jeff (1988) *Seaham lifeboats (1856–1979)*. Coventry: Lifeboat Enthusiasts Society.

Motherwell, William (ed.) (1827) *Minstrelsy ancient & modern*. Glasgow: Wylie. 2nd edn, 1846.

Mount & Page [1760s] *A new chart of the Newcastle trade*. Cited as MP.

Nicholls, F.F. (1973) *Honest thieves: the violent heyday of English smuggling*. London: Heineman.

Normandale, Fred (2006) *First of the flood*. Scarborough: Bottom End.

Oppenheimer, Stephen. *The origins of the British*. Constable and Robinson.

Osler, Adrian (2002) 'Pilots of the Tyne', pp.252–269, in *Pilots*, vol.2 *Schooner and open boats of the European pilots and watermen*, T. Cunliffe, with . Osler. London: Chatham *et al*.

Osler, Adrian (2000) 'The cobles: Celtic boats in Anglo-Saxon Northumbria?' [response to K.Thier], *The Mariner's Mirror*, 86, pp.347–348.

Osler, Adrian (1990) *Mr. Greathead's Lifeboat*. Newcastle: Tyne & Wear Museums.

Osler, Adrian (1979–80) 'The study of Northumbrian small craft, 1800 to the present day', *Tyne & Tweed*, 34, pp. 8–12.

Osler, Adrian & Barrow, Tony (1993) *Tall ships two rivers – six centuries of sail on the rivers Tyne and Wear*. Newcastle: Keepdate.

Palgrave, F.M.T. (1896) *A list of words and phrases in everyday use by the natives of Hetton-le-Hole in the County of Durham*. English Dialect Society, vol.74.

Stotty 'n' Spice Cake: The Story of North East Cooking (2nd edition)

Bill Griffiths

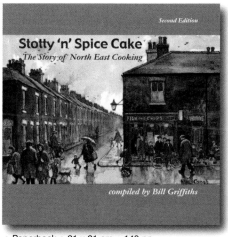

- Paperback • 21 x 21 cm • 148 pp
- ISBN 978-1-904794-21-9 • £9.99

Now in its second edition *Stotty 'n' Spice* brings together recipes, dialect, social history and technology to give us an intriguing insight into how North East kitchen skills, tools and diet options have developed. Bill takes us on a journey through cooking history – from open fire griddle oatcakes and the 'beehive' oven to the widely used, much loved and polished kitchen range and microwavable fast-foods, and looks at how this has impacted on the region's culture.

The relationship between the North East Dialect and the kitchen are examined throughout, explaining where phrases like 'singing-hinny', 'panhaggerty' and 'pikelet' came from.

"…can keep alive regional recipes and cooking methods being lost in the ages of supermarkets and modern kitchens." **The Journal**

"…more than just a regional recipe book. It looks back at how North East kitchens used to be and traditional North East fare and cooking skills, served up with a helping of stories, poems and humour." **Citylife Magazine**

"…traditional recipes, glossaries of baking terms and ingredients, and a whole section devoted to food-related extracts from dialect literature." **The Northumbrian**

Pitmatic: The Talk of the North East Coalfield

Bill Griffiths

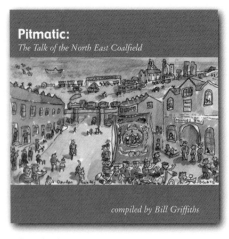

- Paperback • 21 x 21 cm • 160 pp
- ISBN 978-1-904794-25-7 • £9.99

This is more than just a collection of mining terms. It is a heartfelt attempt to bring together the words spoken by miners of the North East pits and how they relate to the wider language-world of the region and its literature of story and song. *Pitmatic* brings together pit literature – its words, jokes, stories and songs – that is fast disappearing and helps attest to the remarkable vitality of the region's dialect and the inventiveness of its speakers.

The last major mine in the North East region closed in 2005 and with it went away of life. Through dialect words, humour, stories and songs *Pitmatic: The Talk of the North East Coalfield* will help you to understand the working and everyday lives of miners. Miners who provided fuel, helped sustain an economy, consolidated communities and created a unique and rich regional culture.

"keepa hadd" "workie-ticket" "aard yakka" "marra" and "bonny on." A few words from Pitmatic.

"Fills a huge gap in the present day knowledge of the subject and at the same time it is an exceptional read." **Beamish Museum**

"It is hoped the book will preserve the dialect for future generations." **BBC Breakfast News**

"...complied by Bill Griffiths, the country's foremost Geordie scholar, the book reveals an exceptionally rich combination of borrowings from Old Norse, Dutch and a score of other languages with inventive usages dreamed up by the miners themselves." **Martin Wainwright, The Guardian**

Pearson, M.R.R. (1979) *Fisher-gansey patterns of North East England*. Newcastle: Esteem.

Pickard, Tom (1989) *We make ships*. London: Secker & Warburg.

Porteous, Katrina (2006) 'Mapping the human landscape: knowledge. Skills and stories in Northumberland fishing communities', *North East History*, 37, pp.68–87.

Porteous, Katrina (2005) *Fishing and fishing communities*. The Maritime Heritage of the North East, leaflet 1.

Porteous, Katrina (1999) *The wind an' the wetter: a Northumbrian poem*. Cullercoats: Iron. Includes glossary pp. 28–40. Cited as WW.

Raine, J. (ed.) (1835) *Wills & Inventories…of the Northern Counties*, pt 1. Durham: Surtees Soceity, vol.2.

Raine, J (ed.) (1841) *The correspondence etc. of the Priory of Coldingham*. Durham: Surtees Society, vol.12.

Raistrick, Arthur (1971) *Old Yorkshire Dales*. London: Pan.

Ray, John (1674) *Collection of English words, not generally used*. London: 1674, 1737.

Rennison, R.W. (1987) 'The development of the North-East coal ports 1815–1914'. PhD, Newcastle University.

Runciman, Walter (1924) *Before the mast and after*. London: Fisher Unwin.

Ryder, M.L. (1998) 'Animal hair in Medieval ship caulking throws light on livestock types', *Environmental Archaeology*, 2.

Salmon, John (1885) *The Coble*. South Shields: Learmouth.

Sandahl, Bertil (1951) *Middle English sea terms 1. The ship's hull, 2. Mass, spars and sails, 3. Standing and running rigging.* Essays and Studies in English Language and Literature, S.B.Liljegren (ed.) 3 vols, Upsala, 1951, 1958, 1982.

Sanderson, S.F. (1969) 'The Tweed salmon cobles', *Studies in honour of Iorwerth C. Peate*, G. Jenkins (ed.). Routledge, pp.273–280.

Sanderson, Thomas (1873) *Chips and shavings of an old shipwright, or life, poems and adventures of Thomas Sanderson*. Darlington: Bragg.

Seller, John (1671) *The English Pilot*. London.

Seymour, John (1974) *The Companion Guide to the Coast of North-East England*. London: Collins.

Sharpe, Sir Cuthbert (1834) *The Bishoprick Garland*. London.

David Simpson (1991) *Shore of the Saints*. Durham: North Pennine.

Smith, Graham (1994) *Smuggling in Yorkshire 1700-1850*. Newbury: Countryside Books.

Smith, Ian (1993) *Northumbrian coastline: Berwick upon Tweed to North Shields*, 2nd edn. Warkworth: Sandhill.

Smylie, Mike (2004) *Herring: a history of the silver darlings*. Stroud: Tempus.

Smyth, Admiral W.H. (1867) *The Sailor's Word Book*. Reprint, Conway Maritime Press,1991, 2006.

Stainthorpe, Fred (c.2001) *Home and Away*.

Starkey, D.J., Reid, C., & Ashcroft, N. (2000) *England's Sea fisheries: the commercial sea fisheries of England and Wales since 1300*. London: Chatham.

Surtees, Robert (1816) *History & antiquities of the Co. Palatine of Durham*. 4 vols, London: 1816–1840. Reprint, 1972. Wakefield: EP.

Sykes, Bryan (2006) *Blood of the Isles*. Oxford Ancestors.

Terry, R.R. (ed.) (1931) *Salt sea ballads*. London: Curwen.

Terry, R.R. (ed.) (1926) *The shanty book*. Part 2, *Sailor shanties*. London: Curwen.

Their, Katrin (2002) *Altenglische Terminologie fuer Schiffe und Schiffsteile – Archaeologie und Sprachgeschichte 500–1100*. British Archaeological Records, International Series no.1036.

Their, Katrin (2001) 'The cobles: a response to Adrian Osler's letter', *The Mariner's Mirror*, 87, p.98.

Their, Katrin (2000) 'The cobles: Celtic boats in Anglo-Saxon Northumbria?', *The Mariner's Mirror*, 86, pp.131–139.

Tinniswood, J.T. (1949) 'English galleys 1272–1377', *Mariners' Mirror*, 35, pp.276–319.

Tyneside: A Christmas annual for Tynemouth, North & South Shields and district (1890) South Shields.

Umpleby, A, Stanley (c.1935) *The dialect of Staithes*.

Ungar, Richard (1985) 'Dutch design', ch.14 in C.O.Cederlund (ed.) *Postmedieval boat and ship archaeology*. British Archaeological Records, International Series no.256.

Walker, Jim (2006) *By net and coble: salmon fishing on the Tweed*. Spital: Blackhall.

Walton, Isaac (1797) *The Complete Angler*, 6th edition with notes by Sir John Hawkins. London: Rivington.

Watts, V.E. (2002) *A dictionary of County Durham place-names*. Nottingham: English Place Name Society.

Watts, V.E. (1976) 'Comment on *The evidence of place-names* by Margaret Gelling', pp.212–222 in *Medieval settlement: continuity and change*, P.H.Sawyer (ed.). London: Arnold.

Westall, Robert (1977) *The Watch House*. London: Macmillan.

Whitmarsh, David (2000) 'Adaptation and change in the fishing Industry since the 1970s', ch.24 in *England's Sea fisheries*, D.J.Starkey(ed.). London: Chatham.

Whittle & Laurie (1819) *Chart of the coasts of Northumberland & Durham from Sunderland Point to Berwick including the Farn Islands, Holy Island, etc.* Cited as WL.

Whitwell, R.J. & Johnson, C. (1926) 'The Newcastle Galley', *Archaeologia Aeliana* 4th series, 2, pp.142–193.

Wood, Herbert (1937) *Spare time sailing: being a record of 40 years' sailing and cruising experiences off the North-East coast*. London: Brown.

Wright, Joseph (ed.) (1898–1905) *English Dialect Dictionary*. 6 vols, Oxford: English Dialect Society.

Wright, Reginald (1985) *Black Hall Rocks & Blackhall*.

Yorkshire dialogue between an awd wife, a lass, and a butcher (1673). Reprint,. in F.W. Moorman (ed.) *Yorkshire Dialect Poems 1673–1915*, London, 1916.

Stotty 'n' Spice Cake: The Story of North East Cooking (2nd edition)

Bill Griffiths

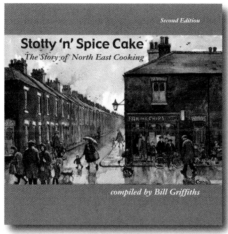

- Paperback • 21 x 21 cm • 148 pp
- ISBN 978-1-904794-21-9 • £9.99

Now in its second edition *Stotty 'n' Spice* brings together recipes, dialect, social history and technology to give us an intriguing insight into how North East kitchen skills, tools and diet options have developed. Bill takes us on a journey through cooking history – from open fire griddle oatcakes and the 'beehive' oven to the widely used, much loved and polished kitchen range and microwavable fast-foods, and looks at how this has impacted on the region's culture.

The relationship between the North East Dialect and the kitchen are examined throughout, explaining where phrases like 'singing-hinny', 'panhaggerty' and 'pikelet' came from.

"…can keep alive regional recipes and cooking methods being lost in the ages of supermarkets and modern kitchens." **The Journal**

"…more than just a regional recipe book. It looks back at how North East kitchens used to be and traditional North East fare and cooking skills, served up with a helping of stories, poems and humour." **Citylife Magazine**

"…traditional recipes, glossaries of baking terms and ingredients, and a whole section devoted to food-related extracts from dialect literature." **The Northumbrian**

Pitmatic: The Talk of the North East Coalfield

Bill Griffiths

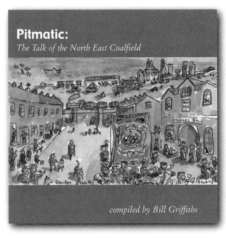

- Paperback • 21 x 21 cm • 160 pp
- ISBN 978-1-904794-25-7 • £9.99

This is more than just a collection of mining terms. It is a heartfelt attempt to bring together the words spoken by miners of the North East pits and how they relate to the wider language-world of the region and its literature of story and song. *Pitmatic* brings together pit literature – its words, jokes, stories and songs – that is fast disappearing and helps attest to the remarkable vitality of the region's dialect and the inventiveness of its speakers.

The last major mine in the North East region closed in 2005 and with it went away of life. Through dialect words, humour, stories and songs *Pitmatic: The Talk of the North East Coalfield* will help you to understand the working and everyday lives of miners. Miners who provided fuel, helped sustain an economy, consolidated communities and created a unique and rich regional culture.

"keepa hadd" "workie-ticket" "aard yakka" "marra" and "bonny on." A few words from Pitmatic.

"Fills a huge gap in the present day knowledge of the subject and at the same time it is an exceptional read." **Beamish Museum**

"It is hoped the book will preserve the dialect for future generations." **BBC Breakfast News**

"...complied by Bill Griffiths, the country's foremost Geordie scholar, the book reveals an exceptionally rich combination of borrowings from Old Norse, Dutch and a score of other languages with inventive usages dreamed up by the miners themselves." **Martin Wainwright, The Guardian**